READINGS IN
RUSSIAN HISTORY

Volume II / The Modern Period

✓ **W9-BAZ-607**

Volume II /

READINGS IN
RUSSIAN HISTORY

The Modern Period

Edited by *Sidney Harcave*

State University of New York, Harpur College

Thomas Y. Crowell Company, New York, Established 1834

PREFACE

A BOOK OF readings such as this is assembled through the generosity of scholars and writers who at some time or another have been engaged in the study of a common concern—in this case, Russian history. And it is a particularly unselfish kind of generosity that prompts a writer to allow his treatment of a specific aspect of a subject to be fitted into the anthologist's broader design. His work must usually be shorn of its careful documentation and footnoting; it may be made to stand alone as representative of a position subsequent study has led him to qualify or revise entirely; it may even be disengaged from its original context (if a book chapter, for instance) with a consequent loss in force of argument, in logic of interpretation. But because such liberties have been taken with the works selected for this book, it has been possible in a relatively limited space to present a survey of Russian history quite different from that of the mere recorder: a survey from the viewpoint of the thinker and the doer.

In the articles and essays here reprinted, the reader will observe the historian in his highly skilled competence: Rostovtzeff, suggesting a new approach for studying the origins of Russia; Toynbee, taking the long view of Russia's place in the Western world; Obolensky, rigorously examining Toynbee's view; Platonov, marking the limits beyond which the student of Ivan IV may not go. He will observe also some of the raw elements of change that, as they build in pressure, are capable of markedly influencing the course of Russian history: Tarle's trial-by-press, Belov's experiences with collectivization, Jasny's interpretation of the welter of Soviet statistics.

The degree to which we may truly understand Russia's past, and the conditions and events of her present, depends upon the work of just such men as are represented here: those who dig out, organize, and present knowledge previously unknown to us; those who critically examine the varied array of evidence, perhaps accepting one item, rejecting another, modifying a third, and amplifying a fourth. Although these serious analysts of historical materials may often disagree with the judgments of others, as well as with their own earlier ones, their dissent must be taken to indicate not a perverse contentiousness, but rather their working premise: that no historical judgment is final.

In its first section, "The Scope and Nature of Russian History," this book includes treatments of the over-all features, the broad and persistent problems, of Russian history. Thereafter the arrangement is generally chronological, beginning with Kievan Russia and concluding with the Russia of today. With a few exceptions, the selections—many not readily available elsewhere—are presented uncut, reproduced as in the original save for the correction of obvious slips in typography and punctuation. To provide maximum space for text, however, most footnotes have had to be either abridged or omitted.

In view of the quality of the pieces and the stature of their authors, it has seemed unnecessary to do any extensive editing beyond selecting and arranging the items so as to provide the substance, clarity, and balance appropriate to "readings" in Russian history. The brief introductory comments on the general features of each work and the short biographical notes are intended primarily as aids to orientation. The authors speak for themselves.

Readers will find that the authors sometimes differ from one another in their spelling of Russian names: for example, Golicyn (or Golitsyn), Tsarskoe Selo (or Carskoe Selo). Such variations result from using different systems of transliteration (there is no standard one, alas). The Russians employ the Cyrillic alphabet, and the various systems of transliteration aim at converting the sounds of Cyrillic letters into those of our Latin alphabet. Though the lack of uniformity in spelling may be a bit annoying, one finds that, in the actual pronunciation of names, there are no greatly disturbing differences among the systems.

Another possibly confusing feature results from variations in designating dates in Russian history. Until 1918, Russia used the Julian calendar, which, by the twentieth century, had fallen thirteen days behind the Gregorian calendar. Some writers give dates in Russian history according to the Russian usage; others, according to Western usage. As with transliteration, there is no accepted rule, and authors are free to use whichever calendar they please; but generally there is some indication in the writing as to which has been used.

It is hoped that the use of this book will encourage further reading in Russian history. Almost all the selections provide clues to other informative and interesting sources. For additional bibliographical listings, the interested reader might turn to a basic textbook in Russian history, or to *The Russian Review, The Slavic Review,* and *The Slavonic and East European Review,* which provide bibliographies of recently published books and articles. And among guides to still broader fields, there are two of superior quality: Philip Grierson's *Books on Soviet Russia, 1917–1942* (1943), and Charles Morley's *Guide to Research in Russian History* (1951).

Some authors have extended the spirit of scholarly generosity to include more than the agreement to have their work included in this book. I sincerely appreciate the help of the many who have given their time to make suggestions or revisions, to expedite arrangements, or to express encouragement. I am particularly indebted to Professor Philip E. Mosely, who, to me as to many others, is the friendly embodiment of interest and competence in Russian history and Soviet affairs. Publishers, editors, and others concerned with the materials chosen for this book (identified on the first page of each selection) have been consistently responsive and helpful in the arrangements for reprinting; I am most grateful to them. And I am glad to hold a salute of appreciation for the skilled bookman who is the director of Crowell's college department, John T. Hawes. Librarians are always invaluable assistants to anyone using their materials, but I have received from them more help than anyone has a right to expect. To Miss Janet Brown, Reference Librarian at Harpur College, I owe special thanks for the resourcefulness and energy she employed in my behalf when I was assembling and preparing this material. Finally, I acknowledge with thanks the "very present help" of Norah, my wife, from the beginning to the end of this undertaking.

S. H.

Binghamton, N.Y.
December, 1961

CONTENTS

ix

SOVIET RUSSIA

IMPERIAL RUSSIA:
FROM EMANCIPATION
TO REVOLUTION
1861-1917

1 /

THE AGRARIAN
POLICIES
OF RUSSIA
AND THE WARS *

By the end of his reign, in 1855, Nicholas I recognized that the agrarian problem was the most critical one facing Russia; and almost half a century later Plehve, the Minister of Interior, declared that it was still the most serious of the several major domestic problems. Even today the agrarian problem is acute in Russia. To be sure, its nature has changed in the course of a century, but there is little indication that it is disappearing. Professor Timoshenko's analysis will be found to complement that of Professor Portal (see pp. 22–29). The backwardness of Russian agriculture and industry is shown to have been more than an economic phenomenon; it was a social and political one as well.

THE AGRARIAN POLICIES of Russia, as they developed during the last three-quarters of a century, were determined to a considerable extent by the agrarian relations created at the emancipation of the serfs in 1861. Serfdom developed in Russia with the growth of the Russian monarchy, and to a certain extent it must be regarded as the price that had to be paid for the building and preservation of that vast empire. Every period of expansion of the empire or of military struggle for its preservation was accompanied by a further spread and tightening of the system of bondage. This was true in the second half of the sixteenth century under John the Terrible, during the decades following the period of unrest (*smuta*)

* Vladimir P. Timoshenko, "The Agrarian Policies of Russia and the Wars," *Agricultural History*, XVII (October, 1943), 192–210, abridged. Reprinted by permission of the author and the publisher.

The author is Professor Emeritus at Stanford University. He was born in Russia and received his education there and in the United States. Much of his work was done in the Food Research Institute at Stanford, where he pursued his special interest in agricultural economics, with particular attention to Russia. His *Agricultural Russia and the Wheat Problem* (1932) is a major work in the field.

in the beginning of the seventeenth century, and also at the beginning
of the eighteenth century under Peter the Great. The well-known Russian historian and politician, P. N. Miliukov, has pointed out that during
the last period the political growth of the Russian state surpassed its
economic development. The tax burden of the population had been tripled
during the first quarter of the eighteenth century, while the population
itself had decreased by 20 percent. As Miliukov said, Peter the Great raised
Russia to the rank of a European power at the cost of the economic ruin
of the country. His characterization of the social costs of the growth of
Peter's monarchy is courageous, particularly because it relates to a period
regarded by the majority of Russian historians as one of the most brilliant
in Russian history.

The aggravation of the Russian peasants' state of bondage, at least
up to the first quarter of the eighteenth century, had not been mainly for
the benefit of some privileged class, but was motivated by the interest of
the state itself. The old Russian aristocracy had been, to a considerable
extent, exterminated or suppressed by the autocratic monarchs of Moscow, particularly by John the Terrible; and new state servants, forming
the upper strata of Russian society, had replaced it. Vast land areas and
the peasants settled on those lands were distributed among them, or their
inherited patrimonies were secured for them, only on condition of, and
in proportion to, their own service to the state. Landlords were at that
time as much servants of the state as the serfs were their bonded servants.

The agrarian system of serfdom, however, had changed its social-
economic meaning substantially by the second half of the eighteenth
century. Instead of securing services of all classes of society for the state,
as it had done before, it had degenerated into a system ensuring the
services of the lower agrarian classes for the benefit of the upper class of
landlords, while the landlords had been liberated from obligatory services
to the state.

During the sixteenth and seventeenth centuries, the upper class of
state servants had accumulated immense landed property, and by the
middle of the eighteenth century, they had almost completely subjugated
the peasant class. This enormously increased the political power of the
landlords. They had not succeeded in securing formal acknowledgment
of their political power by some kind of constitution, but their actual influence upon state affairs had become very great. In 1762, a proclamation
of Peter III had freed them from obligatory military and civil services,
and the inalienability of their landed property was proclaimed a few
years later by Empress Catherine II. But no relaxation of the bondage of
the peasant class took place.

On the contrary, in the second half of the eighteenth century, the
system of bondage was intensified and spread to new areas. In the

Ukraine, where the Cossacks' revolution against Poland in the middle of the seventeenth century had liberated Ukrainian peasants from their Polish landlords, and where serfdom had only been in the process of gradual restoration in the first half of the eighteenth century, the system of serfdom was consolidated legally by Catherine II. With the final abolition of the last vestiges of Ukrainian autonomy in the second half of the eighteenth century, the last obstacle to strengthening there the system of bondage in its most extreme forms disappeared. Millions of acres of state lands, mainly in Ukraine and in other southern provinces just regained from Turkey, with several hundred thousand peasants settled thereon, were granted by Catherine II to her numerous favorites and to other state servants. The end of the eighteenth century must be regarded, thus, as the climax in the evolution of bondage in Russia. However, this system, with practically no legal changes, continued to dominate Russian social organization through the middle of the nineteenth century, in spite of the fact that its corrupt influences upon the whole social and state organization of Russia were recognized not only by many Russian progressive thinkers of that time but also by the monarchs who ruled Russia during that period.

Both Alexander I and Nicholas I were enemies of the system of serfdom; and both tried, if not to abolish it completely, at least to reform it in favor of the serfs, mainly for reasons of security to the state. However, their efforts in this direction were not strong enough and had no practical results, except for the decision of Alexander I at the beginning of his reign to cease further distribution of state lands settled by peasants to private ownership. Although this decision stopped further expansion of serfdom, the system itself experienced no changes, and the situation of serfs rather deteriorated toward the end of his reign. The Napoleonic Wars and the militaristic system developed by Alexander I for the protection of legitimistic interests in post-Napoleonic Europe, a policy also continued by Nicholas I during his reign, were to a great extent responsible for the deterioration of the situation of serfs and for the timidity of the rulers in their attempts to reorganize the agrarian system of serfdom. A new serious shock to the country from the outside was necessary in order to bring the system of bondage to an end.

Such an external shock was provided by the Crimean War of 1854–56 and the humiliating conditions of the peace that followed. In this war, the plans of Nicholas I for the further expansion of his empire at the expense of the decaying Turkish Empire were checked by a coalition of the Western Powers (Great Britain and France), with the inimical connivance of the central European states (Prussia and Austria), which were tired of the legitimistic tutelage of Russia, and were afraid of her further expansion in the Near East. The conditions of the Parisian peace

forbade Russia to hold her warships in the Black Sea and abolished her
protectorate over the Danubian principalities (the present Rumania)
and the entire Christian (Orthodox) population of Turkey.

During the war some sincere Russian patriots even became defeatists,
because they thought that a defeat might contribute to a reorganization
of the Russian Empire upon more liberal bases. The defeat and the
humiliating conditions of the peace demonstrated not only to Russian
society but also to the people at the top of the political system and to the
new Emperor Alexander II himself, how completely unprepared economically Russia was for that war. All understood that the system of serfdom was the principal obstacle to the necessary economic and administrative reorganization of the country. The severe disturbances concurrent
with the recruiting of peasants for the army and navy demonstrated also
that the security of the state itself was endangered by the system of
bondage. This particularly affected Emperor Alexander II, who became
after that time a sincere and energetic partisan for the liberation of serfs.
Landlords also were frightened by increased disturbances of serfs, and
this facilitated the emancipation of serfs in 1861.

THE BASES OF THE 1861 REFORM

The conditions upon which the agrarian system of serfdom was
abolished in Russia in 1861 indicate that, under certain circumstances,
social reforms may be accomplished with less perturbance and with more
social justice under a system of political autocracy than under a democratic government. At least, the results of the emancipation in Russia
were more favorable for the peasants than those obtained earlier in the
countries of central Europe. Also the abolition of serfdom in Russia did
not result in civil war as in the United States in connection with the
emancipation of slaves. This was true in spite of the fact that the interests
affected by the abolition of serfdom were much wider than those affected
by the emancipation of slaves in America.

Generally speaking, the reform of 1861, as finally accepted, was more
radical than it appeared in the earlier declarations of its authors. Some
historians explain this by the fact that Alexander II was disturbed by
certain political claims raised by some of the representatives of the
nobility during the elaboration of the reform. Consequently, he decided
to rely more upon the peasant class. For this reason conditions of the
reform became more favorable for the peasants.

By the time of the emancipation, the plan of allotting to serfs land
sufficient to secure their existence as farmers had become more popular
among Russian bureaucratic groups than it had been in the earlier
decades of the nineteenth century, when the serfs of the Baltic provinces
were liberated without land. At that time, the Russian peasantry was

threatened with being deprived of the land in its possession in the case of emancipation. The idea of landless emancipation of serfs was still very popular among certain groups of landlords, particularly in the areas to the south with valuable fertile black soils. The government, however, under the impetus of social and revolutionary movements in western Europe, and for reasons of security to the state, was afraid of proletarianization of peasants, and favored emancipation with land. Furthermore, a large group, if not the majority, of landlords also favored emancipation with land, as their own possessions of livestock, machinery, and other forms of capital were not sufficient in order to organize farming on the land that would remain in their possession after the reform, with the use of hired labor. They expected to rent their lands to their former serfs, and were, therefore, interested that these preserve their households intact with necessary livestock and implements.

The leading principle of the reform in relation to the allotment of lands to former serfs, at least as it was understood by the most statesmanlike of the bureaucrats responsible for its preparation, was to leave the land they held before the reform in the possession of the liberated serfs. However, since the proportion of peasant holdings in the total land area of estates varied greatly from one case to another, it was necessary to establish certain correctives to this principle. On some estates that had not organized their farming on a large scale, nearly all of the productive area was held by serfs, who paid their landlords established dues (*obrok*). There existed, on the other hand, particularly in the fertile black-soil area, plantation-like estates; and their number had increased during the recent decades before the reform, with expansion of the market for agricultural commodities. On such estates, a large proportion of the serfs were landless laborers working wholly on the landlord's farm, with no more than a vegetable garden for their households. Consequently, local maximal and minimal norms were established for the allotment of land to every male person of serf households. When actual holdings of serfs exceeded the maximal norm, the landlord could require that the excess be cut off from those holdings. On the contrary, when the holdings of the serfs were below the minimal norm (it was equal to one-third of the maximal), additional land was to be allotted to them.

Under pressure of interested groups of landlords, these norms were established, however, in such a manner that practically no additional allotments were required, while peasants lost a considerable portion of their prereform holdings. Some authorities estimate that from one-sixth to one-fifth of the total area of land held by serfs before the reform was taken from them. These losses were particularly large in the fertile black-soil area, especially in the middle Volga provinces and the northern provinces of Ukraine, where peasants lost on the average from one-fifth to two-fifths of their prereform holdings.

In contrast to this, former serfs received on the average more land than they had held before the reform in the western provinces of Russia where landlords were mainly of Polish origin. This was done for political motives, in view of the separatist tendencies of many of the Polish gentry that resulted in the Polish insurrection of 1863.

Still another group of serfs received very small allotments. Under pressure of certain landlords' groups, an article was introduced at the last moment in the Statute of Emancipation, permitting landlords who were willing to surrender all claims for dues, services, and redemption payments to make to their former serfs an outright gift of an allotment equal to one-fourth of the maximal norm. When the peasants were willing to accept such an allotment, a settlement might be arranged on this basis. More than half a million peasants chose to accept such "beggarly allotments," as they were called later, mainly in order to escape the redemption payments for land that they regarded as fixed at too high a level.

The redemption payments for allotted land were fixed, under pressure of the same landlord interests, at a level out of proportion with the market value of land at the time of the reform. Although it was the policy of the government that no redemption fee should be paid for the personal liberty of serfs, this was actually concealed in the high dues imposed for the use of land allotted to the former serfs and, consequently, in the redemption payments for this land. Furthermore, by fixing rates of payments for the first units of the allotted land relatively higher than for the following additional units, and by high appraisal of farmsteads, the payments were proportionally much higher for serfs who obtained relatively small allotments.

These distortions of the fundamental principles of the Great Reform resulted in unfavorable economic consequences immediately after the emancipation. From the very beginning large groups of liberated serfs were not sufficiently provided with land, and at the same time were burdened with heavy payments for it. This relates particularly to the situation in the central agricultural area of Russia and in the northern Ukraine. As will be shown later, the economic situation of the peasant class in these regions became particularly difficult, and special measures were necessary to alleviate the situation.

Another aspect of the emancipation of 1861 was responsible for the fact that the unfavorable consequences of the reform were aggravated rather than removed during the few decades immediately following the emancipation. The reform had not made former serfs completely free. It liberated them from the authority of their landlords, but it made them dependent on the peasant commune—*mir*.

Most of the public powers exercised by the landlords over their serfs before the emancipation passed then to the peasant communes. As the Great Reform was dictated mainly by interests of, and had in view the better security of, the state, the idea of concentrating considerable power over former serfs in the hands of the commune originated among the sincere partisans of the reform within the bureaucracy. The commune was to guarantee the fulfillment by individual peasants of their obligation to the state and to the former landlords, before their allotted land was completely redeemed. According to the law, the commune became collectively (jointly) responsible for the payment of the taxes of its members and of the redemption payments on the allotted lands. Furthermore, these lands were allotted to the commune rather than to individual peasants, even in those communes where no repartition of land took place, and where the land was in hereditary holdings of separate peasant households.

Because of these responsibilities, the communes assumed control over the economic activity of their members, who could not leave the community, even temporarily, without permission of the commune (passport system). True, the Statute of Emancipation (article 165) made it possible for the members of a commune to complete the redemption payments for their land any time, then to require separation of that land from the commune, and to dispose of it freely. However, for economic reasons, only a few members could do this; and later, by a special law (December 14, 1893), this possibility also was made dependent upon the consent of the commune.

Such communal organization was introduced not only among former serfs of private landowners, but also among appanage peasants and state peasants. At the time of the emancipation, the last group of peasants was even more numerous than that of serfs. The terms of land reform for these two groups (a special statute of 1863 and the statute of November 26, 1866 respectively) were more favorable than for the serfs of private landowners, since they received much larger allotments of land with lower payments. But their social organization was based on the same principles as that of former serfs. Thus, with the exception of the nobility and those representatives of other classes that had acquired large land property, the whole rural population was organized separately from other social groups, and formed a special estate or class. Regarded as a lower social stratum, they did not enjoy the same rights as other estates, and their civil life was regulated mainly by customary law instead of by the general civil code enjoyed by other classes of the population.

The isolation of the peasant class from other classes of society even increased, to some extent, in the middle of the 1880s, when political reaction resulted in a further subordination of the peasant communal organization to the local administrative organs of the government. It closed for peasants many fields of economic activity and kept them artificially in rural communities. This inevitably resulted in the overcrowding of the countryside and a consequent economic deterioration of peasant farming—situations that were later to call for various measures of agrarian policies.

The agrarian policies of the Czarist government preceding the revolution of 1917 may be conveniently divided into two separate periods: (1) the four decades from the Great Reform until the Russo-Japanese War and the abortive revolution of 1905, and (2) the shorter period between the two revolutions of 1905 and 1917. The earlier period may be characterized as a period of stability, or rather of stagnation, of agrarian relations, while the later was a period of feverish governmental activity directed toward a new reorganization of agrarian relations in order to stem the peasants' revolutionary movement intensified by the unsuccessful Russo-Japanese War.

1861–1904

During the twenty years following emancipation in 1861, no special measures of agrarian policy were undertaken by the government. These years were practically the period of the execution of the reform, since, on estates where no agreement about the condition of the redemption of allotted land had taken place earlier, the compulsory relation between landlords and their former serfs was not to terminate formally for twenty years. According to the Statute of Emancipation, the redemption of the allotted land could take place either by mutual agreement of the landlord and his former serfs or by the initiative of the landlord. The redemption of allotted land was, thus, not compulsory for the landlords. But in spite of this, a great majority of them chose the redemption, mainly because they needed free money. By 1881, agreements had been reached for the redemption of about six-sevenths of all allotted lands.

The reform of 1861 was followed by a period of rapid expansion of railroads, built mainly with foreign capital. Building was particularly intensive between 1868 and 1875, when on the average about one thousand miles of railroad was added annually. The railroads were designed to connect the main agricultural regions with Moscow and St. Petersburg, the principal domestic markets for agricultural products, and with the export harbors. Consequently, both domestic and foreign markets for agricultural commodities, mainly grain, increased greatly during the years following emancipation.

Nevertheless, agricultural production on large estates, unfavorably affected by the reform of 1861, declined during the following decades. Most of the landlords did not possess enough capital to reorganize their enterprises on a capitalistic basis, in spite of the fact that the government advanced the redemption payments for land ceded to the peasants. Consequently, crop areas on the large estates were reduced in most of the agricultural regions after the reform. Most of the landlords changed their status from agricultural producers to agrarian renters, particularly in the central agricultural area of Russia. This did not reduce their income from rents, but their importance as organizers of agricultural production declined greatly.

The agricultural production of the peasants, on the other hand, expanded considerably after the reform and acquired more of a commercial character. However, this increased activity did not mean that peasant farming was developing under favorable conditions. On the contrary, the peasants had to increase their sales on the market mainly because of the heavy burden of redemption payments and taxes, and their expansion of crops on land rented from the manors indicated that they were not sufficiently provided with allotted land. Private and official investigations during the 1870s showed clearly that the heavy burden of taxation and of redemption payments and the deficiency of allotted land were the principal causes of the unsatisfactory economic condition of the peasants. The findings of these investigations did not result, however, in any practical changes of policy on the part of the government during the 1870s.

The Balkan War of 1876–78 was partly responsible for the postponement of governmental action, as it caused considerable strain on, and finally resulted in serious disorganization of, governmental finance. Not until the beginning of the 1880s did the government undertake a series of measures to alleviate the situation of the peasants. These measures, resulting in substantial immediate reduction of specific state revenues, were undertaken in spite of the deflationary policy of the government at that time, and in spite of the political reaction that followed the assassination of Czar Alexander II. This indicates the urgency of the situation.

The first among these measures (the law of December 28, 1881) was designed to make obligatory the redemption of the allotted land and to sever finally the compulsory relation between landlords and former serfs on the estates where the redemption of land had not yet been agreed upon. At the same time, the annual redemption payments were substantially reduced, on an average, by about one-fourth to one-third of their previous level. This brought the payments for allotted land into closer agreement with their market value.

In recognition of the insufficiency of the peasants' allotments of land, the government also undertook several measures to increase the peasants' landholdings. It facilitated leases of state lands; it regulated, in a somewhat unsatisfactory manner, the migration to the thinly populated border areas; and finally it created a special Peasants' Land Bank (law of May 18, 1882) in order to facilitate for peasants the purchases of private lands, mainly by parceling large estates. However, the operations of the Peasants' Land Bank were too cautious and too limited during the first period of its activity (until 1895), and the loans were too expensive for peasants. Perhaps the most important of all measures taken by the government at the time was the abolition of the poll tax paid by peasants. It is true that the government compensated for the loss of revenue from this direct tax by introducing various indirect taxes that fell mainly on the same peasants. But the abolition of the poll tax might have had some judicial importance, since it might have put an end to the lower social standing of the peasantry as a class and might have discontinued its isolation in the village communities from other social classes.

In connection with this reform, Minister of Finance Bunge planned to abolish the collective responsibility of the peasants for taxes and other payments to the state, thus liberating them from the tutelage of the communities. However, reactionary influences did not permit the fulfillment of this last reform, and the isolation of the peasantry from other classes of the Russian social structure continued for several decades. Moreover, from the middle of the 1880s, under the influence of a further political reaction, it became a direct policy of the government to establish still greater political tutelage over the village communities, to strengthen the role of the land commune, and to make abandonment of the commune more difficult for its members. During the last two decades of the nineteenth century, the social isolation of the peasant class, thus, became even stronger than it had been before. Withdrawal from the rural community became still more difficult, and the ties with rural life stronger.

It must also be borne in mind that, from the mid-1880s to 1900, Russian agriculture, as well as agriculture throughout the world, was much affected by the decline of prices. Even though the alleviations granted to peasants in the beginning of the 1880s might have been sufficient to improve their situation at current prices and under current market conditions, they were of small help at the low prices prevailing after 1885. In addition, during the second half of the 1880s and the beginning of the 1890s, Russian agriculture suffered much from the unfavorable weather that culminated in the crop failure and famine of 1891.

In spite of the unfavorable conditions of peasant farming, the rural population increased rapidly after the emancipation, in contrast to its relatively slow growth before the reform of 1861. Consequently, the countryside became more and more overcrowded, and peasants felt the shortage of allotted lands with greater and greater acuteness. It is true that the peasants had expanded farming considerably on lands rented from the estates. They had even succeeded in purchasing considerable land from these estates, since the manor economy had also passed through a serious crisis during this period. The Russian nobility disposed of nearly half of its lands during the forty years following the reform of 1861, and a great portion of the land remaining in its possession was rented to peasants.

However, the expansion of peasant farming was not wholesome economically. The condition of land lease, never regulated by specific laws in Russia, was not favorable for peasants. Most of these renters must be classified, according to American terminology, as "croppers," and not as tenants. Usually peasants rented land from estates for one crop. In many instances, rent was paid in kind and not in money. Conditions of this type of land lease were particularly unfavorable for small renters. Under the necessity of increasing their crop areas for production of food for domestic consumption, peasants were ready to pay rents exceeding normal commercial income from rented land. Consequently they did not receive for their work even usual rural wages, which were very low in Russia.

In addition to being economically disadvantageous for peasant renters, such forms of land lease stood in the way of technical progress not only on peasant farms but also on manors. Very little large-scale farming was organized on most manors, particularly in the central agricultural area of Russia. By far the greater portion of manor lands was cultivated by peasants with their primitive implements and techniques.

The overcrowding of the countryside was stimulated further by the forms of landholding predominating among the Russian peasants—the partitional land commune. Under this system the allotted land was redistributed from time to time among the households of the community in proportion to the total number of members, to the number of male members, or to the number of adult male members (workers). Hence, the growth of a family was regarded by peasants as one means of expanding their holdings. Consequently, the shortage of land did not serve as a stimulus for birth control; on the contrary, it tended to raise the birth rate.

As a result of these developments, Russian agriculture was brought, by the middle of the 1890s, to an impasse, from which it could not be helped out even by the more energetic measures of agricultural policy that the government found it advisable to apply about that time in order to alleviate the pressure of the rural population. Little help could come also from the increased tempo of industrialization of Russia during the last decade of the nineteenth century and the beginning of the twentieth century.

Impressed by the overcrowding of the countryside, the government changed its policy in relation to rural migration to the borderlands in the 1890s. During previous decades, it had rather retarded the spontaneous movements of peasants to new frontiers, and the southern steppes of European Russia were settled during that time without governmental assistance. About 1890, the government decided to stimulate and assist the migratory movement of the surplus rural population into Siberia. In the middle of the decade, a special committee of the Siberian railroad showed considerable activity in preparing land for new settlers, in extending loans to them, and in facilitating their transportation. Nearly 1,500,000 agricultural migrants crossed the Asiatic frontier between 1895 and 1905.

About the same time, the Peasants' Land Bank increased its activity in financing peasants' purchases of lands from large estates. The statute governing the bank was changed in 1895, its financial resources increased, and the interest rate on loans extended to purchasers of land was lowered. As a result, peasants succeeded in purchasing more than 14,000,000 acres during the decade 1896–1905 with the assistance of the bank, compared with 6,500,000 acres purchased during the preceding longer period 1883–1895. Both the migration to outlying areas and the redistribution of landownership in the interior agricultural area were important during the last decade preceding the revolution of 1905. Unfortunately, these policies came too late to be of much help in improving the agrarian situation in the central agricultural area of Russia. Alone they could not solve the difficult agrarian problem of European Russia at that stage of its development.

At that time even the rapid industrialization of the country, particularly the very ambitious plan of railroad building financed mainly with foreign capital, did not improve the situation of Russian agriculture much. Rapid industrialization could proceed only under the protection of high tariff duties, and these were raised several times beginning with the early 1880s. By raising prices of manufactured goods, the tariff policy could not help but be injurious to agricultural interests. In order to bring in the foreign capital essential for industrialization, it was necessary for Russia to accept certain political commitments, and this resulted in large military expenditures which inevitably increased the burden of taxation carried mainly by the peasantry. It was also necessary for Russia to reorganize her monetary system on the gold standard. This was done by Minister of Finance Witte and not without considerable success. But the preparation of a successful monetary reform, and the maintenance of the gold standard later, involved a deflationary policy. Russian agriculture, which was the principal export business at that time, inevitably had to suffer from that policy.

Consequently, Russian agriculture continued to be depressed during the end of the nineteenth century and the first years of the twentieth century, in spite of the rapid industrial development that took place during these years. The peasants, who were particularly affected by this depression and the heavy taxation, became more restless. Serious agrarian disturbances broke out in 1902, especially in northern Ukraine, but they were brutally suppressed.

At this conjuncture came the Russo-Japanese War, one of the most unpopular wars in the history of Russia. In spite of the fact that the

Japanese attacked Russia first, Russian liberal society accused the Russian government—its imperialistic policy—of being responsible for the war. Defeatist sentiments were widespread even among the more conservative groups of Russian society, to say nothing of the radical groups, which saw in a military defeat their best chance for overthrowing the Czarist autocracy. The revolution came in the fall of 1905. It was started by political strikes of workers in the cities and on the railroads, but soon spread to the countryside. A wave of serious agrarian disturbances rolled over the whole country, including the Baltic provinces, where the rural population consisted mainly of agricultural laborers, rather than peasants—a situation resulting from the emancipation of the serfs without giving them land in the early nineteenth century.

After a period of confusion, during which Czar Nicholas II was forced to grant a constitution, the revolution was defeated—first in Moscow and the Baltic provinces and later throughout the whole country. By this time the leaders of conservative groups, composed mainly of the landed aristocracy, understood that they could not succeed in maintaining their political power for long without radical changes in agrarian relations. Although unsuccessful, the agrarian revolution had taught them that the governmental policy must be changed, radically and rapidly. Thus, instead of the indecision and slowness characteristic of the government's agrarian policy during the preceding two decades, a feverish activity is peculiar to the policy of the following decade.

1905–1917

The most characteristic feature of the governmental agrarian policy during this period was its complete reversal in relation to the land commune and to the social isolation of the peasantry within their village communities as a separate rural class. During the two preceding decades the government had favored greater isolation of the peasantry and had made serious efforts to preserve and even to strengthen the land commune as the basis of the peasants' agrarian organization. Now it strove to abolish the land commune as soon as possible and to introduce instead unlimited private ownership of the land allotted to peasant households by the heads of those households. By this policy it hoped to build from the upper strata of the peasantry an economically strong and politically conservative group of small agricultural entrepreneurs, who, because their interests would be common with those of the manor owners, would align themselves against the group of poor peasants with their revolutionary tendencies. The bureaucracy was disappointed in the rural community as a conservative force in society and began to see in it an organizational center around which the revolutionary tendencies of all groups of peasantry could easily be coordinated. Some sign of the change in the position of the bureaucracy and of the conservative agrarian groups in respect to the land community appeared before the revolution of 1905, but it became more common and more pronounced after the agrarian revolutionary movements of 1905–06, in which all groups of peasantry marched together.

The new agrarian policy found its best expression in Stolypin's agrarian reform (proclaimed by the decree of November 9, 1906, which was replaced later by the law of June 14, 1912). The reform was announced after the defeat of the political revolution and the dissolution of the first Duma elected according to the relatively liberal election law. Political purposes were not the only reason for Stolypin's reform; it also pursued important economic and agronomic-technical purposes. An important feature of this reform was that it proposed not only to introduce private property instead of the community of land but also to eliminate strip farming by replacing it with separate farms. In regions where it was difficult for topographic and climatic reasons to do away completely with village settlements, as in the southeastern steppe area, it was planned at least to collect numerous field strips into one or a few fields but to leave farmsteads in the villages. Special regional committees for arrangement of land had even been organized before the proclamation of the agrarian reform of November 9, 1906, but the proclamation reoriented their activity with a view to performing important functions in connection with the agrarian reform.

Critics of the Stolypin agrarian reform from the liberal and socialistic groups of Russian society usually concentrated their attention on the political aspects of that reform, and, affected by its political purposes, could not see its beneficial economic and technical results impartially.

The agrarian reform of November 9, 1906 had been preceded by several important governmental acts in relation to the peasants, to which the reform itself was a logical conclusion. At the climax of the revolution, the redemption payments for the allotted land had been abolished by the manifesto of November 3, 1905, in order to appease the riotous peasantry. The legal significance of this was that, according to the Statute of Emancipation of 1861, henceforth peasants had to become unlimited owners of the land allotted to them at the time of the emancipation. Still earlier (by the law of March 12, 1903) the joint (collective) responsibility of the rural community for the payment of taxes had been annulled. Finally a decree of October 5, 1906 cancelled certain limitations of the civil rights of peasants. This last decree signified a decisive stride in the direction of abolishing the lower social standing of the peasants among other social groups.

Since the purpose of the decree of November 9, 1906 was to accelerate the process of the dissolution of the land communes, the decree had been formulated by the counterrevolutionary government in such a way that it provided certain groups among the membership of the land communes with economic incentives for their abandonment. These particular aspects of the reform were justly criticized by many as being unfair to other members of the communes. But it would be going too far to say, as did many of the populist critics of the reform, that the dissolution of the land commune was artificially imposed on the peasants by the government.

The rapidity with which the members of the communes abandoned them during the first years after the proclamation of the reform (about one-fifth of the total number of households belonging to the land communes asked for the separation of their land during the period 1907–10), and the diversity of the membership that applied for separation, point to the spontaneous character of the process of dissolution of land communes. The governmental decree was nothing more than an additional shock that precipitated that spontaneous movement. Households abandoning land communes included not only those who, favored by the decree of November 9, 1906, tried to secure ownership of larger quantities of land than they could claim at the next repartition, but also households with smaller allotments. The well-to-do peasantry hastened to separate its land in order to improve its farming, but a large group of poorer peasants, even larger than the former group, also asked for separation of their land. Some of the latter were already occupied in the cities and hastened to break their nominal relation with the rural communities. Others, planning to migrate to the new settlements on the borderlands, were interested in the separation of their land in order to sell it and to obtain the money necessary for organization of farming in the new place. Both these tendencies must be recognized as economically wholesome, contributing to the alleviation of over-population of the countryside.

The process of dissolution of the land community, however, proceeded faster in the western provinces of European Russia, where the land communes had been dying before the reform, and in the southeastern prairie provinces, where there was more space for the development of commercial families. In the central agricultural area of European Russia, the region most overcrowded, the peasantry continued to stick to the land community longer. Here, perhaps, the reform came too late to permit the development of commercial farming among the peasants. The countryside was already too overcrowded and the shortage of land too acute.

Stolypin's agrarian reform was only one of several measures applied by the Russian government after the revolution of 1905. Several of these had for their purpose further expansion of peasant farming, both in the old agricultural area of European Russia and in the new regions of agricultural settlement in Asia. The government recognized that a pressing shortage of agricultural land in the possession of peasants existed in certain agricultural regions and that expansion was necessary. But, in contrast to liberal and radical opinion, the government opposed any extraordinary noncommercial methods of realizing that expansion. Its position was that peasants should purchase necessary land from neighboring manors on usual commercial bases, or, if that was impossible, they should migrate to the new agricultural areas, while the liberal and radical groups demanded that agricultural lands be compulsorily transferred from the manors to the poor peasantry. The moderate liberal groups insisted on the compulsory purchase of most of the manor lands at prices fixed on a moderate level by the government, while the radical socialistic groups demanded pure confiscation of these lands, and their nationalization or socialization.

It must be said that, under the influence of the revolutionary agrarian movement of 1905–06, not only the government changed its position regarding the peasant class; the revolutionary parties did likewise. This relates particularly to the left wing of the Social-Democratic Party, the Bolshevists. Before the revolution of 1905, the agrarian program of the Russian Social-Democratic Party was rather moderate; it required only a certain expansion of peasant landholdings by correcting some of the injustices of the great reform of 1861. After the revolution, the leader of the Bolshevists, Lenin, competing with the radical populists for the revolutionary leadership of the peasantry, advanced a more radical agrarian program, requiring pure confiscation of all manors and the nationalization of all lands. In his opinion, the damage that might be caused by the revolutionary destruction of a few well-organized large agricultural enterprises (if this should happen in the process of revolution) would be more than compensated for by the great advantage that would come from the dismemberment of those manors which were renting most of their land to peasant croppers under conditions disadvantageous to the peasants. Later—in the revolution of 1917—Lenin, in order to win the peasantry for the revolutionary cause, fully accepted the agrarian program of the radical wing of the populist (Socialist-Revolutionary) party, which he combated as Utopian during his whole life.

The policy of the government after the revolution of 1905–06 was to assist peasants in purchasing land from manors by extending to them cheaper credit from the Peasants' Land Bank, and to facilitate migration to the new agricultural areas in Asiatic Russia for those peasants who could not expand their landholding in their neighborhoods. It must also be recognized that the imperial government achieved great results in both directions before the war of 1914–18 and the revolution of 1917.

The financial resources of the Peasants' Land Bank were enlarged by a decree of November 3, 1905, and the same decree permitted it not only to make loans to small purchasers of land, but also to buy large estates upon its own initiative in order to parcel them later among the peasants. In August 1906, the government transferred to the bank for such parceling all appanage land that could be used for agricultural purposes as well as similar land in European Russia belonging to the state. By decree on October 14, 1906, the interest rate paid to the bank by its debtors—small purchases of land—was lowered to 4½ percent, which was below the cost of credit to the state itself. This subsidization of credit for small landowners cost the state about 75 million dollars between 1906 and 1917. During these years, the Peasants' Land Bank succeeded in transferring more than 25 million acres of land in European Russia to the peasants. There can be no question that the operation of the bank during that period was the largest government-organized operation of this kind.

Still greater results were achieved by the government during that period through acceleration of rural migration to Asiatic areas. It will be recalled that migration to Siberia proceeded rather rapidly during the preceding decade. Some Russian economists, knowing the situation of rural resettlement at first hand, even asserted in 1905 that most of the agricultural lands there were already exhausted by the previous wave of migrants, and that, consequently, further migration to Siberia must inevitably slow down. However, the government did everything possible to increase the reserve of land for the new settlements. It even violated the land rights of the native nomadic tribes (Kazakhs and Kirghizs), as well as of the old Russian settlers. Fiscal assignments for expenses connected with preparation of these lands for new settlers were greatly increased during the period. The government thus succeeded in preparing about 60 million acres of land for new settlers during the short period from 1906 to 1910—about double the area made available during the longer period of 1893–1905. As a consequence, nearly three million people moved from European Russia to the Asiatic provinces between the revolution of 1905 and the beginning of the war in 1914. The whole agricultural colonization of Siberia was practically completed by that time. Before the present war, very little agricultural migration to Siberia had taken place since the revolution of 1917. Siberian agriculture, so important for Soviet Russia in its present struggle, was actually developed by the counterrevolutionary government of Imperial Russia before World War I, and by the peasant settlers who have worked hard there since that time.

The importance of the rural migration to Siberia for the solution of the agrarian problem in European Russia is frequently understated by those who point out that during these years this migration took only one-fourth of the natural increase of rural population in European Russia. However, not all of European Russia was overpopulated. If only the overpopulated regions are considered, the migration to the Asiatic provinces during 1906 to 1913 took about a half of the natural increase of the rural population in that area.

Rural migration to Siberia had still another important consequence. Rapid colonization of Asiatic Russia substantially increased markets for products of the manufacturing industry. The growth of Russian industry during the period 1906–14 was generally more rapid than during the previous decade or two, and the rapidity of industrialization in Russia during this short period may be compared advantageously even with that in the United States. Hence, the countryside was relieved of at least a portion of the remaining natural increase of its population by those seeking employment in cities. Industrialization, by increasing local markets for the products of intensive agriculture, contributed also to an intensification of agriculture in European Russia.

During this period the government greatly increased its assistance to peasants for improvement of their agriculture. The principal objective of the collection of field strips and of the improved arrangement of land, envisaged in Stolypin's agrarian reform, was to do away with the traditional three-field rotation in peasant farming and to replace it by improved methods of peasant agriculture. But, in spite of the extreme rapidity with which the rearrangement of land proceeded during the years before the war of 1914, the advantages for peasant agriculture could be felt only slowly. More rapid effects resulted from direct agronomic assistance to small farmers, which was greatly enlarged during that period. Indeed, it suffices to say that the number of agronomic personnel employed by the central government of Russia increased from 1907 to 1912 about ten times, reaching nearly 1,400 in the last year. The number of those employed by provincial governments in 1912 exceeded 3,000, a number five times larger than that employed in 1907. In 1913 there were more than 1,700 district *agronoms,* who were equivalent to the American county agents. Only in the United States and there only after the first World War was this number exceeded by any country. Agricultural education was greatly expanded during these years, but the colleges could not supply a sufficient number of *agronoms* to fill all of the vacancies. During these years were developed the agronomic personnel and the agronomic institutions that later assisted in the restoration of agricultural production after the agrarian revolution of 1917–20 and the famine of 1921–2.

Another important source of assistance for the peasant farmer during this period was agricultural cooperation. In no other country did agricultural cooperation develop faster than in Russia from the revolution of 1905 to World War I. This was a spontaneous action of the rural population itself. Frequently the government was even suspicious of this movement for political reasons. But, subordinating it to its control, the government nevertheless assisted it financially and technically. In 1914, Russia had 13,000 cooperative credit associations with ten million members, by far the greater part of which were in rural localities. Every other farm was a member of some kind of cooperative association. A cooperative organization of dairy farmers in Siberia was doing an important export business, mainly with Great Britain, before World War I.

Not only Stolypin's reform, but all aspects of agrarian policy must be taken into consideration in order to appraise the magnitude of the work undertaken by the Russian government in the short period between the revolution of 1905 and World War I. The Russian government of this epoch was not lacking in energy and even in skill in its attempts to solve the agrarian problem in the eleventh hour of its long history. Unfortunately, the World War came before the results of these efforts could definitely appear. However, in retrospect, even the Russian economists who cannot be suspected of political sympathy with the Czarist government recognize that Stolypin's agrarian reform, in combination with other measures, made a great stride in the direction of solving the Russian agrarian problem. They recognize that the mobilization of landed property developed rapidly after 1905, that the direction of this mobilization —from large estates to small farmers—was economically wholesome and democratic, and that the whole national economy of Russia greatly profited from this process. No matter what the political purpose of the authors of the agrarian reform of 1906 was, it greatly accelerated the process of the conquering of Russian agriculture by the democratic peasantry.

Lenin himself recognized that Stolypin's agrarian reform was not reactionary economically. On the contrary, he saw that it facilitated and accelerated capitalistic development, and, for this reason, must be recognized as an economically progressive reform. He opposed it for political reasons, namely, that it was preparing a Junker type of capitalistic evolution of agriculture in Russia with a political and economical dominance of large agricultural entrepreneurs. He preferred the American farmers' type of capitalistic agriculture, which he believed would be established in Russia by a successful agrarian revolution of the peasants. In his opinion, a revolutionary agrarian reorganization would result in more rapid development of productive forces and better economic conditions for the masses of the peasantry than could be expected from Stolypin's reform.

.   .   .   .   .

THE PROBLEM OF AN INDUSTRIAL REVOLUTION IN RUSSIA IN THE NINETEENTH CENTURY *

The question that Professor Portal considers has one thing in common with many questions that are considered in this book: it suggests the difficulty of attempting to fit Russian developments into compartments of Western European origin. Terms such as "industrial revolution," "feudalism," and "nobility" are derived from Western European history and sometimes cannot be used in their original sense when applied to Russian phenomena.

THE TERM "industrial revolution" has been used so often and in so many different economic contexts that it has finally come to have no fixed meaning, and one is justifiably hesitant to use it.

If, nonetheless, one chooses to use the term, he must re-establish its true meaning. To do so is particularly necessary when one is attempting to determine whether or not and when an industrial revolution, comparable to the one that occurred after 1780 in England and later in France and Germany, actually took place in Russia, a country so markedly different from the Western states in geographical position, social development, and political structure.

An industrial revolution has quantitative as well as qualitative characteristics. The latter, which come first to mind, involve the socio-eco-

* Roger Portal, "The Problem of an Industrial Revolution in Russia in the Nineteenth Century," a translation from *Forschungen zur osteuropäischen Geschichte,* I (1954), 204–16, abridged. First given as a lecture at the Eastern European Institute of the Free University of Berlin in 1953. Translated from the German by S. Harcave. Reprinted by permission of the author and the publisher.

The author holds the chair of Professor of Slavic History and Civilization in the Faculty of Letters of the University of Paris. The economic history of Russia has been the focus of much of his work, an example of which is his *L'Oural au XVIIIe Siècle* (1951).

nomic character of industrial establishments. . . . [To understand such establishments] it is necessary to consider their social structure, giving attention to both the legal and the actual status of employers and employees. Without the replacement of an involuntary labor force [by a free labor force] there can be no industrial revolution. And, as that takes place, there is a growth of population in the new industrial centers, followed by the appearance of new social strata, more or less distinct from the original ones. . . .

The qualitative characteristics alone are not of such significance as to justify the use of the label "industrial revolution." Quantitative characteristics, particularly on a mass scale, must be present. Technological changes and changes in the way of life must be of such an order as in fact to transform the industrial geography and the social structure of the country.

. . . . .

From this broad definition it is easy to see that one should not make general use of the term "industrial revolution," that it is hardly applicable to periods before the eighteenth century, and that one should restrict its use exclusively to those fundamental social changes that are so closely linked with the beginning of machine production.

As is known, first England and then France and Germany were the scene of successive fundamental industrial changes that occurred in the course of a century, beginning roughly in 1780. Did Russia experience a comparable development? . . .

To be sure, if one judged only on the basis of qualitative characteristics, he could discover the beginnings of an industrial revolution in Russia as early as the end of the eighteenth century. Such is the opinion of Yakovlev, the Soviet historian, who finds an industrial revolution in Russia between 1790 and 1825.[*] Actually such a position is untenable, but the evidence he used enables us to establish the noteworthy and remarkable features of the industrial revolution of Russia.

At the beginning of the nineteenth century, those technological innovations that were already known in the West were introduced. Spinning machines made their appearance in 1798 at Alexandrovo, a suburb of Moscow, at the same time that cotton spinning was introduced. By 1805, steam was used to operate these machines. . . . In 1815, the Berd factory of St. Petersburg launched its first steamship; and, in 1825, it built its first steam engine. That is the chronological framework within which Yakovlev places the so-called industrial revolution in Russia.

It should be noted that, of the two most important branches of industry, textile manufacture and metallurgy, the latter experienced a marked advance in 1837, when the puddling process was introduced in

[*] V. Yakovlev, "Vozniknovenie i etapy razvitiya kapitalicheskogo uklada v Rossii," Voprosy Istorii, 1950, No. 9, pp. 90–104.

a factory in the Urals. In 1860, this process was used in 50 per cent of the iron production. Yet the use of charcoal was customary in the process, and transportation was still at a primitive level. Moreover machinery, whether imported or manufactured, was still a rarity in the textile industry . . . and in transport.

At the beginning of the nineteenth century most of the cotton looms were utilized by artisans working in their cottages, while only a few were in the possession of factory owners. It is estimated that in 1860 there were 90,000 hand-operated looms as against 10,000 power looms, the latter accounting for one-fifth of the total production. The silk, linen, and hemp industries maintained their antiquated ways well into the second half of the century. In the woolen industry, power looms did not appear until the 1840's, and it was not until 1879 that machine production of wool reached 46 per cent of the total.

The steam engine, that typical machine of the industrial revolution, did not come into widespread use until the middle of the century. In 1843, in the Moscow area, there were some 1,300 industrial establishments and about eighty steam engines. . . . As late as 1866, only 16 per cent of the woolen mills used steam power. . . . In 1861, two hundred steamships were in use on the Volga and her tributaries. How trifling is this number in comparison with the tens of thousands of ships in the unmechanized river fleet.

From the examples cited, one can conclude that a technological revolution, involving not only the utilization of machines but also such an increase in number as to make possible a change in the conditions of production, can in no sense be traced back in Russia to the beginning of the nineteenth century. . . .

We can establish the fact of a rapid and massive change in technological development only after 1860. . . . In 1871, for the first time power looms accounted for more than two-thirds of the woolens produced. And, although 85 per cent of the sugar industry was using steam power as early as 1860, the use of such power did not become general until the seventies. . . .

It must be kept in mind that one industrial sector remained backward: that was metallurgy, which was still primarily represented by the plants of the Urals. Here is evident a peculiar feature of Russian economic development in the nineteenth century, namely the difference between the various industrial regions in the beginnings of the great changes. . . .

This uneven character must be stressed. We find it also in the financial conditions of industrial establishments and in the system of industrial credit, which are generally affected by technological progress. Even though there is evidence of a certain limited industrial capitalism in Russia in the first half of the nineteenth century, there was no real credit system. In contrast to the Western countries, Russia did not, even in 1860, have any capital market. The small number of banks in operation were either deposit, mortgage, or loan offices for the state. Stock companies handled a negligible amount of capital. Only in the second half of the century did the situation change, and then only gradually.

The establishment, in 1864, of the railroad companies on the one hand and of the State Bank on the other resulted in the development of a credit system, but it was of little service in industry until the eighties. Of course, one can note the expansion of banking between 1869 and 1873, permitting a rather laborious growth of the capital market, a growth nourished for the main part by foreign capital. But we must wait until the nineties and the beginning of Witte's policies to be certain of the establishment of a financial structure that is not dependent on the development of industry. This lack of capital, even at a time when industrial technology offered all sorts of possibilities, is likewise a peculiarity of the Russian scene. The industrial revolutions of the Western countries developed in a different climate and a different milieu. They were supported by wealthy commercial capitalism, linked to an old credit system. They developed rapidly and completely, unlike nineteenth-century Russia. These reflections . . . lead us to place the beginnings of the industrial revolution in Russia in the second half of the nineteenth century and to note that it occurred in two stages, the first in the seventies and the second in the nineties, with a very marked lull between them.

Is this point of view supported by what is known of the changes in the social structure? Russian industrial development before 1860 took place within the framework of a serf or half-serf society, consisting of three categories: serfs required to provide a specific amount of labor; a fairly small number of state peasants; and serfs who could contract their services. The latter serfs, whose only tie to their owners was the payment of dues, were actually, if not legally, a kind of proletariat in relation to their employers and constituted a disruptive element in the feudal system. It is on the basis of the growing employment of dues-paying (*obrok*) serfs at the end of the eighteenth century that Yakovlev is able to designate the period between 1790 and 1825 as the period of the beginning of the industrial revolution.

Indeed industrial development did, in a certain sense, create a precedent for the liberation of the serfs long before the legislation of 1861. But this semi-proletariat produced by industry was no new phenomenon; as far back as 1771, about 32 per cent of the industrial workers, excluding those in mines, were free—that is, capable of entering into contracts. Their number increased, not so much in the first quarter of the nineteenth century as in the second, when it grew from 54 per cent in 1825 to 87 per cent in 1860. There is then no social transformation, no revolution, but a lengthy movement toward the creation of a proletariat in the modern sense of the word. This development was quite incomplete since landlords continued to use large numbers of serfs in their own establishments, such as mills and distilleries, or to arrange for their use in metallurgy. . . .

Insofar as a social transformation occurred, it was the result of the law liberating the serfs and took place after 1861. Even so, the effects of the law became visible slowly; its effective influence in the sixties was limited by the transitional policies employed. Moreover, since the labor force was already, in 1860—actually, if not legally—semi-proletarian, it cannot be argued that the situation of the workers was directly and markedly changed in the period immediately following. But it can be said that the law freed the labor market, established new legal relationships in production, and opened the way for the emergence of a genuine proletariat. . . .

. . . . .

The most convenient measure for industrial development is the number of workers rather than the number of factories. . . .

. . . . .

In 1830 there were about 250,000 workers in a population of fifty million; and in 1860 about 860,000 in a population of seventy million. The ratio of the labor force in the total population had hardly changed and remained at less than 1 per cent.

If we were to make a growth curve for population and another for the labor force, we would find that, until 1830, the two were continuously parallel. After 1830, the curve for the labor force approached that for the population; only after 1871, and especially between 1871 and 1875, did it shoot up suddenly and cross the population curve. However the real growth of industry, measured by the number of employed workers, began only in the nineties. There were 1,400,000 workers in 1887, and slightly less than three million in 1900. To be sure, the population grew in the intervening years from 110 million to 130 million, but the ratio of the labor force to the total population had doubled in fifteen years.

To evaluate this accelerated growth properly we must not forget that we are starting from a low base. If we compare Russia's industrial development with that of other large industrial states, Russia's backwardness is obvious. The French labor force in 1861 was estimated at 1,300,000, approximately the same as that of Russia in 1887, thirty years later. But the French population was thirty-five million in 1861, while Russia's population in 1887 was three times as large.

Since it is not a question of comparing Russia with other industrial nations, but of determining at what point in her history her socio-economic development was such as to merit the designation of industrial revolution, we must look more closely at the process of acceleration in the nineties. The decade was marked by brisk activity: between 1890 and 1900 the production of cast iron, of sugar, and of cottons doubled. The amount of coal and oil transported was tripled. In this period the Trans-Siberian Railroad was built. In these years, large-scale industry was finally established in the Ukraine with the result that the industrial picture of Russia was substantially altered; in contrast to developments in the Ural industrial region . . . a modern, completely equipped industry relying on coal was built in the Ukraine, one that far outstripped the Urals in production by the end of the century.

The social consequences of this industrial growth are no less noteworthy. First of all, there came the ruin of the handicrafts, which began to disappear in the second half of the century as the result of competition with the factories. Also, industrial growth led to the movement of workers to the cities and even to the establishment of new cities in connection with the development of the Ukrainian industrial region and the construction of the Trans-Siberian Railroad.

By this time, it is finally possible to see the long-range effects of the Law of 1861. The law had not only placed a free labor force at the disposal of the factories. It had also changed the psychological conditions in which the industrial development took place; it had made possible rapid improvement in the standard of living and, with it, the accelerated expansion of the consumers' market. Thus ended the limited market, almost exclusively peasant, that had kept the social system in a relatively passive condition. Possibilities that had not previously been sensed now opened up, and they were quickly noted by both government and business. The contrast between the timidity of Kankrin's industrial policies in the first half of the nineteenth century and the real daring of a Count Witte after 1893 gave sharp expression to the new optimism of official circles.

But was the expansion of the domestic market in fact so great that it can be given as a sufficient explanation for the industrial upsurge of the nineties? It was, if it is understood that this upsurge was based first of all on the needs of the state and on the construction of the railroad system . . . and not on the spontaneous growth of demand. Producers' goods constituted an important part of the swift industrial growth at the end of the nineteenth century, in contrast to consumers' goods. . . . One must look beyond the turn of the century, to the years 1910–1913, to find well-established industry dependent on an expanded consumers' market. . . .

If one applies the term industrial revolution to the nineties, he must do so with reservation. If one takes into account the significance of the transformation in the socio-economic structure . . . with respect to this or that geographical area in isolation (e.g., St. Petersburg or the Ukraine) or with respect to this or that industrial sector (cotton or metallurgy) alone, then the term industrial revolution is justified. If, however, one wishes to evaluate the consequences of the speeding-up of industrial growth for Russia as a whole, it soon becomes clear that these consequences were limited and that the industrial revolution did not produce those widespread phenomena characteristic of the West.

If at this point we had to answer the question posed at the beginning—was there an industrial revolution in Russia in the nineteenth century?—the answer would be yes. One would agree that during the second half of the nineteenth century in Russia, beginning in the seventies, an industrial revolution took place, but it was an incomplete revolution incapable of effecting fundamental and rapid changes at the same time, except in certain limited geographic and economic sectors.

After 1880, the Ukraine experienced a fundamental and rapid change that deserves the name of revolution. This may in no way be said of the Urals, where, with the exception of certain factories, the traditional socio-economic structure persisted, even into the early part of the twentieth century. We are dealing here with large regions, each of which is comparable in size to England or France. From this fact, it can be seen that the differential growth was determined for a long time by the boundless expanse of the Russian Empire and the distance of industrial centers from one another. The chief characteristic of an industrial revolution . . . (industrialization of the same economic sphere in the entire country) is not to be found in Russia.

Now, did the industrial upturn of the nineties produce a fundamental change in Russian society? The ratio of workers to peasants in 1900 was still low. And if one excludes foreigners and members of the nobility from his count of factory owners and managerial personnel, he is left with a negligible number of persons who are primarily manufacturers. It can be asserted that the industrial bourgeoisie was of no consequence in the last quarter of the nineteenth century. Its real development came in the early part of the twentieth century and was interrupted by the change of regime in 1917.

It is not only the limited development of Russian industry that accounts for the fact that peasant society changed as little as it did. One must take into account also the fact that industry could absorb only part of the rapidly increasing population. It is evident that the industrial revolution exerted little direct influence on the great majority of the Russian people, the people of the countryside—90 per cent of the population. In fact, the peasant mass continued to weigh heavily on the entire Russian society, including even the social elements created by industrialization.

A considerable part of the labor force was no longer identified with the land, but many still had two occupations, being peasants and factory workers in turn, a phenomenon that was rare in the Western countries, except among handicraft workers. A true industrial revolution creates new and influential social strata. From this point of view, the industrial revolution [in Russia] produced very limited consequences in the nineteenth century.

. . . . .

3 /

RUSSIA AND
PANSLAVISM IN THE
EIGHTEEN-SEVENTIES *

The Pan-Slav movement is more than a century old and has been
espoused by various ethnic and political groups, to whom it has
represented different things. To some it has been a cultural movement
to strengthen the solidarity of the several Slavic groups; to others, a
political movement to aid in the struggle of Slavic minorities for
national rights. In both the Tsarist and the Soviet periods, Pan-Slavism
has sometimes been discouraged by the government, and sometimes
used by it for political purposes. In Tsarist times, the period described
by Professor Sumner, the movement drew much of its strength from
popular support. For that reason, it was a more important and complex
force than it has been in recent times.

W‌HEN TWENTY YEARS after the Crimean War the near eastern
question again absorbed the attention of Europe, among the various
changes in the setting of the crisis of 1876–8 as compared with that of
1853–6 appears conspicuously the new force styled panslavism. It is the

* B. H. Sumner, "Russia and Panslavism in the Eighteen-seventies," *Transactions of
the Royal Historical Society,* 4th Series, XVIII (1935), 25–52. First given as a
lecture to the Royal Historical Society in 1934. Reprinted by permission of the
publisher.
The author (1893–1951) spent most of his life at Oxford University—as student,
teacher, and scholar. A graduate of Balliol College, he served as Fellow of All
Souls College, then of Balliol, and, from 1945 until his death, he was Warden of All
Souls. He was both a gifted teacher and a scholar, his scholarly interests being
primarily, but not exclusively, directed towards Russian diplomatic history. *Russia
and the Balkans* (1937) and *Peter the Great and the Ottoman Empire* (1950) are
the products of that interest. His *A Short History of Russia* (1949) well illustrates
his gift for thoughtful analysis.

purpose of this paper to attempt some analysis of its growth and its main elements with a view to indicating its position and potentialities on the eve of the crisis of 1876. Since panslavism was in general not so much an organised policy, or even a creed, but rather an attitude of mind and feeling, it was at the time correspondingly difficult to gauge its power, just as it is now to analyse its different elements. At least there is no doubt that during the late 'seventies panslavism bulked in the eyes of Buda-Pesth and Vienna, of Constantinople and London as the most dangerous force in Russia, and as will be seen in the course of this paper there was indeed much in it to give good ground for the denunciations of foreign alarmists.

One major difficulty in giving specific meaning to the vague, general term panslavism was that when and in proportion as it gained wide influence it did so very largely by transforming itself into a very pronounced form of Great Russian nationalism. It was in fact during the 'sixties and 'seventies in a period of transition when the watchwords that appealed to the older generation were sounding less clearly and did not chime in harmoniously with the harsh clanging of a younger generation. In a sense it was the difference between panslavism, or slavophilism as it had been originally styled, and panrussianism. What had begun as the religious and intellectual strivings of small coteries of Muscovite landowners ended by being transformed into crude appeals to nationalist mass-emotions.

The slavophil movement, which grew up in the two decades before the Crimean War and attracted considerable attention abroad under the description of the struggle between the slavophils and the westernisers, had neither any organisation nor any clear political programme. The conditions of the later years of Nicholas I's reign made the open expression of political opinions almost impossible, but a further reason for the predominantly non-political character of early slavophilism lay in the fact that for the majority of the slavophils it was the outcome of individual struggles to express a satisfactory philosophical and theological formulation of their religious convictions and a justification of their view of the world: hence the vein of quietism, of social and political conservatism which runs through much of the writings of the slavophils,—it is particularly noticeable in Ivan Kirievsky. Yet they were by no means conservatives of the official Uvarov brand; they tended to look upon the state and the machinery of law as acting only by force and as entirely secondary in comparison with the living reality of a community (obshchina) morally free and morally united in the collective realisation of faith. They were first and foremost steeped in Orthodoxy. But they were also intellectuals, belonging to the middle or upper strata of the nobility; well off and well educated; acquainted with western thought and literature; specially influenced by Schlegel and Hegel. The opposition between them and the westernisers was ultimately due less to divergence of historical or political views than to differences of temperament and psychological approach,—the one religious, the other rationalistic. Nearly all of the slavophils were closely bound to the Russian land, for they were not only serf owners, but were born, bred and resident much of the year on their country estates.

Like spreading oaks, these families grew in the easy soil of serfdom, their roots invisibly intertwined with the life of the people and drawing life from its waters, while their topmost branches reached up into the air of European culture.*

Instinctively they represented the country as against the town. Their one town was Moscow, and that was a great, sprawling clutter of gardened houses, peasant huts, and countless churches. St. Petersburg was psychologically and physically, just as it was symbolically, entirely alien to them. Thus bound to Moscow, thus linked with the land, they inevitably reacted profoundly against the catastrophic failure of the St. Petersburg bureaucracy, largely non-Russian in personnel, in the Crimean War. In the "liberal" years that ushered in Alexander II's reign, when the press was relatively free and political activity to some extent possible, the slavophils entered the lists prominently in the struggle for reforms, above all of course concentrated on the fundamental problem of serfdom. It was thus in the sphere of internal reforms that the slavophils first openly appeared upon the political scene. Though bitterly critical of the breakdown of the foreign policy of Nicholas and his Baltic German diplomats, their efforts were in the first place mainly directed to saving Russia herself. Only a healthy, cleansed Russia could come forward as the saviour of Slavdom. In this respect at least they had come round to the point of view of the westernisers.

Prior to the Crimean War slavophil circles had in general taken little sustained interest in the non-Russian Slavs. The linguistic and cultural revival which began among Czechs, Serbs, and Bulgars in the first half of the century looked far more to Russia than *vice versa*. Russians when they travelled abroad went normally to Germany, Switzerland or the West, not to the Balkans or the Slav lands of the Austrian Empire. The official world looked askance at any incipient panslav stirrings, and Nicholas I, only too thoroughly supported here by Nesselrode and his closest confidants, frowned severely upon any Slav movements which might infuse a further dose of revolutionary principles, above all if they infected the Habsburg Empire. No raising of a Slav banner was possible without a break between St. Petersburg and Vienna, and such a break Nicholas was, to his

* M. Gershenzon, *Istoricheskie Zapiski*, pp. 44–5 and 94–5 (2nd edition; Berlin, 1923); referring to such families as the Kirievskys, the Koshelovs, the Homyakovs, or the Samarins.

cost, the last to think possible. Only on the very eve of the Crimean War did he as a last resort sanction an appeal to the Christians of Turkey to rise in common defence of Orthodoxy,—but not of Slavdom. It as at this point that there came into play the first attempts of the slavophil movement to influence foreign policy. These were due mainly to the activities of the energetic and widely known Pogodin, one of the few among the friends of the earlier slavophils to interest himself vigorously in the other Slav peoples.

Professor of history at Moscow University, Pogodin was the leading representative of the type of academic propagandist and philanthropist which was to be very prominent in the panslav movement in the 'sixties and 'seventies. Though stoutly Orthodox himself, his Slav interests and sympathies were founded rather upon the historical achievements of the past than upon a spiritual basis of the reuniting and redemptive powers of Orthodoxy. As for the present, he conjured up a picture of brother Slavs groaning under the yoke of the foreigner and gazing expectantly at Russia, by whose undisputed and unaided might they were to be rescued. This breezy optimism of Pogodin was rudely shattered by the Crimean War, but he was possessed of a buoyant perseverance and he had the invaluable capacity of giving some life to vague sympathy by harnessing it to practical and organised work. Almost alone of the slavophil sympathisers of his generation he lived on in activity for long after the war (he did not die until 1875), and he was one of the founders, and the second president, of the Moscow Slavonic Benevolent Committee.

This committee was set up with the approval of Alexander II in 1858 with the declared aim of assisting the Southern Slavs to develop their religious, educational and other national institutions and of bringing young Slavs to Russia to be educated. In practice it concentrated almost entirely upon the Bulgars, upon whom it had an important, though by no means always the desired, effect. From the start it was closely connected with the Church, and various ecclesiastical dignitaries both in Moscow and the provinces gave the movement influential assistance. It had the backing of the Department of Asiatic Affairs in the Foreign Office, and in particular the energetic support of Ignatyev. The St. Petersburg committee, founded ten years later, was largely directed by professors of the university and concentrated mainly on relations, by no means always amicable, with the Czechs. Similar committees were also set up in 1869 and 1870 in Kiev and Odessa, where the Bulgarian colony served as its nucleus. The membership of all four was very small: they did not issue propagandist literature on any scale in Russia until 1876 and they had no regular press of their own. Their influence within Russia was not widespread before 1876; outside Russia and especially in Bulgaria they were by then of definite importance. But their greatest effect probably lay less in their actual achievements than in the exaggerated alarm which their activities in the Balkans and Austria-Hungary had inspired in the world of diplomacy and journalism.

The most spectacular achievement of the Moscow Committee had been the holding in 1867 of a Slavonic Ethnographic Exhibition in Moscow which was much advertised in Russia, and much commented upon abroad as a thin cultural cloak for political propaganda. On the whole it was not much more than a platonic declaration of Slav sympathies, and no effect was given to the one practical proposal put forward (by the Czechs not the Russians), namely, the organisation of a permanent Slavonic institute and of biennial Slavonic cultural congresses. Its Russian organisers hailed it as for the first time arousing Russia to the Slav question and as converting what had been an abstract, literary question into a living problem of actuality. Yet these same men eight years later, when the eastern question again festered into a crisis, had to confess that Russian ignorance of and apathy towards their Slav brethren were still only too widespread. By 1875 not so very much had changed since 1860 when Turgenev's *On the Eve* depicted the father of the heroine as unable to distinguish her Bulgarian revolutionary lover from "a vagrant Montenegrin."

But at the least the Slavonic committees did form a skeleton organisation which might be rapidly expanded if circumstances were favourable, for besides the rigid Muscovite patriotism which was their core they now had, what they never had before, powerful supporters in both the Winter Palace and the Anichkov Palace and powerful allies in a new stream of anti-foreign hostility. Of their Muscovite core the most typical representative was the leader of the Moscow Committee, Ivan Aksakov, a man of vigorous personality, who rose to the height of his career in the crisis of 1876 to 1878.

Born in 1823, sprung from the central Russian land and bred in something of the atmosphere of his father Sergei's *A Russian Gentleman*, Ivan Aksakov belonged spiritually, like Dostoyevsky two years his senior, to the older slavophils born in the first decade of the century. With him as for them the roots of Slav feeling lay in absorbed devotion to the Orthodox church. With them likewise his main energies lay outside any professional or official service. Neither learned nor widely read, but passionately outspoken with all the conviction of a doctrinaire fanatic, he became the prophet of the small circle of the Moscow Slavonic Committee, announcing in semi-apocalyptic terms the divine mission of Russia, the freeing of her brothers in faith and blood from a foreign religious and political yoke. This historical mission of Russia, her moral right and duty, is founded in the fact—never argued nor "proved," merely didactically stated—of Orthodoxy as the one pure form of Christianity, the essential basis of true civilisation, of which the Russian Slavs are the only true and effective repository and upholders. Over against Slav Orthodoxy is set the old decaying Romano-German world of the West, with its poison of unbridled rationalism and individualism, its cancer of internecine competition, and its ruinous social and industrial struggles. As for almost all the earlier slavophils Catholicism is the symbol for western civilisation, and for Aksakov the arch-enemy. Protestantism bulks far less, appearing merely as a subsidiary form of declension from the true principles of Christianity. Thus the Catholic Slavs have been guilty of the great betrayal. The Slavs stand at the parting of the ways; either the way of the West, of Rome; or the way of the East, of Orthodox Moscow. For the Czechs and Croats there may be some hope if they return to Cyril and Methodius, to Orthodoxy; to the Poles Aksakov offers nothing but the cup of irreconcilable bitterness. The essential prerequisite for the idea of panslav fraternity is the idea of the highest spiritual unity in faith: secure the purity of the Slav ideal of faith and church, then all things will be added unto you. Hence political combinations, the political aims of Russian foreign policy are left vague and unanalysed. All the strength of the Slavs lies in Russia; all the strength of Russia in her Slavdom. Russia cannot achieve healthy national development save through realisation of her vocation as the great Slav power, through a break with the post-Petrine, Petersburg period of her history. Just as Russia is unthinkable apart from Slavdom, since she is both spiritually and materially the leading expression of it, so also is Slavdom unthinkable apart from Russia.

These views are little else than a restatement of those of Ivan Kirievsky and Homyakov, but the emphasis is now laid in Orthodox Slavdom rather than on Greco-Slavonic Orthodoxy, a significant transition towards the newer panslavism. And further, while earlier writers, as too Aksakov's contemporary Dostoyevsky, hankered after some synthesis which should save western civilisation from the consequences flowing from the over-developed rationalism of its philosophical and theological bases, Aksakov was content to summon Orthodoxy and Slavdom to do battle with the principle of evil. Russia's messianic calling was no longer to be that of the saviour of humanity at large, but was now limited to Orthodox Slavdom alone. On the other hand, he took over from his predecessors, besides their fundamental religious outlook, their antipathy to institutional forms of constraint and regulation and their criticism of or hostility to Peter the Great and his semi-German successors with their tentacular bureaucratic despotism and their desertion of true Russian ways of life for western importations. Thus the *mir* and later the *zemsky sobor* became slogans for slavophil or panslav groups as genuine, national products of Muscovite Russia; thus the Holy Synod was repudiated as an erastian creation of Peter which had shackled the true life of the church and bent it into subservience to the state: thus the governmental machine was attacked as an alien incubus, controlled by

Baltic Germans and other non-Russians, totally unable to respond to the deep currents of national life; thus, finally, the dynasty itself was the target for accusations of being but a German brand of military autocracy without roots in the soil of Russia.

Such an attitude of mind, to some extent traditional among certain sections of the landed power, owing much now to the reaction against the régime of Nicholas I and something to the economic and social dislocation following on the emancipation of the serfs and other reforms, was by no means confined to Aksakov's followers. With different colourings and different trappings, it was common to many among the landowning class for whom St. Petersburg meant government by bureaucrats, loss of power, and economic displacement. Here were potent feelings, essentially unconnected with panslavism, which yet might be utilised by it in an assault upon St. Petersburg foreign policy if that policy refused to move in consonance with the true aspirations of the Russian people as the standard bearer of the Slav cause.

This anti-governmental element, together with the anti-dynastic streak, in the panslavism of Moscow circles helped to make them profoundly antipathetic to Alexander II himself and to most of the high functionaries of the St. Petersburg machine. Yet they were not without allies or sympathisers in the very highest circles of the court. The Empress and, later, the wife of the Tsarevich with all the enthusiasm of converts to Orthodoxy imbibed the traditional view of the mission of Orthodox Russia and surrounded themselves with a circle of ardent devotees of Homyakov's and Tyutchev's brand of religious, poetising nationalism, of which the Countess Bludova's salon was the most conspicuous centre. There reigned Tyutchev's dreams of a "great Graeco-Russian Orthodox Empire" which should gather together Slavdom with "the Pan-Slavonic Tsar" at its head, and

> as ye gaze,
> To east and west, to south and north,
> The sun's glad tidings shall ring forth,
> The summons of his conquering rays.

In such an atmosphere, and with Pobedonostsev as tutor, the future Alexander III had been brought up. He was probably not deeply influenced by this mixture of panorthodox and panslav symbolism, but he was as Tsarevich generally supposed to be an adherent of panslav ideas, a supposition which could find confirmation in the undoubted fact that a number of his entourage, as well as his wife, were warm supporters of the cause. These court allies were not an initiating force, but if a crisis arose in Turkey, if feeling rose high, they might act as a powerful influence on Russian foreign policy and as invaluable collaborators with Aksakov's following in Moscow.

Although Aksakov and his like fiercely denounced Peter the Great and so much that followed after him, they omitted from their counts the expansion of Muscovy into the Russian Empire. It was Peter and his house of Holstein-Gottorp who had annexed the Baltic provinces, the southern steppes, the Crimea, Poland, Finland, Bessarabia, the Caucasus, great tracts of Asia. This tremendous heritage was silently accepted. So far from there being any murmur of undoing any part of this work, Moscow and the panslavs were the loudest in demanding that the borderlands be fully absorbed in the great Slav mass of central Russia, the core of the old Muscovy. The Polish revolt of 1863 had unleashed again century-old hatreds and fears. Katkov in his *Moskovskiya Vedemosti* had led the first great press campaign which Russia had known, with resounding effect against the Poles and against foreign intervention. In the years which followed the old "Congress Poland" was swept away, mercilessly dragooned within the framework of the administration common to Russia proper (a framework that largely consisted of a state of siege), while "the western lands," Lithuania, White Russia and the right-bank Ukraine, were subjected to every measure of russianisation. Contemporaneously was initiated a campaign of the same nature in the Baltic Provinces and Bessarabia; and, to show without mistaking that Russian meant Great Russian alone, the Little Russian or Ukrainian cultural revival of the time was successfully attacked by Moscow, above all by the prohibition in 1876 of the use of the Ukrainian "dialect" for any academic or literary purposes. Symptomatically two of the men most actively associated with this denationalising, russianising policy were among the most prominent of the slavophil or panslav Muscovites of the day: Prince Cherkassky (1824–78) and Yuri Samarin (1819–76), both of them friends of Aksakov.

Completely different in character and attainments, they were both at one in regarding the problem of nationality within the Russian Empire as requiring urgent and drastic handling. Samarin admirably summed up an increasingly widespread feeling when he ridiculed the ideal of a denationalised empire in which Russians, Poles and Germans lived side by side but apart from each other "comme qui dirait la reproduction très en grande de l'hôtel Ragatz (he was writing from Brussels) où Russes, Américains et Français venaient, sans se connaître, s'asseoir à la même table d'hôte"; over against this he set a Russia in which a Russian "would feel like a Frenchman feels in France or an Englishman in England," entirely at home.

For Samarin and Cherkassky the only solution possible for the great western fringes of the empire was an undeviating policy of russianisation: of the success of this in the central Polish provinces with an overwhelming pure Polish population they were admittedly doubtful, but it could at least serve to stifle the nationalistic chauvinism of the upper classes until such time as the Polish peasantry had been transformed by the new legislation for which both men were largely responsible. Samarin had been one of N. A. Milyutin's right-hand men in working out the details of the abolition of serfdom in Russia and was subsequently employed in the somewhat similar task of agrarian reform in Poland. An earlier period of administration in the Baltic Provinces had likewise given him first-hand practical experience of the Letts and Esthonians and their Baltic German landowners. Prince Cherkassky, a wealthy Tula landowner, had taken a prominent part in the emancipation of the serfs and also worked with Milyutin and Samarin in Poland and distinguished himself in the campaign for reuniting the Uniats with the Orthodox Church. For three years (1868–70) he was still more in the public eye at the head of the Moscow City Council, until his protest against reaction, in concert with Aksakov and Samarin, called down the displeasure of the Tsar and he was forced into retirement. Both were noted members of the Moscow Slavonic Committee, though Cherkassky, unlike Samarin in his closing years, did not deeply concern himself with the Slavs outside Russia until he ended his life, in 1878, as civil administrator of Bulgaria.

Both men are significant in the panslav movement in that unlike Aksakov or the earlier slavophils, and unlike the professorial type represented by Lamansky, Miller or Grot, they were active in administration and politics and were well-known public figures. Cherkassky in particular represents the doer—by fits and starts—as opposed to the thinker or prophet. Samarin, endowed with an exceptional capacity for hard work, combined practical ability with deep intellectual and religious interests grounded in him by his early upbringing and his student years at Moscow university. Himself a considerable theologian as well as the author of the widely influential *The Borderlands of Russia*, the text-book of the "russifiers" of the 'seventies, he may be accounted a bridge between the older type of slavophil steeped in the learning, the rites, and the mysticism of Orthodoxy and the newer type of forceful administrator, diplomat or soldier to whom such a religious and philosophical grounding was of little or no concern. Both men are also, above all, significant as leading protagonists of the transformation of the idea of panslavism into that of panrussianism. To the success of such views on internal policy was largely due that continuance in western countries of the picture of Russia as the brutal oppressor of her subjects and peoples which remained one of the strongest springs of Russophobia in England and elsewhere.

At the same time this internal aspect of developing panslavism was paralleled by the note of hectoring domination or overweening pride which was becoming more and more marked in relations with the Slavs outside the empire. It is of course obvious that views such as those of Aksakov sketched above would raise in an acute form the fundamental contradiction contained in the combination of panslavism and Orthodoxy. A thousand years of the history of the western Slavs were virtually ignored. More than half of the Slavs living outside Russia dwelt within the bounds of the Austro-Hungarian empire; and the great majority of these were Catholic and had been for centuries deeply affected by westernising influences. Still more formidable was the problem of the Poles, the second most numerous of the Slav races and with their long and great tradition of civilisation binding them to Catholicism and the West. It was impossible in the long run to ignore them, and yet at this period that was the deliberate attitude of the Russian panslavs, hot with the acrid fumes of 1863. At the Slavonic Ethnographic Exhibition held in Moscow in 1867 to display to Russia and the world at large the fraternal union of Slavdom the Poles were conspicuous by their absence. In all the round of speeches on that occasion the Poles were scarcely mentioned save by Pogodin who called upon them to rejoin the Slav brotherhood by humbling themselves before the Russian Tsar. At the close Rieger, the Czech leader, remonstrated in cautious terms. Promptly Cherkassky, true to his reputation, arose to pour forth minatory reproaches on any meddling with what was a purely Russian question.

It is evident that panslavism as long as the Orthodox Church remained as its basis could only be applied in the main to the Slavs in Turkey. Only in proportion as it shed its ecclesiastical and religious elements, might it be capable of appeal to the majority of the Slavs in Austria-Hungary, or to the Poles. Even then there would remain the stumbling-block of the lack of any common language. It was symptomatic that Safarik's correspondence with Pogodin was written in German, and that the proceedings of the Prague Slavonic congress of 1848 were likewise conducted in German. The Russians in their attempt to impose Russian as the common language for all Slavs encountered the most emphatic opposition: unedifying and fruitless wrangles with Lamansky, Hilferding and other Russian philologists in the panslav camp were the only result.

Lastly, a third stumbling-block in the path of panslavism lay in the fact that, although Russia was indisputably the only effective political and military Slav power, her claims to cultural predominance seemed thin and arrogant in the eyes of many western Slavs. Thus Homyakov's *Address from Moscow to the Serbs*, in 1860, with its tone of dictatorial superiority, had aroused much ill-feeling in Serbia. Palácky and others were not behindhand in repudiating any idea of Russian hegemony; and the same antipathy to the patronising dominance of Moscow was scarcely veiled during the celebrations of the 1867 Ethnographic Exhibition. Despite the reforms of the early 'sixties, Russian Tsardom ran counter to the traditions and aspirations of every other Slav people. Emancipation at the hands of the Russian Tsar might mean but an exchange of domination. Gorchakov, always an opponent of panslav schemes, was justified in writing, "Je ne vous dissimule pas qu'il m'est difficile de croire, à une sympathie sincère, des races Slaves pour la *Russie Autocratique.*" However much some of the Czech leaders might blind themselves to the nature of Russian Tsardom, the trees of liberty were likely to have very queer blooms if transported from the banks of the Neva or the Moskva. Certainly they were not recognisable along the Vistula.

These three major obstacles to the development of panslavism were abundantly apparent throughout Alexander II's reign. Towards its close they became less apparent to foreign eyes when a different form of panslavism was in the ascendant which put either no or little store on the test of purity of religion, or on the overcoming of linguistic differences, or on the civilising mission of Russia, but proclaimed a nakedly political programme for the annihilation of the Habsburg and Ottoman Empires through the military might of Russia. This may be said to mark the final stage of the development of panslavism into panrussianism, and this was the form in which during the eighteen-seventies panslavism was above all represented to the rest of Europe, mainly through the work of two men, the one forgotten, the other still remembered: Rostislav Andreievich Fadyeev and Nikolai Pavlovich Ignatyev.

Fadyeev (1824–84) was a military man, belonging to a country family of the nobility serving in the army or civil service. His father rose to be governor of Saratov: his mother was a Dolgorouki. He himself served for twenty years in the Caucasus, where he became an ardent supporter of expansion in Central Asia and a lifelong henchman of Prince Baryatinski, the conqueror of Shamyl and "the pacifier of the Caucasus." In 1867, inspired by the field-marshal chafing in retirement, he joined in the attack then being engineered on D. A. Milyutin's army reforms which he subjected to drastic criticism in a series of articles entitled *Russia's Armed Forces.* As a result he was forced by Milyutin to retire from the active army, and he soon joined forces with Chernyaev, the Central Asian lion of the day who had likewise been broken by Milyutin, and with his swashbuckling friends grouped round the violent nationalist paper *Russky Mir.* From this period dates Fadyeev's championship of the Slav cause, first pronounced in strident tones in his *Opinion on the Eastern Question* (1869), which at once made his name in the Slav lands. In January 1875 he went to Egypt to reconstruct the Egyptian army at the invitation of the Khedive,—an invitation which apparently was extracted by the intrigues of Ignatyev. This task was undertaken as a practical means for working towards the disruption of the Ottoman Empire, in the hope of being able in five or six years to utilise the Khedive's army against his suzerain in conjunction with a rising of the Balkan Slavs. Events moved too quickly; and in any case Ismail Pasha intended his army for a very different use, against the Abyssinians. Fadyeev hurriedly set out for the real scene of action and was back in Russia at the end of May

1876. The authorities succeeded in stopping him from proceeding to Serbia as he intended, but they allowed him to re-enter the active army, and he gaily continued his career as a stormy petrel figuring prominently, after war had been declared by Russia, in Belgrade and Cettinje.

It is not surprising that the views of such a man on the Slav question should present radical differences from the ideas already analysed. Fadyeev had no interest in the past, no concern for the slavophil tradition of emphasis on the spiritual and cultural union of the Slavs, no feeling for the unique mission of the Orthodox Church and the civilisation based upon it, no rooted belief in the virtues of the Russian peasant. He looked upon the Moscow slavophils as having finished their rôle and as having, since the emancipation of the serfs, no practical programme. Significantly he lived, in his later years, in St. Petersburg or Odessa, not in Moscow. He had the mentality of a militant adventurer. He could be direct and briefly to the point, but was apt to be carried away by fantastic exaggeration and atrabilious judgment. Of the Slav lands he knew little at first hand, and he had never visited any of them until his unwelcome appearance in Serbia in 1877; but he imbibed much from his friend Ignatyev and from the panslav group in Odessa. Above all he had a perfectly clear idea as to two fundamentals in the Slav question—force and Austria-Hungary.

His first book, *Russia's Armed Forces* (which appeared in 1867 and was soon translated into German with an alarmist, anti-Russian preface by Julius Eckardt), contained little of a political or non-technical character and panslavism is only incidentally urged, and in relatively moderate terms, but it enunciated without qualification the doctrine that force is the sole final arbiter in international affairs and the inevitable prerequisite for any great nation with a mission to fulfil. That the eastern question could only be solved by war on a great scale was even more emphasized in his *Opinion on the Eastern Question*. This brief, easily read, violently provocative outburst from Fadyeev was the most influential of all the expressions of panslav views of the time. First published in 1869, it was rapidly translated into most European, and all the Slav languages, and was generally taken abroad to sum up the quintessence and real programme of panslavism.

Its resounding keynote was the watchword attributed to Pashkevich, "the eastern question can be solved only in Austria, not in Turkey; the way to Constantinople lies through Vienna." The eastern question can only be terminated by war on Russia's western frontiers, for it is not a question affecting only the Slavs in Turkey, but the Slavs in Austria-Hungary as well, and the Poles: *i.e.*, it is "the Pan-Slavonian Question." Austria-Hungary cannot without committing suicide act otherwise than in a sense diametrically opposed to Russia: free Slav states in the Balkans would be impossible for the Austrians and the Magyars with their subject

Slav races. "Austria can hold her part of the Slavonian mass as long as
Turkey holds hers, and *vice versa.*" Turkey is looked upon as being in
complete decadence, and neither her army nor her fleet are regarded as
of any consequence. Militarily Russia can always forestall her western
opponents not only in the Balkans, but on the Bosphorus: with 100,000
men to mask the Bulgarian fortresses and a striking force of another 150,-
000 she can be in Constantinople in six weeks. But, her line of communications is fatally threatened by the strategical situation of the
Austrian Empire. Hence the necessity of settling with the Habsburgs and
of annexing Eastern Galicia and Bukovina, with their brother Slavs
"groaning on the Russian borders."

Russia's "historical individuality" is now pronounced, but it is not
realised, and it can only be realised by expansion as the welder of the
Slavonic world. She cannot be consolidated save as the centre of her
Slav and Orthodox world of eastern Europe.

The whole of Europe stands up against the historical development of Russia, threatening, as it does, a still greater breaking up of present systems . . .

The historical move of Russia from the Dnieper to the Vistula was a declaration of war to Europe, which had broken into a part of the Continent which
did not belong to her. Russia now stands in the midst of the enemy's lines—
such a condition is only temporary: she must either drive back the enemy or
abandon the position.

She "must either extend her pre-eminence to the Adriatic or withdraw
again beyond the Dnieper." Save for the members of her own family, the
Slavs and the Orthodox, Russia has, and can have, no reliable allies. Least
of all must Prussia (which Fadyeev already regarded as virtually united
Germany) be accounted such, for she will stand with Austria-Hungary
for the traditional German preponderance in the Danube valley, and for
continued Germanisation of the Slavs. "Russia's chief enemy is by no
means Western Europe, but the German race in its enormous preten-
sions." Thus foreshadowing developments of the late 'eighties, he went
on to argue that "all the more substantial interests of Russia and Prussia
are much more antagonistic than those of *Russia and France.*"

Fadyeev was not a whit depressed by his picture of an irreconcilably
hostile Europe in the struggle that was inevitably to come. Russia must
stand alert and prepared to act alone—with her Slav allies. He did indeed admit as a weakness the small amount of interest that had hitherto
been shown in these allies by Russia and her omission to establish herself
as their undisputed leader, but he readily comforted himself with the
recommendation that time and propaganda would rectify the mistakes
of the past. In any case the immense sympathies of the Slavs for Russia
could be securely counted upon as her greatest asset when the opportunity came and her armies struck victoriously against their common

foes. Then seven hundred thousand Slavs (a typically exaggerated figure) would rise in arms to fight on Russia's side. The Rumanians were to be won over by the gift of Transylvania; the Greeks by the gift of Thessaly, Epirus and the Isles, but nothing more. Unlike Aksakov and others, Fadyeev was ready enough to supply some outline at least of the political aims of the struggle for Slav emancipation. The objects were two-fold: to secure to each branch of the Slavs its independent political and social life; and to combine with Russia in some form of confederation in which Russia was to be militarily and internationally predominant. "Each tribe requires a Sovereign of its own for its domestic affairs, and a great Slave * Tzar for the affairs of all collectively." Thus foreign policy and military affairs must be in the hands of the Tsar. He added that it was very desirable that Russian Grand Dukes should sit upon the new Slav thrones. Russia however was to make no annexations, except in the case of Eastern Galicia and Bukovina, and of course the southern districts of Bessarabia torn from her in 1856. Constantinople was left in the vague position of a free city for the confederation. As for the Poles, they were summarily offered the alternative between entry into a Slav confederation and ruin. "The Polish nation will have to choose between the position of a younger brother of the Russian people and that of a German province."

Such a programme of panslavism, aiming nakedly at a Russian domination of the whole of eastern and south-eastern Europe to be realised through the overthrow of the Austrian and Turkish empires, however reckless in what it assumed and fantastic in what it omitted, could rouse all the more alarm abroad when in the course of the eighteen-seventies the renown of the Russian ambassador at Constantinople came to be widely spread as the able, unscrupulous, tireless propagator of closely similar ideas. It was above all the influence of Ignatyev which transmuted the aspirations of the Moscow panslavs into one of the main realities of the eastern crisis when it came to a head in 1876.

Ignatyev (1832–1908) was a man of exceptional abilities and ingeniously flexible determination, whose active life was entirely spent in the army, in the foreign office and in diplomacy. He made his name, when only twenty-eight, by his resounding success in the Far East in securing for Russia the 1860 Treaty of Pekin. From 1861–64 he was Director of the Asiatic Department of the Foreign Office, which dealt not only with purely Asiatic countries but with Turkey in Europe as well. In 1864 he took over the Constantinople legation (it was not raised to the rank of an embassy until three years later), and he remained at that post continuously until just before the outbreak of the Russo-Turkish war in 1877. He came to be on increasingly bad terms with, and finally

---

* Slav was frequently at this time spelt in English Slave, thus evoking a wholly different range of associations from those suggested to Slavs themselves by their common name,—*Slava* meaning glory.

the avowed rival of, his nominal superior Gorchakov, and he never acquired the real confidence of the Tsar; but he had multiplied connections
with the court, the army, the big landed nobility (to which he himself
belonged), and especially with the Slavonic Benevolent Committees.
By 1875 he stood out not merely as a diplomatist but as a leader on whom
was pinned much of the hopes of Russian nationalism and whose influence both in Russia and in the Balkans was of the greatest practical
consequence.

Ignatyev in sketching in his memoirs his general policy in the Near
East laid down three aims which Russian diplomacy must follow: the
revision of the 1856 Treaty of Paris (including the suppression of the
collective guardianship of Turkey by the powers), the command of Constantinople and Straits, and some form of common action by the Slavs
under the direction of Russia. His attitude to panslavism is predominantly
political, the religious and cultural aspects being merely means which
could be useful adjuncts for the attainment of Russian predominance
in south-eastern Europe. Ignatyev was not a man for whom the Orthodox
Church meant any deep religious experience or mystical communion.
His attitude during the struggle between the Greeks and the Bulgars
over the Exarchate is an excellent illustration of the way in which political calculations were the determinant factor. He knew that a schism
would lead to internecine struggles among the Eastern Churches and
a general lowering of the prestige of Orthodoxy which would be not at
all to Russian interests: hence his original policy appears to have been
to secure a compromise which would provide some nucleus for the nas-
cent Bulgarian nation but which would not entirely alienate the Greeks.
But as the prospect of any such agreed settlement receded he was quite
prepared to tip the scales more and more decisively in favour of the
Bulgarian extremists. Unable to prevent the Greeks from offering un-
yielding opposition, he appeared undisguisedly as the main protagonist
of those in the Russian diplomatic service who thought in terms of Slavdom rather than in those of Orthodoxy. There could be no stronger contrast than that between Ignatyev and his subordinate Leontyev, occasionally, though with doubtful justice, classed as a slavophil. Leontyev
was for some ten years in the consular service in the Balkans and Constantinople. There his first-hand acquaintance with both Bulgars and
Greeks served to fortify his convictions as to the primacy of "Byzantin-
ism" (the Greek-Orthodox culture and view of the world) and caused
him to recoil in horror from the deliberate rending of the Orthodox world
by the Bulgarian intelligentsia in the name of that false nationalism,
linked up with the principles of 1789, which for Leontyev was the curse
of Slavism. For Ignatyev, on the other hand, the whole question of the
Exarchate was simply one as to how could be secured for the Bulgars

"un noyau national qu'on serait libre de développer ultérieurement"; and by "on" he meant primarily Russia.

The difference between the panslavism of Ignatyev and his like, and the philosophical and religious slavophilism of the older type, is equally well illustrated by Ignatyev's frank repudiation of any pretence at idealism in his championship of the Slavs. Sooner or later, he held, Russia must fight Austria-Hungary for the first place in the Balkans and for the leadership of Slavdom: only for the attainment of this task should Russia make sacrifices for the Slavs under Austrian and Turkish rule and be solicitous for their freedom and growth in strength. To aim merely at emancipating the Slavs, to be satisfied with merely humanitarian success would be foolish and reprehensible. Slowly they must be united in the form of a defensive union subordinated to the general military, diplomatic and economic direction of Russia. Against Gorchakov he insisted that the Slav standard should be borne exclusively by the Russian Tsar: better to adjourn any idea of solving the Balkan question or of liberating Bosnia and Herzegovina from the Turkish yoke rather than yield anything to the inevitable rivalry of Austria-Hungary.

All Ignatyev's efforts were directed towards working for the time when the development of Russia's strength and favourable conditions in Europe would allow of the attainment of a purely Russian solution of the eastern question, *viz.*, the Straits at the disposal of Russia and the creation of brother states in blood and faith linked to Russia by adamantine ties. Of first importance was the command of Constantinople and the Straits, as necessary for the security of Russia's Black Sea coast-line as for her political and economic expansion. She must be master of Constantinople by one of two means, either by complete diplomatic predominance there, as was largely achieved between 1871 and 1875, or by direct conquest if the opposition of the Turks and the powers rendered the former policy impracticable. Ultimately in any case a radical solution of the eastern question would have to be found involving the disruption of the Ottoman Empire in Europe, and defiance of the Habsburg Empire: if the other powers combined with Turkey against Russia, Constantinople and the Straits must simply be conquered, and the Greeks, Bulgars and Armenians won over to act as obedient tools of Russian policy.

Thus with Ignatyev, as with Fadyeev, predominated the ideas of an independent, anti-European policy of force, and of a Russia whose destiny was to utilise the growing nationalism of the Slav peoples so as to facilitate the disruption by her own might of the Austro-Hungarian as well as of the Ottoman Empires, leaving in their stead south-eastern Europe (and for Ignatyev above all Constantinople and the Straits) under her unquestioned control. Ignatyev himself was to play his hardest

for these high stakes in 1878 when with the signature of his treaty of
San Stefano for a moment he was at the zenith of his power, only to
taste the bitterness of defeat three months later.

Of this newer type of panslavism no theoretical or systematic exposition was supplied by Ignatyev or Fadyeev. This lack was met by Danilevsky's *Russia and Europe,* subsequently styled "the bible of panslavism."
Though first published in 1869 it was not very influential in Russia or
much known abroad until a later period. Ponderous, very lengthy, and
graceless in style, it was certainly not designed for wide consumption.
It did, however, introduce a new note which helped to give it some
immediate vogue. Danilevsky (1822–85) had been trained as a student
mainly in botany and the natural sciences and throughout his career,
which was that of a government inspector of fisheries and other departments of agricultural economics, he retained the closest interest in them;
Darwin becoming his particular bugbear. From his botanical studies
he derived the idea of the struggle for existence as the dominating factor
in the relation between states; force was justified as an inevitable, natural concomitant of the development of any healthy species. *Russia and
Europe,* built up with much parade of scientific argumentation, seemed
to give to panslavism the *cachet* of science as then fashionable.

Danilevsky's political views, apart from their setting and presenta-
tion, are closely similar to those of Fadyeev. He, too, denies the conception of humanity or civilisation as a whole, and places in the forefront that of the struggle between different cultural-historical types,
based mainly on language groupings. While in general agreement with
the other slavophils or panslavs as to the opposition between the Romano-German civilisation of Europe and the civilisation of the Slav
peoples, he considers this opposition to be fundamental in the sense
that it is insuperable. Thus he, too, repudiates anything in the nature of
Dostoyevsky's striving towards a universal brotherhood to which Russia should guide, not merely her Slav brothers, but the whole suffering
world. Slav civilisation, above all as represented by Russia, is inevitably
destined for a glorious future, but this future depends upon the political emancipation of the Slavs from western Europe, and such independence can only be attained by war. Thus only can the eastern question
receive its final solution. Danilevsky has no doubts as to the outcome.
His political outlook and reasoning are, as with nearly all the panslavs,
extremely optimistic. Russia is taken as a match even for a combined
Europe, and the Slavs can have the fullest confidence in their moral superiority over a Europe diseased through centuries of violence and now
through economic dissensions and the undermining threat of socialism.
Victory is assured, and will bring to birth a Slav federation under the
leadership of Russia, into which must enter, besides the Poles, the non-

Slav Greeks, Roumanians and Magyars, and the capital of which is to be Constantinople.

Here again is apparent the unsubstantial sketchiness of panslavism as a political programme. It was in fact, except in the case of Ignatyev, far less a political programme than a political manifesto. With too little backing of real knowledge of the Slav lands and with insufficient facing up to the obstacles in its path, panslavism was much more of an emotional force than a planned creed of Russian imperialism. It is significant, for instance, that on the vital question of the future of Constantinople there was no agreement among the Russian nationalists. All were indeed agreed that Constantinople "must be ours"; but there were wide differences as to what exactly that meant. When the crisis of 1878 was reached, the lack of any clearly thought-out solution was only too evident. While Dostoyevsky feverishly preached the necessity and rightness of the annexation of Constantinople by Russia as the head and guardian of Orthodoxy, and while pious Orthodox circles, and particularly the Court devotees, would not be satisfied "until they sat cross-legged upon the crescent of Santa Sofia," Fadyeev and others urged some kind of internationalisation in the form of a free city, and Danilevsky and Leontyev on the other hand diatribed against such an idea as converting what should become the capital of a Slav or an Orthodox confederation into a hotbed of hostile intrigues of every description.

Such were the main strands going to make up the tangled web of panslavism in the eighteen-seventies. Clearly it was not the organised power or carefully worked-out plan which it was represented to be abroad. Yet the foreign view of it, though exaggerated, had sensed correctly the fundamental element of danger which lay in it. The panslavs, divided and few in numbers though they were, represented a sounding-board of the new, restless Russian nationalism. Through them, with their connections with the Moscovite nobility, the Orthodox Church, the court, the diplomatic service and the army, this nationalism might, if events abroad gave the requisite shock, be capable of effectually diverting or even directing the policy of the Tsar and his immediate advisers. An outbreak in the Balkans, massacres of Christians, tales of heroic resistance, could be made to arouse again among the immense mass of the illiterate population of Russia the old traditional feelings that God had made the Turks to be the oppressor of the Orthodox and the Russians to be their saviour. With the tiny minority of the educated this same appeal of the panslavs to religious and humanitarian sympathy for the Balkan Christians could bulk large, while they could also, of course, appeal to mere, ordinary chauvinism; in the case of a few to a deep and solid interest in Slavdom; in the case of many to a desire to escape from aimlessness and inaction by plunging into a cause. This last element in the panslav appeal in the late 'seventies brings out one of the two deepest motive forces lying beneath the turgid and often bombastic externals of pan-slavism. In its call to self-confidence, to action, to a belief in Russia as a mighty power destined to shape the history of the world and fulfil a mission of her own, it responded to a deep craving for national recognition, all the keener when the humiliation of the Crimean War was set in such sharp contrast with the achievements of Italians and Germans in moulding their national future. And as a second motive force lay the reaction, so explicit in all forms of slavophilism or panslavism, against the claim of West-European civilisation to set up as the one, true civilisation to which all other peoples are or should be adapting themselves, a reaction which still remains, in different guise, one of the most potent influences in the Russia of to-day.

4

POBEDONOSTSEV ON THE INSTRUMENTS OF RUSSIAN GOVERNMENT *

From 1881 to 1905, Constantine Petrovich Pobedonostsev was regarded as the spokesman of reaction in Russia, also as the originator of the reactionary policies that were being followed. During the reign of Alexander III, the reputation that Pobedonostsev enjoyed was, on the whole, deserved. After the accession of Nicholas II, in 1894, his influence declined, although both supporters and opponents of the regime continued to attribute to him power that he no longer had. Nevertheless, it is quite proper to think of him as the symbol of the period of reaction from 1881 to 1905, for he was the country's most articulate and intelligent defender of Russian autocracy and the most effective spokesman for the view to which the last two tsars, both of them his pupils, subscribed.

Konstantin petrovich pobedonostsev, who was the Over Pro-curator of the Holy Synod or the lay administrative head of the Russian Orthodox Church from April 1880 through October 1905, is known to history as the "evil genius" or the "Grand Inquisitor" of the reigns of Alexander III and Nicholas II, when he was considered the intellectual

* Robert F. Byrnes, "Pobedonostsev on the Instruments of Russian Government," *Continuity and Change in Russian and Soviet Thought,* edited by Ernest J. Simmons (Cambridge: Harvard University Press, 1955), pp. 114–28. Copyright, 1955, by the President and Fellows of Harvard College. Reprinted by permission of the author and the publisher.

The author, Professor of History at Indiana University, has made a study of conservatism in modern Europe, with particular emphasis on Russia and France. His *Antisemitism in Modern France* (1950) represents one phase of that study; his work on Pobedonostsev, another. He is preparing a book on the latter and has published several articles on the subject.

49

and political leader of the reactionary forces in Russia. This essay will
not attempt to discuss Pobedonostsev's career as a reactionary statesman,
or to determine to what degree his reputation is deserved, but it will
seek to analyze his political philosophy, with emphasis upon his views
concerning the instruments by which Russia was governed and should
be governed.

Pobedonostsev was born in Moscow in 1827 and died in St. Petersburg in 1907. His life thus approximately spanned the eighty years sepa-
rating the Decembrist Revolution and the Revolution of 1905. He entered
service in the bureaucracy in 1846, beginning as a law clerk in the Eighth
Department of the Senate. He rose steadily, becoming a Senator in 1868
and a member of the Governing Council in 1872. He was a prolific author, editor, and translator throughout his entire career. There are probable more data available in the West concerning Pobedonostsev's activities and opinions than concerning those of any other nineteenth-century
Russian statesman because of the quantity of his published works, the
governmental and other records which have been published, the care
with which he collected letters and other source material (much of
which he published late in his life, and some of which was published
after 1917), and the large number of his Russian and foreign acquaint-
ances who wrote memoirs containing information concerning him.

A thorough examination of this immense mass of data reveals that
Pobedonostsev's philosophy remained remarkably constant throughout
his long life. Indeed, he reprinted, without change, in the 1890's or in
the first decade of the twentieth century several books which he had
written or translated originally in the 1860's. There were, of course, exceptions, and there were minor variations in his views from time to
time, as new issues arose. However, the variations and new concepts were
almost invariably developments of Pobedonostsev's established concepts.
Thus, when he advocated the parish school system in the 1880's and
1890's, he was in fact just developing into practical and concrete form
ideas he had expressed twenty years earlier concerning education by
the church. Even his most daring essay, his bitter indictment of Panin's
administration of the Ministry of Justice, which was published in London in Herzen's *Golosa iz Rossii* (Voices of Russia), was a faithful
representation of views he held throughout his life concerning sound
administrative principles. Pobedonstsev's statements in the Governing
Council in 1905 and 1906 are very similar to those made in the Panin
article, which was written in 1858.

Pobedonostsev had firm ideas concerning the issues most fundamental to any political philosophy. To begin with, he was convinced that
by nature men were evil and unequal. He repeated frequently that
"every man is a lie" and that "every word said by man is an idle word
of self-delusion." He shared the views of Hobbes, though he had never

read Hobbes. He shared too the view expressed by Dostoyevsky's Grand Inquisitor that man is "weak, vicious, worthless, and rebellious." He told an English journalist that neither the spiritual instincts nor the moral restraints of the Russian people were adequate to subdue "the ferocious passions that lie dormant in their breasts" without the aid of physical sanctions. He believed that the Slavs were by nature sluggish and lazy and that they required firm leadership. He was convinced that the Russian man was inferior to all others, and he once described Russia beyond the imperial palaces as "an icy desert and an abode of the Bad Man."

Pobedonostsev's ruthless attack upon rationalism or "the fanaticism of formal logic" was a corollary of his views concerning the nature of man. He derided those who believed in the perfectibility of man. He severely condemned those who assumed that man could reason or that reason could be an effective tool for any but a tiny minority, whom he called "the aristocracy of intellect." He believed that the search for truth makes the average man a dangerous "rational fanatic" and threatens the unity and very existence of society. "True, sound intelligence is not logical but intuitive, because the aim of intelligence consists not in finding or showing reasons but in believing and trusting." The great essential and living truths are above the mind, and the great mass of men can receive ideas only through feeling.

Speculative, abstract thought in particular drew Pobedonostsev's wrath, and he declared that abstract principles were "destructive, suicidal, and sinful." He saw man, except for the minority, as an object of soft wax molded and formed by three forces utterly beyond his control: the unconscious, land, and history. Probably no statesman or politician in modern times, even Hitler, has so directly attacked rationalism and openly glorified the unconscious as Pobedonostsev did. Noting that "the healthy do not think about health," he urged that society be allowed by man to operate as an organ of the body does, "simply and unconsciously."

Pobedonostsev believed that, except for the minority, man's knowledge should be restricted to the sacred books and the "correct version" of his national history. He would have accepted the apothegm of Barres that the necessary foundation of a state is a cemetery, for he saw the "congenial seed" of a state in "the unconscious sphere of feeling, accumulated hereditarily from our ancestors." Since the capabilities of all but the minority are so limited, man must realize simply that his roots are in the past and that he derives from his ancestors. More he cannot understand.

Pobedonostsev's views on government reflect not only his concept of the nature of man, but also his ideas concerning the nature and character of societies and of the differences between societies. Pobedonostsev equated society and religion, and he would have accepted Professor

Toynbee's thesis that the great religions have created the different characteristics which make one "civilization" distinct from another. The role of the church in each society (Pobedonostsev considered Russia both a state and a society) was to create a "community of believers" and to answer "the deep-rooted human need for unity of belief."

From his belief that the character of a state or society was shaped by its "national faith" or by its church, Pobedonostsev drew the logical conclusion that no healthy state or society could have more than one creed. The Roman Empire collapsed because it tolerated many beliefs, which meant it had no faith or principle. Indeed, any state which tolerates more than one creed will be torn apart by conflict. Accordingly, Pobedonostsev believed that the states of continental Europe were doomed to civil war and destruction. He predicted that freedom of religion would ultimately disappear in the United States, because otherwise the Catholic Church would grow so strong as to threaten the very existence of Protestantism, which was the historical American creed.

Pobedonostsev believed too that each society or state possessed distinctive political and social beliefs and institutions which helped to shape its character. Each nation's development represented an organic process based on immutable laws. Each state was thus a prisoner of its past, and Pobedonostsev believed that historical research was beginning to reveal why the various states had different institutions and philosophies. Thus, he explained that some states, such as Russia, had centralized, authoritarian governments because in their distant past the emphasis had been upon communal life and upon firm control over the family by the father or by the patriarch; consequently, each person remained dependent, political power was respected and became more highly concentrated, and strong central government developed. On the other hand, "the Anglo-Saxon and Scandinavian states" had decentralized, democratic governments because in their distant past the emphasis had been upon individualism, and the father did not acquire absolute power in the family; consequently, democratic local government developed, and central authority remained comparatively weak.

Pobedonostsev, of course, was severely critical of parliamentary democracy, and he believed that representative institutions in the states of continental Europe were fatally stricken. However, he was convinced that constitutional and democratic government would continue to flourish in those states in which it developed from historical roots. Thus, all systems were consecrated by history. The principal problem, from his point of view, rose when a continental European state, such as France or Russia, sought to graft an alien institution upon its old foundations. This he considered fatal, particularly in those states where there were several national groups.

Pobedonostsev believed that each faith is intolerant and uncompromising and that it was both impossible and dangerous for one state or society to attempt to borrow ideas and institutions from another or to impose its customs and beliefs upon another. The idea of an active Orthodox mission or a Pan-Slav mission was, therefore, foreign to his philosophy. He believed Russia should concentrate upon attaining unity and increasing its national strength. He wrote nothing concerning the "third Rome" (the belief that Moscow was to succeed Rome and Constantinople as the capital of the universal empire), or concerning Russia's "sacred mission" of carrying civilization to the rest of the world.

While Pobedonostsev believed that other states and other religions as well would continue to thrive, at the same time he made clear that they should have no influence within Russia. In other words, he accepted "peaceful coexistence" and believed that the world should consist of a group of independent states which meet "only at the top," as they had during the greatest periods of absolute monarchy in Western Europe.

Pobedonostsev considered stability the supreme virtue of a political or social organism. His political philosophy glorified static relationships, with old institutions, traditions, and customs embodying the sacred ideas. Change was necessary, even in the most shielded and isolated society, but it would be minor, gradual, and elemental. If one compares Pobedonostsev's aims with those expressed in the preamble of the American Constitution, it becomes apparent that he sought two of the goals sought by the American leaders, unity and tranquillity. For the founders of the United States, however, unity and tranquillity were not to the same degree ends as they were for Pobedonostsev. They were also means to the attainment of three other goals, justice, the general welfare, and the blessings of liberty. Of these, Pobedonostsev says nothing.

For Pobedonostsev, government was maintained by three kinds of instruments: those which coerced or repressed, those which educated, and those which offered and provided rewards and incentives. He considered the coercive and repressive instruments the most vital, but he devoted more attention to the instruments for indoctrination. He ignored incentives, except for the ruling elite.

Pobedonostsev thought first of the state, as naturally as an American thinks first of the individual. He agreed with Rousseau that "the union of its members" makes the state one and that this union derives from the obligations which bind the members. However, he was not clear concerning the source of the binding obligations. Fundamentally, he asserted that the state was an expression of truth and represented the national will. The state's power was based "solely on the unity of consciousness between the people [narod] and the state, and on the national faith." He advised the tsar always to speak of "the people" of Russia, never of "the peoples," and he believed there was a mystical connection existing between the narod and the state.

The autocracy was the foundation upon which Pobedonostsev's political philosophy was erected. He bitterly opposed constitutional and democratic government for Russia, particularly because it restricted the powers of the ruler and divided power in such a way as to make government impossible. He was opposed even to advisory councils, such as the *Zemski Sobor*. Parliamentary government surrendered control in the state to parties, which meant that the true rulers were party organizers, vote manipulators, and eloquent demagogues, all interested in personal profit and none interested in the welfare of the state. Democratic government, in other words, "satisfied the personal ambition, vanity, and self-interest of its members," and prevented men of genuine ability from governing.

Pobedonostsev believed that power should be tightly concentrated and that there could be no institution or individual whose powers did not derive from the power of the state, which was absolute. Even though he first became prominent as a scholar of Russian civil law, he denounced the rule of law for distributing power and allowing conflict within the state. He even defended Russia's passport system in his *Course on Civil Law* on the ground that the passport identified the bearer as a citizen of Russia and provided him the autocracy's protection against local government.

Pobedonostsev's emphasis upon absolutism was constant, but it was strengthened by his experience with the Pan-Slav movement in 1876 and 1877. The drive to free the Balkan Slavs had inflamed even Pobedonostsev temporarily, but he soon realized that the government would have to control all such popular movements or face the danger that they might turn against the state in distrust and then in enmity. As a consequence, after 1877 he was particularly insistent upon autocratic government, the "binding" of Russian society, and international peace.

The uses of absolute government for Pobedonostsev are quite clear. It was, first of all, to distinguish between good and evil, light and dark. It was to provide "rational direction," by means of "calm, humane, indulgent, and arbitrary administration." It was, of course, to ensure stability. Above all, by using force and by ensuring equality for all, it was to prevent the rise of nationalisms in the multinational Russian empire.

Pobedonostsev would have agreed with Ammianus Marcellinus that "life is never sweeter than under a pious king." His ideal monarch was Louis IX, King of France in the second half of the thirteenth century, when everyone in each of the "estates" knew his place, social peace prevailed, the church and the state ruled in harmony, and the king, a saint, sat under a tree and decided those few disagreements which arose within the society.

However, his opinion of most Russian rulers was not favorable, and the autocrat in his view was most important as a symbol. He had a high regard for Peter the Great, because Peter saw the needs of his age clearly, used the established institutions when possible to increase the state's power and authority, and revised the established institutions when necessary. He praised Alexander III for knowing Russian history and traditions and for reflecting "the nature of his land and of his people." However, he was sharply critical of Alexander I, who knew neither Russia nor the Russian people and who sought to introduce dangerous foreign ideas. He condemned Nicholas I for using only lackeys in his administration, for isolating his court from the *narod*, and for placing his personal interests above those of the country. He was particularly critical of Alexander II, whom he called "a pitiful and unfortunate man" guilty of wasting and dishonoring the power given him.

Pobedonostsev's autocrat had several functions, the most important of which was setting a high standard for all government officials by working hard, by surrounding himself with serious and able men, and by living a sober Christian life. The autocrat was to represent the *narod's* interests, and by his travels and his presence at ceremonies he was to strengthen the love of the *narod* for the state. In addition, he was to select tough, able, and energetic executive aids and to accept their advice in directing the state. These executive agents for Pobedonostsev were the principal instruments of rule, and efficient operation of the entire system depended upon them. Essentially, he sought to modernize the autocracy. His advice to Alexander III was, "cherchez des capables," and his letters to the tsar constantly reiterated that a few able men in responsible positions could resolve Russia's principal problems.

These executives were first of all to be men of courage, willing to accept responsibility and to speak frankly to the tsar. They were to be hard-working, practical, efficient; they were to have organizing ability; they were to operate in a system which had clear lines of authority and responsibility. In other words, they were to possess the qualities which Pobedonostsev believed the Russian bureaucracy lacked, for he had great contempt for the craven and irresponsible "typical bureaucrat," who, he believed, delighted in eliminating efficiency and personality from government.

In their advice to the Russian ruler, these aides were to consider "history, tradition, the actual position of the state, and the needs of national life." However, they were to ignore and smash Russia's laws and institutions whenever they believed this was required in the state's interests. Pobedonostsev justified violent and arbitrary governmental action and angrily denounced the moralistic interpretation of history and of politics. He emphasized that "the rulers of the world" have always acted forcefully, and he believed that superior men should be beyond criticism in life as well as in history. Thus, although he had been trained as a jurist and a scholar and as a young man had hoped to become the Russian Savigny, as a statesman he was intellectually dishonest. For example, he deliberately distorted the meaning of some of the books and articles he translated.

It is clear that Pobedonostsev had little interest in the landed nobility and that he preferred representatives of the middle classes for these executive positions. Indeed, he stated in the fifth edition of his *Moscow Collection* in 1901 that the landed nobility as a class had ceased to have power and influence in Russia. He constantly praised the middle-class virtues, and he placed particularly high value upon self-made men. He apparently never visited a landed estate, except for brief visits to his father-in-law's Smolensk property when he and his wife were enroute to Salzburg for vacation. His three-volume *Course on Civil Law* is a mine of information concerning Russian property law and the various kinds of landholding before 1861, but even the final edition in 1896 shows that Pobedonostsev failed to analyze developments on the land after the emancipation of the serfs. Indeed, his very significant 1889 essay, which advocated that "family plots" be "indivisible and inviolable," reveals that he was totally ignorant concerning developments in Russian land-ownership after 1861.

It is obvious that Pobedonostsev was more interested in the policy-making instruments of government than in the administrative instruments. As a consequence, while he constantly interfered with the operations of the administrative departments, especially the various censorship offices, he did not devote much thought to the ordinary operations of government and he never mentioned the army or the police. According to him, the principal governmental instruments of the autocrat and his executive associates were law and the judicial system, the censor, the intellectuals, the printing press, and the Orthodox Church. The final instrument, and one of the most important, was the family.

Pobedonostsev had a thorough appreciation of law and the judicial system as instruments for the state. When he was a young man, he had hoped to publish a history of Russian judicial procedure since the middle of the seventeenth century. He spent the two decades after 1846 accumulating and analyzing the materials for his study of serfdom and for his essays on the history of Russian judicial procedure, which lifted him into prominence in the years just before serfdom was abolished. His three-volume *Course on Civil Law* was a significant contribution to Russian historical scholarship. His master's thesis and many of his articles ridiculed the overcentralized, complicated, ritualistic, and corrupt judicial system, and he was an important member of the committee which drafted the judicial reform of 1864.

Even during the years when Pobedonostsev supported judicial reform, he asserted that law and the judicial system should be servants of the state. For example, he insisted that the state should have the deciding voice in determining whether an issue involving the state should go before the courts, and he consistently opposed permanent tenure for judges. He considered law a superlative conservative force. Thus, he used it to prevent civil marriage and divorce. He recognized its contribution to uniformity throughout the empire. He valued it as a defense for private property and for traditional property relationships. Above all, he advocated the use of Russian law "to safeguard the dominant religion" and to deny rights and privileges to non-Orthodox religious groups and to national minorities, especially the Poles and the Jews.

Just as Pobedonostsev's heavy reliance upon law and the judicial system reflects his early interest in legal scholarship, so also his ideas concerning both censorship and propaganda reflect his career as an intellectual. He grew up in a family of intellectuals and in a close university circle, and he came as a boy to know and to respect scholars and writers, such as the Aksakovs, Lazhechnikov, the historical novelist, and Pogodin, the celebrated historian. He was brought up to assume that study, writing, and publishing were important achievements to which an educated man naturally devoted his life. Everyone who became acquainted with him, from his closest colleagues to foreign visitors such as Senator Beveridge, was astonished at his capacity and love for intellectual work and at the depth and range of his knowledge.

Pobedonostsev believed that the great dangers to Russia derived from intellectuals and the ideas they produced and carried. He considered freedom of the press a Western device for inundating Russia with lies. He hoped to isolate Russian intellectuals from the West. Consequently, the censor was an important instrument. He reorganized and invigorated the Holy Synod's censorship, he intervened to nominate and remove individuals from the various censorship offices under the Ministry of Interior, and he maintained close scrutiny of Russian intellectual life to guarantee that control remained thorough and effective. He paid especial attention to Russian newspapers, and he bombarded the censors with evidence of slackness and with fervent exhortations. Whenever he visited a library or a bookstore, he examined the shelves for forbidden books. He persuaded the censors to close heretical or dangerous plays, and he watched shop windows as well as art galleries to prevent the display of posters, paintings, or statues which might harm the state or the church. Above all, he sought to restrict and to destroy the influence of men such as Count Leo Tolstoy, whose doctrines he considered a direct challenge to the security of the state.

Pobedonostsev believed that repression could halt or control hostile or harmful ideas, but that indoctrination of the proper views was vital to ensure triumph. The principal burden for indoctrination he placed upon the Orthodox Church and its schools. However, he was aware that artists and other intellectuals were significant and that incentives

and rewards would assist in winning their support. Therefore, he urged
government encouragement and aid for papers and journals which were
sympathetic to government policies. He obtained awards and promotions
for scholars and publicists whose works supported his views. Finally,
he provided grants and honors for "truly Russian" composers and musi-
cians, such as Tchaikovsky and Anton Rubinstein.

Pobedonostsev was not an original thinker, but fundamentally a
propagandist. He was particularly interested in promoting the publication of literature which advocated his goals or which criticized his opponents. He devoted especial attention to the Holy Synod Press, and
he made it one of the largest and most efficient in Russia. He used this
press mainly to print and to distribute enormous quantities of literature
for the Orthodox Church and its parish schools. However, he also used
it to publish historical works which represented his point of view, or
which he believed would stimulate an interest in and love for the history of Russia. For example, it was the Holy Synod Press which first
published Kliuchevskii's famous *Course in Russian History.*

For Pobedonostsev, the Orthodox Church was the state's principal
servant and weapon. The Church was to act as a cement for society.
No state could have more than one religion, regardless of the number
of races it contained, for other beliefs and churches would be "agents
of disintegration." "He who deserts the Orthodox belief ceases to be Russian, not only in his thoughts and acts but also in his way of living and
in his dress."

The unity which the Church provided Pobedonostsev called the "community of believers." He asserted that "the Church and the Church
alone has allowed us to remain Russian and to unite our scattered
strength." Thus, when many of his contemporaries in Western Europe
were developing systems labeled "integral nationalism," Pobedonostsev
sought an "integral Christianism." He considered that this system above
all ensured equality: the Orthodox Church more than any other was "a
house where all are equal."

The Church was to accomplish its mission by providing and supporting the traditions, the loved ceremonies and spectacles, and the revered
beliefs. It was to preach submission to authority and to invest the important acts of life with a sacred aura. It was, above all, to control education, particularly in the primary grades. Pobedonostsev had firm and
clear ideas on education, and he was a staunch advocate of a national
parish school system. These schools emphasized the "four R's," reading,
writing, arithmetic, and religion, and they placed a great stress upon
singing. Pobedonostsev believed that schools must fit the people, and
he sought to provide children [with] "the basic elements of intellectual
and moral culture." He asserted too that primary school education should
not be a step toward higher education for most children, but should

concentrate upon inculcating sound habits and feelings and upon leaving the children "in that place and in that milieu in which they belong." Pobedonostsev, of course, attacked rationalism and "the logical man"; it was natural, therefore, for him to advocate trade schools as well as the parish school system. He had a deep scorn for most university professors and wanted to restrict advanced education. It is worthy of note that most of the friends about whom he wrote essays late in life were well-educated people who devoted their lives to primary schools in the countryside.

The Church was also to help eliminate the religious and national minorities. Pobedonostsev boasted of freedom of belief in Russia, but he considered all non-Orthodox religious groups "enemies of the state because the laws of the Orthodox Church are the laws of the state." He characterized the Old Believers as "dark, ignorant, stagnant in thought, and distinguished by deceit, slyness, meanness, and frivolity." He charged the German Lutherans in the Baltic provinces with seeking to destroy the Orthodox Church and the Russian state.

Pobedonostsev had a particular interest in gaining for Orthodoxy the Russian border territories and those areas of Central Asia and Siberia not yet fully under Russian political and cultural control. He hoped to seal these areas off from outside influence and to acquire that community in Orthodoxy which he considered fundamental. Thus, he sought to restrict all religions but Orthodoxy, to promote Orthodoxy and Russian culture, and to crush all minority nationalist feeling. He used his influence upon the tsar to maintain firm, nationalistic administrators in those areas, he built schools and churches, and he persuaded the tsar to send icons, grant money to schools, and in other ways demonstrate his interest. While he was frank and even eager in the use of "firm power" to crush the "mad dream" of national independence held by some minorities, he hoped above all to convert them to Orthodoxy. In 1889, for example, he had two Orthodox Baltic Germans placed on the Governing Council, citing their loyalty to the state as proof of the success his mission was enjoying.

Pobedonostsev's ideas concerning the Church's role in "extending and fortifying the empire" are demonstrated clearly by his own writings and by those of his closest friends, Nikolai Il'minskii, who was the founder of the Kazan Teachers' Seminary for Non-Russians and who also was a member of the Holy Synod's Educational Council. Il'minskii persuaded Pobedonostsev that Mohammedanism represented a serious threat to Russia and that a religious and cultural counterattack alone could save the Volga area and Central Asia from the Tartars and Mohammedanism. Il'minskii saw that "the primary education of non-Russians in their own language is the most certain means of persuading them to adopt the Russian language and Russian culture." He encouraged the cultural diversity of the national groups along the Volga and in Central Asia, and he sought to make their cultures "national in form, but Orthodox in content." He began with a school for baptized Tartars, and trained a native Orthodox priesthood for each national group. Soon he had more than one hundred schools for non-Russians in the Kazan area alone. These schools trained thousands of teachers and missionaries to carry Orthodoxy and Russian culture to the various national minorities. Il'minskii, with Pobedonostsev's support, also established a translating commission, which translated and published hundreds of thousands of copies of Orthodox texts in the various minority languages.

There were two religious and racial minority groups whom Pobedonostsev believed it was impossible to convert or to assimilate in entirety. The Jews should be erased from Russian public life; one third would be converted, one third would "wander away" across the frontier, and one third would die out. While this was being accomplished, their influence was to be restricted in every way possible. Pobedonostsev, therefore, supported the government's anti-Semitic campaign during the reign of Alexander III, although he sought to curb the popular movement against the Jews.

The Polish enclave was an object of Pobedonostsev's bitter hatred also, for he believed "the existence of a Polish state means slavery and oppression for all of the Russian people." He asserted that he did not know "a single Catholic who is not hostile to us and who does not dream of seizing our western provinces." The Polish problem was, of course, indissolubly linked with that of relations with the West. Pobedonostsev sought to incorporate Poland into the empire so that this problem would become only a domestic issue. He helped delay the long negotiations from 1878 through 1883 with the papacy, and during the late 1890's he fought resolutely against allowing a papal nuncio to reside in St. Petersburg. He declared to the tsar in 1899 that the Polish-Lithuanian issue was "a matter of life or death" for Russia. Since he believed religion could not be separated from nationality, acceptance of a nuncio would only give the Poles, the Catholics, "the Latins," a nest of intrigue inside Russia.

For Pobedonostsev, the primary instrument for controlling and educating man was the family, "the foundation of the state" and "the eternal element of prosperous societies." He was extremely well informed concerning European and American scholarship on the history of the family in all societies, and his most important translations were those of the studies of the family made by Heinrich Thiersch and Frederic Le Play.

Pobedonostsev described the family as "the spiritual and cultural nursery for citizens," and he assigned it the functions of maintaining tradition, ensuring social stability, harnessing and controlling man's most fundamental instincts, and providing for the orderly perpetuation of the human race. The parental power, "the only power established by God in the Decalogue, is the highest power." The function of the parents, especially the father, was to repress the child's evil instincts, to instill a knowledge of and respect for the Decalogue, and to provide the proper moral and physical education so that the child would become a patriotic, dutiful, and hard-working adult.

In summary, a brief analysis of Pobedonostsev's political philosophy and a quick survey of his state's armory of instruments reveal several striking characteristics. To begin with, his ideas concerning the nature of man were fundamental to his entire philosophy and "justified" the arbitrary and authoritarian government he advocated. In addition, his belief that the character of the state was shaped by its national religious faith and its traditional political and social institutions provided a base from which he could oppose "alien" ideas and institutions.

Nevertheless, Pobedonostsev's system was not so secure as it appeared. Perhaps this can be shown most clearly by neglecting for the moment the obvious weapons in the state's hands and by identifying some of the principal instruments or elements Pobedonostsev ignored or slighted. First of all, neither the army nor the police play an important role. In addition, Pobedonostsev did not appreciate the significance of a political facade, and there is a striking absence of color and trappings. However, it is in his treatment of the established nineteenth-century political trinity, the throne, the altar, and the aristocracy, that the most serious lacunae appear. For Pobedonostsev, of course, the main bulwark of the state was the Church. The other two members of the trinity, though, were very shaky indeed. Pobedonostsev was a fervent supporter of autocracy, but his advocacy was based neither on functional nor on religious grounds, and his arguments were generally vague. His autocrat was in effect a figurehead. Finally, he sought to replace the aristocracy or the nobility with a group of middle-class executive managers and efficiency experts.

5

THE HIGH COST AND THE GAMBLE OF THE WITTE SYSTEM: A CHAPTER IN THE INDUSTRIALIZATION OF RUSSIA *

In the nineteenth century, Russia still adhered to the Julian calendar and was therefore twelve days behind the West, which followed the Gregorian calendar. Efforts to change the calendar were strongly opposed by Pobedonostsev, who also opposed even more significant changes. On the other side was Witte, who sought to accelerate the process of change. Yet these two men shared the same basic belief in Russian autocracy. Pobedonostsev believed that autocracy could be preserved by preventing change; Witte believed that it could be preserved by encouraging and harnessing economic growth.
Both were wrong.

STUDENTS of the Five Year Plans are familiar with the over-reaching ambitions, the inflated claims, the disputed accomplishments, the misleading statistics, and the appalling human costs of "socialist industrialization" in Soviet Russia. They have generally ascribed these phenomena to Bolshevik theory and practice. It comes as a surprise then to find the criticism of the early Five Year Plans foreshadowed, in almost identical terms, in the attacks made upon the earlier policy of rapid industrialization in Russia which is linked with the name of Sergei Witte, the Czarist Minister of Finance, 1892–1903. He, too, paraded

* Theodore H. Von Laue, "The High Cost and the Gamble of the Witte System: A Chapter in the Industrialization of Russia," *The Journal of Economic History*, XIII (Fall, 1953), 425–48. Reprinted by permission of the author and the publisher.
The author is Associate Professor of History at the University of California (Riverside). He is preparing a lengthy study of Witte and has already published several articles on the subject. He is also the author of *Leopold Ranke, the Formative Years* (1950).

seemingly impressive results and dubious figures, and he, too, was forced
to exact dire sacrifices from popular welfare. Despite the profound dis-
similarities between the Soviet system and the Witte era (they must
go unstated here) there exists, it would seem, an underlying continuity,
pointing to more fundamental necessities and profounder tragedies that
backward countries with strong nationalist and imperialist tendencies
must face in the precipitous development of their resources. One special
difference, however, should be noted in this context. The distaste for the
bitter fruits of forced industrialization, muted in Stalinist Russia, could
frankly, although not entirely freely, be expressed in the eighteen nineties, when Witte's policies attained their full effect. The subsequent discussion of Witte's policies and their consequence is drawn from that public protest.

I

What, to begin with, were the essential features of the policies that
went by the name of the "Witte system"? Were they different from
those pursued by his predecessor Vyshnegradskii? Unquestionably
Witte, who, on September 11, 1892, in the aftermath of the great famine
of 1891, took over his difficult office, continued many fiscal techniques
and economic policies of his predecessor. He always considered the tariff
of 1891, enacted under Vyshnegradskii, the cornerstone of his system,
withal he acknowledged all the protectionist and fiscal necessities that
had shaped that tariff. Moreover, after some initial hesitation, Witte
accepted and realized Vyshnegradskii's ambition to put the ruble on the
gold standard. Witte also adopted and furthered Vyshnegradskii's practice of taxing the population to the utmost; for that reason he created
the vodka monopoly. He zealously promoted the export trade by forcing the peasants to throw their grain on the market when it was cheap,
by the regulation of freight rates, and a host of other measures. Like
Vyshnegradskii, Witte played the foreign stock markets for the benefit
of the Russian treasury. And like his predecessor he assiduously balanced
the budget and obtained, by purposely underestimating the government
revenue, a respectable yearly surplus. He continued and strengthened
the alliance between the Ministry of Finance and the *kupechestvo*, the
industrial, commercial, and financial community of Russia, an alliance
symbolized by the tariff of 1891. And last but not least, Witte inherited,
although scarcely by design, all the fortuitous conditions of an upswing
in the trade cycle.

And yet, there was a novel element in the Witte system, which transformed it from a policy aiming at a balanced budget into a comprehensive economic policy which consciously covered all of Russia's economic
life. Vyshnegradskii's chief ambition had been to balance the budget.
He had accomplished it, business fashion, by tailoring government ex-

penditures to government income, by taxing highly, and by practicing "a salutary caution in the expenditure of government money." Railway construction, for instance, made little progress during his term of office. In his six years fewer rails were laid than in a single good year of his successor's term; in 1891, the year of the famine, only 127 kilometers were built. But the famine ruined Vyshnegradskii's policy of fiscal parsimony. He had squeezed the peasants so hard that they had no reserves left against a bad year; and he had made no effort to develop the resources of Russia to keep pace with her growing needs. Though the budget was balanced, the peasants starved and Russia remained poor, Witte, by contrast, looked beyond the traditional resources of the budget. As a railway director he had succeeded in making railways prosperous by tapping the economic resources of the areas they served; now he was elevated to his high office in order to repeat his previous successes on a larger scale. He was to make the government prosperous by developing the potential wealth of the Russian lands.

The new point of view, which transformed the policies of the Minister of Finance into a comprehensive economic system, was clearly set forth in the first Budget Report written by the new minister:

> Government economy has its limits; refusing justified claims upon government expenditure can inflict serious difficulties upon the normal development of the civil and economic life of the country. Our fatherland overflows with all kinds of natural riches, but it has not yet utilized those riches in any desirable degree for the increase of its wealth. Financial policy should not fail to pay attention to the undesirable effects of excessive economy in meeting the growing demand, but on the contrary should consider as its task giving reasonable assistance to the development of the productive forces of the country. Such a policy should give better results also in regard to the finance of the government and raise not only the welfare of the population but also its paying powers and increase the sources of government revenue. In order to attain these ends one must above all aim at removing the unfavorable conditions which cramp the economic development of the country and at kindling a healthy spirit of enterprise in accordance with the natural conditions and demands of our national industries.

In the same report Witte also stated his conviction that the government had the right to take the initiative in all matters relating to the needs of the people. In a young country with unlimited tasks but limited resources like Russia, the government should direct industry according to the reasons of state policy.

In his memorable Budget Report for 1893 Witte laid the foundations of national planning of Russian industries. His dominant aim was the creation of Russian national industries, as he believed that no modern state could be powerful without modern industries. A follower of Friedrich List, he accepted modern industries as the chief civilizing factor in society, as a source of prosperity to the people and power to the government.

The means that Witte employed for the realization of his ambition were largely those evolved or prepared by his predecessor: the tariff, the gold standard, the influx of foreign capital, forced export, advantageous freight rates, and close co-operation with Russian capitalists. But, in line with his effort "to give reasonable assistance to the development of the productive forces of the country," he added as a contribution of his own a huge public works program in the form of the construction of the Siberian railway and other no less significant lines. Through railway construction Witte intended to expand the heavy industries, build up the industrial potential, particularly of southern Russia with its coal and iron deposits, and give employment to all sorts of subsidiary industries. An active program of railway expansion, justifiable on strategic, political, and economic grounds as an indispensable prerequisite for the development of a modern Russia, would thus serve both as flywheel and steering wheel of economic activity in Russia. Its benefits would be felt, Witte was convinced, in all phases of Russian life, not least in agriculture itself. He argued, as had List, that in modern society agriculture could benefit most effectively from the rapid progress of trade and industry. Despite strong pressure from the public he took very few direct measures for the promotion of agriculture. Whether or not his measures benefited agriculture, there is no question that the phenomenal industrial boom of the eighteen nineties was not so much the spontaneous effect of a favorable phase of the trade cycle (although that too played its part) as of Witte's determination to assist by all possible means "the development of the productive forces of the country."

By trying to stimulate all sides of Russian economy through the activities of the Ministry of Finance, Witte made himself "the responsible director of the great productive association of the Russian people." The task which he had set himself at his accession propelled him inevitably along a road which in the discussions of the Association of Russian Trade and Industry during the early years of the First World War, led to a modern concept of planning. In the Secret Memorandum of 1899 to the Emperor—he would never have used such language in public —Witte himself anticipated that trend, as he commented on the economic changes that had occurred in Russia after the emancipation of the serfs:

As a result of such fundamental transformation every major measure of the government more or less affects the life of the entire economic organism. The solicitude shown to various branches of industry, a new railroad, the discovery of a new field for Russian enterprise—these and other measures, even if partial and of local application only, touch the entire ever more complicated network and upset the established equilibrium. Every measure of the government in regard to trade and industry now affects almost the entire economic organism and influences the course of its further development.

In view of these facts the Minister of Finance concludes that the country, which in one way or the other is nurtured by the commercial and industrial policy of the government, requires above all that this policy be carried out according to a definite plan, with strict system and continuity.

But even more than a degree of economic planning was involved. The economic regeneration of Russia which he envisaged required also a social regeneration; it called for the energetic and enlightened cooperation of the Russian people, freed from all hampering tradition. It was not surprising then that Witte in his Budget Report for 1896 heaped such praise on the capitalist virtues of initiative and speculation which, he said, were creating flourishing new industries.

That kind of speculation arouses and sustains the keen intellectual force which guides and leads labor, capital, credit, exchange, which invents better techniques of production, which develops demand, finds and opens new sources of profit, broadens the field for national enterprise, shows ever new possibilities to entrepreneurs, introduces into production unexplored techniques, provides capital for existing enterprises—in a word that kind of speculation appears as the most energetic promoter of industrial progress, taking upon itself all those tasks which are connected with every forward step in the field of economics.

He hailed the progress of capitalism not only in industry but also in Russian agriculture and wanted to establish the proper legal framework for it in peasant society. As a young railway official he had learned that national chauvinism and religious intolerance make bad business; later as Minister of Finance he was guided by similar wisdom. And finally in his last years at the Ministry of Finance, when his "system" was disintegrating during a protracted industrial depression, he groped toward the recognition that a political adjustment was needed in order to give reality to the economic reorganization which he considered essential for the survival of Czarist Russia. The bold estimate of Witte's work by his friend and onetime adviser E. J. Dillon, was not too far from the truth: "Witte's method consisted of a series of economic, social and political changes gradually adopted. For one thing, he would have educated the entire people and endeavored to qualify the State, or a department of it, to discharge the function of social direction." In "the function of social direction," which Witte stumblingly and hesitantly assumed as Minister of Finance, lay both the triumph and the weakness of his historic role.

No survey of the Witte system would be complete without a reference to its propaganda efforts. The great task which Witte had set himself required the support of the Russian public. From the beginning of his career as Minister of Finance we find him unusually alert to the value of publicity. Under his management the annual Budget Reports of the empire became instruments of public enlightenment. Through them Witte took issue with the criticism of his opponents; they constitute an invaluable commentary on his policies and the economic condition of Russia. Written in a layman's language they appealed to the intelligence of the Russian (and foreign) reader and informed him of weighty problems of the national future. They tried to enlist his support in a great national effort. The impassioned voice of Witte could be clearly heard between the lines. Judging by the comments in the contemporary press they were eagerly read. Some magazines reprinted them in toto, others commented extensively. Of all ministers of the Czar, Witte alone had a politician's feeling for public relations for the promotion not only of his own personal career but also of his larger aims and of Russian credit abroad.

The extent of Witte's publicity effort was impressive for its time. He not only saw to it that he enjoyed a good press in Russia; he organized Russian participation in all great world's fairs of the time: the Chicago Columbian Exhibition of 1894, the Paris Centennial Exposition of 1900, and the Glasgow International Exhibition of 1901. For each he issued a splendid volume on Russian trade and industries written by the foremost experts. He maintained a host of writers abroad, particularly in France, whose task it was to refute all attacks on his system and to advertise the economic advance of Russia and the attractions of Russian investments. Finally he enlisted the help of the professors who supplied him with scientific data for his arguments and conclusions. Russian credit abroad and his own success as Minister of Finance depended on persistent efforts to disseminate the official optimistic picture of Russian economy. But he also served notice that henceforth Russia wished to be considered economically and industrially a great power.

II

While the Minister of Finance thus sought to advertise and justify his system, the Russian public remained doubtful or even grew hostile. From the beginning of his ministerial career Witte had faced bitter opposition. At first it was confined to the pamphleteer Cyon. But already in 1896 the Third Congress of Russian Trade and Industry, held at Nizhni Novgorod, voted against Witte's policies. At the time of the adoption of the gold standard (1897) the majority of the State Council, the highest legislative body of the empire, had warned of the dire consequences of Witte's policies for the welfare of the rural population and the balance of payments of the empire. While the industrial boom of the nineties lasted, Witte was able to brush off lightly these criticisms. But after the outbreak of the industrial depression in 1899 the opposition redoubled its efforts. In February 1899 even the Emperor turned, although only for a brief

Was the Emperor offended?

moment, against Witte's economic policy. Through Witte's quick efforts
the opposition of the Emperor was overcome. Yet within the government
and among the public the criticism of Witte's economic policies mounted
steadily until August 1903, when he was forced to give up the Ministry of
Finance.

As an advocate of rapid industrialization with the help of high
tariffs and the influx of foreign capital Witte antagonized not only all
agrarian interests from the narodniks on the left to the agrarian exporters
on the right but also the nationalist industrialists. Witte's most dangerous enemies in this coalition were those who had access to the Court, including the grain exporters and the nationalists of Katkov's school. They
employed some clever and well-informed pens.

There was no lack of damaging charges that could be brought against
the Minister of Finance. It was said, for instance, that the statistics of
industrial production which Witte had presented in his Budget Report
for 1897 were rather exaggerated. In that report he had written that
the annual product of Russian industries was valued at about two
billion rubles, whereas that of agriculture amounted only to one billion
and a half. As they stood, these figures did not allow closer scrutiny;
the information upon which they were based was not submitted; yet
they were not accepted by Witte's critics. More detailed study of specific data as given in official publications aroused still greater doubt of
the validity of Witte's claims. In the *Handbook for the Department for
Trade and Industry* (a department in the Ministry of Finance), edited
by Blau in 1896, the value of all cotton goods produced annually was
given as 531 million rubles. Upon closer inspection of the methods by
which this figure was obtained, it turned out that the full value of the
raw material, of the semifinished goods, and of the finished articles
had simply been added together. In the *Statistical Survey* for 1897
(published in 1900) the accounting mistake was admitted in a footnote, but the figure was upheld, as it was said that the cotton manufacturers had belittled their output in order to escape taxation. In the
Budget Report for 1900 the original figure from Blau's *Handbook* was
cited again. Yet according to calculations made by Sharapov, the real
value of the cotton goods produced annually was only 266.6 million
rubles, half of the official figure. The methods used in compiling the
statistics of the cotton industry, it was asserted, had also been applied
to evaluate the output of the Russian machine-building industry; the
value of coal, steel, etc., had been added in full to the market value of
the finished machines. In short, the official figures for the industrial
output, of which Witte had boasted, were found vastly inflated. Con-
versely, the inferiority of agriculture had not been so great as Witte
assumed. According to Taburno, the value of the agricultural product
in 1901 was 3.4 billion rubles and that of industry 3.9 billion. But as this

latter figure contained the duplications mentioned above, the real value was said to be nearer three quarters of that figure, which thus gave the lead still to agriculture.

Witte's statistics on increased consumption were found equally untrustworthy and misleading. The official *Statistical Survey for the Factory Industry, 1892–1900* had claimed, for instance, an increase in the consumption of cotton goods from 3.16 *pud* per head to 4.32 in the years 1892–1900, for iron and steel products from 0.54 to 0.99 *pud*, for anthracite from 4.28 to 8.53, and for pig iron from 0.58 to 1.36 *pud*. But it was pointed out that except for cotton goods the increase hardly benefited the consumer, as practically all production of heavy industries was absorbed by railway construction. And regarding the slight increase in the consumption of cotton goods, it was argued that this was caused rather by a shift of a part of the population from the home-spun of the self-sufficient village to the exchange economy of the towns and represented no real improvement. The economist Butmi checked the official figures on the consumption of cotton goods against the figures of raw cotton available to Russian mills and found that at least between 1892 and 1899 the consumption of raw cotton per head had actually declined. If there had been an increase in the consumption of cotton goods, it had been at the expense of their cotton content; that is, of their quality. As for the consumption of sugar, the government claimed an increase of 2.92 pounds per capita; Butmi only of 0.9 pound. Of tea there seems to have been a slight real increase; but it was again explained away by the shift to urban consumption. The consumption of kerosene was claimed by the Budget of 1902 to have grown by 28 per cent between 1892 and 1900. Butmi, basing his investigations on figures released by the collector of indirect taxes, found an actual decline by 4.9 per cent between 1893 and 1899. Witte officially denied the accuracy of Butmi's findings but did not submit the more reliable figures which he said he had in his possession. In short, Witte's opponents concluded that there had been no noticeable improvement of popular consumption, even during the boom years of the nineties. The severest criticism, however, was leveled against Witte's budgets and his boasts of their constant growth and their soundness. Were they based on the prosperity of Russia or were they merely an exercise in juggling figures for appearance's sake?

Let us look first at Witte's claims that the increased tax yield represented higher levels of consumption. Of an actual increase in the tax revenue there could be no doubt. It had risen from 701.8 million rubles in 1892 to 1,040 million in 1901. But neither could there be any doubt that the tax burden had also increased. Miliukov pointed out that it had been raised between 1883 and 1892 by 29 per cent, while the population increased only 16 per cent. Between 1893 and 1902 the tax burden had risen by 49 per cent, while the population increased only 13 per cent.

More specifically, between 1889 and 1902 the tax on sugar had been increased by 106 per cent, on matches 100 per cent, on kerosene 50 per cent. As these figures proved, the indirect taxes had risen tremendously, 108 per cent, it was said, between 1881 and 1901; five sixths of the tax revenue was drawn from them by 1900. And while Witte continued to argue that they were paid only by those who could afford them, his critics showed convincingly that many taxed items constituted part of the peasants' household economy, such as tea, vodka, matches, and kerosene.

The famous vodka monopoly, one of the major accomplishments of the Witte administration, was again a highly controversial topic. The official explanation for its creation, much advertised by Witte, was a humanitarian and moral one: it was designed to curb drunkenness. In connection with it, tearooms and reading rooms were opened under the patronage of members of the imperial family. Few students of the Russian taxation, however, were deceived by this flimsy camouflage of an obvious fiscal necessity. By taking the manufacture and sale of vodka under state management, the Ministry of Finance succeeded in augmenting by one fourth its revenue from the former impost on the sale of vodka, while according to all contemporary testimony no change in the frequency or intensity of drunkenness could be observed. For the consumer the result was a slight rise in the price of vodka, which fell as another burden especially upon the peasants who would not dispense with the liquor. Furthermore, the significant increase in government revenue was not entirely an absolute gain, as it deprived certain local administrative bodies, such as the peasant *volost*, of the revenue derived from the licensing of taverns. In other words, the government appropriated a tax source from local authorities, at the expense of the services performed by these local bodies.

Of the effects of such intensive resort to indirect taxes (not to mention the tariff, another form of indirect taxation), more will be said subsequently. Suffice it to observe now that Witte's confident interpretation of the growth of his tax income could hardly be justified. As Professor Khodskii had said at the Nizhni Novgorod congress, in many cases the extreme taxation of an item of popular consumption had led to the curtailment of the demand for it. In short, the increased tax yield did not represent greater public well-being.

In regard to the soundness of Witte's budget, critical analysis of the income other than from taxes led to some very damaging results. Shvanebakh, scrutinizing the budget for 1900, found that among certain nonrecurrent sources of income, valued at 127.2 million rubles, several were entirely fictitious and others considerably exaggerated. He thus reduced the entry to 85 million rubles. He furthermore checked the figures given for the revenue from state enterprises, state railways, post and telegraph, state forests, and the vodka monopoly, the total revenue of which was listed as 597.6 million rubles. Upon examination it turned out that the 374 million rubles listed as revenue from the state railways consisted entirely of operating costs. As a matter of fact, the state railways had had a deficit of 31.6 million rubles. In a similar manner Shvanebakh calculated the net revenue from post and telegraph at 15 million (instead of 50 million), from state forests at 40.4 million (instead of 55.7 million), and from the vodka monopoly at 30.3 million (instead of 117.9 million). The relatively high net profit of the state forests, he discovered, was the result of unpardonable parsimony in their upkeep, for which future generations would have to pay. At the end, Shvanebakh had reduced Witte's impressive figure of 597.6 million rubles to a mere 54.2 million. Adding this figure to the 85 million from other sources mentioned above, he obtained the sum of 139.2 million rubles instead of Witte's 724.8 million. The total revenue recorded in the budget for 1900 had thus shrunk from 1,704.1 million rubles to 1,114.2 million. It was no wonder, therefore, that the impressive increase in government revenues claimed by Witte was received with grave mistrust by his enemies. Sharapov thus found that the official figure for the increase of revenue, given as 73 per cent between 1890 and 1900, should be pared down to a mere 22 per cent. And that small rise was easily explained by the increase in taxation that had taken place in the meantime.

It is difficult to evaluate the results of these and other critical analyses of Witte's figures. They were undertaken by men who were as partisan as Witte himself; their interest was to belittle his accomplishment and to prove the continued misery of the mass of the Russian people. Yet whatever the reliability of their counterclaims, they established beyond doubt that Witte's imposing figures had a hollow ring. The revenue of the Russian empire was not as large as it appeared from the government's statements. The truth, indeed, was admitted by the economist Migulin, one of Witte's spokesmen: no matter how skillfully masked, the budget always faced a deficit, which was covered by foreign loans officially designated for railway construction but in fact required for fiscal reasons.

Unfortunately the position of a Russian Minister of Finance, as well as of Russian credit abroad, made such window dressing indispensable. Witte would not have lasted so long in office if he had not disguised so well the hardships of the transition period in an era of rapid industrialization.

Before long the criticism of Witte's figures, which rose in a steady crescendo after the outbreak of the depression and was hardly checked by the censor, was heard officially within the government. Witte's bitterest detractors, the extreme Slavophiles of Sharapov's circle, had long tried to enlist the support of the State Comptroller, whose task it was to watch over the accounts of most branches of the government. While T. I. Philippov was State Comptroller the criticism of Witte in his official reports to the Emperor had been mild and restrained. But when in 1899 General of the Infantry Lobko assumed that post, his office became the center of Witte's reactionary enemies. Behind the closed doors of the government Lobko made it his business to puncture the inflated claims which Witte advanced. He did so very effectively on January 10, 1902, during the final hearings on the budget for 1902 in the plenum of the State Council. The Minister of Finance had just referred, in celebration of his tenth year in office, to the large cash reserve in the treasury as proof of the brilliant financial condition of the government, when Lobko curtly announced that according to his calculations the cash on hand resulted merely from the French loan recently contracted. Still more dramatic was the session of the State Council a year later on January 11, 1903, when the budget for 1903 was examined. Witte had proudly reported that his budget now had passed the two billion mark and that the government's expenditures, which he had succeeded in covering by a corresponding increase in revenues, had almost doubled in his ten years as the Ministry of Finance (from 1,050.0 million rubles to 2,071.7 million). Whereupon the State Comptroller submitted his own analysis which showed that Witte's conclusions had been based on figures that were not comparable. According to his own statistics the increase in government expenditures had been only from 946 million rubles to 1,348 million; that is, 42 per cent instead of the nearly 100 per cent claimed by Witte.

The same session of the State Council gave a resounding demonstration of the decline of the "Witte system." Witte, who had always maintained an optimistic front, was now forced to admit, at least in the relative secrecy of the State Council, that after three years of the industrial depression and a decade and more of an endemic agricultural crisis "the paying powers of the population" were exhausted. Not that he blamed his own work for this; the reason lay in the construction of strategical railways insisted upon by Kuropatkin, the Minister of War. Now he pleaded that all government departments should exercise the strictest economy, because further taxation was inadmissible. This had also been the conclusion reached by Vyshnegradskii before his fall. After ten years of the Witte system, which, it will be remembered, was designed to increase the paying powers of the population, Russia had not escaped from the old impasse. Witte had finally come to face the obstacle that his opponents had always quoted against him: "the exhaustion of the paying powers of the population," which in contemporary parlance was synonymous with the misery of the Russian peasantry.

III

It is not the purpose of this paper to discuss the details and the extent of the deep-seated crisis of Russian agriculture at the end of the nineteenth century. Suffice it to say that contemporary economic literature abounded with heart-rending descriptions of the appalling undernourishment in the famine areas, of hopelessness, stagnation, ignorance, and poverty in the villages throughout Russia but particularly in the central black-soil provinces. And even where conditions, by Russian standards, had improved, they were found to be far behind those of western Europe.

The reasons for such misery stood out clearly to most contemporary economists. Russian agriculture suffered partly from the decline of the grain price in the world market, but partly also from its inability to adjust itself to the new conditions of capitalist economy. It had neither the intelligence nor the means to improve its methods by its own initiative. It was caught helplessly between a falling income and high, sometimes rising, prices for manufactured goods. Its slightest surpluses were ruthlessly taxed away by the state, which spent every kopek for heavy industries and railways which at the time had only a very remote connection with the peasant market. Witte's frequent denials notwithstanding, the government made no serious effort to improve the conditions of the peasants, although occasionally it made a minor concession in the payment of the tax arrears, or in the forms of tax collection. It took no steps to uphold the grain price by buying up grain stores and providing storage facilities. It did not further popular education in the village, nor build roads for local transportation, nor provide cheap credit for the needs of the rural population. Even the measures that Witte eventually proposed for the improvement of peasant economy, the legal change in their status which implied the abolition of the commune, relied for any results on the initiative and scant resources of the peasants. At the most the government undertook investigations. After having established a Special Conference on the Needs of the Landed Nobility in 1897 it created in the fall of 1899 a Special Conference under V. I. Kovalevskii to study the impoverishment of the central black-soil regions. In November 1901 this conference, which had accomplished nothing, became the Special Conference on the Impoverishment of the Center under V. I. Kokovtsov; it did not hold its first meeting until October 1903. At last, in February 1902 the Special Conference on the Needs of Agriculture was founded, of which Witte was made chairman. Its work attracted much attention, but its conclusions were not carried out until the revolution of 1905 and after. The prevailing opinion, vainly combated by Witte, was that industrialization impoverished the peasant, or at least prevented any improvement of his position. The resources of the government, it was argued, should have been spent on the promotion of agriculture, the primary source of income for the Russian people.

The deplorable state of Russian agriculture was in itself a grave charge against the minister who had made himself "the responsible director of the great productive association of the Russian people." But it appeared in a still more serious light if seen in relation to the "Witte system" and the promotion of industrialization. How could Russian industries be expected to prosper if there was no mass market for their products?

The huge public works program, which Witte, in contrast to his predecessor, had undertaken in order to stimulate Russian economic life, depended for its progress not upon domestic revenues but upon the continuation of foreign loans. When the international complications of the late nineties, the Fashoda crisis, the Spanish-American War, the Boer War, and the Boxer rebellion, curtailed the international money market; the railway construction and the attendant industrial boom in Russia also came to an end. And when the state orders ceased, Russian industry, which had hitherto depended so largely upon them, had no internal market to fall back upon. The industrial stagnation, although world-wide, became a serious industrial depression in Russia, because Russian industries had grown without any relationship to the domestic consumer. The development of the market had not followed the pace of state-fostered industrialization. In this way, the depression seemed to justify the dire predictions which narodnik writers like Vorontsov and Daniel'son had made for decades about the fate of capitalism in Russia, and refuted the Marxist analysis about the development of the Russian market. After 1899 the narodnik argument that Russian capitalism could not prosper because it had no domestic market, although modified by the recognition that Russian capitalism had come to stay, was very much in the foreground of the attack on the Witte system.

It was General Lobko, the State Comptroller, who soon pleaded this doctrine in his annual reports to the Emperor. In his report for 1900, printed with the Emperor's comments in May 1901, he commented briefly on the world-wide depression, which had hit Russia with special intensity because the growth of her industries had not been paralleled by the growth of the purchasing power of the domestic market. A year later, when the crisis had deepened, he returned to this question with a lengthy charge:

At present there is no more doubt that the crisis is caused by the artificial and excessive growth of industry in recent years. Industry, based on the protective tariff, extensive government orders, and the speculative increase of cheap foreign capital, grew out of proportion to the development of the consumers' market, which consists chiefly of the mass of the agricultural population, to which 80% of our population belongs. An entirely sound existence for industry is guaranteed only by a corresponding development of the domestic market representing a sufficiently broad and constant demand for manufactured goods. That condition is particularly important for a young industry developing under the influence of protective tariffs, as it is in no position to count on the international market. Furthermore, the economic condition of our agriculture cannot be called satisfactory. The strenuous efforts of the government to plant industries has not been accompanied by equally intensive measures for the support and raising of the agricultural base of the welfare of the Russian people. In view of the inadequacy of the government measures the negative sides of the protective system show up all the more strongly in the agricultural population. The chief burden of that system lies undoubtedly upon the agricultural mass, seriously impairing its purchasing power. It has to bear almost the entire burden of direct and indirect taxes. As a result the demand of our domestic market cannot keep up with the excessive growth of our industry. The equilibrium between industry and the domestic market has been destroyed and with it the basis of successful economic development. This, according to my deepest conviction, constitutes the chief cause of the present difficulties.

What Lobko stated so emphatically in May 1902 was indeed the prevailing opinion of the time. Everywhere the same complaints of the Witte system were heard. The State Council had long been convinced of their justice. Even Polovtsov, an important member of the State Council, and Kuropatkin, the Minister of War, who at that time were friendly to Witte, spoke to him about his mistaken policies; the latter in addition deplored the deteriorating physical conditions of rural recruits. The industrialists too took up the cry and blamed the minister for their troubles. The "local people" called into consultation by the Special Conference on the Needs of Agriculture voiced the dissatisfaction with the Witte system at the grass roots level. It is no exaggeration to say that the discontent against it was part of the rising popular agitation against the autocratic regime. And as if to drive home the charges against Witte, in the spring of 1902 the peasants rose in revolt in the very areas of Poltava and Kharkov, which were among the worst hit by the agricultural crisis.

At the end of his career as Minister of Finance Witte faced a bitter indictment of his economic policies from practically all groups of Russian society. For the sake of rapid industrialization, it was said, he had vastly increased both Russia's foreign debt and her dependence upon foreign creditors in the future; her foreign debt was the largest held by any government in the world. In order to facilitate the influx of foreign capital he had introduced the gold standard at great cost to the Russian people, perpetuating thus, in order to prevent the outflow of gold, the necessity for an excessively high tariff. And, in order to support his pet industries, Witte taxed the population to exhaustion, absorbed the savings from local savings banks into the treasury, and

curtailed badly needed social and cultural services. He thus sapped the
initiative of the Russian peasants, kept them in their primitive condition, ruined their health, denuded their forests—all in order to construct a huge network of poorly built, often wasteful railways and
heavy industries to support them, none of which stood in any profitable
relation to the consumers and their crying needs. Such system could
end only in the utter ruin of Russia.

IV

The political consequences of the upsurge against the Witte system
are not within the scope of this paper. But it is necessary to ask in
conclusion why Witte so long defied the pressure of public opinion
and ignored the widespread concern for the well-being of the Russian
peasant population. To be sure, he readily conceded that the protectionist system exacted heavy sacrifices particularly from the agricultural
population. They paid for Russian industrialization, he wrote in the
Secret Memorandum of 1899, not out of a surplus but out of current
necessities. But he never took so serious a view of these sacrifices as
his opponents; to him they constituted not an indictment of his system
but an incentive for it. The reason for this reaction lay only partly in
the fact that as a man trained in railroad affairs he was not familiar
with peasant conditions. More important, it was conditioned by his
estimate of the required tempo of Russian industrial development. The
crux of the controversy over the Witte system lay in the question of
tempo: how rapidly must and can Russia develop her industries? All
the other problems, the tariff, foreign capital, taxation, etc., were of
secondary importance.

Witte's opponents started from the narodnik premise that the development of industries, which most of them accepted as indispensable,
should proceed organically, as it had in England. The creation of an
adequate market should precede the creation of industry. They wished
to build up the domestic purchasing power by improving agriculture
and fostering the handicraft industries, hoping that both would expand
side by side until the market could support crafts that had grown into
large industrial enterprises. They would expand local credit facilities
to enable the peasants to rationalize and improve their economy; and
they would appropriate funds to expand the network of local high-
ways. In short, they would build Russian prosperity slowly, from the
bottom up, relying largely on Russian resources of skill and ingenuity.
To be sure, they disagreed among themselves over the extent and the
nature of the help that might be drawn from western Europe. The extreme nationalists of Sharapov's circle wanted to exclude the outside
influences altogether. The liberals of Ozerov's stamp hoped for the

gradual assimilation of European ways as part of the economic advance of Russia. Yet both were agreed that the tempo of industrialization under Witte was too fast and that the cost to the consumer and to the well-being of the Russian people was too excessive.

Witte, on the other hand, took the opposite course. He argued that the Minister of Finance was committed to rapid industrialization. "One can differ," he wrote in his Budget Report of 1897, "over the question which is preferable: the intensive development of industry over a short time or a weaker and thus also considerably slower forward movement? But one cannot deny that once the government adheres to the protective system in the course of a rather lengthy period and with undeviating strictness and determination, any premature interruption of it would be a serious political mistake and cause deep tension in the economic organization of the country." Rapid industrialization once undertaken could not be interrupted. He spoke the truth when he implied that the decision over the tempo was not really his; it had been made by Alexander III and the men who designed the tariff of 1891. And even that generation had been propelled on its course, as Migulin pointed out, by the policy of Alexander II and his Minister of Finance, Reitern, to build Russia's railways with the help of foreign capital. "Of course, gradual development out of our own resources," Migulin continued, "and work with the help of the savings accumulated by our own labor proceeds more cheaply and has more lasting results. But time does not wait; life goes full steam ahead. Even so we are behind all western peoples; and by walking slowly one does not go far, despite our proverb to the contrary. We have to live in a more rapid tempo and, whether we want to or not, we must resort to the services of foreigners." Kankrin, he said, had been the last Russian Minister of Finance who could afford to proceed slowly and soundly. After the Crimean War Russia could no longer tarry, unless she wanted to fall behind again. "But a great nation cannot wait"—that was the passionate appeal of Witte, repeated in his Budget Reports and speeches; "a modern great power had to have modern industries." As a young railroad official in Odessa, the most capitalist and open-minded city of the empire, he had absorbed from the railroad kings of the seventies the spirit of modern technology. He saw far more prophetically than any other dignitary in the government the necessity of industrialization, if Russia were to continue to play the part all her leading men assigned to her. In this view he was at one with Peter the Great and the promoters of the Five Year Plans. Yet, as he admitted in his *Memoirs*, his message found no response in the inner circles of the empire. Few shared his willingness to brave the hardships of rapid industrialization. Nobody acquainted with the history of Russia during the First World War can deny the justice of

Witte's plea; and by that time he had a few more followers. But during his term as Minister of Finance he was a prophet without honor in his own country.

The student of Russian society in this time finds a strange inconsistency in the books and documents that deal with the task of domestic and foreign policy. They indulge in almost unlimited ambitions of social improvement or territorial and economic expansion. Whether one takes a representative liberal like Ozerov, the Moscow economist, or the nationalists of Sharapov's school, or Migulin—not to speak of the millennial hopes of the revolutionaries—one finds that Russian society was in revolt against its backwardness or its weakness in world politics. And yet, very few men realized that their dreams could come true only by a concerted effort for rapid industrialization such as Witte had attempted. Not convinced of the need for rapid industrialization they naturally were unwilling to face the brutal costs. Witte, on the other hand, never grasped his opponents' point of view. To him their apprehensions appeared merely a sign of stupidity, malice against him personally, or sheer selfishness. He resembled the Bolsheviks in his ruthlessness and his optimism; he had neither the deep sympathy, the imaginative sensitivity, nor the rooted esteem for Russian traditions that enabled his opponents to see so clearly the full scope of the gamble and the revolution which his system implied. And he could find in the arguments thrown against him no valid answer to his insistence that his system represented the only feasible way by which Russia could catch up quickly with the advanced western nations.

But even at best, as the pessimists protested, there was no guarantee that his system would succeed. The implicit hope—and it was never more than a hope—was that the unfolding of Russia's natural riches would proceed more speedily than her foreign indebtedness and her domestic impoverishment, and that there would be a margin of earnings large enough to release Russia eventually from dependence upon the foreign rentier (and his government) and from her peasant poverty. This was the crucial gamble of the Witte system, a bold wager on Russia's undeveloped resources both human and natural. And to make the wager convincing to his contemporaries Witte had to promote an optimistic attitude. As he wrote in his Secret Memorandum of 1899, the accumulation of native capital, once started with foreign help, would increase by geometric progression: millions would give rise to billions. In support of such extravagant expectations he cited the example of the United States, where such miracles had really happened, without conceding that Russia was not the United States (as his opponents never tired of pointing out).

He assumed that, once his huge railway project was under way and the flywheel of industrialization spinning full tilt, the intelligent and

God-fearing Russian public would take over the task: "the best school for industry is industry itself." Through investing in industry an illiterate peasant could become a captain of industry, so he wrote in his Secret Memorandum, thinking no doubt of I. S. Bliokh, the amazing self-made railway king, whom he had known in his earlier days. The Russian people, Witte was convinced, would follow in Bliokh's footsteps and become resourceful and energetic capitalists. Deriving his theoretical equipment from Friedrich List, he could not but see his task in this over-simplified light. In the United States and in Germany tariff protection and foreign capital had been the only extraneous stimuli required for a phenomenal economic upsurge. There had been enough capable and enterprising people to take advantage of favorable natural conditions; the market had kept pace with industrial advance. In Russia, however, the task was far more difficult. For one thing, the twin problems of industrial promotion and governmental finance always seemed to interfere with each other and hampered the process of industrialization. Another difficulty lay in the necessity of the state's assuming a far more important role than List had anticipated. Furthermore, even at the height of his optimism Witte could not deny the fact that the commercial and industrial community of Russia was unpardonably sluggish and unable to co-operate fully with his plans. And finally, as Witte dimly recognized at the end of his career as Minister of Finance, Russian society and government as he had found them were incompatible with the economic order which he envisaged.

The truth was that in 1903 nobody in Russia (or anywhere else) could see the tragic dilemma of a backward country beset with ambition to rival the model nations of the West. There was only confusion and bewilderment over Russia's economic future. Even those who agreed with Witte's general principles, like Migulin, found fault with his careless handling of funds, his neglect of the consumers' market, and his lack of attention to details, which came from an insufficient realization of the difficulties involved. It was a great step forward when Ozerov advocated a commission for the scientific study of the conditions governing the industrial development of Russia. But even he, in his call for greater discipline of work and thought and for a pragmatic approach to the problem, had no perception of the magnitude of the task.

By 1903 Witte had failed, and for the next decade the government and a large segment of the public turned their attention to peasant affairs. Industrialization, to be sure, continued, not quite as feverishly and with less reliance on government orders. Yet the World War found Russian industries still insufficient for the great task at hand. Witte's ambition had not yet been realized and his warnings had not been heeded.

6

PLEKHANOV AND
THE ORIGINS OF
RUSSIAN MARXISM *

Agrarian Russia did not seem to provide the proper habitat in which
Marxism might flourish. Yet flourish it did; and to Plekhanov goes
much of the credit—or responsibility—for introducing Marxism into
Russia. It is doubtful that he would ever have acknowledged the
Soviet variety of Marxism as his legitimate offspring: in the first year
of Soviet rule (and the last year of his life) he actually repudiated it.
But the kinship can be traced; and the Soviet leaders, doing so, credit
Plekhanov with the founding of Russian Marxism.

It was in the year of Karl Marx's death that Russian Marxism
was born. In 1883, five people in Geneva, Switzerland, joining together
as the "Emancipation of Labor" Group, launched the fateful movement
that was to lead fifteen years later to the formation of the Russian Social-
Democratic Labor Party, and was to have such phenomenal consequences in 1917 and thereafter. The outstanding leader of the new revolutionary organization was George Plekhanov, who is rightly called the
"father of Russian Marxism."

It was not for lack of acquaintance with Marx's work that the
Marxian movement began in Russia at this relatively late date. Literate
Russians had had ample opportunity to familiarize themselves with
Marxian ideas inasmuch as (1) the works of Marx and Engels were ad-
mitted freely into the country at mid-century and for some time there-
after, (2) *Das Kapital* was legally published in Russia in 1872 and sold

* Samuel H. Baron, "Plekhanov and the Origins of Russian Marxism," *The Russian
Review*, XIII (January, 1954), 38–51. Reprinted by permission of the author and
the publisher.
  The author is Associate Professor of History at Grinnell College. The article
by which he is represented here is one of several that Professor Baron has written
on Plekhanov. He is now preparing a longer study on the subject.

well, (3) the revolutionary underground published illegally other works of Marx and Engels in the seventies and eighties, and (4) Marxian writings were not infrequently discussed in the periodical press. Leading Russian thinkers, such as Belinsky, Chernyshevsky, Lavrov, Bakunin, Tkachev, and Mikhailovsky, all had knowledge of some of Marx's works, and several of them had high praise for some aspects of Marxian thought. The important revolutionary organization, *Narodnaya Volya* (The People's Will), wrote to Marx in 1880: "The class of advanced intelligentsia in Russia, always attentively following the ideological development of Europe and sensitively reacting to it, has met the appearance of your works with enthusiasm."

But if advanced Russians had had a considerable exposure to Marxism, if various persons had a warm respect for Marx and some of his ideas, prior to 1883, Russian thinkers familiar with that system of thought agreed in failing to accept a thorough-going Marxism with its economic, political, sociological, and philosophical implications. Radical Russians had not taken Marx's ideas as a basis for their revolutionary activity for, in general, they considered that, while Marx had laid bare the roots and workings of capitalist states, his diagnosis and prognostications were inapplicable to Russia. It was rather the doctrines of populism (*narodnichestvo*) that held almost universal sway in Russian socialist circles. Marxism began to win adherents only when, as a consequence of repeated failures of populist movements to attain their ends, faith in the ideas and methods of those movements weakened. Then there was resumed that quest for "an algebra of revolution" that had engaged advanced Russians for decades. In the course of this renewed quest, Plekhanov, who had been an enthusiastic populist in the first years of his revolutionary career, was drawn to Marxian thought, which appeared to him to offer a more realistic and practicable basis for the Russian revolution. A study of his experience and of the development of his ideas with respect to Russia's social evolution reveals Plekhanov's reasons for abandoning populist views in favor of a Marxian approach. But the lessons that Plekhanov drew from his experience and studies had more than a personal significance; they provided the rationale for defections of other revolutionists from the populist ranks and for the consequent buildup of the Russian Marxian movement.

In 1874, the young nobleman Plekhanov was a brilliant, first-year student at the Mining Institute in Petersburg. In that turbulent decade, the universities were hotbeds of revolutionary propaganda. The times were such that a classroom could be used for a revolutionary meeting, while a professor acquiesced in such activity by foregoing a scheduled lecture. Under such conditions, Plekhanov, like so many other youths, was drawn into revolutionary activity and, gradually, he abandoned his studies. The sentiments he felt when, as a neophyte revolutionist, he en-

countered his first representative of the masses illustrate well both the
romantic nature of the populists and the gulf that tragically separated
them from those they yearned to help.

When I met Mitrofanov for the first time [he wrote] and recognized that
he was a . . . representative of the people, in my soul there stirred a feeling
of compassion. . . . I very much wanted to converse with him but did not
know how and with what expressions. . . . It seemed to me that the language
of . . . [the student] would be incomprehensible to this son of the people
. . . and that I would have to use the absurd manner of speech of our revolutionary pamphlets.

By December, 1876, Plekhanov, then an agitator for the revolutionary
organization "Land and Liberty" (*Zemlya i Volya*), was prepared to
burn his bridges behind him. In that month, he addressed an illegal
demonstration of students and workers on the Kazan Square in Petersburg. The meeting was broken up by the police and, in order to escape
arrest, Plekhanov fled abroad. Thereafter, he was wanted by the authorities; when in his native land, he was obliged to remain incognito.

Some months later, when he returned to Russia, Plekhanov showed
unexampled energy for the cause of rebellion. The broad scope of his
activity as an agitator can be seen in the series of revolutionary proclama-
tions—the first products of his pen—which he addressed to students,
workers, Cossacks, and "educated society." His vigor and talent soon
brought him to a position of leadership in the then dominant populist
organization, "Land and Liberty"; and, early in 1879, he was made an
editor of its periodical publication.

But even in 1879, while Plekhanov was a populist, he was a populist
with a difference. His first revolutionary assignment had foreshadowed
his future rôle, for it involved propaganda not among the peasants but
among the Petersburg workmen. The aim of the populists in mingling
with the workmen was to recruit propagandists for activity among the
peasants, those who were expected to provide the mass basis for the
revolution. But in order to win the confidence of the workers, the revolutionists had to take part in the workers' struggles. Thus Plekhanov came
to participate in strikes, to share the experiences of the workers, and to
write propaganda and manifestoes for them. While those who were trying to activate the peasants were having little success, Plekhanov obtained a positive response from the workers among whom he carried on
agitation. The significance of this was not lost upon him and, even as a
populist, he pointed to the socialist inclinations of the city worker and
to the useful rôle that the latter might play in the social revolution.

Early in 1879, there appeared in the journal, *Land and Liberty*, a
long article in which Plekhanov detailed his populist views. He expected
that Russia would soon produce a great revolution, a revolution that

would establish an anarcho-socialist order. The revolution would be consummated when the intelligentsia, dissatisfied as it was with the political and social order, would, by agitation, succeed in arousing the great mass of discontented peasants and in directing their fury against the existing régime. The revolution would bring the destruction of the state and the distribution of state and noble lands among the peasants. The character of the new society would be determined by the anarcho-collectivist nature of the peasants who were the overwhelming majority of the Russian people. The age-long desire of the peasant for freedom and self-government would lead to the destruction of the coercive, centralized state and its replacement, from the bottom up by a "free federation of free communes." Since the peasants were organized in collectivist-type communes, it was deduced that the future society would be collectivist in nature, with property collectively owned and with production, whether agricultural or industrial, organized on a collectivist basis. Although much was left unsaid, it was clear that, to Plekhanov's way of thinking, Russia would attain socialism through the revolutionary action of the peasantry and without passing through a capitalist stage of development.

This general scheme was by no means peculiar to Plekhanov, the influence of Bakunin is all too clear, and some such outlook was common to most of the revolutionary populists of the period 1876–1879. But what is arresting about Plekhanov's analysis is that in 1879, he already showed concern that his system should be consistent with Marxian principles as he then understood them. Thus he said: "Let us see to what the teaching of Marx obligates us . . . in view of the necessity of establishing the points of departure of our program." Unlike other Russian populists, he argued that Marxian principles were relevant not only to capitalist so- cieties, but to all societies. However, this did not signify that all societies must have identical histories; for, "weaving and combining variously in various societies, they [Marxian principles] give entirely dissimilar re- sults. . . ."

It was significant that the article under consideration was entitled "The Law of the Economic Development of Society and the Tasks of Socialism in Russia." The title suggested, and the contents of the article confirmed, that Plekhanov was at one with Marx in identifying "the economic history of society" as the determining factor in social evolu- tion. He held up to criticism the "utopian" socialists of the thirties and forties who, considering the mind all and life nothing, had supposed that a happily-conceived plan for a well-proportioned and smoothly-function- ing society could, by virtue of skillful use of propaganda, be translated into reality without reference to the stage of economic development ex- isting at a given time and place. Arguing, in effect, that his own populist views could not be described as utopian, Plekhanov insisted that the peasant commune was stable, that its collective ownership of land and the collectivist habits of work and thought that it created among the peasants provided a real and sound basis for socialism in Russia. If Russia differed from the West in this regard, if Russia could attain socialism in a unique way, it was only because the peasant commune had fallen in the West, and with it, the collectivist instincts of the people. When those instincts were replaced by individualism, the possibility of socialism in the West vanished until such time as the growth of large-scale, factory production with its socialization of labor had once again restored the social spirit that had decayed with the decay of the commune. The very cornerstone of Plekhanov's system, then, was the belief that the commune provided the basis for Russian socialism, and that the commune "does not bear within itself the elements of its own doom." In terms of his own theoretical premises, it followed that if the commune should disintegrate, the social conditions essential for the establishment of socialism would no longer obtain in Russia and, in that case, only a utopian could speak of the likelihood of socialism there in the near future.

The early influence of Marx upon him is important in helping to explain Plekhanov's later, definitive, conversion to Marxism; but it is clear that, in 1879, the young revolutionist did not qualify as a Marxist. Plekhanov believed that Marxian principles supported the outlook and program of the populists. But this was, at least in part, an erroneous judgment; for Plekhanov, like most of the populists of that time, considered that the revolution would destroy the state and open the way to an anarcho-federalist order, while Marxists held that a state, and a strongly-centralized state, was essential for the transition to socialism. Very shortly before the publication of the article discussed above, he had described all of Russian history not as "the history of class struggle," but, in anarchist terms, as "an unbroken struggle of the state with the commune and the individual." And so poorly oriented was Plekhanov in questions of Western socialism that he grouped Marx and Engels with Rodbertus and Dühring as "the brilliant pleiade" of socialism, in 1879, that is, a year after Engels had published his celebrated attack upon Dühring.

Nevertheless, Plekhanov's exposure to some Marxian ideas clearly had produced a strong impression upon him. For the present, he could both be a good populist and be faithful to Marxian precepts, as he then understood them, since there seemed to him to be no contradiction between the two. But in time, his faith in the populist creed was shaken, while a more extensive contact with the primary sources of Marxism strengthened his conviction as to the validity of that outlook. Within a very few years, he became persuaded of the essential incompatibility of populism with Marxism; and this led to his renunciation of populism.

When within "Land and Liberty" there developed a strong tendency to abandon agitation among the peasants and workmen in favor of a terroristic, political struggle with the government, Plekhanov led the fight against the terrorists. When dissension within "Land and Liberty" led to its dissolution in the fall of 1879, Plekhanov became a leader of the new, anti-terrorist organization, "The General Redivision" (*Chernyi Peredel*), which, in opposition to the terrorist "People's Will," affirmed its adherence to the traditional views and methods of "Land and Liberty." But Plekhanov's faith in the old populist outlook was soon weakened by the failure of "The General Redivision" to compete successfully with the terrorists in attracting fresh forces. When even those who remained loyal to the old populist ideas showed little inclination to carry propaganda to the countryside, doubts arose in Plekhanov's mind as to the correctness of the views of the "redivisionists."

Around the same time, his doubts were compounded by his encounter with Orlov's book, *Communal Property in the Moscow District.* Orlov presented such persuasive data on the decline of the peasant commune, that Plekhanov was obliged to revise his opinion concerning its indestructibility. Soon afterward he acknowledged that economic differentiation was proceeding among the commune members, that the commune "is being divided into two parts, each of which is hostile to the other. . . ." Yet, he insisted that the causes of the decline of the commune were external and that they would cease to operate if the socialists should succeed in igniting the revolution, if they should bring the peasants "from a passive expectation of a general redivision" to "an active demand for it." For the moment, Plekhanov seemed able to reassure himself, but he reported later that Orlov's work "strongly shook" his populist convictions. By raising serious doubts about the stability of the commune, the book tended to undermine the very foundation of his populist outlook.

As uncertainty came to take the place of conviction, Plekhanov began to deplore the inadequacy of his knowledge and the difficulty of supplementing it under the repressive conditions of Russian life. Hence, he was not entirely displeased when, late in 1879, some of his revolutionary comrades urged that he and other leaders of "The General Redivision" go abroad until such time as the situation was more auspicious for revolutionary work. Plekhanov welcomed the opportunity to secure the information which would quiet his doubts and verify his views. Half in jest, he remarked that he was going abroad "to study and to attain there the scholarly level of a master's or a doctor's degree."

In January, 1880, Plekhanov made his way to western Europe and immediately plunged into the study of history, political science, and socialism. The works of Marx fascinated him and, in order to gain more complete access to them, Plekhanov undertook to learn German. Beginning in the fall of 1880, he lived in Paris for almost a year, engaging in intensive study at the *Bibliotheque Nationale* and, in his spare time, making the acquaintance of such leaders of Western socialism as Jules Guesde. His sojourn in the West made a profound impression upon Plekhanov. Experience of Western conditions and increased familiarity with Western socialist political and economic conceptions gave him the perspective for a critique of "Russian socialism." Thus his trip abroad had unexpected results, inasmuch as he did not acquire information that could bolster the populist position; on the contrary, for as Plekhanov recalled many years afterward, "the more we became acquainted with the theories of scientific socialism, the more doubtful became our populism to us, from the side of both theory and practice." The changes effected in his views were soon evident and, indeed, it is possible to trace, in his writings between 1880 and 1882, Plekhanov's rejection, one after another, of the fundamental theses of populism. In a period of fifteen to eighteen months he renounced the doctrine of a unique social evolution for Russia, abandoned hostility to politics and political struggle, and ceased to identify the peasantry as the mass basis of the Russian socialist revolution.

By September, 1880, (nine months after he had gone abroad), Plekhanov was contending that the next stage for Russia would probably be a bourgeois-constitutional régime. This judgment, dropped rather casually in an article, revealed the profound change that had taken place in Plekhanov's outlook in a short time. It signified that Russia would not have a unique social development, involving a leap from her contemporary situation to a socialist order, but instead would experience an intervening capitalist stage. But Plekhanov was not yet prepared to make these affirmations. That for him the situation was not yet entirely crystallized was apparent when he indicated that while the agrarian question was still the chief concern of the socialists, "Russian industry is not standing still." And "along with this, the center of gravity of economic questions is being transferred to the industrial centers." By January, 1881, the idea that the next socio-political formation for Russia would be a bourgeois-constitutional régime had passed from probability to certainty for Plekhanov. While the implication was unavoidable that Russia's economic evolution would therefore parallel that of the West, it was only at the end of 1881 that Plekhanov unequivocally stated that Russia was launched on the capitalist phase of development and that "all other routes are closed to her."

The adoption of the point of view described above meant that Plekhanov no longer regarded the peasant commune as a basis for a direct transition to socialism; but nothing was said of this, nor were detailed and reasoned arguments given for his change of front before the publication of his important works of 1883 and 1885 respectively, *Socialism and Political Struggle* and *Our Disagreements*. In those works, and especially in the latter, it became clear that additional study of Russian economic data, on the one hand, and on the other, mastery of Marxian economic theory had led him to formulate his new conception of Russian social evolution.

Plekhanov's new convictions concerning Russian social development led to a revision of his views as to the tactics the socialists must follow. Although they worked for the destruction of the state, the populists, prior to the formation of "The People's Will," did not regard theirs as a political fight. As anarchists, they were opposed to political struggle, since such a struggle signified to them the acceptance of the state principle. Their aim was not to win political rights within the state system, not to reform that system, nor even to capture the state and utilize it for the implementation of their social program. They sought an end to all states, since the latter were considered instruments of coercion and oppression. The members of "Land and Liberty," and of "The General Redivision" after it, believed that their socialist convictions—for they were anarcho-socialists —obliged them to devote all their energies to agitation among the masses, revolving around their *economic* needs. Only in consequence of such activity would there be called into being the popular rising that would destroy the state and permit the development of the anarcho-socialist order. The populists thought that political liberty was intimately associated with, and beneficial mainly to, the bourgeoisie; political freedom and the struggle to attain it had little or no relevance, they thought, to the needs of peasant Russia—needs which were preeminently economic.

Plekhanov had shared these views, but in September, 1880, he wrote: "We know the value of political liberty . . . ; we greet every struggle for the rights of man." If this was a notable departure from his earlier views, Plekhanov, as yet, was prepared to accord to political struggle and political liberty only as secondary importance. He still urged that the people everywhere and always were concerned about economic rather than political questions. Therefore, if the socialists were to become a power, and if the people were to register gains at the time of a revolution, the socialists must carry on agitation among the peasants centered around economic demands. This would guarantee that with the coming of a revolutionary crisis, the socialists would not constitute a "staff without an army," but instead, would have massed forces behind them sufficient to ensure consideration of the popular needs. If, on the other hand, the socialists should be drawn into a political struggle against absolutism, they would lose contact with the economically-minded masses, and the latter, lacking awareness, unity, and leadership, would gain little or nothing from the overthrow of absolutism.

Plekhanov, in common with many other populists, was still inclined to treat politics and economics as mutually exclusive, unrelated spheres; but for Plekhanov, this situation did not last. In January, 1881, advancing another step toward what was to be his life-long position, he articulated, although yet imperfectly, that synthesis of political struggle and socialism which was to be one of his major contributions to Russian revolutionary thought. In the ensuing months, he clarified his thinking further and, in the spring of 1882, in his foreword to the second Russian edition of the *Communist Manifesto,* Plekhanov plainly enunciated a social-democratic strategy. It was indeed appropriate that he should have done so at that time and in that place, for within the *Communist Manifesto* appeared the formula toward which he had been groping. No longer did he place "political struggle" (the fight for political rights and political hegemony) in opposition to socialist activity (agitation among the masses designed immediately to bring the destruction of the state and a socio-economic revolution). Plekhanov had come to believe that "political struggle" and "socialist activity," so far from being mutually exclusive, were intimately inter-related, that neither could be overlooked in favor of the other, that only *by way of* political struggle could socialism be attained. Plekhanov commended the *Manifesto* as a corrective to the one-sidedness of those socialists who, like the members of "Land and Liberty" and "The General Redivision," opposed political activity, and of those, like the partisans of "The People's Will," who became so engulfed in the political struggle against absolutism as to forget about the creation of a mass movement, which alone could ensure the future of the socialist party. Plekhanov's premises were these: Even though the coming upheaval be a bourgeois rather than a socialist revolution, the masses have much at stake. With the fall of absolutism, they should win political rights which would greatly increase the possibilities for developing the campaign for economic emancipation, for socialism. The tactic that Plekhanov recommended to the Russian socialists, therefore, was much the same as that which Marx had urged upon the German Communists in 1848. The socialists must fight alongside of the bourgeoisie to the extent that it is revolutionary in its struggle with absolute monarchy, but, at the same time, must not for a moment slacken its drive to develop in the minds of the workers the clearest possible consciousness of the antagonism of the interests of the bourgeoisie and the proletariat. The Russian socialists must draw the workers into the struggle against absolutism as allies of the bourgeoisie, but must make plain to the proletariat that its interests dictated the inauguration of an all-out struggle against the bourgeoisie on the morrow of the overthrow of absolutism.

Finally, it followed that, if capitalism was to dominate the economic life of Russia, the proletariat, that inevitable by-product of capitalist development, rather than the peasantry, would provide the mass basis for the socialist revolution. In September, 1880, when he first suggested that Russia stood on the eve of a bourgeois revolution, Plekhanov advised that propaganda for factory workers be published. However, through most of 1881, his uncertainty was reflected in the continued reference to "the toilers" and "the people" as the chief support of the socialists. But, at the end of 1881, around the same time that he imparted to the venerable Russian revolutionary leader, Lavrov, his conviction that Russia could not escape capitalist development, he designated the city workers as the only group from which something significant could be expected in the revolutionary movement. Thus, if earlier he had seen socialism coming to Russia by way of a peasant revolution, on the basis of the peasant commune, and without a prior stage of capitalist development, Plekhanov now argued that the socialist revolution was thinkable only after a considerable period of capitalism, which would produce both the productive system requisite for a socialist economy and the proletariat, the class which would overthrow the capitalist system and inaugurate the socialist order.

Plekhanov's evolution had brought him to a position which represented an innovation in Russian revolutionary thought; at the same time, it represented a triumph for the Western statement of the socialist problem. He was now convinced that "in Russian history, there is no essential difference from the history of Western Europe." Consequently, he maintained that the problems of the Russian socialists could best be illuminated by the study of west European social development and Western socialist teachings. Plekhanov thus took his place in the tradition of the Russian "Westernizers." As Peter the Great had applied military and administrative techniques to Russia, as the Decembrists and the men of the thirties and forties had hoped to "westernize" Russia in the political sense, now Plekhanov adopted a Western version of socialism and set out to make it the ruling socialist tendency. As Peter had fought the tradition-bound clergy and boyars, as the "Westernizers" of the time of Nicholas I had done battle with the Slavophiles, now Plekhanov undertook to demolish Russian, populist socialism. Now he declared that he was ready to make of Marx's *Capital* "a Procrustean bed" for the leaders of the revolutionary movement.

In early 1881, as a result of an apparent convergence of views of the "redivisionists" and the terrorists, collaboration between the two factions had been suggested by Plekhanov. Some months later, when collaboration had in fact been established, Plekhanov's views once again diverged from those of the terrorists as he moved toward Marxism. Although for two years the factions were in uneasy association, it was apparent that each was trying to use the other. The "redivisionists" (now become Marxists) wished to capitalize on the popularity of "The People's Will," while trying to infuse that organization with a new social-democratic content. The terrorists intended to turn the well-known names and the experience and talents of the former "redivisionists" to their advantage without, however, allowing the social democrats to gain a predominant voice in the organization. The differences between the two factions were so great they could not live in connubial bliss; nor did one succeed in assimilating the other. Plekhanov and his comrades proved unwilling to sacrifice their principles for the sake of unity, while the terrorists showed themselves unwilling to accommodate themselves to Plekhanov's "Procrustean bed." But if Plekhanov's circle had failed in its attempt to win over the revolutionary movement from within, its members then resolved to create a new revolutionary organization for the propaganda of their ideas. When, in September, 1883, they founded the "Emancipation of Labor" Group, it was in order to take over the leadership of the revolutionary movement and thus, in the end, to stamp the imprint of Marx's thinking deep into Russian life.

TWO TYPES OF
RUSSIAN
LIBERALISM *

History tends to give more attention to movements that succeed than
to those that fail. On the whole, this is as it should be, for the first
task of a historian is to search for the antecedents of that which
occurred. Yet, unless he accepts the notion of historical inevitability,
he must also ask why one alternative course was followed rather than
another. Russian liberalism was an alternative to Russian Bolshevism,
and in its heyday—roughly from 1903 to 1917—it gave promise of
becoming the voice of the Russia that was to be. The new Russia,
however, spoke with another voice. Had circumstances in 1917 been
different, the liberal movement might have had an opportunity to
prove itself. The strengths and weaknesses of two representative
figures of that movement are examined here by Professor Karpovich.

THE WEAKNESS of prerevolutionary Russian liberalism has become a common-place in historical literature. Too often, it has been asserted as something self-evident, and thus not in need of further investigation. This attitude has been based largely on an a priori reasoning,
the weakness of Russian liberalism being deduced from the weakness of
the middle class in Russia. The latter, in turn, has been rather assumed
than investigated. Moreover, another broad assumption has been involved—that of an organic connection between liberalism and middle

* Michael Karpovich, "Two Types of Russian Liberalism: Maklakov and Miliukov,"
Continuity and Change in Russian and Soviet Thought, edited by Ernest J. Simmons (Cambridge: Harvard University Press, 1955), pp. 129–43. Copyright, 1955,
by the President and Fellows of Harvard College. Reprinted by permission of the
publisher.
    The author (1888–1959) was born and educated in Russia. World War I
interrupted his career as historian; during the latter part of the war he served in
the Ministry of War and, from 1917 to 1922, was secretary to the Russian Embassy in Washington. After his embassy service, he chose to remain in the United

classes, as if it were natural and almost inevitable for a middle class to
favor a middle-of-the-road policy. Coupled with this, there has been a
fairly common tendency to identify the middle class with the business
community, the bourgeoisie in the Marxian sense of the term.

The validity of neither of these basic assumptions can be taken for
granted. The designation of a social group as a middle class merely indicates its central position in a given society, and consequently the
nature of the middle class can vary from one country to another, in accordance with the country's social structure. Thus it might be argued, as
it has been argued in the case of the Polish *szlachta,* that the bulk of the
Russian gentry was a middle class as distinguished from the landed
aristocracy. Much more important, however, is the other point—the one
referring to the relationship between the middle class and liberalism.
We know from historical experience that under certain conditions
middle-class groups might support extremist political movements, as in
the cases of Italian Fascism and German Nazism, for instance, or that at
least they might retreat from their liberal positions as they did in France
under the Third Empire and again in Bismarck's Germany. On the other
hand, the history of European liberalism cannot be reduced to that of
the "businessman's creed," as Laski attempted to do. This was only one
of its component parts, and de Ruggiero convincingly demonstrated the
primary importance of other elements that went into its make-up—such
as religious dissent and the defense of "ancient liberties" by the privileged estates of feudal origin.

It is neither necessary nor possible for me to discuss these general
questions in the present paper. The purpose of the foregoing remarks was
to point out the complexity of the problem and the need for its further investigation. The history of Russian liberalism has been sadly neglected.
To many, the a priori assumption of its weakness seems to have been
fully justified by the course of events in Russia since the Revolution.
Why should one pay much attention to a political trend which could
not achieve any lasting results and which suffered such a crushing defeat? The answer to this question is twofold. In the first place, the historical process does not know any "ultimate" results—any "final" defeats
of victories. And secondly, the importance of historical phenomena
should be assessed as of the time when they occurred, and not only in
the light of the historian's *post factum* wisdom. Certainly, *vae victis* is
not a principle for historians to follow!

States. He joined the faculty of Harvard University and taught Russian history
there until his retirement. Aside from numerous articles, Professor Karpovich published little; he had undertaken, in cooperation with Professor Vernadsky, to write a
ten-volume history of Russia but had not completed his part of the work at the time
of his death. His only book, *Imperial Russia,* appeared in 1932. But his bibliog-
raphy is not the measure of his stature: he was a gifted teacher and scholar whose
chief monument is the work of his many students.

As elsewhere, liberalism in Russia was not a homogeneous move-ment. It proceeded from different social groups, and various motives induced people to join it. This lack of homogeneity was clearly reflected in the make-up of the Constitutional Democratic Party founded in October of 1905. It has been repeatedly pointed out that it came into being as the result of the merging of two forces: the zemstvo liberals, on the one hand, and the liberal-minded part of the professional class, on the other. Strictly speaking, this is an oversimplification. There were other elements in the party which by their social provenience did not belong to either of the two groups, and inside each of the latter there could be found a considerable variety of political attitudes and aspira-tions. By and large, however, one can accept the accuracy of this sum-mary characterization of the two main components of the Cadet Party, and it is in the light of this division that I am going to discuss the two types of Russian liberalism as exemplified by Maklakov and Miliukov respectively.

Vasilii Alekseevich Maklakov, born in 1869, was exactly ten years younger than Pavel Nikolaevich Miliukov. If I begin my discussion with Maklakov it is because he represents some of the prevailing trends of the zemstvo liberalism which historically preceded that of the profes-sional class. Not that he was a zemstvo worker himself, but it so hap-pened that his political education was greatly influenced by the zemstvo liberal tradition. In his reminiscences, he speaks of his father and those around him as being imbued with the spirit of the Great Reforms of the 1860's, strongly favoring their continuation and extension, but re-maining rather indifferent to politics. He also pictures them as being resolutely opposed to the terroristic activity of the *Narodnaia Volia*. Both in the secondary school and in the university, he found the Russian youth of the time on the whole sharing the attitude of their elders. Ac-cording to his observations, even the student disturbances of 1887 and 1890, during the years when he himself was a student at the University of Moscow, as yet were devoid of "politics." The great majority of the students were motivated by the concern for academic freedom and their own corporate rights as well as by a feeling of "student solidarity," and they resented the attempts of some of their more radical colleagues to inject into the movement general political slogans. When in 1890 the Moscow students organized a memorial service for Chernyshevskii (d. 1889), this again was an expression of their sympathy for a man who suffered for his convictions rather than a political manifestation. In his last volume of memoirs, speaking of himself as he was at the age of twenty, Maklakov says that all his sympathies were "with those repre-sentatives [of the period] of Great Reforms who wanted to continue to improve the [Russian] state on the bases of legality, freedom, and justice, taking for their starting point that which already existed in reality . . . ."

Characteristically, a trip to France that he made in 1889 served for him as a "lesson in conservatism." What impressed him was the picture of a country where "rights of the state could be reconciled with the rights of man" and where even the opposition "showed a concern for what had been created by history." The centenary of the French Revolution made him read the recent literature on the subject, and from this reading he derived a "new, historical understanding" of the Revolution—as opposed, one must assume, to the romantic and idealizing interpretation of it that was current among the Russian radicals of the time. It is not without significance that of all the revolutionary leaders Mirabeau became his favorite hero.

While in Paris, Maklakov got in touch with some leaders of the French student organizations, of a professional rather than a political nature. Their existence and the character of their work largely inspired young Maklakov in that active part which, upon his return to Russia, he took in the attempts to develop nonpolitical student organizations at the University of Moscow (mutual-aid societies and the like), within the rather narrow limits of the then existing legal possibilities. Thus he was one of the early leaders of what later became known as "academism" (a term which acquired a derogatory meaning for the opponents of this tendency from among the radical students)—in a sense, a student counterpart of that "economism" among the workers which was supported by some of the early Social Democrats and served as a target for Lenin's violent diatribes. For Maklakov, however, it was a step in the development of his liberalism, not in opposition to, but in harmony with the general program of "improving the Russian state" by starting from "that which already existed in reality."

During these years, Maklakov was greatly influenced by his association with the so-called Lubenkov circle, one of the traditional Russian discussion groups, in this case gathered around an eminent Moscow jurist and consisting of various public leaders mostly from among the zemstvo workers. A decade later, Maklakov became a recording secretary of a similar discussion group known as *Beseda* (here best translated as "Symposium") and headed by D. N. Shipov, subsequently one of the founders of the Octobrist Party. Together with some more politically minded zemstvo constitutionalists, the *Beseda* included also, besides Shipov, such other representatives of the "purer" zemstvo tradition as N. A. Khomiakov and M. A. Stakhovich. Both Lubenkov and Shipov had definite Slavophile leanings. While not accepting the original Slavophile doctrine in its entirety, and certainly not sharing its almost anarchical aberrations as exemplified, for instance, by Konstantin Aksakov's political theory, they still showed a strong affinity with Slavophilism in their somewhat diluted antistatist attitude, their emphasis on "public work" as distinguished from, if not opposed to, political activity, their relative indifference to forms of government and strictly defined constitutional formulas, as well as in their traditionalism. There can be no doubt that the influence of these men left its traces on Maklakov's brand of liberalism.

There was one point, however, where Maklakov substantially differed from the Slavophiles, and the difference can be defined by calling him a Slavophile who had learned the necessity of legal guarantees for the preservation of human rights and freedom. After several years of intense preoccupation with historical studies which led Maklakov to think of an academic career, he decided to shift to jurisprudence and to become a lawyer. The final choice was made not on the basis of either intellectual interests or practical considerations, but in response to the call of civic duty. This is what Maklokov himself has to say on the subject: "My brief life experience had shown me . . . that the main evil of Russian life was the triumph of arbitrariness that went unpunished, the helplessness of the individual in the face of administrative discretion, the lack of legal bases for his self-defense. . . . The defense of the individual against lawlessness, in other words, the defense of the law itself—this was the substance of the Bar's public service." This defense of the individual, however, was not to be waged in a spirit of aggressive partisanship, and the lawyer's task was to seek for a synthesis between the rights of the state, on the one hand, and those of the individual, on the other. Here, in a nucleus, is that philosophy of compromise which became characteristic of Maklakov the politician.

The role played by Maklakov's legal career in the development of his liberal views has more than a mere biographical interest. It has a broader significance in so far as it points toward another important element in the make-up of Russian liberalism—the Russian counterpart of the German *Rechtsstaat* idea which while not necessarily connected with political liberalism eventually led many of its exponents to strive for the abolition of autocracy and the establishment of a constitutional regime.

Unfortunately, in the case of Miliukov, we are not in a position to trace the formation of his political views as fully as it can be done for Maklakov. Miliukov's personal memoirs as yet have not been published, and the manuscript so far has remained inaccessible to scholars. Several chapters of Miliukov's political reminiscences, published in an *émigré* Russian periodical in Paris, in 1938–39, cover a rather limited period (1904–06) and are not as self-revealing as Maklakov's much more personal writings. The same is true of Miliukov's other political works. Nor is there any adequate biography of Miliukov available. All one can do under the circumstances is to indicate those points in which Miliukov's political upbringing seems to have differed from that of Maklakov. We knew from Miliukov himself that in his youth he was strongly influenced by both Spencer and Comte, and that as a university student he was seriously interested in Marx's writings. As the same intellectual fare was typical of the radical youth of the period, one might assume in Miliukov a somewhat greater affinity with their *Weltanschauung* than one could expect in the case of Maklakov with his mildly Slavophile leanings. While being associated with the moderate wing of the student movement, Miliukov watched with sympathy the *Narodnaia Volia's* assault upon autocracy, seeing in their terroristic activities "one of the means of political struggle." This is significantly different from that attitude of unreserved condemnation of political terror which, according to Maklakov's reminiscences, prevailed in his milieu a decade later. If the latter reflected the views of the moderate zemstvo majority, Miliukov's position agreed with that of the somewhat more radical minority among the early zemstvo liberals. One of them, I. I. Petrunkevich, who even attempted to form a kind of working alliance with the revolutionaries, later became Miliukov's chief political mentor.

In the volume of essays dedicated to Miliukov on the occasion of his seventieth anniversary, S. A. Smirnov dates Miliukov's "actively political attitude" from the famine year of 1891, while V. A. Obolenskii asserts that he already was a "convinced liberal and democrat" at the time of his graduation from the university. The fact remains, however, that in Miliukov the politician matured much more slowly than the scholar. For a number of years after graduation, he was almost completely absorbed in historical research and teaching. Within the period 1892-1903 appeared all of his most important scholarly works, beginning with the *National Economy of Russia and the Reforms of Peter the Great* and ending with the third volume of *Outlines of Russian Culture*. Miliukov's intensive scholarly activity went on even after his academic career had been brusquely terminated by his dismissal from the University of Moscow on rather flimsy charges of a political nature. One is tempted to say that Miliukov became an active politician almost in spite of himself.

Miliukov's real political activity began in the first years of the century, simultaneously with the general revival of the opposition sentiment in the country, and more particularly in connection with the formation of the Union of Liberation. From the outset, he took an active part in the Liberation movement, in contrast to Maklakov, who, according to his own admission, remained on the periphery until the establishment of the constitutional regime. The difference, of course, was not accidental. Miliukov joined the movement with an intention of forcing its zemstvo elements to adopt a more radical attitude and to ally themselves more closely with the professional intellectuals on the Left. To Maklakov, such a development was a source of serious doubts and misgivings. In retrospect, he sees the initial strength of the Liberation movement in the fact that it was primarily a zemstvo movement, organically connected with the "era of Great Reforms" and nurtured in the tradition of public work performed within the framework of local self-government institutions. It was losing rather than gaining strength in allying itself with other public elements which were devoid of practical political experience. These new allies differed from the majority of the zemstvo men not only in their final aims, but, which was more important, also in the choice of means for the achievement of the immediate objectives. Under their influence, "the Liberation movement became too indifferent to that dividing line which should have separated the evolution of the state from the evils of a revolution."

Maklakov has been accused by some of his critics of evaluating past events from the vantage ground of wisdom acquired in the course of subsequent historical experience. But while to some extent this is true, there is enough evidence to permit us to believe that in a large measure his present judgment reflects the attitude he had at the time when the events he is evaluating were taking place. This attitude explains his relative aloofness from the Liberation movement. It explains also the casual way in which he joined the Cadet Party and accepted election to its central committee. He freely admits that he was not a very good Cadet, and it is on the record that on several important occasions he found himself in disagreement with the majority of the Party members and with its leaders. In its turn, the Party, while glad to make use of Maklakov's remarkable oratorical gift as well as of his legal erudition and ability, did not look upon him as a dependable Party regular.

It would be impossible, within the scope of this paper, to follow the Miliukov–Maklakov controversy through all the stages of its development. Nor is it necessary for my present purpose. What is of importance is the fundamental cleavage between these two outstanding representatives of Russian liberalism, the difference in the main premises and the general spirit of their political actions. In this case, as in that of many other Russian political trends, the Revolution of 1905 played the part of a catalyst. In Maklakov, it strengthened his fear of all and every revolution, his conviction that revolutionary methods were not only undesirable but in the long run futile. He counted on the evolutionary process in the course of which the regime was bound to change "under the pressure of life itself." In his opinion, it was preferable to try to contribute to the regime's peaceful evolution and not to aim at its complete overthrow. The "historical state power" had one decisive advantage on its side: the people were in the habit of obeying it. It was precisely this inertia of obedience that would be destroyed by a revolution, and with it would go that legal continuity which was so important for the normal growth of a nation. The results could be foreseen on the basis of historical experience: the new government issuing from the revolution either would be so weak that it could not maintain itself in power or else it would be forced to become a ruthless dictatorship.

Maklakov had no illusions as to the nature of the Russian regime of the period. But he still thought that it would be amenable to the pressure of organized public opinion had the liberals used every opportunity to reach an agreement with it, on a program of gradually introduced reforms. In this lay the historical task of Russian liberalism. Maklakov felt that the liberals were missing their chance of contributing to Russia's peaceful evolution by assuming an uncompromisingly hostile attitude toward the regime and thus allying themselves with the destructive revolutionary forces in the country. This appeal to the Acheron (the symbol of the "lower world" in Greek and Latin poetry) was bound to end in the liberals' undoing: their cause would be lost whether revolution won the victory or suffered defeat.

In the eyes of Maklakov the failure of the Russian liberals to approach their political task in a proper spirit became obvious after the proclamation of the constitutional regime. The October Manifesto of 1905 opened a real opportunity for the peaceful solution of Russia's problems, and it was up to the Cadet Party to lead the way in this undertaking. But for this a kind of psychological demobilization was necessary. Unfortunately, the Party could not get rid of its "wartime psychology," and instead of seeking a lasting peace with the government, which could be based on a compromise only, insisted on continuing to wage the struggle until the "final victory." In this connection, Maklakov cites an extemporaneous speech made by Miliukov in Moscow, upon the receipt of the news of the Manifesto's publication, in which he said "that nothing was changed, and the war still was going on."

It is on the basis of these general premises that Maklakov has severely criticized the Cadet policies of the years 1905–07. The main points of his indictment can be summarized as follows:

The maximalism of the Party's programmatic demands, such as, in particular, the convocation of a Constituent Assembly which could not be realized unless there was a complete capitulation on the part of the imperial government;

The Party's uncompromising attitude toward both Witte and Stolypin who, according to Maklakov, could and should be used as allies rather than abused as enemies;

The peremptory way in which the Cadet leaders rejected the idea of Cadet participation in the government advanced both by Witte and Stolypin;

The Party's tendency to use the Duma as a tribune for antigovernmental agitation rather than for constructive legislative activity;

Its dogmatic insistence on the immediate revision of the Fundamental Laws, aiming at a universal franchise, reduced powers of the

upper chamber, and ministerial responsibility—matters which, in Maklakov's opinion, could be settled gradually as the constitutional regime
grew stronger and took firmer roots in the Russian soil;

And finally the issuance of the Vyborg Manifesto—essentially a revolutionary measure in so far as the dissolution of the Duma and the appointment of new elections were in accordance with the constitution.

Maklakov admits that the other Cadet leaders neither wanted a
revolution nor acquiesced in its eventual triumph. But he feels that,
unlike himself, they were not afraid of it—some because they did not
believe in the possibility of its victory, others because they thought that
it could be stopped in its initial stages. Meanwhile, "as the threat of the
revolution might have forced the government to make [further] concessions, they continued to play this card, not realizing that they were playing with fire."

Once more it should be mentioned that, because of the nature of the
material available, Miliukov's views cannot be presented in the same
systematic fashion in which I have tried to summarize Maklakov's "political philosophy." The two volumes in which Miliukov has collected his
articles and papers, written in 1905–06, contain precisely what their
subtitle indicates—a running comment of a publicist on current political
events, and his later writings (those of the *émigré* period) likewise do
not offer any exposition of the author's liberal creed. Even the two
articles written in response to Maklakov's criticism of Cadet policies have
the nature of *ad hoc* contributions, and they merely touch upon the
divergent premises underlying the controversy.

Miliukov begins his defense of the Cadet Party by a characteristically
empirical reference to the actual conditions in which the Party had to
formulate its program and to make its tactical decisions. The Party, he
reminds Maklakov, was not living "on abstractions and armchair
(*kabinetnye*) deliberations." Its position was shifting now to the right
and now to the left, "together with the life of the Russian society." Elsewhere he refers to the psychology of the time—that surge of emotion
which was caused by the events of 1905, and from which the rank and
file of the Party did not remain immune. He points out that the Party
leaders, while trying to maintain the central position, were forced to
make occasional concessions to the more impatient spirit of many of their
followers. He insists, however, that the Cadet program, while "radical,"
was not Utopian. What Miliukov means by "radical" becomes clear from
his reference to "neoliberalism" as a kindred movement in Western
Europe. Back in October 1905, in his opening address at the first ("constituent") convention of the Constitutional Democratic Party, he made
the same comparison in slightly different terms: " . . . our Party stands
closest to those groups among the Western intellectuals who are known
under the name of 'social reformers' . . . our program is undoubtedly

the most Leftist of all those advanced by similar political groups in Western Europe."

In a different context, Miliukov accuses Maklakov of stressing the tactics at the expense of the program, attaching more importance to the means than to the aims. He argues that under certain conditions even a liberal might become a revolutionary, and that thus one cannot equate liberalism with a strictly legal way of political action. It is equally erroneous to confuse a defense of the rule of law with that of a given positive law, as Maklakov's reasoning tends to do. Nor should one ascribe such a decisive order to the other.

If, in these last arguments, Miliukov opposes to Maklakov's traditionalism his own historical relativism, in another case, when dealing with a proper approach to political problems, he blames his opponent for an excessively relativist point of view. Miliukov sees the chief defect of Maklakov the politician in his attempt to transfer into the sphere of politics the psychology and methods of a lawyer. The latter inevitably acquires a professional habit of "seeing a share of truth on the opposite side, and a share of error on his own." A politician cannot allow himself the luxury of such an indifferent and "objective" attitude toward "the contents of truth." Here Miliukov is striking at the very heart of Maklakov's "philosophy of compromise."

Apart from this theoretical disagreement, a radically different interpretation of political events was involved in the controversy. Miliukov did not share in the least Maklakov's optimistic appraisal of Russia's chances of peaceful evolution after the proclamation of the constitutional regime. I have cited above Miliukov's admission that at the time of the publication of the October Manifesto he did not see in it any real change that would induce him to stop fighting the government. Twenty-five years later Miliukov still asserted the correctness of his original diagnosis. Referring to Nicholas II's statement that after the revision of the Fundamental Laws "autocracy remained the same as of old," he declared the Tsar to be closer to the truth than Maklakov, "even from the formal point of view." He also stoutly maintained that the Cadet leaders had been right in repelling the overtures of both Witte and Stolypin, as in neither case had there been any evidence of sincerity. By joining the government on conditions that were proposed to them, Party representatives would have walked into a trap: while being unable to exercise a decisive influence on governmental policies they would have compromised themselves in the eyes of the people.

How these considerations affected the tactical line which was followed by Miliukov in 1905–06 can be seen from the various statements made by him at that time in his capacity as party leader. Thus in his opening address at the first Party convention he expressed himself as follows: ". . . in fighting for our aim we cannot count on any agreements and compromises [with the government], and we should raise high the banner already unfurled by the Russian liberation as a whole, striving for the convocation of a Constituent Assembly . . ." This was said a few days before the publication of the October Manifesto. But in its closing session, which took place on the morrow of this event, the convention adopted a resolution (undoubtedly edited by Miliukov) in which it reiterated that "in so far as the state Duma cannot be recognized as an adequate [organ of] popular representation, the aim of the Constitutional Democratic Party remains the same as before—namely, [the convocation of] the Constituent Assembly." As to the Duma, "it can serve for the Party only as one of the means towards realization of the above-mentioned aim, while a permanent and close contact should be maintained with the general course of the liberation movement outside the Duma."

The last sentence obviously implied a coordination of the Cadet Party's efforts with the activities of the parties of the Left. This subject was discussed by Miliukov at the convention in the following terms:

Between us and our allies, not adversaries, from the Left (this is how I prefer to call them) there also exists a certain dividing line, but it is of an altogether different nature from the one that we have drawn to the right of us. Together with them we stand on the same Left wing of the Russian political movement. We do not join them in their demands for a democratic republic and nationalization of means of production. To some of us these demands are generally unacceptable while others consider them as being outside [the realm of] practical politics. But so long as, in spite of different motives, it remains possible for us to march together to a common goal, both party groups will act as a single unit.

In the course of time, the difference between Miliukov and Maklakov lost a good deal of its sharpness as far as *tactical* problems were concerned. Events themselves took care of that. By the fall of 1907, the revolutionary energy was totally spent, and there were no visible prospects of its resurgence. The government had recovered its control over the country, and there was a conservative majority in the Duma. The Cadets had to adjust themselves to the new situation. "To preserve the Duma" now became the official slogan. This meant to make the best of the existing circumstances, and to take part in the legislative activity, modest as its scope might be. In this way, the Cadet Party, still led by Miliukov, was moving to the right, in Maklakov's direction. But there was also a reverse process, this time affecting the moderates of the Maklakov type and even those to the right of him. As yet it has not been studied by historians, but it surely can be traced as a slowly but steadily developing trend in the life of the last two Dumas. As the Duma was growing more sure of itself, even its conservative majority was becoming less and less inclined to acquiesce in the arbitrariness of the administration or to overlook its inefficiency. By the end of the period, the opposition spirit in the Duma was by no means limited to the Cadets and those to the left of them. Thus was prepared the ground for the formation of the Progressive Bloc in 1915 and through it for the first Provisional Government.

All this, however, does not deprive the controversy as it developed in 1905–06 of its considerable historical interest. It was then, in a period of crisis, that the two different concepts of an appropriate liberal policy found its fullest and most articulate expression. Essentially, the Russian liberals faced the same problem with which the Social Democrats were struggling at the same time: What was the nature of the transformation Russia was undergoing, and what were its possible limits? Closely linked with this problem was another question: What were the forces in the country that would be able to bring this transformation to a successful conclusion? Maklakov saw the historical need of the hour in the continuation and completion of the Great Reforms of the 1860's, in the establishment in Russia of a political order based on the rule of law and self-government, and he believed that it could and should be effected in an evolutionary way, without the destruction of the existing political and social structure. In his eyes, even a thorough democratization of the latter was not immediately feasible and could be left to the future. For the time being, lasting reforms could be achieved only under the direction of those elements in the country which were prepared for the task by their previous practical experience in the field of public or governmental work. This was why the liberals had to ally themselves with those groups to the right of them which recognized the necessity of reforms, and why they had to seek an agreement with the government whenever an opportunity presented itself. Maklakov minimized the danger of reaction for which he saw no solid base in the prevailing trends of national life. To him, the main danger was on the left and not on the right. It was the danger of uncontrollable and chaotic revolutionary outbreaks, spurred, even if not provoked, by demagogic policies and appeals.

Miliukov expected from the Russian crisis much more far-reaching results than those envisaged by Maklakav. In his concept, the introduction in Russia of a full-fledged parliamentary regime was an immediate necessity and not a program for a more or less remote future. Unlike Maklakov, he considered the country ripe for popular sovereignty, and he felt that it was the duty of the liberals to wage a battle for this aim so long as there was a chance of its attainment. A much more politically minded person than his opponent, he also wanted the constitutional guarantees to be fully spelled out at once. The extreme importance that he attached to institutional arrangements, which to his critics was a sign of his doctrinaire spirit, in reality proceeded from his firm belief in the logic of political institutions. He did not neglect the social aspects of the

Russian problem, and he emphasized the immediate necessity of a radical agrarian reform as vigorously as he fought for political democracy. I know that the Cadet agrarian project, of which Miliukov was one of the sponsors, appeared rather modest as reflected in the peculiarly slanted looking glass of the Russian political life of the time. The fact remains that it proposed compulsory alienation of private property on such a scale as would be deemed revolutionary in any one of the contemporary Western societies. Miliukov knew, of course, that his political and social program could neither win any support among the Russian moderates nor serve as a basis for an agreement with the government. Thus, in pursuing his aims, he was forced to look for allies among the Left-Wing opposition parties, much as he disliked some of their objectives and methods. If Maklakov minimized the danger of reaction, Miliukov at that time apparently minimized the danger of revolution. To him, the real enemies were on the right not on the left.

It is not the purpose of this paper to pass judgment on the respective merits of the two political approaches I have tried to outline on the preceding pages. What I want to point out is that both stood in a direct and close relationship with the realities of prerevolutionary Russian life and both had their roots in the native tradition.

Maklakov could cite as his predecessors those public leaders and enlightened bureaucrats who throughout the nineteenth century, from Speranskii on, were concerned with the problem of introducing legality into the Russian government, the mid-century defenders of individual and civil liberty, the architects of the Great Reforms, and the moderate zemstvo liberals. Miliukov's political genealogy would include the Decembrists, Herzen in some of his phases, the more radical zemstvo constitutionalists of the Petrunkevich type, and those of the late nineteenth-century revolutionaries who were prepared to subordinate all other aims to the more immediate task of obtaining a constitutional regime for Russia.

Neither Miliukov nor Maklakov were any more "uprooted" than was the whole liberal movement in Russia, the two different aspects of which they exemplified. Too much has been made of the alleged absence of a social base for a liberal party in Russia. Strictly speaking, none of the Russian political parties had a stable and properly organized social base. If the revolutionary parties benefited from a mushroom growth in a period of national excitement, as happened both to Social Democrats and Socialist Revolutionaries in 1905, the moment the revolutionary wave receded the suddenly acquired social base began to disintegrate, and before long party organizations were reduced to their former, more than modest, proportions. After all, the liberals too had their periods of widespread popularity, first in 1904, and then again in 1906.

It might be argued that the *potential* social base of revolutionary parties was larger than that of the Constitutional Democrats. This is undoubtedly true—if one assumes the inevitability of revolutionary upheavals in imperial Russia. But from this it does not follow that the liberals had no potential base at all. Miliukov and Maklakov agree in their testimony that the Cadet Party was meeting with a mass response among the lower middle class of the cities, and that its ties with this milieu were growing. As the size of this group certainly was not smaller than that of the industrial working class, for instance, it cannot be dismissed as *quantité négligeable*. Apparently, some of these Cadet constituencies survived even the revolutionary turmoil of 1917 as otherwise it would be difficult to account for the two million votes received by the Cadet Party in the election to the Constituent Assembly. Professor Oliver H. Radkey, in his excellent study of the election, speaks of this result as a "washout" for the Cadets. I am inclined to think that on the contrary, with practically all odds against them, the Cadets did surprisingly well.

At any rate, no conclusion can be made on the basis of the Cadet Party's defeat in the revolution as to the actual or potential strength of liberalism in prerevolutionary Russia. The Russian liberals shared the historical fate of all moderate groups caught in a revolution. There is no need of looking for some specific reasons peculiar to Russia for an explanation of this phenomenon. It is one of the concrete examples of that political polarization which we have observed of late in several Western countries, all of them with a much more numerous middle class and a far stronger liberal tradition than Russia ever possessed, and as yet not in throes of a revolution. Obviously, the assessment of the historical importance of Russian liberalism must be made on different grounds.

8 /

RUSSIA AND THE
PORTSMOUTH
PEACE CONFERENCE *

That an aggressive Russia and an aggressive Japan, both interested
in Korea and Manchuria, would inevitably fight was no historical
certainty: imperialistic competition can be resolved by means other
than war. But the inept and irresponsible policies of the Russian
government from 1898 to 1904, for which Nicholas II was chiefly
responsible, not only made inevitable the armed conflict with Japan
but also insured the Russian defeat. The Tsar redeemed himself
somewhat by his policies during the Portsmouth Peace Conference, as
is shown in the following article analyzing an important chapter in
Russian diplomatic history.

THE RUSSO-JAPANESE WAR, which had begun in February, 1904,
as a result of friction between these two countries in Manchuria and
northern Korea, was one long military disaster for the Russian army. The
Japanese army moved from victory to victory, proving its superiority
in the battles of Liao-Yang and Sha-ho in August and October, 1904,
the fall of Port Arthur in January, 1905, and the battle of Mukden in
February and March. On May 27, the Japanese navy proved itself by
virtually destroying the Russian fleet in the battle of Tsushima.

In spite of what seemed to be great good fortune, however, all was
not well with the Japanese. On May 31, the Japanese Foreign Minister,
Baron Jutaro Komura, instructed his ambassador in Washington to deliver a message to President Roosevelt, asking him if he would "directly
and entirely of his own motion and initiative . . . invite the two bellig-
erants to come together for the purpose of direct negotiation."

* Robert K. Godwin, "Russia and the Portsmouth Peace Conference," *The American
Slavic and East European Review*, IX (December, 1950), 279–91. Reprinted by
permission of the author and the publisher.

The author is associated with the U.S. Department of Defense as a Research
Analyst specializing in problems of Soviet foreign policy.

Roosevelt immediately opened discussion on the subject with the Russian ambassador to the United States, Count Kassini. Kassini refused to consider the question sincerely, declaring that Russia was fighting the battle of the white race and could not accept defeat. Roosevelt asked him to transmit to his Government an American invitation to talk over peace terms with the Japanese. Roosevelt, however, did not trust Kassini to deliver his message and decided to ask the American ambassador to Russia, George von Lengerke Meyer, to see the Tsar in person and deliver his invitation.

After some difficulty, Meyer succeeded in obtaining personal audience with the Tsar. Explaining that the proposed conference would be for the good of all humanity and most advantageous to Russia, he managed to get Nicholas to agree to a meeting, providing it be held without intermediaries. When Kassini heard of this, he insisted that Meyer had misunderstood the Tsar. Roosevelt found it necessary to send Kassini's statement to Meyer, who then showed it to the Russian Foreign Minister, Count Vladimir Lamsdorf, along with the original message he had sent to Roosevelt. Lamsdorf then issued a statement declaring that Meyer had not misinterpreted the Tsar's remarks. Roosevelt spoke of this whole episode as "a perfectly characteristic experience, showing the utterly loose way in which the Russian Government works."

Once the question of whether there should be a peace conference at all had been settled, there ensued another squabble over where it should take place. The details of this argument need not concern us here. Russia proposed Paris or The Hague, and Japan proposed Chefoo. They finally agreed on Washington.

Within Russia, the question of who would take responsibility in this politically very dangerous mission became a problem. Lamsdorf wanted to send his friend, Count S. J. Witte, but Witte was at this time out of favor with the Tsar. The Tsar appointed Nelidov, but he insisted that he was not well enough for the trip. The choice then fell on Murav'ëv, but he too declined. The Tsar then agreed to send Witte. Witte told Kokovcev, the Minister of Finance, that the Tsar had "forced" him to go to America, and added, "When a sewer has to be cleaned, they send Witte; but as soon as work of a cleaner and nicer kind appears, plenty of candidates spring up."

As a matter of fact, both Witte and Kokovcev had been involved in unofficial negotiations with the Japanese since sometime in February. Roosevelt's peace offers, which he pretended to make on his own initiative, did not come as a surprise to the Russian government. As early as February 26, Kokovcev's agent in London, Rutkovskij, telegraphed Witte that the Japanese ambassador there wished to see him and talk over peace possibilities. Witte turned this correspondence over to Kokovcev, who forwarded it to Lamsdorf. All his statements to the contrary notwithstanding, Witte must have looked forward to this assignment with some enthusiasm. He already knew that the Japanese wanted peace for their own reasons, but this apparently was not well known to the outside world. If the Japanese eagerness for peace were strong enough, he could appear before the world and before the Imperial Court as the man who had turned defeat into victory by clever negotiation.

Baron Roman Rosen, who had succeeded Kassini as ambassador to the United States in July, was appointed plenipotentiary under Witte. Korostovec and Nabokov were named as secretaries.

The Japanese appointed Komura and Takahira as plenipotentiaries, with Sato, Adatci, and Otchiai as their secretaries.

Both Russia and Japan hoped to end the war, each for its own reasons. Roosevelt also hoped for peace, and so was willing to help all he could. From Roosevelt's point of view, peace would be advantageous to both countries and to the rest of the world as well. He thought it would be to Russia's advantage to get out of the war before she lost more territory. He seems to have been convinced that if the war continued, the Russian army would continue to be defeated. As he wrote to Lodge: "Russia had far better make peace now, if she possibly can, and find her boundaries in east Asia left without material shrinkage from what they were ten years ago, than to submit to being driven out of east Asia." He thought Japan should make peace because the continuation of the war would cost her more than she could possibly gain. In the interests of the United States and the rest of the world, Roosevelt seems to have desired to maintain some form of balance of power in Asia. "While for the rest of us, [he wrote Lodge] Russia's triumph would have been a blow to civilization, her destruction as an eastern Asiatic power would also in my opinion be unfortunate."

Russia wanted peace for three main reasons. First, there was the unsettled situation within the country. Russia was, at this time, passing through one of the great revolutionary periods in her history. The war had never been popular in Russia, and almost everyone connected with the peace negotiations must have realized its end would strengthen the government's position considerably. Meyer wrote in his diary on July 21: "The Russians are putting up a tremendous bluff about wanting the war to go on, but with the condition of internal affairs, there is but one thing for Russia to do—make peace before it is too late. If they do not do so, I cannot foretell what the outcome will be."

The second reason, which may very likely be first in order of importance, was financial. Witte has expressed this opinion on the question:

At the time of my departure [for the United States] our financial position was as follows. We had exhausted all our means and had lost our credit abroad. There was not the slightest hope of floating either a domestic or a foreign loan.

We could continue the war only by resorting to new issues of paper money, that is, by preparing the way for a complete financial and consequently economic collapse.

Kokovcev, in a letter to Lamsdorf, said that from a financial point of view, immediate peace was a necessity, but he added that perhaps financial considerations should not be the deciding factor.

The third and final reason is connected closely with the other two: Russia was losing the war. Some people have argued that the Russian army could have eventually won the war. Kuropatkin has written that "if we had not concluded peace so hastily victory would have crowned our arms." But be this as it may, Russia had not won a battle, and the morale on the home front would not stand for many more defeats.

The Japanese desire for peace seems to have been largely financial. The Japanese had spent great sums of money on the war, and most of these funds had been borrowed from other countries. To continue the war, she would have to borrow more money. This she could not do because she had little or no collateral left. Takeuchi says that the war resources of Japan were completely exhausted by the end of March, and Count Hayashi wrote in his memoirs that "those who know the real circumstances recognize that at the time the negotiations were in progress it was absolutely necessary for us to make peace."

The Japanese could hardly help being aware of the revolutionary situation within Russia, but whether they knew of the Russian financial difficulties is not known. Their insistence on the payment of an indemnity would tend to indicate that they did not. On the other hand, the dire straits in which the Japanese found themselves may have forced them to try for an indemnity even if they knew it would be next to impossible for Russia to pay.

That the Russians knew of Japan's financial position is certain. This knowledge may have been, in fact, the deciding factor in determining the Russian position at the conference. Sir Cecil Spring-Rice wrote Mrs. Roosevelt (for transmission to the President) that "a memorandum drawn up by a clever French financier, just home from Japan, showed clearly that Japan could not continue the war for financial reasons." This same memorandum is referred to by Meyer, who says that it "caused the Tsar to be firm against an indemnity."

As one of the outstanding statesmen of his time and as chief plenipotentiary from his country, Witte held a dominant position among the Russians at the conference. Witte's attitude toward Japan and his plan of action are of considerable interest. He had opposed the war from the very beginning, probably because he did not think it an expedient method of extending Russian influence in the Far East. His informal contacts with the Japanese early in 1905 have already been noted. These contacts must have made the enemy's position and desire for peace clear to him. For some time before the conference he seems to have desired to work out some kind of political rapprochement with the Japanese, perhaps even some form of military alliance. It was his desire that the settlement with Japan be friendly and durable. With such an arrangement in the Far East, Russia could turn her attention to European problems and leave the spread of Russian interests in the East to slower, more peaceful but more permanent, economic devices.

Before the conference opened, Witte sent his friend, the British journalist, E. J. Dillon, to see Count Hayashi in London. The purpose of this maneuver seems to have been twofold. He wanted the Japanese government to appoint Marquis Ito as its plenipotentiary (probably because he had also opposed the war, and was at this time rather old), and he wanted to sound out the possibilities of a Russo-Japanese alliance. Hayashi told Dillon that the appointment of Komura could not be changed, and seems to have indicated that an alliance would be impossible. Witte, however, continued in the early days of the Portsmouth Conference to speak of the desirability of reaching a thorough political understanding with the Japanese.

As a matter of fact, of course, the Russian delegation was required to carry out the wishes of the Tsar. There is no evidence to show that the Tsar desired any kind of alliance with Japan, and Witte could not have concluded such an agreement without his consent. In the face of both the Tsar's and Japan's unwillingness to make an alliance, he was forced to change his tactics.

The Tsar's instructions to the Russian plenipotentiaries were categorical and clear: they were not to consent to the cession of any Russian territory or the payment of an indemnity in any form. Witte's final decision as to the tactics to be employed can best be expressed in his own words:

I resolved to base my tactics on the following principles: (1) Not to show that we were in the least anxious to make peace, and to convey the impression that if His Majesty had consented to the negotiations, it was merely because of the universal desire on the part of all countries to see the war terminated; (2) to act as befitted the representative of the greatest empire on earth, undismayed by the fact that that mighty empire had become involved temporarily in a slight difficulty; (3) in view of the tremendous influence of the press in America, to show it every attention and to be accessible to all its representatives; (4) to behave with democratic simplicity and without a shadow of snobbishness, so as to win the sympathy of the Americans; (5) in view of the considerable influence of the Jews on the press and on other aspects of American life, especially in New York, not to exhibit any hostility toward them—which conduct was entirely in keeping with my opinion on the Jewish problem.

He told Rosen that in his opinion they should "act as broadmindedly as possible in questions that are of no material importance, and stand out for those conditions that are really important and show our compliance so that in case of a rupture the blame should fall on the Japanese."

This was a difficult position to maintain. The Japanese desire to annex Sakhalin and force Russia to pay an indemnity was apparent long before the conference opened, and it was doubtful if they would conclude a peace settlement unless these claims were met. In the early days of the preliminary negotiations, Japan invaded the island of Sakhalin. This move was interpreted by the Russians as an attempt to preclude argument on this question. Rosen claims that Witte wanted to conclude peace as quickly as possible, and was willing to give up the island and pay a disguised indemnity, but that he persuaded Witte that Japan's need for peace was greater than Russia's and such concessions were unnecessary. Rosen seems to have held this unconciliatory attitude throughout the conference.

It was decided that since Washington was uncomfortably hot throughout the month of August, the conference should be moved to New England. The plenipotentiaries lived in Portsmouth, New Hampshire, while the conference itself was held in the government navy yard at Kittery, Maine. The conference opened on the tenth of August and lasted for twelve sessions. The two powers agreed that it should be held without intermediaries and in secret. All communications to the press were to be approved by both powers at the conclusion of each session.

After some difficulties about the extent of the powers of the plenipotentiaries, the Japanese presented their demands. As had been expected, the most important of these were the insistence upon the payment of an indemnity and the cession of Sakhalin. The Russians indicated that they could not agree to these two demands, but they proceeded to discuss the other, less important items. During the first eight sessions (through August 18), the negotiators reached tentative agreement on the following eight problems: (1) that there should be peace and friendship between Japan and Russia; (2) that Russia recognize Japan's paramount interest in Korea; (3) the evacuation of Manchuria; (4) the freedom of China to develop Manchuria commercially; (5) that areas leased from China by Russia be transferred to Japan, subject to the consent of China; (6) the transfer of the southern section of the Chinese Eastern Railway to Japan, Russia retaining the part at the north which was a short-cut to Vladivostok; (7) agreement not to exploit the Manchurian railways for political purposes; and (8) agreement not to make separate conventions for the regulation of railway services.

These questions out of the way, the items concerning an indemnity and the cession of Sakhalin had to be considered. In the course of the sessions from August 16 to 18, it became increasingly apparent that the two nations were in almost hopeless disagreement on these questions. The Japanese continued to insist, and the Tsar continued to hold firm. Kokovcev wrote Witte on August 21 that his message suggesting a disguised indemnity had been returned to him by the Tsar with the words "no land, no indemnity . . ." written across it. Both Witte and St. Petersburg seems to have taken a pessimistic view of the possibilities of agreement. Witte wrote Lamsdorf on August 14 to prepare for a long war, and told Kokovcev on August 17 that there would be no agreement. At one point during this time he wired the Tsar his regrets at the failure of the conference. Dillon says that on the fifteenth or sixteenth, he helped Witte draw up a paper declaring the conference a failure and placing the blame on the Japanese. On August 22, Lamsdorf wrote Kokovcev that Witte had been instructed to break off negotiations if the Japanese would not change their minds.

On August 23 the Japanese proposed that the island of Sakhalin be divided in half, with the Russians paying the Japanese 1,200,000,000 yen for the northern part. Witte refused to accept this proposal, but offered to give the whole of Sakhalin to Japan if she would drop her demand for money. The Japanese refused to accept this compromise. The conference had reached an impasse. Japan now stood before the world as desiring to continue the war for territorial gain and money. This was what Witte had wanted.

As already noted, Witte placed great importance on American public opinion. From the very beginning he had tried to win the American press to his side. His close friend, E. J. Dillon, acted as his press representative along with Korostovec and tried to keep the American newspapers well informed about the movements and "human interest" of the Russian delegation. Many people have written of the "marvelous" shift of public opinion which took place as a result of Witte's carefully planned campaign to prove to the American people that a representative of the Tsar could be "democratic." Mr. Thorson's research, however, seems to prove conclusively that, all textbook accounts notwithstanding, the editorial opinion of American newspapers did not change. They were consistently, both before and after the conference, pro-Japanese and anti-Russian. Witte, however, seems to have believed that a shift did take place. He spoke of it at some length in his memoirs and even wrote Kokovcev a letter in which he explained the shift and pointed out its advantage to the Russians. The London *Times* correspondent at the peace conference reported that Witte was very popular among the Americans but that this popularity did not indicate a shift in American public opinion, although Witte thought it did. This feeling on the part of Witte may have been another reason why the Russians stood firm in the face of continuing Japanese demands.

All sides were in a delicate position. The Japanese did not want to appear to lose the peace after having fought so many victorious battles. The Russians did not wish to give up any land and probably could not have paid an indemnity if they had been willing to. At this time, it looked as if the conference would break up without agreement. Plans were made for Witte to make a tour of the United States after the expected breakup, with the aim of encouraging favorable American public opinion and promoting a loan to help Russia carry on the war.

At this point Roosevelt decided to intervene in an attempt to save the conference. On August 18, he telegraphed Assistant Secretary Pierce (whose job it was to look after the conferees) to have Witte send Rosen or some other person of confidence to see him. Rosen went almost immediately to visit the President. Roosevelt proposed that the Russians agree to divide Sakhalin, buying back the northern half. He agreed to bring pressure on the Japanese in an attempt to persuade them to accept this plan. He suggested that the question of the price to be paid might be settled by discussions between two more or less neutral powers, e.g., England and France. He further asked that this plan be transmitted to the Tsar for his approval.

Roosevelt apparently did not trust the Russian diplomats and decided to approach the Tsar directly. He instructed Ambassador Meyer to see the Tsar and explain this compromise to him. Meyer made arrangements for a personal interview with the Tsar at which he presented the President's proposals. The Tsar insisted that Russia was not defeated, but he agreed to divide Sakhalin on the basis that the southern half was really Japanese. He would not, however, agree to pay for the northern half. This, he said, would be simply a disguised indemnity. Meyer described the Tsar in the following terms:

He appeared to me this time as a man of no force, without any breadth of mind; he has the Russian capacity of passing by misfortunes that have taken place and seeing things in the future as he would have them, and instead of reasoning, resorts to the subterfuge that his conscience tells him that he must do this.

The Ambassador wrote Roosevelt that the Russian public was becoming convinced that everything was settled except the "matter of rubles" and were united in their determination not to pay. Roosevelt then sent two more telegrams, and Meyer saw the Tsar again but the Tsar remained firm.

It should be noted at this point that the Russian foreign office had come into possession of the American diplomatic code and was reading Roosevelt's messages to Meyer before they reached Meyer. He always felt that the Tsar had been briefed beforehand about all of his visits and proposals. While Roosevelt was trying to contact and reason with the Tsar, the Russian foreign office (keeping itself one step ahead of Meyer) was trying to get the French government to intervene. The French, however, soon learned of Roosevelt's messages to Meyer and interpreted the Russian move as an attempt to tie the Tsar's hands and frustrate the Roosevelt intervention. The French judiciously refused to act, but instead supported the Roosevelt proposals.

Germany was also involved in this negotiation. In the early days of these discussions, when Meyer told the Tsar that the German Emperor favored peace, the Tsar said, "I know that. I have a letter on my table now from Emperor William, just received, in which he tells me he so expressed himself to you." At the time Roosevelt intervened, Meyer wrote, "The Tsar then remarked that it was quite a coincidence that each time I came to see him he had had a telegram from the German Emperor (in their private code) urging him to make peace." Roosevelt wrote Spring-Rice: "He [the Kaiser] has done everything he could to make the Czar yield and has backed me up in every way, and I thoroughly appreciate how he has behaved."

As he had promised, Roosevelt also brought pressure to bear on the Japanese. He urged them to accept his compromise proposal or at least not to continue the war in order to get an indemnity. He personally felt that they had a right to Sakhalin, but that to continue the war for money would be contrary to common sense and Japan's own national interest.

The Anglo-Japanese Alliance had been renewed on August 12, and the United States repeatedly urged the British government to bring pressure on Japan to make peace. This the British consistently refused to to, on the grounds that such advice would be improper and go unheeded.

The final session of the conference was to be held on August 26, but when Witte continued to refuse to pay an indemnity, it was postponed until August 29. On the evening of August 27 a high conference of state was called in Tokyo which lasted through the night and was followed by a cabinet meeting the next morning. In these meetings the policy makers in Japan decided that the financial and military position of the Empire was so critical that a continuance of the war to force the payment of an indemnity, or to keep Sakhalin, would be disastrous. They ordered Komura to give up these claims and make peace as soon as possible.

When the conference reconvened on August 29, Witte, carrying out direct orders from the Tsar, took the offensive and categorically refused to pay any indemnity in any form, offering to let the Japanese keep the southern half of Sakhalin. These, he said, were his final conditions and if they were not accepted, the conference was over. After a moment of silence, Komura accepted the Russian proposal. In the words of Korostovec:

At last Komura, in a well-controlled voice, said that the Japanese Government, having for its aim the restoration of peace and the bringing of the negotiations to a successful conclusion, expressed its consent to Russia's proposal to divide Sakhalin in two, without indemnity being paid. Witte calmly replied that the Japanese proposal was accepted and that the line of demarkation of Sakhalin would be reckoned the fiftieth degree.

The final treaty was formally signed on September 5 and ratifications were exchanged at Washington on the twenty-fifth of November, 1905. The main provisions of the treaty were as follows: Russia acknowledged that Japan possessed "paramount political, military and economic interests" in Korea; the two countries agreed to evacuate Manchuria; Russia agreed to transfer her lease on Port Arthur, Talien and adjacent territories to Japan (and they agreed to mutually engage to obtain China's consent to this transaction); Russia agreed to transfer to Japan, without compensation and with the consent of China, the railway between Changchun and Port Arthur; Russia agreed to work out fishing rights along the coasts of Russia with Japan; and Russia agreed to cede to Japan the southern half of Sakhalin Island, using the fiftieth degree of north latitude as the line of demarkation.

This final settlement was essentially a compromise and as such it was not entirely satisfactory to either power. Under the circumstances, however, the restoration of peace was of paramount importance to both. Roosevelt seems to have served both sides with the same impartiality in spite of his obvious preference for the Japanese. The American President did not mediate. For the most part, he served as a convenient instrument for getting the two countries together within the framework of diplomatic protocol. When the conference seemed about to dissolve without agreement, he intervened. Whether this intervention was necessary may never be known. It is very likely that both nations were merely stalling for time, and that the weaker, financially, was bound to make concessions sooner or later. Roosevelt may have hurried the process along, but since so much depended on the whim of the Tsar and his estimate of the strength of his empire, the final significance of Roosevelt's intervention cannot be ascertained from the evidence now available.

9

THE *VEKHI* GROUP
AND THE MYSTIQUE
OF REVOLUTION *

The years between the 1905 Revolution and World War I were critical
ones for Russia, for they were years of change in both tempo and
direction. The rate of change in industry and agriculture was
accelerating; the country was experimenting with constitutionalism;
efforts were being made to introduce universal primary education. For
the intelligentsia it was a period of self-examination and
re-examination in the light of the events of 1905 and their aftermath.
The issues debated by various groups provide a background for
understanding the Revolution of 1917.

Tʜɪs ɪs the story of a debate which engaged most, if not all, of
the best intellects of the present century in pre-revolutionary Russia. It
started some time before the 1917 revolution as an argument about the
Russian intelligentsia. It continued in exile, after the revolution, as a
dispute on the historical meaning of the revolution. Every one of the
main participants in the debate is now dead, and its subject matter belongs to history. But some of the issues involved may still be of importance today.

The general character of the *intelligent* of the opening of this century is familiar to all. His outlook was still moulded by the radical heroes
of the generation of the 1860's and 1870's—Chernyshevsky, Pisarev, Mikhaylovsky. At the end of the 19th century the influence of Marx and En-

* Leonard B. Schapiro, "The *Vekhi* Group and the Mystique of Revolution," *The
Slavonic and East European Review*, XXXIV (December, 1955), 56–76. Reprinted
by permission of the author and the publisher.

The author was born in Scotland, but lived in Russia during his childhood years.
He has had two careers, one as a lawyer and one as a scholar. From 1932 to 1955,
he was engaged in the practice of law, with time out for war service. Since 1955,
he has been on the faculty of the London School of Economics and Political Science, where he is now Reader in Russian Government and Politics. He is the author
of *The Origin of the Communist Autocracy* (1955) and *The Communist Party of
the Soviet Union* (1960).

gels had also made itself felt. The Russian *intelligent* believed passionately in progress, in utilitarianism, in the perfectibility of human society—if the right formula could be found. The autocracy and its supporting bureaucracy were anathema—not to be against them in spirit, if not in action, was a betrayal of all that was noble in man. This radicalism of outlook, though not without its naïve side, which was born of the fact that most of the intelligentsia had had virtually no experience of practical government activity, certainly had the appeal of nobility. But there was some truth in the reproach later to be made by S. L. Frank that it also had something of the slave mentality about it in its attitude to the government: all ills spring from the government, which is no part of us, and with which we have no concern except to revolt against it.

Early in the century a group of young philosophers, most if not all of whom had been much influenced by marxism, broke both with marxism and with some of the main philosophical and social foundations inherited from the radical thinkers of the 1860's and 1870's. This group, which included S. N. Bulgakov, N. A. Berdyayev, S. L. Frank, P. I. Novgorodtsev and B. A. Kistyakovsky, joined together to publish a volume of essays under the title *Problemy Idealizma* (Problems of Idealism). The ideas of this volume, though they ran directly counter to the sacred beliefs of the radical intelligentsia in that they were critical of both positivism and materialism, were expressed on a sufficiently academic plane not to arouse either violent controversy or very wide attention. As Frank wrote many years later, although regarded as heretical, 'they were nevertheless condescendingly forgiven by radical public opinion as a relatively innocent piece of crankiness, even if not without its dangers'. In the Preface to *Problemy Idealizma* the editor, Novgorodtsev, drew attention to the fact that philosophical idealism was not a novelty for the Russian public. At the height of the development of positivism, this doctrine had been boldly assailed both by Vladimir Solov'yov and by Boris Chicherin. The volume included essays criticising the historical theories of Marx and Engels, criticism of Auguste Comte and of Mikhaylovsky, and an essay on the revival of natural law doctrines.

But, although unobtrusive, this volume, which already signalised a break with marxism by a number of its former adherents, was to prove the forerunner of a much more dramatic attack. The main influence in this development came from Petr Berngardovich Struve. Struve, seven years older than Frank, with whom he was closely linked in friendship, was the most prominent of the renegades from marxism, if only by reason of the fact that it was he who in 1898 had drawn up the manifesto of the Social Democratic Party. He parted company with marxism in 1901, and in 1902 founded a paper in Stuttgart, *Osvobozhdeniye* (Liberation) which became the leading influence in the formation of the party of National Liberation (Kadets) in 1905. Struve became a member of the Kadet party, and sat as a deputy in the short-lived Second Duma in 1907. After the dissolution of the Duma he retired from politics to academic work, and to work on *Russkaya Mysl'* (Russian Thought), first as joint editor with the historian Kizewetter, and after 1911 as sole editor. Already by 1907 a vast gulf separated Struve from the party which he had done so much to create. Before 1905 Struve had urged in *Osvobozhdeniye* that Russian liberalism should express its solidarity with the revolutionary tendencies. After the revolution of 1905 he believed that the time had come for liberalism to break with the revolutionary tradition from which the party had in large measure drawn its inspiration. This the Kadets were unable or unwilling to do. In his memoirs of the period of the First and Second Dumas V. A. Maklakov traces the victory of bolshevism to this factor above all, and Struve would probably have agreed with this judgment. But in 1907 Struve was almost alone in his belief that the primary duty of the liberal forces was to strive for some sort of working agreement with the monarchy, so that reform could take place on the solid foundation of order. In order to appreciate the originality of this outlook one must see it in the psychological setting of the radical intelligentsia of the period, and nothing could show this better than the following passage from Frank's unpublished memoir of Struve. Struve, writes Frank, brought a new note into the typical outlook of the intelligentsia of his day. 'This note', Frank continues, 'I can only describe as government consciousness. Oppositional and particularly radical public opinion felt itself oppressed by the government and completely estranged from it. State power was "they", a strange and inaccessible compound of court and bureaucracy, pictured as a group of corrupt and mentally limited rulers over the real "national and public" Russia. To "them" were opposed "we", "society", the "people", and above all the "caste" of the intelligentsia, concerned for the welfare of the people and devoted to its service, but by reason of its lack of rights capable only of criticising the government power of arousing oppositional feelings, and secretly preparing a revolt. Petr Berngardovich had within him, and displayed from the very first, the embryo of something quite different from the usual—*tranchons le mot!*—slave consciousness (which was alas! destined in practice to triumph and to determine the fate of Russia). He always discussed politics, so to say, not from "below", but from "above", not as a member of an enslaved society, but conscious of the fact that he was a potential participator in positive state construction.' This new outlook took shape, mainly in the columns of *Russkaya Mysl'*, after 1907. In his reflections on the 1905 revolution, written after the dissolution of the Second Duma, and in later articles, Struve urges compromise, and denounces hatred and vengeance as political motives so far as liberals are concerned. He emphasises throughout that what is needed is not a question of tactics, but of a 'political and moral re-education of the Russian intelligentsia', to emancipate it from its outworn heritage of the period before 1905. But at the same time, the government must be founded on the idea of law, 'which excludes all absolute power, however disguised and however justified'. The only solution is for the 'state and the nation to grow organically into one'.

These three ideas—the need for a moral re-education of the intelligentsia, for a legal order as the foundation of government, and for the fusion of state and nation—became the foundation for a volume of seven essays published in 1909 under the title *Vekhi* (Landmarks) by a group of thinkers whose views were both close to those of Struve and influenced by him. Some of them had already contributed to *Problemy Idealizma* in 1903: N. A. Berdyayev, S. N. Bulgakov, S. L. Frank and B. A. Kistyakovsky. The newcomers were M. O. Gershenzon and A. S. Izgoyev. We have it on both Struve's and Frank's authority that *Vekhi* was not in any sense a joint effort—each author wrote independently, and without consultation with the others. The publication of this slim volume of essays was a bombshell. It ran into five editions in a short time. It provoked violent attacks from the Kadets, from the Socialist Revolutionaries, from Lenin, from a whole number of outraged individuals, in books and in articles. The leader of the Kadets, P. N. Milyukov, toured Russia for a series of public meetings organised by his party for the denunciation of *Vekhi*. The violence of the reaction is sufficient indication of the fact that emotions were engaged as much as, if not more than, intellects. In his memoir, to which reference has been made, Frank gives the following explanation: in contrast to the mild and academic *Problemy Idealizma,* he writes, *Vekhi* embodied 'criticism of the basic sacred dogma of the radical intelligentsia—the "mystique" of revolution. This was regarded as an audacious and quite intolerable betrayal of the age-old sacred testament of the Russian intelligentsia, the betrayal of the tradition handed down by the prophets and saints of Russian social thought— Belinsky, Granovsky, Chernyshevsky, Pisarev—and a betrayal of the age-old striving for liberty, enlightenment and progress, and a going over to the side of black reaction.' He adds that it was not only the revolutionaries, but also the more moderate liberals who rose up against *Vekhi*. This was not surprising, since the liberals were quite as much the target of criticism as the revolutionaries and were often little behind the revolutionaries in 'revolutionary mystique'.

Let us examine the contents of this explosive volume. The Preface, by M. Gershenzon, from whom incidentally the suggestion to publish the volume had emanated, stresses that the only platform common to all the seven authors is 'the recognition of the primacy both in theory and in practice of spiritual life over the outward forms of society, in the sense that the inner life of the individual . . . and not the self-sufficing elements of some political order is the only solid basis for every social structure'. It is indeed the case that an acceptance of the religious basis of life is common to all the authors of *Vekhi*—a fact which, no doubt, contributed to earning them the charge of being 'reactionary' from their radical and rationalist opponents. In the first essay, N. A. Berdyayev examines the attitude of the intelligentsia to philosophical systems. His main thesis is that the value of the different philosophies, from the point of view of their absolute truth, has been subordinated in Russia to the utilitarian and social purposes which it was considered those systems could serve. This attitude, although inspired by the noblest of motives, has led to a general failure to seek and recognise truth for its own sake, and those who devote themselves to this pursuit fall under the suspicion of being reactionaries. (In a footnote to the second edition of *Vekhi* Berdyayev points out that the accuracy of his criticism has been confirmed by the character of the polemics evoked by his article.) Owing to historical reasons, says Berdyayev, the following misfortune has befallen the Russian intelligentsia: 'Love for egalitarian justice, for the general good and national well-being has paralysed love of truth, has almost destroyed any interest in truth.' But love of truth in the absolute is the *sine qua non* of all real philosophy. Even economic materialism, he argues, when transplanted onto Russian soil, has lost its objective analytical character, which had a grain of truth in it, and has suffered a change, whereby the subjective element of class warfare has been elevated to first place. As against that, the truly Russian thinkers such as Chaadayev, Dostoyevsky, or Solov'yov have been misunderstood or ignored. The reason for this is that the systems of these philosophers do not lend themselves to adaptation for use in the fight for socialism. 'We only recognised that philosophy as true', says Berdyayev, 'which helped us to fight the autocracy in the name of socialism.' His conclusion is that the intelligentsia must cure itself of its 'inner slavery', for only thus can it free itself from the external oppression upon which it is accustomed to throw all the blame for its own *malaise*.

S. N. Bulgakov, writing on 'Heroicism and Askesis', examines those elements in the outlook of an essentially atheistic intelligentsia which are derived from religious traditions, in order to point the contrast between these elements and the true Christian tradition. Puritanism in living, self-denial, a sense of guilt and repentance—not, of course, before God, but before the people—are all relics of Christianity. But their spiritual character is set at naught by the atheist materialism which has been slavishly copied from the West, along with socialism and belief in progress. For in adopting these Western beliefs, the intelligentsia has ignored the essentially Christian heritage in the West of the Roman Church and of the Reformation, which does not exist in Russia—freedom of person, and of speech, and the rights of man. In the result the Russian intelligentsia is propelled by an unrestrained passion for the betterment of mankind, which is essentially hubristic, and which sacrifices the means to the hoped for end. This is the 'heroicism' of the intelligentsia in contrast to the true humility of Christian 'askesis'. S. L. Frank, in a much more profound and brilliant essay, 'The Ethics of Nihilism', is also concerned with the problem from the religious aspect. He sees the main characteristic of the intelligentsia as 'nihilistic morality'. Like Bulgakov he recognises the pseudo-religious morality of the *intelligent*. But this morality is based on nihilism, in other words on the denial of any absolute values. Hence, it seeks its foundation outside absolute values, and finds it in the *narodnik* mystique of 'the people', in the idea of service and devotion to the welfare of 'the people'. In a passage of quite extraordinary perceptiveness, especially if one recalls the date when it was written, Frank points out that the conflict between marxism and *narodnichestvo* is really illusory. In fact, he says, 'the victorious and all-devouring *narodnik* spirit has swallowed and annihilated marxist theory and at the present time the difference between avowed *narodniki* and *narodniki* who profess marxism is reduced at most to a difference in political programme and sociological theory, and has no significance as a difference of a cultural and philosophical nature'. Today, forty-six years later, in the better perspective which the passage of time has brought, it is easy to see that the victory of bolshevism in 1917 was at least as much a victory of *narodnichestvo* as of marxism. Developing his idea, Frank, with equal foresight, traces the spiritual odyssey of the nihilist-moralist. The love of man yields in him to the love of an idea—an abstraction, human happiness. 'Ready to sacrifice himself for this idea he does not hesitate to sacrifice others.' He sees his contemporaries either as victims or as enemies. Out of great love for mankind is born great hatred for men—and the believing *narodnik*-socialist has become a revolutionary. The *intelligent*, Frank writes, must seek escape from the danger of nihilistic moralism in creative religious humanism.

The remaining essays are less directly religious in their main ideas, though the acceptance of a religious belief is common to all of them. B. A. Kistyakovsky, who for some years edited in Moscow a periodical called *Kriticheskoye Obozreniye* (Critical Survey), in which ideas akin to those of *Russkaya Mysl'* found an outlet, writes 'In Defence of Law'. He sees the main vice of the Russian intelligentsia in its failure to acquire any consciousness of the importance of law and legal order. Russia has made no contribution whatever to the development of legal ideas, while the absence of legal order in daily life has in turn led not only to an ignorance of the nature of a state founded upon law, but even to an illusion that the Russian people through some innate sense of truth has found a superior form of social life to that provided by the external truth of a legal order. Kistyakovsky quotes from the witty satire of B. N.

Almazov on the views of Konstantin Aksakov, of which the following is a rather lame translation:

> For reasons entirely organic
> We have not been endowed with at all
> That quality wholly satanic—
> Common-sense in the matter of law.
>
> Russian natures broad and wide
> Seeking truths eternal,
> Cannot be constrained inside
> Lawyers' rules infernal.

Such views, says Kistyakovsky, are not however confined to the Slavophils. He quotes tellingly from the works of Mikhaylovsky; and also the famous passage from Plekhanov's speech at the Second Social Democratic Congress to the effect that if the parliament freely elected after the revolution should prove to be a bad one, it should be dispersed. Our principle must be, said Plekhanov, with more enthusiasm than latinity, *salus revolutiae suprema lex.* (It should be added that in the last article which he wrote Plekhanov bitterly deplored the attempts made in January 1918 to justify the dispersal of the Constituent Assembly by references to this speech.) The main moral of Kistyakovsky's essay is that in the absence of a sense of the importance of legal principles among the radical intelligentsia, it is impossible for the courts of law to acquire their proper place in the life of the country.

Of the remaining essays, A. S. Izgoyev's on the youth of the intelligentsia paints a fairly deplorable picture of the moral life of university students. The progressive views of the fathers, he says, have led to a breakdown of family influence, which in turn has led to a decline in moral standards among the sons. As evidence he adduces the results of a questionnaire submitted to over ten thousand Moscow students on their sex life, which are certainly somewhat staggering. Much of the rest of what he criticised was, as Izgoyev recognised, at least to the same degree the fault of the authorities as of the students. As the result of restrictions on freedom of ideas, the student had become suspicious, conspiratorial and over-interested in politics to the detriment of his studies. His ideal was the revolutionary, his enemy the state. The further to the 'left', the nobler he felt himself to be; the nearer to the shadow of the gallows, the more he believed he was fulfilling his holy duty. In consequence, says Izgoyev, 'the great majority of the deputies in the Dumas, with the exception of thirty to forty Kadets and Octobrists, have not displayed any of the knowledge which is necessary for the government and reconstruction of the country'. M. O. Gershenzon's essay on 'Creative Self-Knowledge' is the wittiest, but least profound in the volume. Gershenzon, who was in some respects out of tune with the other six contributors, does not add much to the ideas developed in the other essays, but perhaps his attack was more telling because of the popular nature of the style. At all events, it was Gershenzon's essay that aroused the most violent reactions. His main thesis is that the intelligentsia, carried away by romantic notions, has lost all touch with reality and all capacity for concrete work. For the past half century, he says, 'A handful of revolutionaries has been going from house to house, knocking at every door, shouting "Out into the streets, everyone. You ought to be ashamed of sitting at home." And all living creatures poured into the town square, the lame, the blind and the halt, not one of them stayed at home. For half a century they have remained in the square, jostling one another and exchanging abuse. At home there is dirt, beggary, and disorder—but what does the householder care about that? He's out in the world, saving the people—and of course that is easier and more entertaining than doing the household chores at home.' Meanwhile, these revolutionary *intelligenty* remain oblivious of the fact that between them and the people is a vast gulf. In fact, the people hate us with a deep hatred, says Gershenzon. 'Such as we are, so far from dreaming of union with the people we ought to fear the people more than any executions by the government and bless this government which alone, with its prisons and bayonets, still protects us from the people's fury.' This last sentence aroused a special storm of protests. Struve was also later critical of it, pointing out that it was not the intelligentsia but the propertied classes which had to be protected with prisons and bayonets from popular fury. In a note to the second edition of *Vekhi*, Gershenzon explained that what he had meant was not that the intelligentsia *ought* to bless the government, but that it is in the circumstances *compelled* to do so, i.e., 'müssen' and not 'sollen'. (The word used by him in Russian was 'dolzhny'.) In a later reprint of the article he omitted the whole sentence. 'Better late than never' was Struve's comment, though in the light of later events Gershenzon does not appear today to have been so very wide of the mark. In contrast to the remaining authors, it is fair to say that there is a bitterness about Gershenzon's essay which is completely absent in the others. There is less charity, more censure, less recognition of the fact that the plight of the radical intelligentsia was not so much a moral fault as a tragedy of history. Gershenzon, incidentally, was the only one of the *Vekhi* group to remain in Russia after the Civil War—all the others, except Kistyakovsky who died at the end of the Civil War, went into exile. He enjoyed a high reputation as a literary critic, and was allowed by the Soviet authorities to publish several volumes, some of a deeply religious content, before his death in 1925. A selection of his letters to his brother was published posthumously in 1927. He was allotted a substantial article in the first edition of the Great Soviet Encyclopaedia, which has not survived in the current edition.

Struve's article, 'The Intelligentsia and the Revolution', is the most remarkable in the volume, and one of the best from Struve's pen. The ideas developed in it had first been jotted down by him in 1907 as notes for a chapter of a book. That they represented a very fundamental part of Struve's outlook is evident from the fact that echoes of them are to be found both in his earlier writings in *Russkaya Mysl'* and in his later work. The intelligentsia, he argues, is the social element which in contemporary Russian society has taken up the *rôle* once played by the *kazachestvo* in the 17th and 18th centuries—that of an antigovernment jacquerie. Not all intellectuals are *intelligenty*: the essence of the *intelligent* is his 'standing apart' (*otshchepenstvo*) in relation to the government, and, as an expression of the same 'standing apart', his irreligious nature. The beginning of the intelligentsia can be dated from the taking over from the West of atheistic socialism—the first *intelligent* was Bakunin. Thus Radishchev and Chaadayev are not forerunners of Bakunin and Cherny-shevsky—they belong to two quite different and quite irreconcilable spiri-tual orders. In this sense, the great 19th-century writers were not *intel-ligenty*. In the atheism and in the 'standing apart' of the *intelligenty* from the state lies the key to the understanding of the results of the revolution of 1905. The Manifesto of 17 October 1905 marked the most fundamental change in the political structure of Russia for centuries; it should, but for the intelligentsia, have marked the consummation of the revolution. But the intelligentsia failed at this point in its duty. Instead of cooperat-ing with the government, it tried to rouse the masses to revolt. Because of its irreligion, the intelligentsia failed to realise that its real moral duty to the people was to educate them, not to arouse them. This left the al-ternatives of despotism or mob rule. In defence against mob rule, the autocracy inaugurated the present (1909) despotism (for such it then seemed). But the mistake of the intelligentsia was not one of tactics: it was a moral mistake. As Struve says: 'Fundamentally it was due to the conception that the progress of a society is a stake to be won at the gam-bling tables of history by appealing to the aroused masses, and not the fruit of the perfection of individual men.' These words sum up the es-sence of the idea which inspired the publication of *Vekhi*. Economic development, Struve concludes, will in part lead to the *embourgeoise-ment* of the intelligentsia and thus in time bring about its reconciliation with the government. But equally important remains the moral duty in the realm of ideas, man's mastery over himself.

It should be apparent by now that in their criticism of the intelli-gentsia the *Vekhi* group were appealing to what they believed was the real, Russian, tradition. Indeed, as Bulgakov puts it, one of the main

complaints of the *Vekhi* group against the radical intelligentsia was that
they had borrowed the empty shell of atheistic socialism from the West,
without its important Christian substratum or heritage of law, order,
and social morality. The Russian tradition to which *Vekhi* appealed was,
first, that of the sombre pessimist, Chaadayev, who was the first to analyse the consequences to Russian society of the fact that Russia had never
experienced either the Christian social order of the Roman Church, or
the humanistic revolt of Reformation and Renascence. The ideas of
duty, justice, law and order which in Western society were the 'ideas
which are breathed in with the very air' had in consequence never taken
root in Russia. Next Pushkin, who combined love of liberty with love
of order, and who was both conservative in recognising the importance
of preservation, and liberal in seeing the need for reform, who could
remain personally attached to the emperor without being blinded by the
nature of the society around him. His well-known letter to Chaadayev
of 19 October 1836 is much quoted by members of the *Vekhi* group.
(In 1937, Frank published an essay of great penetration on Pushkin
as a political thinker, for which Struve wrote an introduction and some
addenda.) Another influence on *Vekhi* was Boris Chicherin, the legal
philosopher, and particularly his collected essays, published in 1862,
which included the famous letter of protest to Herzen on the policy of
Kolokol. In the Preface he speaks of the necessity of 'pointing to the
elements of power and law, forgotten in our literature, but just as necessary to society as freedom itself. Sensible civil life is only possible when
freedom is united to these principles.' Solov'yov was another obvious influence, and so was Dostoyevsky. Dostoyevsky's genius is so manifold
that no doubt many sides of it were influential at different times. But at
least two aspects of his thought can be singled out in this context. First,
his opposition to all forms of utilitarian philosophy as a basis for the
social order. Secondly, his profound analysis of the mystique of the revolutionary, and his foreboding of the terrible danger implicit for Russia
in the revolutionary philosophy. As for Solov'yov, it was not only his
philosophical idealism which influenced the *Vekhi* group. Its members
saw in Solov'yov's teaching a revival of the Christian humanism of Eras-
mus and St Thomas More: Solov'yov had recognised the essentially Christian nature of humanism—so long as it was not atheistic humanism—as
a corrective to the defects of the Christian past. Another reason why
Solov'yov was influential was because, like Dostoyevsky, he shared that
vision of impending doom which obsessed so many of the non-socialist
intellectuals of the early 20th century. It would seem natural to add Turgenev, not only the Turgenev of *Fathers and Sons*, but more especially
of the *Letters to Herzen* published in Geneva in 1892. But there is little
direct trace of Turgenev's influence among the *Vekhi* group—though
Gershenzon wrote about him, mainly from the literary aspect. Perhaps

the *Vekhi* authors felt something of that hostility which Turgenev aroused, and still arouses, in so many Russians, for his unashamed adoption of Western European life, in the train of Madame Viardot. Dostoyevsky's feelings for Turgenev spring immediately to mind. And, after all, the *Vekhi* group were first and foremost nationalists and patriots.

If one had to attempt a rough summary of the position of *Vekhi*, one could say that they stood midway between the Slavophils and the Westerners. They accepted the Slavophil veneration of Russian national tradition, while rejecting their romantic idealisation of innate Russian virtues as a substitute for the more usual civic virtues. They accepted the Westerners' desire to learn from the countries of the West, while rejecting their atheism, their socialism, and their utilitarianism.

It was suggested above that the very violence of the reaction to the publication of *Vekhi* shows that emotions were engaged as much as reason. The quality of the rejoinders rather confirms this. Since the extreme right-wing welcomed what it regarded as a useful attack on the revolutionaries, it was very easy for the revolutionaries to say in one voice: 'the liberals have joined up with the reactionaries'. This, in the main, was the burden of the socialist revolutionary reply to *Vekhi*, which was published in the form of a volume of essays. Ivanov Razumnik in a very witty pamphlet summed up the *Vekhi* position as: 'pereat mundus fiat iustitia'. (The authors of *Vekhi* might well have replied that there is quite a strong case to be made for this maxim.) Lenin, in characteristic fashion, made political capital out of the split in the liberal ranks. *Vekhi*, he wrote, with less regard for truth than was usual even for Lenin, was typical of the whole Kadet outlook. It showed that Russian liberalism, under the guise of attacking the intelligentsia, was really attacking democracy, and was thus identified with *Moskovskiya Vedomosti* and Pobedonostsev. Then, as an afterthought, he added that the Kadet leaders' attack on *Vekhi* was just hypocrisy.

The Kadet reply appeared as a volume of eight essays, edited by I. Petrunkevich. Apart from the longest essay, that of P. N. Milyukov which takes up nearly half the book, it cannot be said that the intellectual level is very high. The appeal is rather to the emotions than to the head. 'The authors of *Vekhi*', writes Professor N. A. Gredeskul (who was later to cooperate with the bolsheviks) 'have left out nothing more nor less than the main actor on the historical scene—the people. . . . The intelligentsia is only a superstructure upon the people.' Milyukov's essay is witty, a brilliant piece of advocacy in the sense of scoring debating points against an adversary, but somewhat devoid of political realism. It was Milyukov's tragedy that he believed that he was a liberal, when he was in reality a radical. He ends his essay with numerous quotations from Graham Wallas's *Human Nature in Politics* and with a plea for a 'scientific spirit in politics'. The *Vekhi* plea for the moral rearmament of the *intelligenty* is reactionary and dangerous. 'Just imagine', he says, 'such words as "purification" or "repentance" on the lips of a European intellectual.' It was in all sincerity that Milyukov, a highly civilised historian, saw himself in 1909 as the equivalent of a Western European liberal politician. Yet it was Milyukov who, in 1905, at the foundation congress of the Kadets, had welcomed the revolutionary parties as 'our allies on the left,' and it was his Kadet party in the First Duma which refused to vote even moral censure on terrorism as a method of political struggle. Perhaps the emotional nature of the opposition to *Vekhi* is best illustrated by a pamphlet written in reply by a passionate disciple of Chernyshevsky. 'The name of Chernyshevsky', he writes 'brings to us the spirit of unconquerable courage, creative energy and plans for widespread reorganisation. His spirit exudes refusal to bow before the present in the name of a better future. The volume *Vekhi*, on the contrary, smells of a kind of elderly impotence, preaching moderation and meticulousness; it is steeped in the love of quiet and order.'

So ended the great debate of 1909 and 1910, and passed into history. But the voice of some members of the *Vekhi* group was to be heard again for a fleeting moment, and in rather dramatic circumstances. In the course of 1918, after the revolution, on the initiative of Struve, the main participants in *Vekhi*—Struve, Frank, Berdyayev, Bulgakov and Izgoyev —joined with six others, including Vyacheslav Ivanov and Novgorodtsev, to publish another volume. The publication was fraught with difficulty —Struve, who had by then joined the side of Denikin, was living illegally in Moscow; Frank was in Saratov. But the difficulties were overcome, and the volume was completed, set up and printed in Moscow by the autumn of 1918, when Struve left for Finland. The title, *De Profundis* (*Iz Glubiny*), was chosen by Frank. But though printed, the volume was not published; it was overtaken by the renewed wave of bolshevik repressions which followed upon the attempt on Lenin's life in the summer of 1918. The printed copies remained lying in the printing office of *Russkaya Mysl'*. Three years later, in 1921, apparently around the time of the Kronstadt revolt, the printers of their own accord 'published' the book, by putting it out for sale in Moscow. It is to be presumed that most of the copies were confiscated—at any rate it is unlikely that more than two copies ever reached the outside world.

It could not be expected that this volume, written under the terrifying impact of the revolution, should contain the mature wisdom which distinguished *Vekhi*. The authors would not have been human if they had not pointed out, as Struve does in his preface to *Iz Glubiny*, that *Vekhi* had foreseen the catastrophe, but that the warnings were ignored. It is worth pausing for a moment to consider to what extent the mystique of revolution, which *Vekhi* set out to combat and which afflicted the radical intelligentsia, in fact contributed to the victory of the bolsheviks.

V. A. Maklakov, for example, blames the liberal constitutionalists of the Duma for persuading the Grand Duke Michael to abdicate, and implies that they were infected with the revolutionary virus. This is a somewhat doubtful judgment: the temper of February 1917 was incompatible with monarchy and probably no amount of political wisdom on the part of the Duma could have saved it. But the revolutionary mystique played its part in the bolshevik victory in two other respects. First, if it had not been for this mystique, with its concomitant inability to see reality separately from the preconceived theoretical idea of that reality, Lenin would possibly not have been the extremist he was. Revolution, which after all is at best a painful necessity, was to Lenin an obsession. His standard of judgment of men was, even after the revolution was over and done with, according as to whether they were more or less 'revolutionary'—a completely meaningless judgment charged with emotional overtones. Hence, he could only feel safe with the most 'revolutionary' of men around him. And hence, the disastrous decision to ensure monopoly of power for the bolsheviks, from which most of the consequences of the Soviet form of dictatorship flowed. It had little, if anything, to do with marxism: it was the result of obsession with a mystique, and a mystique which was much more *narodnik* than marxist in character.

The second way in which the revolutionary mystique led to bolshevism was in making cooperation between the so-called bourgeois parties and the socialists, after the February revolution, a forlorn hope. It was a two-way process. On the one hand the majority of the Kadets, but no longer Milyukov himself, who still regarded themselves as the heirs of the revolutionary tradition, were quite unable to perceive that those rather rough and absurd bolsheviks were not, in their hearts of hearts, still 'the allies of the left' that they had appeared to be to Milyukov in 1905. On the other hand the socialists, even when they were capable of understanding the necessity for cooperating with the 'bourgeois' parties for the maintenance of order, were swayed more by their hearts than by their heads—with the disastrous consequence that they actively helped to increase the state of anarchy in the country (which they themselves, when their heads were in control, feared), from which Lenin alone could emerge the victor. The memoirs of Sukhanov, for example, fully bear out this view—in fact, Sukhanov himself was the most typical *intelligent* that ever lived.

Thus, the authors of *Iz Glubiny* could scarcely be blamed if they were tempted to say: 'We told you so.' In fact this forms a very small and incidental part of the book, which is deeply religious in tone— markedly more so even than *Vekhi* was. As in *Vekhi*, the authors emphasise again and again the need for moral self-perfection, for repentance, and the incompatibility of materialistic socialism and egalitarianism with the Christian way of life. The consolations of religious faith are the main solution which they offer for the catastrophe which had befallen the country. In his Preface, Struve points out that in spite of differences of views, the one conviction common to all the authors is that 'the positive beginnings of social life are rooted in the depths of religious consciousness'. For the rest, the articles in the volume are in the main a restatement of the bases of the faith which ruled *Vekhi*, with, perhaps, an added concreteness, the product of bitter experience. Izgoyev's article, 'Socialism, Culture, and Bolshevism', is one of the most interesting. The main argument is that the cause of the Russian disaster was not so much bolshevism, as socialism in the form which it took in Russia. 'The Russian Socialists,' he says, 'had they found themselves in power, would either have had to remain simple chatterers, doing nothing to put their ideas into practice, or else to have done from A to Z everything that the Bolsheviks did.' This argument is of course a familiar one in the mouths of most marxist historians of bolshevism, as a justification of bolshevism. What Izgoyev meant, one need hardly say, was an indictment of socialism. He went on to argue that the only hope was to retain a few healthy grains which were contained in socialism, and to renounce for ever all the rest. Berdyayev in his article on 'The Ghosts of the Russian Revolution' emphasises that the revolution had finally shattered the illusion of religious *narodnichestvo*, from which even Dostoyevsky had suffered, that the religious spirit of the Russian people would provide a safeguard against the anti-Christ of socialism. Novgorodtsev, writing on 'The Ways and Tasks of the Russian Intelligentsia', also, analyses Russian socialism and liberalism. Liberalism in Russia, he says, lacking the experience of long practical work in the business of government, was emotionally attracted to socialism, without realising that Russian socialism was devoid of any liberal elements; it was in essence *narodnik*, and its father was Bakunin. Novgorodtsev preaches conservatism, in the fine words of Burke, from his *Reflections on the Revolution in France:* 'Our political system [Burke, of course, is referring to England] is placed in a just correspondence and symmetry with the order of the world and with the mode of existence decreed to a permanent body composed of transitory parts. . . . The whole, at one time, is never old, or middle-aged, or young, but, in a condition of unchangeable constancy, moves on through the varied tenor of perpetual decay, fall, renovation and progression. . . . In what we improve we are never wholly new, in what we retain we are never wholly obsolete.' Struve's essay, though not perhaps equal to his best, contains some penetrating observations. He points out, for example, that the idea of 'class' in bolshevik Russia is a purely emotional one, and does not correspond to objective realities. It is not classes which determine class enmity; it is enmity which creates division into arbitrary classes. Where the idea of 'class' divides, the idea of 'nation' unites. Therefore the ultimate regeneration of Russia must come from the idea of national-

ism. Struve probably meant by this not the gradual evolution of bolshevism into a national state, but the forcible overthrow of the bolsheviks by the resurgence of a national movement. Struve never accepted
the idea that bolshevism could in time evolve into anything essentially
different from what it started as. He regarded it as an usurpation by evil
men of the rightful traditional powers of the state, and as such an usurpation something which could only be overthrown by force. Consistently
with this view he—alone of all the *Vekhi* group—took an active part to
the best of his powers in the physical struggle against bolshevism.

So ended the first part of this debate, of which the second part was
pursued in exile. Reassembled in emigration, after the vicissitudes of the
Civil War, some of the participants in *Vekhi,* and particularly Struve
and Frank, posed the question: what attitude must we adopt to the revolution? A group of lesser spirits, mostly former Kadets, but whose views
certainly did not represent Milyukov, or the majority of the Kadets,
had answered this question with startling simplicity: accept it, and co-
operate with the bolsheviks. They expounded their philosophy of national bolshevism in a volume of essays called *Smena Vekh* (A Change
of Landmarks) published in 1921, and in a periodical of the same name
which appeared in Paris from October 1921 until March 1922, and subsequently in a daily called *Nakanune* (On the Eve) published in Berlin. The choice of the name *Smena Vekh* was probably in part due to
the fact that two of the members of the group, Yu. V. Klyuchnikov and
G. Ustryalov, had at one time been close to *Vekhi*. The very nature of
the arguments used by this group was a melancholy reflection on the
total failure of some of the Kadet intelligentsia ever to understand what
Vekhi was about. The intellectual level is not very high—about the same
as, say, that of the arguments used by Vichy supporters to justify collaboration with the Germans. With the introduction of NEP, bolshevism has
now become a national doctrine. The longer we intellectuals oppose it,
the more we encourage bolshevik excesses. We bow to the will of the
Russian people—and so forth. Inside Russia, *Izvestiya* and *Pravda* welcomed the new movement in identical terms. Meetings organised by Professor Gredeskul, another ex-Kadet, proclaimed the new doctrine. But
five intellectuals, including A. S. Izgoyev (who had not yet succeeded
in leaving Russia), were courageous enough to publish a volume of protest, in guarded but unmistakable terms, against what they regarded as
a betrayal of the ideas of *Vekhi.* Meanwhile the Communist Party Conference in August 1922 showed beyond doubt that, whatever hopes might
have been placed on Lenin, his successors, i.e., Stalin and Zinov'yev, now
that Lenin had virtually lost his influence through illness, had no intention of following up the economic concessions of NEP by any political
relaxation.

Of course the simple political chicanery of *Smena Vekh* could not even become a debatable issue for men of the calibre of Struve or Frank, whose reaction was confined to regret that the name of *Vekhi* had been so unscrupulously abused for such a purpose. But there was between 1921 and 1923 a discussion of some moment between the two men on the meaning of the revolution in its historical perspective, which forms a fitting conclusion to this sketch of the controversies raised by the emergence of the *Vekhi* group. By 1921, Struve was in Sofia, and had revived his old periodical, *Russkaya Mysl'*. This appeared for some years thereafter, first in Sofia and then in Prague. It was opened, of course, to a much wider range of contributors living in emigration than former supporters of *Vehki*, but some of the original *Vehki* names—notably Struve himself, and Izgoyev after 1922—reappeared in its pages. It was to be expected that a good deal of controversy should have developed on the historical meaning of the revolution, on the attitude which should be adopted to it, on prognosis of its future development. Struve's own position remained clear and uncompromising. 'For me,' he wrote in 1921, 'idealisation of the revolution which took place in 1917 and in the subsequent years is at one and the same time a religious and moral lie, and an historical and factual untruth, self-deception and deception of others.' There is no hope of salvation in mystical faith in the 'people' and its ability ultimately to transform the character of the revolution. The only real faith in the Russian people is the faith that it will ultimately overthrow the communist regime. He describes *Smena Vekh* as 'the most monstrous phenomenon in the whole history of Russian spiritual development'. It represents, he says, the exact antithesis of *Vekhi*, which was a denial of the validity of revolutionary ideology in the name of certain basic religious, cultural and social principles. (A. S. Izgoyev, in the pamphlet published inside Russia in reply to *Smena Vekh*, to which reference has been made, had also written: 'We must judge this or that action of the government in the light of our conscience and our consciousness, and not change our conscience and consciousness according to whose hands happen to hold government power at the moment. . . . Outside this principle there is neither freedom, nor human dignity, nor spiritual strength.' It must have been very nearly the last time that such words appeared in print in the U.S.S.R.) Struve further rejected arguments based on the analogy of the French revolution—that when the turmoil and violence of the revolutionary period is over the revolution will be seen to have accomplished salutary and necessary progress. The analogy between the two revolutions, he maintained, was false: the French revolution, for all its violent nature, in fact achieved the objects which it set out to achieve, and in fact put into practice its main ideas. In contrast, the bolshevik revolution put into practice from the start the very reverse of what had been its avowed principles—not socialism, but inequality; not freedom, but dictatorship; not a militia, but an army; not nationalised land, but private peasant holdings. In one of his articles Struve concluded that pre-revolutionary Russia 'was in all respects immeasurably nearer to a free and prosperous Russia founded on peasant ownership' than was Soviet Russia.

The best of Struve's thought on the meaning of the Russian revolutions in historical perspective is contained in two lectures which he delivered inside non-bolshevik Russia in 1919, and reprinted in 1921. The theme running through these remarkable essays is that the only hope of salvation lies in the restoration of the state as a result of the rebirth of national consciousness. 'State' is thus contrasted with bolshevik rule, to which Struve would probably have denied the quality of a state, because it lacked order; while 'national consciousness' is contrasted with the class hatred fostered by bolshevism—the idea which was already developed in Struve's contribution to *Iz Glubiny*. The foundation for this idea of state *plus* nation Struve found in historical parallel, and particularly the parallel which he saw between the Russian revolution and the *Smuta* —the period of the troubles in Muscovy in the 17th century. (On this question, Struve, and probably all the *Vekhi* authors, had derived a great deal from S. Th. Platonov's great study of the period, which had first been published in 1899.) The parallel Struve saw particularly in the importance in each case of a foreign interest in the trouble—Poland and Germany, respectively. The lesson he derived from the *Smuta* was the fact that order in the 17th century was restored by a national movement of the middle classes, supported by the only intelligentsia which then existed, the clergy, and guided by the idealistic motives of safeguarding the faith, and the church, and of saving the state from ruin. Then it was the middle classes, and not the people, who had the necessary qualities to restore the state: so it would be again, if those who should be the intellectual leaders of this class, and who had failed in 1917, would realise their mission. The tragedy of Russia in 1917 was primarily due, according to Struve, to what he calls 'the abnormal, the deformed attitude of the Russian educated class towards the state and its activities'. After 1905 political freedom and democracy could have been possible, on two conditions: sincerity on the part of the government in putting reform into practice, and recognition by the Kadets of the greater danger from the left than from the right, and a consequent will to co-operate in reform. Neither condition was fulfilled: hence Lenin's triumph became possible. By 1921 at all events, Struve did not dispute that restoration of the old order was impossible. But he never swerved from his belief that without restoration of some moral and legal order by overthrow of the bolsheviks there could be no development of reforms on the basis of order. 'New life—old might' was the slogan he proposed, by which he meant a new, not entirely foreseeable form of government order, but one drawing national inspiration from the Russian past.

Two years later, in 1923, Frank published his criticism of Struve's views on the revolution, also in *Russkaya Mysl'*. It was wrong, argued Frank, to throw the main blame for the bolshevik revolution on the intelligentsia. The very embitterment of the intelligentsia was itself but a symptom of the national disease. What was happening was the death of the Russia of the nobility, the *dvoryanstvo,* and its replacement by a peasant Russia—the 'advance of the inner barbarian'. It was incorrect, argued Frank, to explain the collapse of the monarchy by such factors as the war, the faults of the emperor, and the like. The only reason why the old Russian state had been able to stand up, in spite of the vast chasm between the peasants and the state, was because of the monarchy: the monarchy had been the only institution deeply rooted in the consciousness of the people, in contrast to institutions like the courts, or local administration. But after 1905 a loss of faith in the monarchy had occurred, the change that V. V. Rozanov described as 'the collapse of the great fetish', and with this collapse the entire old order was doomed. Frank saw the essentially peasant character of the revolution precisely in its indifference to government and forms of government. (Chicherin had, incidentally, previously discovered this characteristic in the Russian people throughout history—indifferent to the nature of power and ready to submit, the Russian people, says Chicherin, 'in cases of extremity, when the state was threatened by collapse, would rise as one man, restore order, and then once again abandon all power and all state activity to the government'.) The return of the old order, according to Frank, was inconceivable, if only because of the physical destruction of the very social and political material out of which it had been constructed. Therefore the revolution must be lived through as a purifying catharsis, accepting the fact that the peasant state has replaced the old state. Whatever the future may bring in the way of regeneration can only come as the result of the moral regeneration of the whole people, helped on by the bitter disappointment which it has suffered in reaping tyranny where it had hoped to reap freedom.

This summary only gives a very bald idea of the profound historical and psychological analysis which this fine article contains. The controversy between Frank and Struve is perhaps now more remarkable for its analysis of the situation than for the solution it offers to any practical problem. If one had to venture a judgment on the dispute after some thirty years one might say that perhaps Struve underestimated the actual physical destruction that Soviet rule would entail of the class upon which ultimately he placed his reliance. Equally, Frank may have underestimated in 1923 the extent of the moral corruption of a nation which communist rule would produce, and which makes moral regeneration appear difficult to conceive. The difference of approach to the problem by the two men was perhaps due to a difference of temperament; yet, each stressed a vital aspect of the philosophy of *Vekhi*. To Struve, the more practical man of action, the first requirement was a state order, without which there could be no freedom and no progress. For Frank, the deeply religious philosopher and mystic, the predominant idea was the primacy of moral and spiritual forces over material circumstances. But these two elements—freedom under order, and the primacy of spirit over material forces—together make up *Vekhi*.

The importance of *Vekhi* lies not in what it achieved, but in the light which it throws on Russian liberalism on the eve of the revolution. Our historical assessment of the Russian revolution is so much consciously or unconsciously coloured by the influence of marxist historians that there is a risk that we may view the entire Russian liberal movement merely as something that stopped half-way on the road to revolution for lack of courage or consistency or class consciousness, and thus fail to distinguish the very different strands of which it was in fact made up. There is a grain of truth in the marxist view when applied to the Kadets, in the sense that they may have been revolutionaries without knowing it. When the Russian Kadet called himself a liberal, he may have believed that he was using this term as meaning what, say, Gladstone meant by it. But in fact he was in spirit much more the liberal of 1848, in other words more a revolutionary, or a radical. The great service of *Vekhi* was to illuminate this fact for the first time, even if the illumination came too late, and the message fell on deaf ears. But, as well as being pioneers, the *Vekhi* group also symbolised a return to a tenuous but more truly liberal Russian tradition, which recognised that when once a major change in society has been accomplished, the more important ally of liberalism is conservation, and not revolution. Thus Chicherin had written on the morrow of the emancipation of the serfs: 'True liberalism is now measured not by opposition, not by glorification of freedom, not by progressive movements, but by devotion to the manifesto of 19 February which has liberated twenty-three million Russians. . . . Conservatism and liberalism are here one and the same.' Let us concede freely that it was as difficult to see the truth of this in the years which followed the manifesto of October 1905 in Russia, as it had been in 1862. But it was the *Vekhi* group and they alone, of all the progressive intelligentsia, who had the courage and the wisdom to make the attempt.

10

THE RUSSIAN
MOBILIZATION
OF 1914 *

The question of whether or not Russian mobilization in 1914 was
responsible for setting off World War I no longer arouses the keen
interest or provokes the bitter debates that it once did. But the
question is still important. The study of it provided here by Professor
Florinsky is a valuable account of the events and policies that must
be understood in order to assess Russia's position.

INTRODUCTION

Russia is taking very reasonable and sensible precautions, which
should in no wise be interpreted as provocative. Germany, of course,
who has been steadily preparing, now wishes to throw the blame on
Russia—a very thin pretext. However, comments are superfluous.
[Minute by Sir Arthur Nicolson, July 31, 1914, *British Documents on
the Origins of the War* (London, 1926), vol. XI, p. 214.]

THE RUSSIAN mobilization of 1914 continues to occupy a central
place in the controversy which is raging around the problem of responsibility for the outbreak of the Great War. Professor Harry Elmer Barnes
declares bluntly that Russia took "the specific steps which made the
War inevitable, and the *only* steps which made it unavoidable." The purpose of this article is to show the Russian mobilization in its proper setting, its proper background. This is made possible by using Russian
sources some of which are not accessible to the majority of American
readers.

* Michael T. Florinsky, "The Russian Mobilization of 1914," *Political Science Quar-
terly*, XLII, No. 2 (June, 1927), 203–27. Reprinted by permission of the author and
the publisher.
  The author is Professor of Economics at Columbia University. He was born
in Russia and received his education in that country, England, and the United States.

The final decision resulting in the mobilization of the Russian army in July, 1914, and the transition from partial to general mobilization were largely influenced by technical military considerations. Before proceeding, therefore, any further in the discussion of our problem it may be desirable to obtain at least a slight knowledge of its technical aspects which weighed so heavily in the balance for peace or war in the fateful days of July, 1914.

Certain critics of Russia go so far as to maintain that the Russian mobilization began with the declaration of the "pre-mobilization" period on July 26. This assertion, however, does not withstand the test of investigation. The "pre-mobilization" period was introduced in Russia early in 1913. This plan was recommended by a committee presided over by General Lukomsky, accepted by the Council of Ministers, and approved by the Emperor on March 2, 1913. It was modeled on similiar provisions of the German Code and empowered the Government to take preliminary military measures in cases of emergency. The ordinance of March 2 provided for two series of measures. Those of the *first series* included the introduction of censorship, the nomination of army officers to take charge of railway stations, the conditioning of artillery parks, the calling of reservists in the area adjoining the frontier within the limit of ordinary army credits. The measures of the *second series* dealt with railroad defense and provided for the calling of reservists in the area adjoining the frontier, if this, for lack of financial provisions, had not already taken place under the *first series*. Only the last-named measure could be quoted in support of the charge that the "pre-mobilization" period was equivalent to mobilization. On the other hand there is no evidence that the Government in 1914 took advantage of the power of calling reservists, even in that area. General Dobrorolsky and General Golovine both refute this accusation. "In all countries," writes General Golovine, "the term mobilization has a very definite meaning and denotes the transition of the army from peace-time to war-time conditions through the calling of reservists and the requisitioning of horses and carts. . . . On July 26 not a single man in Russia was called to the colors; not a single horse or vehicle was requisitioned." The proclamation of the "pre-mobilization" period on July 26 was accompanied by the issuance of orders for the return of troops to their barracks from the summer quarters; for the immediate promotion of graduating cadets to the rank of officers (under normal conditions the promotion would have taken place in a fortnight, in August); for the establishment, in certain districts adjoining the frontier, of the so-called *voennoe polozhenie* (state of emergency), that is

During World War I he served as an officer in the Russian army. He edited the Russian series of the *Economic and Social History of the World War* and is the author of many books, among them the authoritative *Russia: A History and an Interpretation* (2 vols., 1953).

the transfer of all civil powers to military authorities. None of the measures enumerated above meant mobilization. It is difficult to see how Count Montgelas's assertion can be maintained in the light of this evidence.

In considering the technical reasons which necessitated the declaration of mobilization, one should remember that, because of the apparently close and intimate relations between Germany and Austria, Russia military circles were convinced that a state of war on her western frontier would result in concerted action against Russia on the part of the Central Empires. Moreover, it was generally admitted by Russian military authorities that either Germany or Austria-Hungary would prove a serious opponent, and that an encounter with either would call upon the resources of the whole Russian Empire. The Russian mobilization plan, therefore, contained no provisions for a partial mobilization in case of an armed conflict on the western frontier. Any such mobilization would be a dangerous improvisation upon the original plan of defense and might have in calculable consequences.

Only in a country which has the territorial system of complementing its peace-time forces may a partial mobilization be carried out without endangering the machinery of the subsequent general mobilization. Under that system the mobilization of one or more military districts does not interfere to any considerable extent with normal conditions in other districts. A number of circumstances, however, made the introduction of the territorial system in Russia all but impossible. Even in time of peace the great extent of the empire and its underdeveloped network of railroads necessitated a certain degree of concentration of troops in the areas adjoining the western frontier; while the chief sources for complementing peace-time forces of both men and horses were to be found in the southern and eastern regions of the empire. For that reason the part played by the railroads in carrying out mobilization in Russia was as important as it was arduous and complex. The difficulties of the problem were further increased by the low efficiency of the local administrations and the nomadic character of a portion of the population making up the so-called *otkhozhii-promisli*—a class of day-laborers continually moving from place to place in search of work.

The "Modified Mobilization Plan, No. 18," in force at the outbreak of the war was in process of revision by the General Staff and the new plan was to have been put into operation on January 1, 1915. This new plan contained provisions for partial mobilization. But they dealt exclusively with armed conflicts on the less important sections of the frontier, chiefly in Asia, where the mobilization of a small number of troops was considered sufficient and could be carried out without need of haste.

There was another aspect of the problem which could not possibly be overlooked by the men who were responsible for the military safety of Russia. In case of war against Austria, the strategic plan of the Russian General Staff provided for the concentration of sixteen army corps on the Austrian frontier and for the advantageous use of the favorable strategical position offered to Russia by the encircling line of the Russo-Austrian frontier. The partial mobilization decided upon by the Council assembled at Krasnoe Selo on July 25 not only restricted mobilization to thirteen army corps (while sixteen army corps were required for carrying out the operations planned by the General Staff in case of war against Austria), but also confined the concentration of troops to the districts of Kiev, Odessa, Kazan and Moscow, thus precluding the use of the Warsaw district as a *place d'armes* against Austria. The concentration of troops in the western part of the district of Kiev and the southern portion of the district of Warsaw for an encompassing movement on Austria was an essential part of the plan of the Russian General Staff. The exclusion of the district of Warsaw from the field of mobilization not only would have confounded all the calculations of the General Staff, but also would have exposed Russian Poland to the serious danger of an Austrian attack, before the district of Warsaw could have time to mobilize, in the event that a general mobilization should become necessary.

These were the chief concerns of the leaders of the Russian army. The precarious military position in which Russia would place herself by ordering merely a partial mobilization was an important factor in the situation, as the Emperor and Sazonov were finally forced to admit, though not without a struggle.

A few words may be said here with reference to the well-known Imperial Order of March 12, 1912. This order reads as follows:

In accordance with His most gracious Majesty's decision a telegraphic command to order mobilization in the European military districts on account of political complications on the western frontier, is to be regarded simultaneously as an order to commence hostilities against Austria and Germany. As far as Rumania is concerned the hostilities are not to be commenced without direct order.

This order, however, had been cancelled by the orders of November 26, 1912, and June 26, 1913, which provided that

commencement of war was to be separate in form from mobilization, and the commencement of hostilities was to be ordered by separate telegram signed by the Minister of War, giving the name of the enemy power and the time of the commencement of the war, or was to be made dependent upon the action of the opponent.

There is not the slightest evidence that the Russian Government intended to depart from this decision and to revive the order of March 12, 1912.

Reference is sometimes made to the mobilization of Russia and

Austria-Hungary in 1909 and 1912, as evidence of the fact that Russia's mobilization in 1914 did not necessarily mean war. Although we are fully in agreement with the conclusion, this particular argument does not seem to be valid. Information on the mobilization of 1909 is very scarce. More is known about the mobilization of 1912. Mr. Gooch speaks of "Russia and Austria both of whom carried out partial mobilization" (end of 1912 and beginning of 1913). It seems, however, that these mobilizations, if mobilizations they were, considerably differed from that of 1914. Count Montgelas writes that "the Russian army was simultaneously [in 1912] strengthened by test mobilizations on an extensive scale on the frontier, which were not officially notified [to Germany] beforehand, as formerly." And concerning Austria:

It is true that, in view of the steps taken to reinforce the Russian army not being cancelled, precautionary measures were also taken in Vienna. The strength of the three army corps in Galicia, and of the troops on the Bosnian frontier, was increased by calling up reservists and *Erstaz* reservists. Those were the orders which were erroneously described, even in official documents, as "mobilization."

Very striking is the complete absence of reference to these mobilizations in the diplomatic papers of 1914 and in the comments on the subject, especially those of Russian generals such as Danilov, Dobrorolsky, Golovine and Gurko. One would hardly expect Russian diplomats and soldiers to overlook so valuable a precedent concerning previous mobilizations.

Additional information on what really took place in 1909 and 1912 may be found in the following private letter which the author of these lines was privileged to receive from the former Russian Minister of Foreign Affairs, M. Sazonov:

I may tell you from memory what I know about the mobilization of 1912, the year of the Balkan wars. There was no real mobilization, that is no reservists were called, but something equivalent to it took place. The international situation was extremely tense and we expected an attack by Austria on Serbia as result of the latter's endeavor to establish herself on the shores of the Adriatic. Austria carried out a partial mobilization against Serbia and was unofficially taking preliminary measures for the mobilization of her troops in Galicia. As a counter measure we decided that, in order to give the new contingent of men time to go through the first stages of their military training, the men who would have completed the term of service were to be retained until the spring. Later on an agreement was reached by the Russian and Austrian governments and both parties reduced their armies to normal size. Germany was not yet ready and therefore did not want war. This is why the catastrophe was temporarily averted. This episode is shortly mentioned in my book. As to the mobilization of 1909, I was not in Russia at that time and am unable to give any definite information on the subject. I believe, however, that even if military measures were taken they were of a purely preliminary character. The political situation was highly strained and it is conceivable that our government deemed it necessary to take certain military precautions. I doubt that they could be described as a mobilization.

The evidence given above seems to leave little doubt that the military preparations of 1909 and 1912 were quite different from the mobilization of 1914.

These preliminary remarks are intended to show the line of argument of Russian military leaders, and the technical conditions which made it impossible for them to accept the responsibility for partial mobilization. It may be useful to remember these facts while investigating the course of events which led to the order for Russian mobilization and to the declaration of the war.

The inner story of the mobilization will be more easily understood if we obtain some knowledge of the general state of mind which prevailed in Russian military circles on the eve of the Austrian ultimatum to Serbia. "In Russia," writes General Danilov:

the danger of an expansion of the conflict brought about by the murder of Sarajevo appeared so remote, that in the middle of July I was sent to the Caucasus in connection with the annual field training of staff officers—in spite of my office of Quartermaster General which closely identified me with all problems of national defense. The officer in charge of the Operative Department of the Western Front, Col. Sholkov, went on leave to a seaside resort of the Crimea almost simultaneously with my departure. Our work in St. Petersburg was carried on by our deputies. Before leaving I suggested to the Chief of the General Staff that my trip to the Caucasus should be cancelled, in order to await further political developments, but General Yanushkevich decided that there was not sufficient ground for altering the arrangements already made.

The optimism of the military leaders was shared to a large extent by the diplomats. The diary of the Russian Foreign Office, kept by Baron Schilling and first published by the Soviet Government in the *Krasni Arkhiv* in 1923,* betrays no signs of anxiety until July 22, when Sazonov sent a telegram to the Russian Ambassador in Vienna asking him "to point out in a friendly but firm manner the dangerous consequences of any action on the part of Austria of an unacceptable character with regard to the dignity of Serbia." The preceding entry in the diary gives an account of Sazonov's interview with Count Szapary on July 18. After the departure of Count Szapary, Sazonov told Schilling that "he had had no need to resort to threats, as the Austro-Hungarian Ambassador has sufficiently and emphatically assured him of his Government's love of peace: "*Il a été doux comme un agneau.*" "Even as late as Thursday morning [July 22]," Prince Kudashev telegraphed from Vienna, "nothing pointed

* Published in English under the title *How the War Began* (Allen and Unwin, London, 1925). This publication will be referred to in the following pages as Schilling's diary.

to that dramatic change in the situation occasioned by the handing in of the Austrian ultimatum to the Serbian Government that same evening."

The contents of the Austrian ultimatum became known to the St. Petersburg Foreign Office early on July 24 and took Russian official circles entirely by surprise. At 3 p. m. the Council of Ministers met at Krasnoe Selo and approved the suggestions made by Sazonov, viz. to request Austria to grant Serbia an extension of time for replying to the ultimatum; and to advise Serbia to offer no military resistance to Austria, but to appeal to the Great Powers. At the same time the Council empowered the Ministers of War and Marine "according to the progress of events, to order the mobilization of the four military districts of Kiev, Odessa, Moscow and Kazan, and the Baltic and Black Sea fleet." Mr. Binkley rightly remarks that "the journal of the Council of Ministers [quoted above] . . . strongly testifies that the original intention of the Russian Government (perhaps, by implication, of the French Government also) was honorable and pacific." In pursuance of the policy laid down by the Council, Sazonov sent to Belgrade the same day the following telegram (No. 1487): "In view of the helpless situation of the Serbians, it would be better for them to offer no resistance, but to address an appeal to the Great Powers." On July 25 a Crown Council assembled at Krasnoe Selo and was presided over by the Emperor. The Council approved the decisions taken by the Council of Ministers the day before and ordered the "pre-mobilization" period to be declared as from July 26. The mobilization of the four military districts was decided upon, but only *in principle*. The final proclamation of the mobilization was made dependent on the course of the negotiations. In the meantime Sazonov continued his efforts to bring about the peaceful solution of the crisis. He telegraphed to London and Belgrade suggesting the mediation of England.

What was the attitude of Russian military men towards the declaration of partial mobilization? General Sukhomlinov, Minister of War, and General Yanushkevich, Chief of the General Staff, were both present at the Council of Ministers of July 24 and the Crown Council of July 25. They did not oppose, so far as we know, the decision for partial mobilization. It was, however, greatly resented by the responsible officials of the General Staff. "Partial mobilization," writes General Dobrorolsky, "would make the subsequent general mobilization impossible." And "partial mobilization would be pure folly." The reasons justifying this point of view were given above. General Danilov writes:

It is easy to understand the decision of those members of the Council who had little knowledge of purely military problems and were not acquainted with the technical side of mobilization. They were solely guided by the natural desire of safeguarding the honor of Russia and of avoiding at the same time anything that could suggest a hostile attitude towards Germany. But how can it be explained that General Sukhomlinov, who took part in the Council, deemed it possible to agree even without a word of protest to a decision which put Russia in a very dangerous position? Was it mere negligence or utter incompetence?

General Dobrorolsky maintains that General Yanushkevich was fully aware of the danger of a partial mobilization. But General Danilov contests this view and thinks that the Chief of the General Staff, who was only recently appointed, was not yet sufficiently familiar with the details of the mobilization plan. It took some time to prove to him that the decision of July 25 was full of danger. A hurried scheme for the mobilization of four military districts was drawn up by General Dobrorolsky and his staff, in spite of their conviction that its application would do untold harm to the defense of the country.

While this work was going on at the War Office, on July 25, Sazonov made two more attempts to bring pressure upon Austria. He sent a telegram to Rome (No. 1505) asking that the Italian Government exercise a moderating influence in Vienna. In a telegram to Berlin (No. 1508) he urged the German Government to support the demand addressed to Austria by St. Petersburg. On July 27 Sazonov accepted Sir Edward Grey's suggestion to submit the dispute to a conference of four Great Powers assembled in London. His telegram to the Russian ambassadors at Paris and London ends with the assurance that, if direct negotiations with Austria prove a failure, he is ready "to accept the English proposal, or *any other* calculated to bring about a favorable solution of the conflict." Sazonov also urged Montenegro "to observe a waiting and pacificatory attitude" (Telegram No. 1523).

The gloomy political outlook strengthened the apprehensions of Russian military leaders and induced them to increase the pressure upon Yanushkevich and Sukhomlinov, and through them upon Sazonov and the Emperor, in order to obtain the cancellation of partial mobilization. Quartermaster General Danilov was recalled from the Caucasus and reached St. Petersburg on July 26. The political situation he found there was, in his opinion, so grave that he wired to his family, then in residence in the province of Podolsk adjoining the Austrian frontier, asking them to return to St. Petersburg at once. General Danilov used all his influence to bring about the revision of the decision concerning the mobilization of the four military districts. He drew the attention of General Yanushkevich, not only to the technical, but also to the strategical dangers of partial mobilization. On his special request the Chief of the General Staff agreed to have the whole matter thoroughly examined by a conference which included, in addition to Yanushkevich and Danilov, General Dobrorolsky and General Ronzhin, head of the Department of Military Transportation. General Danilov does not mention in his book the exact date when the conference assembled. It was probably July 28. The argument of his colleagues, coupled (one may assume) with the threatening political situation created by the declaration of war on Serbia by Austria, finally overrode the resistance of General Yanushkevich and he gave orders for the preparation of two imperial ukases—one for the partial and the other for the general mobilization.

Sazonov immediately announced to the various European capitals that, in consequence of the declaration of war by Austria on Serbia, Russia had decided to order partial mobilization (Telegram No. 1539, July 28). The telegram specially emphasized "the absence on the part of Russia of any aggressive intentions regarding Germany." There seems to be little doubt that the decision to bring into operation the military measures decided upon *in principle* by the Council of Ministers of July 24 and the Crown Council of July 25 was due to the declaration of war on Serbia by Austria. "The change in the dispositions of the Minister [Sazonov]," writes Count Pourtalès, "took place only on the 28th, when it became known that the firm attitude of Russia did not prevent Austria from declaring war on Serbia. Undoubtedly the change in the attitude of Sazonov was primarily due to this step of Vienna." This view is also held by von Chelius, who telegraphed to Emperor Wilhelm on July 29 that, in the opinion of Russian court circles, the European war had become "almost inevitable" as a result of the declaration of war on Serbia by Austria.

Let us now consider the immediate events which led to the transition from partial to general mobilization. July 29 was a critical day. There is a certain amount of controversy as to the exact time when different events took place. General Dobrorolsky maintains that the ukase signed by the Tsar and ordering general mobilization was handed to him by General Yanushkevich in the morning of July 29. He then describes in detail his visits to the Ministers of War, of Marine and of the Interior in order to obtain their signatures on the mobilization telegram. It appears from this narrative that the telegram was ready only at about 9 p. m., that is, that it took some ten or twelve hours to have a document of this importance signed by three ministers! This seems extremely unlikely and does not agree with Baron Schilling's diary, which puts the issue of the general mobilization order at a time after 3 p. m., probably not before 5 p. m.

Taking into consideration the fact that Baron Schilling kept his records on the spot and has given a very detailed account of the happenings of those days, while General Dobrorolsky was writing after an interval of ten years, one is inclined to prefer Baron Schilling's evidence. The admission of Schilling's account—and this seems only reasonable— will explain Sazonov's attitude in his conversation, on the morning of July 29, with Count Szapary, to whom he mentioned a "mobilization on a considerable scale" which had been decided upon, as well as his interview, at 11 a. m. on the same day, with Count Pourtalès, whom he informed that a mobilization would be ordered in the districts adjoining the Austrian frontier. Sazonov could not possibly ignore the fact that general mobilization had been ordered (we assume for the sake of argument that General Dobrorolsky's version is correct) and in the circumstance his declarations to the ambassadors of the Central Empires would have been nothing short of wilful deceit or, at least, as M. Renouvin mildly puts it, of an endeavor to *"induire en erreur"* his prospective enemies. An action of this kind was not only hardly compatible with the dignity of the Foreign Minister of a Great Power and with the honorable behavior of a gentleman, but would also have been futile, as general mobilization could not have been kept secret. It seems much more reasonable to admit that General Dobrorolsky made certain mistakes in questions of detail, which is only too natural when a man writes from memory after a period of ten years. M. Renouvin himself is compelled to recognize that General Dobrorolsky's chronology concerning the events of July 30 is defective.

In accordance with Baron Schilling's diary, Count Pourtalès paid a second visit to the Foreign Office at 3 p. m. on July 29 and read Sazonov a telegram from the Chancellor stating that "if Russia continues her military preparations, even though she does not proceed to mobilize, Germany would find herself compelled to mobilize, in which case she would immediately proceed to take the offensive." This communication seems to have dispelled the last hopes Sazonov may still have had. He sharply remarked, *"Maintenant je n'ai plus de doute sur les vraies causes de l'intransigeance autrichienne."* Soon after the departure of the German ambassador, the Emperor telephoned to Sazonov and told him that he had just received a telegram from Emperor Wilhelm urging him not to allow events to develop into a war. Sazonov informed the Emperor of his interview with Count Pourtalès and pointed out the contradictions between the declarations of the German Emperor and those of his ambassador. He also asked the Emperor to allow him to discuss the problem of mobilization with the Ministers of War and of Marine. The Emperor agreed and the conference immediately took place in General Yanushkevich's room. The two ministers and the Chief of the General Staff came to the conclusion that "in view of the small probability of avoiding a war with Germany it was indispensable to prepare for it in every way in good time, and that therefore the risk could not be accepted of delaying a general mobilization later by effecting a partial mobilization now. The conclusion arrived at at this conference was at once reported by telephone to the Tsar, who authorized the taking of steps accordingly." This decision was received with a comprehensible feeling of relief by the men responsible for the defense of Russia. In accordance with the version given in the diary of Baron Schilling, the general mobilization order was issued late in the afternoon. If this chronology is correct, Sazonov was perfectly sincere when he declared to the Austrian and German ambassadors in the morning of the same day that Russia had decided to order a partial mobilization; he did not mention general mobilization for the simple reason that it was not yet decided.

Immediate orders were given for general mobilization. At 9.20 p. m., however, Emperor Nicholas received a telegram from Emperor Wilhelm promising to do his best to promote a direct understanding between St. Petersburg and Vienna, and insisting that military measures would prejudice his rôle as mediator. Emperor Nicholas immediately and on his own initiative cancelled the order for the general mobilization, for which partial mobilization was then substituted. A telegram worded accordingly was dispatched to the officers commanding the four military districts of Kiev, Odessa, Moscow and Kazan at about midnight.

General Sukhomlinov during his trial in 1917 maintained that he disregarded the order of the Tsar and that he went on with the general mobilization in spite of it. His evidence, however, was flatly contradicted by Generals Yanushkevich and Dobrorolsky. Sukhomlinov himself does not insist on his own evidence in his more recent publications. General Dobrorolsky rightly remarks that the very idea of such disobedience to an order of the Emperor could be conceived only after the revolution. It is surprising, therefore, to find that some historians and diplomatists of high standing, for instance, G. P. Gooch and Sir George Buchanan, accept Sukhomlinov's version.

The partial mobilization ordered during the night of July 29–30 was timed to begin on July 30; that is, July 30 was declared the first day of the mobilization of the four military districts.

Early in the morning of July 30 Sazonov had another interview with Count Pourtalès and, on his demand, drafted the well-known formula for the peaceful solution of the crisis. It will be remembered that in the course of the previous day, July 29, Sazonov had telegraphed to the Russian Chargé d'Affaires in Berlin that "the best manner of turning to account the most suitable methods of finding a peaceful solution would be by arranging for parallel discussions to be carried on by a conference of the four powers—Germany, France, England and Italy—and by a direct exchange of views between Austria-Hungary and Russia. . . ." Later the same day, on the receipt of a telegram from Shebeko announcing the general mobilization of Austria, Sazonov telegraphed to London that "nothing remains for us to do but to rely entirely on the British Government to take the initiative in the steps which they may consider advisable."

Another effort to secure peace came in the evening of the same day (July 29) from Emperor Nicholas who, on his own initiative and without even informing Sazonov, telegraphed to Emperor Wilhelm suggesting a submission of the Austro-Serbian conflict to the Conference at the Hague.

July 30 was the day of final decisions concerning Russian mobilization. Here again we have to discard the chronology of General Dobrorolsky and to accept that of Baron Schilling. Sazonov was rapidly losing faith in the possibility of avoiding a world war, and yielded to the pressure brought upon him by the General Staff. At 11 a. m. he discussed the situation with Sukhomlinov and Yanushkevich. The danger of partial mobilization was now fully admitted. Sukhomlinov and Yanushkevich endeavored to induce the Tsar by telephone to cancel his decision of the night before and order general mobilization. The Tsar, however, refused to yield to argument and only reluctantly agreed to grant an audience to Sazonov at 3 p. m. In the meantime, the Chief of the General Staff "warmly pleaded with S. D. Sazonov to persuade the Tsar without fail to consent to a general mobilization." It was decided that Sazonov should communicate the Tsar's decision to General Yanushkevich by telephone. "After that" (in case of a favorable decision), said Yanushkevich, "I shall go away, smash my telephone and generally adopt measures which will prevent anyone from finding me for the purpose of giving contrary orders which would again stop our general mobilization." At 12.30 p. m. Sazonov lunched with Krivoshein and Schilling at Donon's, and at 2 p. m. he left for Peterhof where the Tsar was in residence. He was received by the Tsar, together with General Tatistchev.

During the course of nearly an hour the Minister proceeded to show that war was becoming inevitable as it was clear to everybody that Germany had decided to bring about a collision, as otherwise she would not have rejected all the pacificatory proposals that had been made and could easily have brought her ally to reason. Under these circumstances it only remained to do everything that was necessary to meet war fully armed and under the most favorable conditions for ourselves. Therefore it was better to put away any fears that our warlike preparations would bring about a war, and to continue these preparations carefully rather than by reason of such fears to be taken unawares by war.[*]

Sazonov had to use a good deal of eloquence before he succeeded in overcoming the reluctance of the Emperor. Finally the latter gave his consent, about 4 p. m., and Sazonov telephoned the decision to Yanushkevich at once; he added at the end of their conversation: "now you can smash your telephone." We have quoted Schilling's diary at considerable length because it clearly shows the conflict between the desire for peace on the part of the Emperor and Sazonov, on one hand, and the apprehensions of the General Staff, on whom rested the responsibility for the safety of the country, on the other. It is also apparent from the excerpts quoted above that General Dobrorolsky's assertion that the mobilization order was communicated by Sazonov to Yanushkevich at 1 p. m. is due to a fault of memory. The evidence of Schilling on this particular point is corroborated by General Danilov and M. Paléologue.

[*] Schilling's diary, pp. 64–65.

The catastrophe which hung over the Russian army as a result of the decision of July 29 was now averted. July 31 was the first day of the general mobilization; the first day of the partial mobilization was July 30. But in accordance with the mobilization plan, the first day of the mobilization was allowed for the arrangement of personal affairs of the reservists, and no movement of troops took place on that day. Now that the order for partial mobilization was merged in the order for general mobilization, the reservists of the four military districts where partial mobilization began on July 30 had merely one extra day for arranging their private affairs. The mobilization plan was brought into operation simultaneously throughout the Empire.

We may add that the false report of German mobilization in the *Lokalanzeiger* can no longer be regarded as one of the reasons which determined the declaration of the Russian general mobilization. The views of Count Montgelas on this subject have now been generally accepted even by the friends of Russia, although Bethmann-Hollweg admitted in 1914 that the false news circulated by the *Lokalanzeiger* could be the immediate cause of the Russian mobilization.*

---

* *German Documents,* No. 488.

Professor Barnes's statement of "Sazonov's Apology and Retreat" (Barnes, *op. cit.,* pp. 364 *et seq.*) does not seem to follow from the documents on which it is supposed to be based. Summarizing an interview with M. Sazonov in the *New York Times* of May 11, 1924, Professor Barnes says that: "Sazonov then resurrects the ancient myth of the *Lokalanzeiger* article. He states that he was unwillingly brought to the order for general mobilization by the publication of a false report of the German mobilization in the Berlin *Lokalanzeiger* at 2 P.M. (Russian time) on July 30th. This is a most transparent falsehood." The fact is that Sazonov said something very different. I may perhaps be excused for quoting the interview at some length. "By this time (July 30th)," said M. Sazonov, "my hope of preventing war had very greatly weakened. I had begun to see that Berlin could not be relied upon to moderate the attitude of Austria, as had been the hope not only of myself but of the Emperor. The order for general mobilization had been withheld by the Emperor, in spite of the order of the chief of the General Staff, General Yanuskevitch. Even then it was only after long indecision that the Emperor consented to my telephoning to General Yanuskevitch on the evening of July 30th that the general mobilization should be called. It was at that juncture that the news of the general mobilization published by the *Lokalanzeiger* reached us from our Ambassador. Personally, I still believe that news to be true, although it was immediately denied in Berlin. The telegram announcing the mobilization reached us within two hours of its dispatch. The second telegram from M. Sverbieff, containing the denial, was delayed in a way which is still unexplained, and that delay is responsible for the *impression* (italics are mine) produced in Russia that the irrevocable step had been taken by Germany."

If we examine M. Sazonov's Foreward to Baron Schilling's Diary, his second pronouncement quoted by Professor Barnes, we shall find a reference on page 9 to the *Lokalanzeiger* affair as one of the "facts which preceded" the Russian mobilization or "coincided with it." As I was directly connected with the preparation of the English edition of the Schilling Diary, although by no means responsible for the deplorable translation, I may say here that the word "coincided" was explicitly inserted by M. Sazonov in order to cover the *Lokalanzeiger* incident. It seems clear, therefore, that M. Sazonov never made the statement attributed to him by Profes-

Looking back on the events which determined the decision of Russia, we see the sweeping change which took place in the general outlook of her military and political leaders in the course of twelve days, from July 18 to July 30. On July 18, describing his interview with Count Szapary, Sazonov said that he was *"doux comme un agneau."* On July 29 he sternly remarked to the German ambassador, *"Maintenant je n'ai plus de doute sur les vraies causes de l'intransigeance autrichienne."* The optimism of Sazonov died away under the chilling effect of the uncompromising policy of the Central Empires. The attitude of Russia's military leaders suffered a similar reversal. On July 24 and 25 Sukhomlinov and Yanushkevich accepted without protest the possibility of a partial mobilization. But they soon realized the danger contained in this decision with regard to the military position of Russia. The fading hopes of the diplomats and the growing anxiety of the military leaders were the two dominating factors of the situation. While the former were losing ground the latter were steadily approaching their goal. As M. Renouvin rightly says, the argument which won the day was the technical argument. We have endeavored to trace the rapidly growing importance of the military technical factor. On July 24 and 25 its irresistible logic was understood clearly only by the subordinates, Dobrorolsky and Danilov, but it soon overcame the resistance of Yanushkevich, Sukhomlinov and Sazonov, and

sor Barnes, with whom I heartily agree in his condemnation of "flagrant and easily detected falsification of readily verifiable facts."

Professor Barnes mistakenly infers that the interview with M. Sazonov was obtained by the *New York Times* "in order to offset the effect" of his own article in *Current History* for May, 1924; but as a matter of fact, the idea of interviewing M. Sazonov originated in Europe early in March, 1924, and was carried out at the end of March and the beginning of April. I was among those immediately connected with the matter and I may assert positively that we knew nothing about Professor Barnes's proposed article, being merely interested in bringing forward historical evidence.

At the time when this article was going to press the author received a personal letter, dated March 25, from M. Sazonov, excerpts from which are given below. This letter was written on the receipt of a draft copy of the present article which, however, did not contain the footnote on this page dealing with the *Lokalanzeiger* incident. It is quoted here with M. Sazonov's permission:

"I fully agree with everything that you say," writes M. Sazonov, "but I believe that you underestimate the importance of the declaration of the German mobilization announced in the *Lokalanzeiger* of July 30, 1914.

"It goes without saying that it did not cause our mobilization; this would have been impossible as is shown from the chronology of the events, but in our opinion it justified the step taken and considerably increased the anxiety which we all, and especially our military men, felt as a result of the rumors about military preparations in Germany which reached Petrograd from all sides and of the communications made by Pourtalès to the Foreign Office. I still think, because I do not know of anything that would shake this conviction, that the special edition of the *Lokalanzeiger* was issued intentionally to induce us to take decisive measures without delay, and then to shift all the responsibility to our shoulders under the cover of the also intentionally delayed or, to be exact, detained denial of the mobilization on its way to Russia. Such methods are quite common in German diplomacy and I understand only too well the policy of apology of Bethmann."

finally—after a long struggle—that of the Tsar. We may, perhaps, add that the way to victory for the military argument was paved by the growing certitude that there was no earthly means for escaping a world conflict.

From the point of view of Russian statesmen the proclamation of general mobilization did not mean the end of negotiations. Even after the decision had been taken, Sazonov continued his efforts towards the maintenance of peace. He declared to Pourtalès on July 31 "that the decision taken by the Imperial Government merely constituted precautionary measures" and that, despite Russian mobilization, "peace could be maintained if Germany would consent before it was too late to exercise a moderating influence upon her ally." He also agreed, in accordance with the suggestion made by Sir Edward Grey, to an alteration of the formula proposed by him to Pourtalès the day before. Emperor Nicholas telegraphed the same day to Emperor Wilhelm: ". . . It is technically impossible to stop our military preparations, which are obligatory owing to Austria's mobilization. We are far from wishing war. As long as the negotiations with Austria on Serbia's account are taking place my troops shall not make any provocative actions. I give you my solemn word for this. . . ."

Even as late as August 1 Nicholas was still hoping that war might be averted. On that date he sent Wilhelm the following telegram:

I received your telegram. Understand you are obliged to mobilize, but wish to have some guarantee from you as I gave you, that the measures *do not* mean war and that we shall continue negotiating for the benefit of our countries and universal peace dear to all our hearts. Our long proved friendship must succeed, with God's help, in avoiding bloodshed. Anxiously, full of confidence, await your answer.

And Sazonov, in the course of his last interview with Pourtalès, who brought him the declaration of war, said that "although the order for general mobilization could not be changed, Russia did not refuse to continue negotiations for the purpose of arriving at a peaceful issue out of the present situation." The documents quoted above seem to establish that in the opinion of the Russian Government the declaration of a general mobilization was not understood to mean war.

That Russian mobilization was inevitable under the circumstances was admitted by Sir Edward Grey when he informed the German ambassador on July 31 that "he did not see how Russia could be urged to suspend them [her military preparations] unless some limit were put by Austria to the advance of her troops into Serbia." That this was the view held by the British Foreign Office and not a mere diplomatic support for Russia and pressure on Germany has been amply proved by the recently published *British Documents on the Origins of the War*. The confidential minutes made by the higher officials of Downing Street are of special value in this respect. Commenting on a dispatch fom Sir Edward Goschen, Sir Arthur Nicolson wrote on July 29 as follows: "There have certainly been no indications that Germany has exercised any moderating influence at Vienna. It is going rather far to put the responsibility on Russia who has been willing to adopt any and every course likely to lead to peace. I suppose Germany wishes Russia to join with other Powers in keeping the ring while Austria strangles Servia." On July 31, the day when Grey's dispatch quoted above was sent out, Sir Arthur Nicolson made the following remarks: "Russia is taking very reasonable and sensible precautions, which should in no wise be interpreted as provocative. Germany, of course, who has been steadily preparing now wishes to throw the blame on Russia—a very thin pretext. However comments are superfluous."

Did the representatives of the Central Powers really think that Russia meant war, that her mobilization was ordered for the purpose of precipitating an armed conflict, and that further negotiations were hence made impossible? An answer to this question may be found in the following official documents.

On July 28 the Austrian ambassador at St. Petersburg telegraphed to Vienna: "My impressions were that, in view of the prevailing disinclination to get into conflict with us, the Minister [Sazonov] was clinging to a straw in the hope of still escaping from the present situation." Von Chelius telegraphed to Berlin on July 30: ". . . I have the impression that they have mobilized here [St. Petersburg] from a dread of coming events, without any aggressive intent. . . ." Still more important is the statement made by Bethmann-Hollweg on July 30, 1914, to the Prussian Ministry of State: "The mobilization of Russia had indeed been ordered, but their measures of mobilization are not to be compared with those of Western Europe. The Russian troops may remain for weeks in this state of mobilization. Russia intends no war either, but has been forced to take her measures by Austria." These documents speak for themselves.

It was not the purpose of this article to deny the fact that Russian mobilization was an important factor in the situation created by the Austrian ultimatum; it was intended to show how the mobilization became inevitable in the opinion of the Russian Government and of the Russian military leaders, and its actual bearing on the course of events. The whole situation was perfectly understood and lucidly stated as early as July 27 by Sir Eyre Crowe in a minute on No. 170 of the *British Documents on the Origins of the War*:

I am afraid that the real difficulty to overcome will be found in the question of mobilization. Austria is already mobilizing. This, if the war does come, is a serious menace to Russia who cannot be expected to delay her own mobilization, which, as it is, can only become effective in something like double the time required by Austria and Germany. If Russia mobilizes, we have been warned Germany will do the same, and as German mobilization is directed almost entirely against France, the latter cannot possibly delay her own mobilization for even the fraction of a day. From Sir M. de Bunsen's telegram No. 109 just come in, it seems certain that Austria is going to war because that was from the beginning her intention. If that view proves correct, it would be neither possible nor just and wise to make any move to restrain Russia from mobilizing.

In summing up the contents of the preceding pages we may perhaps be justified in drawing the following conclusions:

1. For technical and strategical reasons partial mobilization presented a serious danger with regard to the defense of the Russian Empire; these considerations therefore necessitated, in the view of Russia's military leaders, the transition from partial to general mobilization; Sazonov and the Emperor yielded to this view after a struggle which lasted for days.

2. The declaration of partial mobilization was the result of the declaration of war on Serbia by Austria.

3. The Russian Foreign Office did all in its power, short of giving Austria a free hand in dealing with Serbia, to bring about the peaceful settlement of the conflict.

4. Technically speaking, the Russian mobilization was not equivalent to war, mobilization and declaration of war being two separate acts.

5. In July, 1914, the Governments of Germany and Austria were aware that Russian mobilization did not necessarily mean war; it cannot be denied, however, that they had their own military problems to reckon with. But this is a subject entirely outside the scope of this article.

SOVIET RUSSIA

11

GERMAN FOREIGN OFFICE DOCUMENTS ON FINANCIAL SUPPORT TO THE BOLSHEVIKS IN 1917 *

A charge made by Kerensky in July, 1917, that Lenin and other Bolshevik leaders were German agents has been the subject of wide investigation since that time. There is little question that the charge was unjustified and that most of the documents used to support it were unreliable; but the question of Bolshevik indebtedness to the Germans is still a moot one, as was shown by the critical reaction to Alan Moorhead's treatment of the question in his *The Russian Revolution* when it was published, in 1958. Dr. Katkov helps us to examine important and relevant data.

DOCUMENT NO. 1 reproduced on pages 160–61 in an English translation will contribute to the elucidation of one of the most controversial questions of recent history: that of the relations of the Imperial German Government with the Russian Bolshevik Party in the period between the fall of the Russian Monarchy and the seizure of power by the Bolsheviks in 1917. The document has been found in one of the files of the German Ministry of Foreign Affairs, now in the custody of the British authorities. It is a typescript of five pages dated 3 December 1917 with a number of corrections and marginal notes. The caption 'Tel. Hughes' provides for transmission by the Hughes direct line telecommunication sys-

* George Katkov, "German Foreign Office Documents on Financial Support to the Bolsheviks in 1917," *International Affairs*, XXXII (April, 1956), 181–89. Reprinted by permission of the author and the publisher.

The author is Lecturer in Soviet Institutions and Economics at Oxford University and a Research Fellow of St. Antony's College. He received his secondary education in Russia, where he was born, and his university education in Czechoslovakia. Much of his earlier work was in the field of philosophy; in recent years, he has worked largely in the field of contemporary Russian history. In the course of an extensive study of the Revolution of 1917, he came upon the documents that are the basis of the article presented here.

tem. The message was addressed by the Minister of Foreign Affairs, Baron R. von Kühlmann, to an official who was to communicate its content orally to the Kaiser. Document No. 2 shows that the message was duly dispatched and received; and that the Kaiser expressed agreement with its contents.

Document No. 2 is the deciphered text of the reply to Document No. 1, dated 4 December 1917, from the German General Headquarters and signed 'Gruenau', an official of the German Foreign Office attached to the person of the Emperor.

The urgency and frankness of the message are due to the circumstances in which it was written. The German Government was at the time about to dispatch a special mission to Petrograd to start negotiations on the return of German prisoners of war and the resumption of trade relations with the newly formed Bolshevik Government. The mission was to be headed by the representative of the Foreign Office, Count Mirbach, and a representative of the GHQ, Admiral Count Keyserling. Besides, the Armistice negotiations in Brest-Litovsk were about to begin. The outcome of the war might well depend to a large extent on the success of these negotiations. The outline of German policy towards Russia had been discussed between the Kaiser and his Foreign Minister at some length on a previous occasion. The Minister had now to draw up the necessary instructions for these various actions. He wished to have the Kaiser's approval of their general tenor, and as the Kaiser was then at GHQ the State Secretary had recourse to telegraphic communication. The text was then filed with other top secret documents concerning, for the most part, affairs involving the Kaiser personally. The Minister felt it necessary to remind the Monarch of certain recent political activities. This takes up the first four or five sentences of Document No. 1, where it is stated as a fact that financial support was given to the Bolsheviks by the Germans in the spring and summer of 1917. These statements are important, for it is difficult to assume that Kühlmann lied to his Sovereign. They make plain that the German Government had given financial support to the Bolsheviks on a considerable scale; that this support was afforded in a continuous flow through various channels and 'under a variety of labels'; and finally that it was given with the aim of weakening Russia as a partner in the Entente and of detaching her from her allies.

These statements of fact differ considerably from the two main opposing views put forward regarding the relations of the Germans with the Bolsheviks.

According to one view, all accusations of contact with the Germans were counter-revolutionary fabrications, invented to mislead and to discredit the leaders of the Revolution. This of course is still the thesis of official Soviet historiography. But the influence of this idea extended far beyond the borders of Communist orthodoxy.

That German agents were seeking to undermine army discipline by inciting soldiers to attack their officers was suspected from the very beginning of the February revolution. When, at one of the earliest meetings of the Provisional Government, in March, the Kadet leader P. N. Milyukov referred casually to interference by German agents, Kerensky, then Minister of Justice and 'the hostage of Revolutionary Democracy', shouted in tones of hysteria that there was no place for him in a gathering where the glorious Russian Revolution could be calumniated as a machination of the Germans; he left the meeting, announcing his resignation, which needless to say, he almost immediately withdrew. Such was the repulsion felt in 1917 at any suggestion of the contamination of the revolutionary process by German influence, that even the arrival via Germany of the sealed train with the Bolshevik leaders did not produce anything like the 'furious barking of the Defencists and the Bourgeoisie', which Lenin had expected. All that happened was that he (Lenin) failed to secure the official approval of the Executive Committee of the Soviet for his decision to take advantage of German favours. Not until the Bolsheviks had developed their propaganda in the army, inciting the soldiers to insubordination and urging fraternization with the German troops, did the Provisional Government start a cautious investigation of possible contacts with the Germans. The collapse of the Imperial police machine and the disruption of the military counter-espionage service (which had worked with the secret police) made this investigation very difficult. However, with the aid of the allied counter-espionage services and following the confession of an agent, recruited by the enemy while a prisoner of war in Germany, certain information was gathered on which legal proceedings against the Bolshevik leaders could be initiated. By the end of June 1917, with the failure of the Kerensky offensive and the progressive decline in army morale, the arrest of Bolshevik leaders for treasonable activities was seriously considered. It has even been suggested that the abortive Bolshevik *coup* in early July was motivated by the hope of preventing these arrests. The political effectiveness of accusations of contact with Germans was demonstrated during the July disturbances. When troops of the Petrograd garrison began to waver in their support of the government and of the Petrograd Soviet against the Bolshevik mutineers, the Minister of Justice Pereverzev arranged for some of the evidence against the Bolshevik leadership to be published by two journalists; these revelations changed the mood of the troops and greatly contributed to the collapse of the rising. Although that evidence was tenuous enough it was widely believed, because it gave to an ordinary patriotic Russian a more plausible explanation of Bolshevik defeatism and how it worked than the Bolsheviks themselves with their Zimmerwald ideology could provide. Kerensky had left Petrograd on the first day of the rising. On his return, by then vested with almost dictatorial powers, he ordered the arrest of Lenin, Zinoviev, and other Bolshevik leaders together with a number of their suspected intermediaries with the Germans. Some of the latter, e.g., a woman by the name of Sumenson and the lawyer Kozlovsky, were in fact arrested in Petrograd on 7 July. Two of the others involved, the notorious A. Helphand (alias Dr Parvus) and his close collaborator Fürstenberg-Haniecki were abroad. At the same time however Kerensky forced his Minister of Justice, Pereverzev, to resign. The reason given officially at the time (and later repeated in Kerensky's numerous personal memoirs) was that, by prematurely divulging the allegations against the Bolsheviks, Pereverzev had wrecked a deeply laid scheme of the Provisional Government— namely to arrest Fürstenberg-Haniecki on the Swedish-Finnish frontier; this individual was believed to be about to cross into Russia carrying large sums of German money and documents compromising the Bolsheviks.

Pereverzev's resignation discredited the revelations published on his orders. His selected publicists, Grigory Alexinsky (former member of the 2nd Duma) and Pankratov (former political prisoner), lacked the authority to sustain the accusations. And indeed very soon after the shock produced by these revelations a significant reversal in the mood of the so-called 'Revolutionary Democracy' took place. First came protests against wholesale accusations aimed at the Bolsheviks as a Party; if some Bolsheviks were German agents or if they had touched German money they should, it was said, be put on trial, but in the new Revolutionary Russia there could be no place for the persecution of a political party as such, however misguided it might be. At the request of the Bolsheviks the Central Executive Committee of the Soviets set up its own Commission for the investigation of the case of Lenin and others, and appealed—pending this inquiry—to all comrades to stop the spreading of slanderous allegations. This Commission later joined the Government's Commission of Inquiry. While these Commissions were leisurely pursuing their investigations the suspicion gained ground that the whole affair had been staged by officers and 'counter-revolutionaries' with the aim of discrediting the leaders of Revolutionary Democracy. The fact that such accusations could have induced the wavering troops of the Petrograd garrison to side in an armed conflict with the Provisional Government convinced the Left that they amounted to a dangerous weapon in the hands of the Kadet Party and the Defencists. And yet, Lenin's flight into hiding (he had disappeared by 7 July when an attempt was made to arrest him) seems to have greatly disturbed many of his followers and associates. The reaction of a man like Sukhanov is highly significant. Having mentioned, in his memoirs, the 'monstrous slander' (of having touched German money) directed against Lenin, Sukhanov goes on to express his amazement at the course of action Lenin had chosen. 'Any other mortal', Sukhanov writes, 'would have demanded an investigation and trial, even under the most unfavourable conditions. Any other mortal would personally and publicly have done everything possible to rehabilitate himself. But Lenin proposed that others, his adversaries, should do this, while he sought safety in flight. . . . In the whole world only he could have behaved in this way'. Sukhanov does not share Lenin's professed opinion, that the impartiality of the Courts under the Provisional Government could not be trusted. Moreover Lenin, according to Sukhanov, could have had no difficulty in disproving 'the nonsensical accusation', which 'in a little time dispersed by itself—like smoke'. The only explanation of Lenin's behaviour which occurred to Sukhanov was Lenin's superhuman nature ('. . . no mortal would . . .'). Kühlmann's revelation should make a less metaphysical explanation at least probable. Lenin might have known—or at least suspected—that the money he was using was German money and that the accusations were in substance true. Then his action would appear only human—all too human.

At that time however the Provisional Government had only indirect evidence against Lenin and not entirely reliable witnesses. The persons arraigned by the Public Prosecutor on 22 July 1917 for organizing the rising and for treason were never put on trial, and those who were arrested were released on bail in September; although, according to the counter-espionage officer Nikitine, some of them had made pretty full confessions. It should be emphasized that if the accusations dispersed 'like smoke' in the turbulent atmosphere of the last months of the Provisional Government they were never proved to be false before an impartial tribunal. Nor were they forgotten, least of all by the Bolsheviks themselves. They became indeed ammunition in the arsenal of Communist propaganda. Lenin refers to them as the 'Russian Dreyfusiade'; Trotsky speaks with temperamental scorn of 'the great slander'; members of the Institute of the Red Professors headed by M. N. Pokrovsky ridiculed them. More surprising is the fact that impartial historians in the West seem—as time went on—to attach less and less importance to accusations which at a given moment threatened to cost the Bolsheviks their popular support in Russia and possibly their very existence as a party. In his monumental history of the Bolshevik Revolution E. H. Carr makes no reference whatever to the 'great slander', to the alleged links between Bolsheviks and Germans, or to the question of German money. In his account of the steps taken for the arrest of the Bolshevik leaders he makes no mention of the treason issue; the reader is left to understand that the intended arrests were merely part of the police measures to suppress the July rising. Of course, even the attempt to examine impartially allegations which have been branded as counter revolutionary, would have caused offence to those who share the 'great slander' school of thought. On the other hand, only by examining all the possible causes of Bolshevik success in 1917 can one provide an explanation for the inevitable course of historical events, and the German money might have been one of these causes even though Kühlmann's estimate of its importance might be self-flattering and exaggerated.

A careful study of the German archives will probably occasion some re-thinking and re-writing of the history of the Russian Revolution. Some of the hero-worship of Lenin might be affected by it. Not only to his own Party, but to the Left wing of the Russian Revolutionary Government, Lenin's personal character was the best guarantee that he had never worked with German money. He himself never claimed, as he well might have after the German collapse, to have successfully carried out a Machiavellian plan, and beaten German imperialism with the German money the Germans had provided. On the contrary, he always maintained that the accusations were a monstrous and malign attack on his revolutionary honour. The result was that those who, like Bernstein, sincerely—and, as we now see, rightly—believed that he was supported by German money were ostracized as counter-revolutionaries or renegades.

The documents here reproduced should do away once and for all with the legend of a Bolshevik Party strictly adhering to the principles of revolutionary ethics which they professed in common with other Russian revolutionaries. Suspicions that Bolsheviks were financially supported by the German Government were not slander but a fair guess.

And yet no comfort can be derived from these documents by those who believed that Lenin and his associates were agents of the German Government or the German General Staff. This view, spread among Russian anti-Communists of all creeds, is shared by Kerensky and has found a protagonist in the former Kadet leader and historian of the Russian Revolution, P. N. Milyukov. According to this view, Lenin came to an agreement with the Germans by which the latter should help him to seize power in exchange for the demoralization of the Russian Army and the conclusion of a degrading separate peace.

The absence of any documentary evidence for the existence of such an agreement between the Germans and Lenin was largely compensated by speculation on the possible motives of both sides in helping each other: did not the Germans show exceptional solicitude in letting the Bolsheviks return home, and did not Lenin repay them by working for the destruction of the Russian army? Those prone to such conclusions found them confirmed by the fact that the Bolsheviks were receiving German money. The evidence for this was not watertight but all these assumptions and guesses formed one consistent although sensational picture, which in a time of acute political struggle had great power over the imaginations of all those unaffected by the spell of revolutionary enthusiasm or of the mystique of Lenin's superhuman personality. The anti-Communist movement in the Civil War found it politically expedient to represent Lenin as a paid agent of the Germans. The 'Whites' were looking for allied support and this—they believed—would be forthcoming more readily if intervention in Russia could be represented as part of the general war against the Central Powers and their allies. In support of this conception, in the winter of 1917–18 a series of documents allegedly smuggled from Petrograd to South Russia was produced. They purported to be originals, photo-copies and copies of State papers taken from the files of the Bolshevik Government, and they purported to prove close and organized contacts between the German authorities and the Bolshevik Party both in 1918 and before. However, for those who already believed that Lenin had received German money, the Sisson Papers—as these documents, since published in the United States, are called—were only belated additional proofs of his being a German agent. Ironically, now that the fact of German financial aid is established there is even less reason to believe that Lenin was a German agent (unless one uses the word 'agent' in a Leninist–Stalinist sense, in which even a scholar carrying out independent research with the help of a fund established by an industrialist qualifies for the title of an 'agent of bourgeois imperialism'). It is obvious from Kühlmann's report to the Kaiser that in giving their support to the Communists the Germans were giving a 'grant in aid' to an independent subversive movement and not financing political agents and spies working on instructions. In the first years of the war the Germans seem to have favoured the various separatist movements of national minorities, but after the fall of the monarchy the Bolsheviks had their day.

The 'various channels and varying labels' of the aid to the Bolsheviks may not be easy to determine. Kühlmann mentions in a telegram to General Headquarters dated 29 September 1917 that action in such matters was undertaken by the German Foreign Office in close collaboration with the Political Section of the General Staff of the Army in the Field (Colonel von Hülsen), and it is possible that details will be found in the German military archives. As far as the German Foreign Office is concerned there can be no doubt that the German Government's official denial, in 1921, of the existence of any documents referring to the financial support of Russian Bolsheviks in Foreign Office archives was less than candid. The files of the Berne Legation contain, for instance, an 'absolute secret' report of 30 April 1917 in which the German Minister in Berne, Baron Romberg, relates his conversation with the Swiss social democrat, Fritz Platten (who had made the final arrangements for the first sealed train and had accompanied Lenin and his fellow travellers from Switzerland to the Finnish border). Platten conveyed the gratitude of the Russians for the efficiency of the arrangements made, expressed his regrets that he was prevented from entering Russia, and gave a hearsay description of the enthusiastic reception given to Lenin on his arrival in Petrograd, where, according to Platten, three quarters of the workers supported him. 'It was clear from what Platten told me', Romberg goes on in his report, 'that the emigrés are very short of money for their propaganda, while their opponents naturally have at their disposal unlimited means. The funds collected for the use of emigrés fell mainly into the hands of social patriots. I am arranging for a confidential agent to investigate the very delicate question as to whether there is any possible way of letting them have money without their finding this objectionable. In the meantime I would be grateful if I might be informed by telegram whether the revolutionaries are already receiving financial help through another channel'.

(*text cont. on p. 162*)

DOCUMENT NO. 1

BERLIN, 3rd December 1917   Add A3   4486
                                                                  Tel. Hughs I.Z.
                                                                  To Tel. No. 1771

Tit. Lersner
No. 1925.

The disruption of the Entente and the subsequent creation of political combinations agreeable to us constitute the most important war aim of our diplomacy. Russia appeared (to me) [1] to be the weakest link in the enemy's chain. The task therefore was gradually to loosen it and, when possible, to remove it. This was the purpose of the subversive activity we caused to be carried out in Russia behind the front—in the first place (vigorous) [1] promotion of separatist tendencies and support of the Bolsheviki. It was not until the Bolsheviki had received from us a steady flow of funds through various channels and under varying labels that they were in a position to be able to build up their main organ, *Pravda*, to conduct energetic propaganda [2] and appreciably to extend the originally narrow basis of their party. The Bolsheviki have now come into power; how long they will retain power cannot yet be foreseen. They need peace in order to strengthen their own position; on the other hand it is entirely in our interest that we should exploit the period while they are in power, which may be a short one, in order to attain firstly an armistice and then, if possible, peace.[3] The conclusion of a separate peace would mean the achievement of the

H. St. to
see before
dispatch

K

Herr
Nadolny
to see

N

[1] Crossed out in the original.
[2] The words 'to conduct energetic propaganda' written on the margin and inserted in the text.
[3] An asterisk in the original text refers to a handwritten marginal note saying: 'There is no question of supporting the Bolsheviki in the future.' It remains doubtful whether these words were included in the text as telegraphed or whether they are of a later date.

desired war aim, namely, a breach between Russia and her Allies. The amount of tension necessarily caused by such a breach would determine the degree of Russia's dependence on Germany and her future relations with us. Once cast out and cast off by her former Allies, abandoned financially, Russia will be forced to seek our support. We shall be able to provide help for Russia in various ways; firstly in the rehabilitation of the railways; (I have in mind a German–Russian Commission—under our control—which would undertake the rational and coordinated exploitation of the railway lines so as to ensure speedy resumption of freight movement) then the provision of a substantial loan, which Russia requires to maintain her state machine. This could take the form of an advance on the security of grain, raw materials, etc., etc., to be provided by Russia and shipped under the control of the above-mentioned Commission. Aid on such a basis—the scope to be increased as and when necessary—would in my opinion bring about a growing rapprochement between the two countries.

Austria-Hungary will regard the rapprochement with distrust and not without apprehension. I would interpret the excessive eagerness of Count Czernin to come to terms with the Russians as a desire to forestall us and to prevent Germany and Russia arriving at an intimate relationship inconvenient to the Danube Monarchy. There is no need for us to compete for Russia's good will. We are strong enough to wait with equanimity; we are in a far better position than Austria-Hungary to offer Russia what she needs for the reconstruction of her State. I view future developments in the East with confidence but I think it expedient for the time being to maintain a certain reserve in our attitude to the Austro-Hungarian Government in all matters including the Polish question which concern both monarchies so as to preserve a free hand for all eventualities.

The above-mentioned considerations lie, I venture to believe, within the framework of the directives given me by His Majesty. I request you to report to His Majesty accordingly and to transmit to me by telegram the All-highest instructions.

St. S.

K.

DOCUMENT NO. 2

A.S. 4607

Telegram

General Headquarters, 4th December 1917, 7.30 p.m.
Received   8.25 p.m.
The Imperial Legation Councillor at the Foreign Office.
Decypher

With reference to your telegram No. 1925 A.S. 4486. His Majesty No. 1819.   the Kaiser has expressed his agreement with Your Excellency's exposé concerning a possible rapprochement with Russia.

(signature) GRUENAU

No reply, telegraphic or otherwise, is to be found in this particular file, and the trail—as so often happens when highly confidential matters are concerned—disappears. There is however a reference to the efforts of Romberg's confidential agent in a file concerned with the activities of another German agent, a certain Alexander Keskuela. This file contains a report from the German Military Attaché in Berne dated 9 May 1917 to his Minister. Romberg's agent, referred to as Herr Baier, had written on 4 May to the Military Attaché that following preliminary soundings with the Bolshevik, Dr Sheklovsky, and the Menshevik, P. Axelrod, he had had a further interview with representatives of the 'various nuances of the peace-minded Socialist Party in Zurich' (Baier does not say who they were) who were interested in promoting an immediate separate peace at all costs between Russia and Germany. The question of financial support had been discussed. Herr Baier had offered to contribute a substantial sum, and had hinted that other wealthy friends of his might do the same. He summarized the result of these negotiations as follows: '(i) The personality of the donor should guarantee that the source of the finances is unimpeachable. (ii) The donor and the intermediary should be enabled to cross the Russian frontier with the money, having secured an official or semi-official recommendation for this purpose. (iii) To facilitate immediate use funds should be brought in cash and not in other valuables, the encashment of which might present difficulties and attract attention. Swiss currency would be the easiest to convey, to convert and to use'. Needless to say Herr Baier considered himself a reliable intermediary for such an operation.

These communications throw some light on the nature of the channels and labels. The peace-minded Russian socialist contacted expressed satisfaction at the idea that wealthy comrades and friends would afford financial support to their propaganda. The peace-minded socialists are obviously none other than the Zimmerwald Left, of whom Lenin was the most extreme defeatist. Melgounoff in his above-quoted book reports a conversation in 1917 in Moscow with the historian Pokrovsky, who told him that the Bolsheviks had received money from German Social Democrats. This might well have been a source acceptable to the Bolsheviks, although socialists of different creed would probably have considered it unsatisfactory. The material published by Nikitine indicates that the sums transferred through Madame Sumenson came from Fürstenberg-Haniecki (a member of the Polish Social Democratic Party). Money coming through this channel could be considered as coming from 'friends and comrades'. 'Dr Parvus' was by then universally known as an agent of the German Government: he had behaved with so little discretion that Lenin refused to see him on his way to Russia and avoided direct contact with him. But Lenin throughout maintained contact with Fürstenberg-Haniecki, who was Parvus's employee in business, associate in politics, and co-conspirator in German intrigues: and in July 1917

Pravda went out of its way to defend the man's revolutionary integrity.

In any case it is now clear that whatever the labels may have been, the money was that of the German Government. Will the German Archives throw a light on whether or how far Lenin was aware of the fact? The content of the high-level document here reproduced seems to indicate that detailed research into the lower strata of German–Bolshevik contacts would prove rewarding.

AUTHOR'S NOTE, 1961: Five years have passed since the Kühlmann letter was first published. One would have expected its discovery to lead to a revision of many views on the 1917 events in Russia. Some of these, however, like many other historical prejudices, die hard. Even in the West, historians show a reluctance to appreciate the full significance of the document. Thus A. J. P. Taylor, in a review of Z. Zeman's book *Germany and the Revolution in Russia 1917–1918*, which appeared in the *Manchester Guardian*, considered that Kühlmann was just boasting; that his claims were not supported by other evidence or witnesses, and that his message to the Kaiser cannot be regarded as an indication that Lenin received money from the Germans. And Taylor is not alone in his scepticism. In this connection the following should be stated:

1. The authenticity of the Külhmann telegram of 3 December 1917 is beyond doubt, and both copies, the one at the dispatching and the other at the receiving end, are preserved in the German archives. It is a carefully weighed summary of the policy pursued by the German Foreign Office toward the Bolsheviks; it was drafted by high-ranking officials of the Wilhelmstrasse, Diego von Berger and Nadolny, and it represents the views of the Ministry and not of Kühlmann personally.

2. The document, and the supporting evidence published by Zeman, do not prove conclusively that Lenin personally knew about the German money which in the summer of 1917 was pouring "through various channels and under various labels" into the Bolshevik exchequer. Cautious and persistent investigation seems to confirm that one of the channels was that established by Lenin's closest correspondent and henchman in Scandinavia, Fuerstenberg-Ganetsky (Haniecki) and the Petersburg lawyer Kozlovsky, who were both accused by the legal authorities under the Provisional Government of forming the main link between the Bolshevik Party and the chief protagonist of the pro-Bolshevik policy of the German Foreign Office, Alexander Helphand (Parvus).

3. Historians in the Soviet Union have taken hardly any notice of the revelations contained in the Kühlmann telegram, except for occasional references to it as being a forgery. And yet the strongest confirmation of the existence of the channel connecting the Bolsheviks with their supporters in Berlin comes from recent Soviet publications. The minutes of the Central Committee of the Bolshevik Party for August 1917 to Feb-

ruary 1918 were re-published in 1958 under the auspices of the Institute of Marxism-Leninism. The edition claims to reproduce the complete text of the minutes. It omits a number of items, however, and the explanation for the omission is given in a note on p. 250, referring to the agenda of the meeting held on 6 August 1917:

> As in the first edition of this collection, here and in all other cases where items have been omitted from the agenda of the Central Committee the editors have removed from the minutes controversial matters concerning Ya. S. Ganetsky, M. Yu. Kozlovsky and others which were discussed at eight meetings in all. Fragmentary minutes on these affairs contain insufficient material to clarify the essence of the questions discussed.

Unfortunately the note fails to indicate what was the precise nature of the "controversial matters" we are not allowed to learn about forty years after the event.

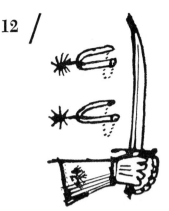

12 /

THE CHEKA *

If the present relations between the Soviet Union and the Western
world were better, the Soviet political police would probably receive
less attention from the West: a hostile attitude towards a country
stimulates attention to its unfavorable rather than its favorable
features. Even so, it is inconceivable that any serious study of Soviet
history would ignore the role of the political police. An understanding
of it is necessary regardless of the final verdict on the currently
popular view that terror is the "linchpin" of Soviet totalitarianism and
that the political police is the instrument of terror. That verdict will
depend not only on what is and has been but also on what is to come
in the development of the U.S.S.R. The historian will certainly begin
his study with a consideration of the Cheka, the first Soviet political
police organization.

THIS PAPER attempts to assemble the available evidence concerning the origin and early development of the Soviet political police. The
difficulties here arise not only from the secret nature of the organisation,
but from the great efforts which have been made to construct a false
image of it for propaganda purposes. Misrepresentation of the police
seems to have followed closely after misrepresentation of the Bolshevik
Party among the very first tasks of Soviet internal propaganda. The task
was well begun under Lenin. Stalin can only be credited with its sim-

* E. J. Scott, "The Cheka," St. Antony's Papers, (London: Chatto & Windus Ltd.,
1956), I, 1–23. Reprinted by permission of the author and the publisher.
    The author is an official of the British Foreign Office. After a tour of duty with
the British Embassy in Moscow, he interrupted his work with the Foreign Office
to spend two years at research in St. Antony's College, Oxford. The selection reprinted here is a product of that research.

plification, by restricting all accounts of the police to a few lines and by concentrating all State historical archives in their hands.

The latest and briefest account of the police, contained in the second edition of the Soviet Encyclopaedia (Volume 9, 1951), gives as its origin a Decree of Sovnarcom of December 20, 1917, which is said to have established the Cheka. The Decree is alleged to have been adopted on Lenin's initiative and to have been based on a note he wrote to Dzerzhinsky, who was appointed head of the organization. The reason for its establishment is said to have been the discovery soon after the Bolshevik revolution of counter-revolutionary plots financed by foreign and Russian capitalists.

Though Lenin is claimed to have founded the Cheka, no evidence has ever been brought forward showing how or when he did so. His note to Dzerzhinsky, on which a Decree organizing the Cheka is said to have been based, is in fact concerned only with drafting measures for conscripting bourgeois labour, and has no reference to an organization such as the Cheka. Nevertheless, Soviet commentators have found it expedient to link the founding of the Cheka to this particular note for the sake of its 'quotable' preamble, in which Lenin pictured the chaos in Petrograd as the product of unscrupulous attempts by class-enemy 'counter-revolutionaries' and 'saboteurs' to 'undermine the government', and declared the necessity of 'extra-ordinary measures' to combat them.

Whether or not Lenin played a direct part in establishing the Cheka, he had long been supplying, in his writings on the theory and tactics of revolution, the theoretical arguments which were used to justify its creation. He had, in particular, proclaimed that the successful consummation of a proletarian revolution depended on the effectiveness with which the resistance of counter-revolutionary classes in the period following the seizure of power was smashed under a dictatorship of the proletariat. In 1908 he had, for example, asserted that the Paris Commune of 1871, 'the first proletarian government', had not endured because it had not followed up its initial victory with a ruthless destruction of the counter-revolutionaries. Already in 1905 he had envisaged the use of terror in the style of the French Jacobins of 1793, 'to settle accounts with Tsarism' after the revolution. It was allegedly in accordance with this Leninist theory that, as Pokrovsky later put it, the Cheka 'sprang from the very essence of the proletarian revolution', and that the terror was 'the inevitable consequence' of that revolution.

The Petrograd Military-Revolutionary Committee, which carried out the seizure of power, numbered among its tasks immediately after the revolution 'the fighting of counter-revolution', and organized a security department for this purpose. Dzerzhinsky, who from the very first was engaged in security work, proposed to the Committee, on December 4, the organization of a special commission to fight counter-revolution. One may suspect that his objective was to reconstruct the security department on broader lines so that it covered not only Petrograd but all Soviet-held territory, and to regularize its position so far as possible in the apparatus on the new administration. It was apparently as a result of Dzerzhinsky's proposal that the Cheka was organized, and was prepared to take over its duties on December 21 after being approved by Sovnarcom on the 20th.

The establishment of the Cheka was first announced on December 26, when the *Gazette of the Provisional Worker-Peasant Government* published the following statement on a page devoted to minor announcements: 'By decision of Sovnarcom of December 7, (20th, new style), the All-Russian Extraordinary Commission for fighting counter-revolution and sabotage, attached to Sovnarcom, has been formed. The Commission is situated at No. 2 Gorokhovaya. Receiving hours: 12 till 5 o'clock.' No Decree establishing the Cheka was ever published by the Press or in the *Collection of Laws of the R.S.F.S.R.* However, what seems to be an extract from a hastily written minute of Sovnarcom's decision approving the organization was first reproduced in the reminiscences of a prominent Chekist, Latsis, in 1926, and then in an article on the history of the police by Pokrovsky in 1927. While Pokrovsky admitted that the decision was not a Decree and that Lenin's note to Dzerzhinsky had no direct bearing on it, he was so successful in exaggerating the significance of these two documents, that later commentators have not scrupled to attribute to the decision the full status of a Decree and to the note the character of a basic directive for the founding of the Cheka.

The statutes of the Cheka, which do appear in the *Collection of Laws*, were not drawn up until November 1918. They declared that it was an organ of Sovnarcom, which appointed the members of its central collegium, and that it worked in close contact with the Commissariats of Justice and Internal Affairs (N.K.V.D.). They also recognized the right of VeCheKa (the 'All-Russian', central Cheka) and the local Chekas to organize armed detachments of troops. But they did not attempt to define the exact functions or powers of the police; Lenin only recommended that this should be done in December 1921 just before the Cheka was transformed into the G.P.U.

The Cheka apparatus developed not only on a territorial basis, in each local administrative centre, but on 'functional' lines, in those organizations, such as the transport system and the armed forces, on whose reliable functioning the security of the regime appeared most to depend. This process began early in 1918, but not until the middle of the year were serious attempts made (by calling an 'All-Russian Conference of Chekas', and by issuing instructions on the organizational pattern to be followed) to co-ordinate it from the centre.

In March 1918 the local Soviets were requested to organize Chekas in the 'Guberniyas' and 'Uyezds', and were informed that henceforward only the Chekas were to have the right to carry out arrests and other measures in the fight against 'counter-revolutionaries'. The chairmen and members of the Chekas were to be elected by the Soviets with the subsequent approval of VeCheKa. Higher level Chekas were empowered to send their representatives to lower level ones, where their vote was decisive, and to reverse the decisions of the lower Chekas. As Bolshevik power established itself beyond the R.S.F.S.R., in the Ukraine, Central Asia and the Caucasus, Chekas were formed in these areas on the same lines as the All-Russian Cheka. One of the first established non-Russian Chekas was the All-Ukrainian Cheka, which at the end of November 1918 was attached to the Ukrainian 'Department of Internal Affairs'.

The formation of 'functional' Chekas began in May 1918 when the control of frontier areas was taken over by special frontier Chekas. In July and September, railway and post and telegraph departments were set up in local Chekas. Transport Chekas ('TeCheKas') were attached to the most important river and rail communication centres. Already in November 1918 the Chekist Moroz declared: 'There is no sphere of our life where the Cheka does not have its eagle eye.'

In February 1919 the task of 'combating counter-revolution and espionage' in the army and fleet was given to a 'Special Department' ('Osobi Otdel') of VeCheKa with subordinate 'special departments' attached to military units and with its agents in foreign territory. The danger of 'counter-revolution' in the armed forces lay not so much in the possible treachery of former Tsarist officers and representatives of the 'counter-revolutionary classes' employed as 'specialists', as in the unreliability and demoralization of the peasant-soldiers. The first task of the 'special departments' seems to have been to attempt to forestall mass desertions and, by employing terroristic methods, to help build up discipline throughout the Red Army. Through the 'special departments', the Cheka during the civil war came to exercise what appeared to be supreme authority over large territories. A resolution of the 8th Party Congress in March 1919 declared that the local 'special departments' were subordinated to the political commissars of Armies and Fronts, while their general direction and control was exercised by VeCheKa. But by 1921, according to Latsis, the 'special departments' were no longer dependent on the political commissars or the Revolutionary-Military Council headed by Trotsky.

Already in March 1918 all newspapers had been obliged to send three copies of each issue to Cheka headquarters for censorship. Failure to do so was punishable by the closing down of the paper. By the end of 1918 the Cheka had developed a system of concentration camps for political prisoners quite distinct from the ordinary prisons maintained by the Commissariat of Justice. In April 1919 the Chekas were ordered to establish forced labour camps, which were subsequently controlled by the N.K.V.D. through the local Soviets.

The Sovnarcom decision of December 20, 1917, formulated the tasks of the Cheka as follows:

1. To investigate and liquidate all attempts or actions connected with counter-revolution or sabotage, no matter from whom they may come, throughout Russia.

2. The handing over for trial by Revolutionary Tribunal of all saboteurs and counter-revolutionaries, and the elaboration of measures to fight them.

3. The Commission carries out only a preliminary investigation in so far as this is necessary for preventive purposes.

From the most imprecise terms of this decision it would seem that the Cheka was originally intended only to carry out investigations and to impose no stronger penalty than imprisonment. But the decision was, as we have pointed out, unpublished till the late twenties when it began to appear in 'improved' histories of the police. There is no reason to suppose that it ever guided the Cheka's actions, or to doubt that the necessity for the Cheka to employ terroristic methods had been envisaged from the start.

Though the terror was first openly proclaimed in September 1918, it was officially encouraged on a mass scale already in June, and the Bolsheviks had had recourse to it on critical occasions since the beginning of the year. Terroristic methods were employed to keep order in Petrograd even before the appearance of the Cheka. The 'special committee for fighting pogroms' which was set up on December 17, declared Petrograd in a state of siege and announced that 'attempts to break into wine-cellars, warehouses, factories, stalls, shops, private apartments, and so on and so forth, will be broken up by machine-gun fire without any kind of warning.' Spontaneous outbreaks of terror directed against the former 'upperclasses' were particularly widespread in the provinces; if local Bolsheviks did not encourage them they were helpless to prevent them The Left Social Revolutionary Commissar of Justice, Steinberg, later maintained that the Bolshevik announcement of December 13 branding the entire Cadet Party as 'enemies of the people' had invited such incidents of mob justice as the murder of the Cadet ex-Ministers Kokoshkin and Shingarev in a Petrograd hospital by a band of sailors on January 20. Lenin told the Petrograd Soviet on November 18, 1917: 'We are reproached with using terror, but we are not using the kind of terror used by the French revolutionaries who guillotined defenceless people, and I hope we will not for we have strength with us.' On December 15 it was Trotsky who told the same audience: 'During the French Revolution the Jacobins brought more honourable persons (than the Cadets) to the guillotine for resisting the people. We have not executed anyone and are not preparing to, but there are moments of popular fury and the Cadets are bringing it upon themselves. They are sabotaging and wrecking, and in every way intentionally aggravating the disorder, and not one of us will undertake to say that the people, if pushed to the extreme, will refrain from this final measure. But we are strong and we do not require such extremes. But everyone should know that the people will not be patient for long and will sweep away the obstacles from its path.' Finally, on January 27, the Presidium of the Soviet heard Lenin, in the course of an address on the food shortage, declare: 'We can achieve nothing unless we use terror, and shoot speculators on the spot.'

On February 23, 1918, immediately after the breaking off of the Brest Litovsk negotiations and the resumption of the German advance, an announcement was published by *Pravda* that the Cheka could 'see no other methods of fighting counter-revolutionaries, spies, speculators, looters, hooligans, saboteurs, and other parasites, then their merciless destruction on the spot'. Anyone attempting to flee from the capital would also be shot on the spot by Cheka detachments. On the next day the first reported case took place of the Cheka shooting without trial. The victim was a certain Prince Eboli, who, according to accounts by Latsis and his colleague Peters, had been 'masquerading as a Chekist' with forged papers in order to extort money. When the L.S.R. Party protested about the shooting Lenin, according to Latsis, would not allow the question to be put on the agenda of Sovnarcom.

After the murder of Volodarsky on June 20 Lenin instructed Zinoviev that the terror should be applied more ruthlessly in Petrograd. The final break with the L.S.R. Party after their murder of Mirbach (July 6), and risings organized by Savinkov at Yaroslavl, Rybinsk and Murom (July 6–21), further increased the slaughter. Early in June, Dzerzhinsky granted a press interview in which he described the character of the Cheka as follows: 'We stand for organized terror. . . . Terror is an absolute necessity during times of revolution. . . . We terrorize the enemies of the Soviet government in order to stop crime at its inception. . . . When confronted with evidence criminals almost in every case confess; and what argument can have greater weight than a criminal's own confession? . . . The Cheka is not a court. The Cheka is the defence of the revolution as the Red Army is. And just as in the civil war the Red Army cannot stop to ask whether or not it may harm individuals, but is obliged to act with the one thought of securing the victory of the revolution over the bourgeoisie, the Cheka is obliged to defend the revolution and conquer the enemy even if its sword does by chance sometimes fall upon the heads of the innocent.'

On September 2, ostensibly as an answer to the attempted assassination of Lenin and the murder of Uritsky, the head of the Petrograd

Cheka, on August 30, VTsIK adopted a resolution calling on 'workers and peasants to reply to the White Terror by mass Red Terror'. The next day Petrovsky, the Commissar of Internal Affairs, issued a circular to all Soviets ordering their Chekas and Militia to 'shoot unconditionally all who are engaged in White Guard activity', and demanding 'not the least wavering, not the least indecision in the application of mass terror'. On September 5 the famous Decree 'On the Red Terror' announced that: 'Sovnarcom, having heard the report of the Chairman of VeCheKa on the activity of the Commission, finds that in the given situation the safeguarding of the rear by means of terror is a direct necessity. . . .' The Decree ordered that:

a. The Cheka should be strengthened by sending to it the largest possible number of Party members.

b. Class enemies should be isolated in concentration camps.

c. Anyone in contact with counter-revolutionary organs should be shot, and

d. The names of all those shot and the reasons for their execution should be published.

An instruction from VeCheKa on September 17 empowered all Chekas to pass and execute sentences in cases of counter-revolution and serious breach of duty without referring them to the Revolutionary Tribunals.

Such an instruction was probably superfluous. Already from the first moment of its existence the Cheka began to undermine the position of the Revolutionary Tribunals and their authority to dispense 'revolutionary justice'. Shklovsky, a member of VeCheKa, wrote: 'The experience of the Cheka plainly indicates the harmfulness of subordinating to any authority an agency discharging such important tasks as the Cheka has assumed. . . . If someone should object that there are revolutionary laws, our reply must be that the methods of the Cheka are those very revolutionary laws, for no one can prove that the Cheka is striking at anyone but the enemies of the proletariat.' The Tribunals, according to their reports of 1918, were powerless to prevent the Cheka from seizing and executing persons whose cases they were in the process of considering, or from transferring others from prison to Cheka concentration camps. The Cheka was seldom concerned to give publicity to the cases it investigated, and apparently only when it was so concerned did it hand them over for trial by Tribunal.

The Tribunals had been established about a fortnight before the Cheka by the 'Decree No. 1 on the Courts', which also abolished all the existing judicial institutions and set up People' Courts. They were to try cases of counter-revolution, profiteering and sabotage, while other crimes and civil cases were to be dealt with by People's Courts. For a short time (December 1917 to March 1918) the Tribunals were under the control of the L.S.R. Steinberg. After his departure they were reor-

ganized so as to consist of three members, one of whom came from the
local Cheka. A supreme Tribunal was attached to VTsIK and Tribunals
were set up in the large towns. There was no right of appeal and the
presence of the accused depended on the Tribunal's decision. The People's Courts were more slowly organized, and much of their work, to
begin with, was done by the Tribunals. They maintained offices in the
local Chekas ('Kameri narodnogo suda pri Che Ka') presumably because the Cheka found itself occasionally able to unload on to them
some of the many minor, non-political, cases which it investigated.

There were many attempts to hand back to the Tribunals some of
the judicial powers which the Cheka had assumed from the first days
of the Terror. None of these attempts had any lasting effect. The Cheka
set up its own three-man courts or 'Troiki', which in April 1918 were reported to have delivered sentences on 400 anarchists in Moscow. At one
period VeCheKa had a 'Special Revolutionary Tribunal' attached to it
for dealing with speculators and officials who committed breach of duty.
It was decreed that this Tribunal be 'guided in its judgments only by
revolutionary interests, and not bound by any forms of legal procedure'.
It was sometimes presided over by Dzerzhinsky. Even the ordinary Revolutionary Tribunals were liable to have Chekists as their president (Peters
was for a time president of the Moscow Tribunal, and Latsis of the Military Tribunal of the Fifth Army.) The Cheka worked in co-operation
with, or was directly represented on, a number of other Tribunals and
semi-judicial organs which at one time or another were empowered to
impose the death penalty. Military Tribunals, Field Court Martials and
Commissions for combating desertion seem to have worked with the
Cheka's 'special departments' in the armed forces. Railway Tribunals
worked with the Cheka's transport departments. At the beginning of
1920 the Cheka's internal security troops ('Vokhr') set up a new system
of Military Tribunals. In May 1920 the Cheka was officially given the
same powers as Revolutionary Tribunals when dealing with any crime
'directed against the security of the State'. As late as June 1921 its powers
to carry out 'extra-legal repression' in areas under martial law were confirmed. In March 1920 the Cheka was permitted to despatch persons
to forced labour camps by administrative decision for up to five years,
if their investigations did not 'reveal sufficient evidence' for the Tribunals
to start judicial proceedings.

It is impossible to gauge with any accuracy the number of victims
of the Cheka's terror. The figures of Cheka shootings and imprisonings
given by Latsis are obviously far too small. He did not even bother to
add them up correctly, and they are contradicted by other official figures.
The figures produced by the Whites are even more obviously far too
large. According to Denikin, 'the Special Judiciary Commission of Inquiry into the Bolshevik atrocities' reckoned the number of victims of

the Bolshevist terror in 1918–19 at 1,700,000. 'But', admitted Denikin, 'their actual number is known to God alone.' Though the terror appears to have got into its stride only during the autumn of 1918, the United States Consul in Moscow reported back on September 3 that 'since May' the Cheka had 'conducted an openly avowed campaign of terror', and that 'thousands of persons' had been 'summarily shot without even the form of trial'. The Petrograd papers had in fact the same day reported the execution of over 500 hostages for the murder of Uritsky, while at least 417 persons were reported to have been shot in connection with the Yaroslavl rising in June. The savagery increased as the Civil War went on, and the Cheka was its chief agent on the Bolshevik side. Latsis already in August had announced that there were no laws in civil war except one, according to which enemy wounded should be shot and no prisoners should be taken. Countless victims fell to the special Cheka troops ('Vokhr' or 'Vnus') which carried out punitive expeditions and raids throughout the war, and also assisted in suppressing the Kronstadt rebellion, and, later, the Antonov peasant rising in Tambov. W. H. Chamberlin gave as his 'probably moderate estimate' the figure of 50,000 for those shot by the Cheka during the Civil War.

According to all accounts the Tribunals had a far smaller share than the Cheka in the terror, yet the available evidence (which is probably more reliable than that concerning the Cheka) concerning their activity is impressive. Even after the end of the Civil War, during the first half of 1921, the Tribunals are stated to have been passing death sentences at the rate of over 100 a month, and prison sentences at the rate of nearly 1,600 a month. Nearly 150,000 arrests were made by the organs of the Commissariat of Justice (i.e., by the Tribunals and the People's Courts) in the first half of 1919. The prisons of the Commissariat in February 1919 held 22,000 persons, 16,794 of whom still had their cases under investigation. Nearly half of these cases were being investigated by the Cheka, and the rest by the Tribunals or People's Courts.

The end of the Civil War placed new responsibilities on the Cheka, particularly in the economic sphere. It is uncertain when the 'Economic Administration' of VeCheKa was first established, but, according to Latsis, it was one of the three main departments of the Central Cheka in 1921 and was responsible for 'combating counter-revolution in the economy'. Inter-departmental commissions consisting of representatives from important economic Commissariats and other organs were attached to VeCheKa to co-ordinate the battle against 'contrabanding and profiteering'. When the granting of concessions to foreign countries for the development of economic resources was discussed at the Eighth Congress of Soviets in December 1920, a delegate proposed that these operations should be controlled, on the political side by the Cheka and the Party, and on the economic side by the Cheka and Rabkrin. The Cheka would no doubt have been permitted to assume these responsibilities if anything had come of the concessions at this time. Though Lenin eventually proclaimed the necessity of restricting its activities to the political sphere, a Party resolution only a few months earlier had called for the Cheka's assistance to control economic life under the N.E.P. regulations and to organize a new export trade.

The terror which the Cheka had practised during the Civil War, in order 'to defend the revolution and conquer the enemy', was scarcely modified by the arrival of peace. As it became more difficult to know whether it was striking friend or foe, the Cheka appears to have cared less, and to have relied on sentencing suspect groups to death or imprisonment *en bloc* for imaginary crimes of which the Cheka 'investigators' conceived them to be capable. Many of the techniques developed by the Okhrana for the purpose of keeping the population under surveillance were adopted, but appear to have been employed with far less discrimination. The direction of this activity lay in the 'secret-political department,' evidently the kernel of VeCheKa, which surveilled both civilian life and (through the 'special departments') the army. That the suppression of religious organizations was also a task in which the department interested itself, is suggested by the fact that the 'Troiki' established in the 'Guberniya' Soviets, to enforce the Decree (of January 23, 1918) on the separation of the Church from the State, consisted of a Chekist and two local officials.

One of the hardest things to establish about the development of the Cheka is the real nature and strength of the opposition it aroused from Bolsheviks as well as non-Bolsheviks, and how smoothly the imposition of the police system was effected. The first active opposition came from Steinberg, the L.S.R. Commissar of Justice in the coalition Sovnarcom which the L.S.R.s entered on December 23, 1917, and left on March 15, 1918. Steinberg used his position to countermand Cheka instructions and attempt to impose legal restrictions on its activities. But these moves were speedily checked by the Bolshevik majority in Sovnarcom. The role of the L.S.R.s in the Cheka itself is more ambiguous. The L.S.R. policy with regard to the Cheka, as explained by Steinberg, was to try to transform it into a 'technical service' at the disposal of the organs of justice and thus to avert the Bolshevik terror, from which the LS.R.s, he claimed, totally disassociated themselves (notably in their leader Spiridonova's open letter to the Bolsheviks of November 1918, which contrasted the 'classical', social revolutionary conception of terror with that of the Bolshevik Party). It was with this aim in view that the Party sought admission to the Cheka and, after overcoming strong opposition from Lenin, were given places in it. Though this account is more convincing than the Bolshevik one, according to which the L.S.R.s were invited to participate in the Cheka by Dzerzhinsky as personal friends and immediately betrayed his trust by undermining its work in order to discredit the Bolsheviks, it is doubtful whether the L.S.R.s ever had an effective policy at all. Their participation in the Cheka was as much a political blunder as their murder of Mirbach and their miniature protest 'rising' in July which led to their being outlawed.

On the occasions on which they were permitted to express their criticism of the regime, the other non-Bolshevik Socialist parties continued to denounce the Cheka. At the Seventh Congress of Soviets in December 1919, Martov protested at the Cheka's 'monstrous growth' (by 1921 it numbered, according to Latsis, 31,000, whereas the N.K.V.D., an important Commissariat even then, reported that it numbered only 2,823). At the Eighth Congress in December 1920, Dan accused it of giving orders to VTsIK about the persons to whom amnesties should be granted. On both these occasions Lenin ridiculed the charges and the Mensheviks who had formulated them. Prominent among the accusations brought against the Bolsheviks by the Kronstadt insurgents of March 1921 was that of having 'brought the workers, instead of freedom, an ever present fear of being dragged into the torture chambers of the Cheka, which exceeds by many times in its horrors the gendarmerie administration of the Tsarist regime.'

The protests of foreigners against the Cheka's terror only provided opportunities for Bolshevik propagandists to practise their skill in polemical writing. Chicherin set a high standard in September 1918 in his replies to the protest delivered on behalf of the Diplomatic Corps in Moscow by the Swiss Minister and to another by the head of the American Red Cross. Trotsky found his best form in his *Defence of Terrorism* (1921) directed against Kautsky. Lenin took the offensive with his refrain: 'The Entente thrust the Terror upon us.' After the Civil War a greater sensitiveness to foreign opinion about the Cheka seems to have developed, and with it the process of attempting to deceive selected foreigners (such as the British Labour Delegations to Russia) who enquired about it.

There was, however, a good deal of internal resistance to the Cheka which could not immediately be discredited as counter-revolutionary. When the central Cheka first enlisted the help of the local Soviets, in March 1918, in setting up local Chekas, the plan seems to have been that the Soviets were to retain a measure of control over them. This was at any rate the view of the N.K.V.D., which was the co-ordinating Commissariat in charge of the Soviets, and which through them already controlled the Militia. An N.K.V.D. instruction to the local Soviets in June 1918, signed by Latsis (who, before becoming a Chekist, began his career in the N.K.V.D.) requested them to organize an administrative department ('Otdel upravleniya') consisting of three sub-departments ('Podotdeli'): Information, Militia and Cheka. But the subordination of the Chekas to the local Soviets was never effected. Relations between them became very strained when both the N.K.V.D. and VeCheKa sent conflicting instructions to the local Soviets, and when the heads of local Chekas and Soviets attempted to arrest each other. At the first conference of representatives of 'Guberniya' Soviets in August 1918 a resolution was passed which formally demanded that the local Chekas be reduced to the status of sub-departments of the Soviets. VeCheKa immediately denounced the resolution and issued instructions to the Chekas to maintain their 'autonomy'.

On October 18 *Pravda* published an article by Dukhovsky, Secretary of the N.K.V.D. collegium, in which he asserted that the relations between the Chekas and the Soviets was one of the most burning questions of the day. The struggle for power between them was sometimes being urged under the slogan, 'All power to the Chekas!' This slogan would replace 'All power to the Soviets!' if the Chekas were not effectively subordinated to the Soviets. *Izvestiya* on October 17, in view of 'the recent press campaign against the activity of the Cheka, and the suggestion that it should be subordinated to a Commissariat', interviewed the Chekist, Peters. Peters was reported as saying: 'In vain do many naive comrades think that the time has come to limit the Cheka's activities. . . . All this noise and lamentation about the energetic and firm measures of the Cheka does not deserve the attention it is given; it could only come from comrades who are occupied in journalism in offices and not in actively fighting the enemies of the proletariat.' This provoked an indignant reply from Olminsky, who remarked that Lenin himself had spent a lot of time occupied in journalism in offices which had not been unprofitable for the proletariat; and from Tikhomirov, in *Izvestiya,* on behalf of the N.K.V.D. The N.K.V.D. it appeared, had sent a circular round the local Soviets requesting their views on relations with the Chekas. Out of 147 replies to this circular, 118 had favoured the subordination of the Chekas to the Soviets. But the opinion of the Soviets, no matter its degree of unanimity, counted little in the councils of the Bolshevik Party, and when the Cheka's powers were 'discussed' by VTsIK in the autumn of 1918 (unfortunately no record of the proceedings appears to be available), the only result was the 'Statutes' of the Cheka, which provided that it should do no more than 'work in close contact with the N.K.V.D.' Friction between the two organs continued for a while, but must finally have subsided after the appointment of Dzerzhinsky in 1920 as head of the N.K.V.D. as well as the Cheka.

Perhaps the most serious threat to the consolidation of the Cheka came from those who wished to see its functions performed by the Revolutionary Tribunals. The Commissar of Justice, Kursky, alleged that 'the wide distribution of Chekas throughout every "Uyezd" of Soviet Russia at the end of 1918 created a natural reaction against the lawless character of their activity, and this was expressed in a quite violent controversy, in the press and at Party meetings, between the partisans of the Tribunals and those of the Cheka.'

The foremost representative of this opposition to the Cheka was Krylenko, who, though his post was that of Chief Prosecutor of the Supreme Tribunal, carried more weight than the Commissar of Justice. Both Latsis and Peters refer (without adverse comment, for Krylenko's reputation was unassailable till the purges of the late thirties) to Krylenko as a persistent critic of the Cheka. It was apparently he who brought about the discussion on the Cheka's powers in VTsIK, and who, according to an American journalist, became known in Moscow as the man who had 'curbed the powers of the Cheka'. His wife, Razmirovitch, also a prominent figure in the Tribunals, is said by Steinberg to have been of assistance in Steinberg's own brief campaign against the Cheka. What is known about Krylenko suggests that he did not oppose the Cheka on account of its 'lawlessness' (though this may have been Kursky's motive) but because he was jealous of a rival system.

Presumably as a result of pressure from Krylenko, numerous Decrees were passed during 1918–21 defining and re-defining the division of responsibility between the Tribunals and the Cheka; but whatever ground the Tribunals gained during the less bloodthirsty periods of the intervention and civil war the Cheka more than made up in times of crisis. Even the transformation of the Cheka into the G.P.U. in 1923, represented at the time as a triumph for the principle of 'revolutionary legality', did nothing to strengthen the position of the courts *vis à vis* the police; and Vyshinsky was bold enough to advance the opinion that the difference between the courts and the O.G.P.U. 'followed the same line' as that which had existed between the Tribunals and the Cheka.

The Tribunals made most headway against the Cheka early in 1919. In January the 'Uyezd' Chekas were abolished; and this, according to Moroz, had been taken by 'some comrades' as a victory in the campaign against the Cheka. (Such comrades must have been disillusioned when it was revealed that these Chekas had not been abolished at all, but simply disguised as 'political departments' in the 'Uyezd' Militia.) In February a Decree was passed, according to which, 'The power of pronouncing sentences in all cases arising in the Chekas is handed over to reorganized Tribunals.' The Tribunals were also permitted to check investigations by the Cheka and to inspect its prisons and free those who had been illegally confined in them. 'Direct punishments' were henceforward to be administered by the Cheka only in areas under martial law. Only a few months later Kursky sorrowfully admitted that it had not been possible to implement 'the humane principles' of this Decree, due to 'the realities of the savage Civil War'. But Krylenko was able to celebrate at least one genuine triumph over the Cheka, and over Dzerzhinsky personally, at the trial in the middle of February by the Supreme Revolutionary Tribunal of the Chekist Kosarev.

Kosarev, according to the report of the trial, had been sentenced to ten years 'katorga' in 1908 for murder and robbery. After the revolution he had secured his release by pretending he had been a 'political', and obtained a job with VeCheKa. In September 1918 Dzerzhinsky had personally appointed him Assistant Chairman of VeCheKa's Control and Inspection Commission, which received and investigated all complaints about illegal actions by Chekists and Soviet officials. He was now on trial, charged with having used his position to extort large sums of money, which had enabled him to lead a luxurious life—according to his own confession he had accumulated 100,000 roubles in the International Bank of Chicago. It appeared that Chekists such as Kosarev were in the habit of accepting bribes from the relatives of persons held under investigation, to transfer cases to the Tribunals. Dzerzhinsky attended the trial in support of Kosarev. He objected to details about the Cheka's work being made public, and characterized Kosarev as 'an experienced and conscientious investigator', denying any knowledge of his criminal past, and hoped he would 'not be sacrificed in the struggle of political passions which has centred round the Cheka'. Krylenko, who appeared as prosecutor (and had probably managed the trial from the start), denied the accusation, in Dzerzhinsky's last remark, that he was more interested in discrediting the Cheka than in Kosarev's innocence of guilt; and demanded that Kosarev be shot and the Cheka purged of all such Chekists, 'who disgraced the revolution'. Kosarev's defence vainly cited the absence of any Decree authorizing the use of the death penalty; he was sentenced to be shot. Not the least part of Krylenko's triumph must have been that *Pravda* carried full reports of the trial which ran over four days.

But Krylenko's victory in the Kosarev case and in other less important ones, reported about the same time, in which Chekists were successfully prosecuted by Tribunals, was small compensation for his failure to appropriate, for any length of time, for the Tribunals any of the Cheka's powers. This failure appears to have rankled long after, judging by the tendentious account of relations between the Tribunals and the Cheka which Krylenko contributed to the Encyclopaedia of State and Law (published under Stuchka's editorship in 1925–7). The account based the Tribunals' claim to perform the Cheka's functions not on any necessity to impose legal restrictions on the terror—there is no suggestion of this—but simply on the alleged fact that these functions had originally been assigned to them and not to the Cheka, which had merely taken advantage of certain regrettable weaknesses in the initial structure of the Tribunals to substitute itself for them as the instrument of the terror.

Krylenko's story, and particularly his explanation of how the Tribunals came to 'yield' their role to the Cheka, is not convincing. He confuses rather than strengthens it by the unusual assertion that the Cheka was founded (for what purpose he does not say) 'long before' the Tribunals, by a Decree of November 2 (November 15, New Style), and that the original text of the 'Decree No. 1 on the Courts' had defined the Tribunals as 'organs for combating counter-revolution'. Perhaps all that can be learned from his account is the extent to which, even in the early years of the regime, the facts of Soviet history were at the mercy of Bolshevik personalities who desired to give it a particular slant.

Not only did the Cheka have to reckon with the opposition of other governmental bodies, which, like the Tribunals or the N.K.V.D. directly blocked the way to its expansion, or which, like the army and the economic Commissariats, resented its incursions into their fields of operation and the arbitrary arrests which deprived them of their personnel; it also could not at first afford to neglect popular feeling.

The Cheka's difficulty lay in the fact that, from the outset, it was obvious that it met the hostility of the very proletariat on whose behalf is was supposedly wielding the terror. Moroz described how during 1918, 'the Chekas came to be considered as something superfluous and even harmful to our revolution. Matters went so far that Chekists were called "inquisitors" and "okhranists". The Chekas themselves were called "torture chambers", "Bastilles", etc.' 'An atmosphere was created', confessed Latsis, 'which killed any desire to work in this necessary organ of state power.' It is uncertain to what extent this abhorence of the Cheka may have been shared by some members of the Bolshevik Party. But at the end of 1918, during the short period when the Cheka was subjected to 'criticism and self-criticism', it came under the fire of a prominent Bolshevik journalist, Olminsky. Olminsky was permitted to write in *Pravda* that there were differences of opinion in the Party, whether and how far the arrests and executions carried out by the Cheka were really necessary, and that he was 'appalled' that under the existing Cheka regulations the local Chekas could shoot nearly any Party member they wished. In another *Pravda* article he protested at the 'scandalous' and 'inhuman' behaviour of a local Cheka at Nikolsk which had stripped and flogged a number of peasants.

Latsis and Peters made a clumsy attempt to explain away the hostility to the Cheka by arguing that its purpose had been misunderstood by the proletariat, who had naively failed to distinguish between its methods and those of their old oppressor, the Okhrana. They further asserted that while the proletariat had boycotted the Cheka, criminals in disguise had managed to slip into its service and 'made use of the title of Chekist agent to blackmail, extort, and fill their pockets'. It was these criminals, and not genuine Chekists, who were responsible for the worst

outrages. For good measure, Latsis also suggested that even genuine
Chekists might be forgiven an occasional lapse, for: 'No matter how
honest and crystal clear a man may be, the work of the Cheka, which is
carried out with almost unrestricted powers and in circumstances which
are exceptionally trying for his nerves, will tell upon him. Only in rare
cases do Chekists remain unaffected by these conditions of work.' These
arguments can have deceived no one, particularly after Dzerzhinsky's
defence of the criminal Chekist, Kosarev, and after a report by a local
Cheka had announced that it had recruited an ex-Okhrana officer as an
agent. (Recruiting of senior Chekists seems to have been carried out at
first by Dzerzhinsky on a personal basis; later it was increasingly staffed
by Party members of several years standing, and they were posted to
and from the Cheka by the Orgbureau of the Central Committee, established in March 1919 and dominated by Stalin. Recruiting of agents and
informers was left to the discretion of the local Chekas.)

By the end of 1918 it was necessary for Lenin to come to the support of the Cheka and he did so by accusing its critics of insufficient
Marxism. The report of his speech shows it to have been an uninspired
performance: '. . . naturally the mistakes of the Cheka attract attention
most of all. A narrow-minded intelligentsia is seizing on these mistakes
without wishing to go further to the root of the matter. What surprises
me about the howls over the Cheka's mistakes is the inability to take a
large view of the question. We have people who seize on particular mistakes by the Cheka, sob and fuss over them. . . . The trouble, of course,
lies not in the Cheka personnel, but in the nature of their activity, which
requires decisiveness, speed and, above all, trustworthiness. When I consider the Cheka's activity and compare it with these attacks, I say: this
is narrow-minded, idle talk which is worthless. . . . Marx said: between
capitalism and communism lies the revolutionary dictatorship of the proletariat. The more the proletariat crushes the bourgeoisie the more furi-
ously will it strike back. . . . When we are reproached with cruelty, we
wonder how people can forget the most elementary Marxism. . . . It
is quite understandable that alien elements should attach themselves
to the Cheka. We will knock them off by self-criticism. The important
thing for us is that the Chekas are directly carrying out the dictatorship
of the proletariat, and in this respect their role is invaluable. . . .'

At about the same time Lenin publicly corrected one of the chief
exponents of the terror, Latsis, whom he was nevertheless careful to describe as 'one of the best, experienced communists', for pushing 'elementary Marxism' too far in the terror. Latsis had urged his subordinates
not to seek for evidence that their prisoners had opposed the Soviets,
but to settle their fate on the basis of their class, origin, education and
occupation, for this was 'the meaning and essence of the Red Terror'.
Lenin announced that this was 'rubbish', and that what Latsis had really

wished to say was only that: 'the Red Terror is a forcible suppression of the exploiters who attempt to restore their power.'

In this way Lenin apparently hoped to bring to heel both 'rightist' and 'leftist' deviators on the subject of the Terror, without making clear how the Marxism which he quoted at them guided the work of the Cheka in practice, or whom precisely the Terror was directed against.

It was necessary to keep the connection between Marxism and the Cheka vague, in order to represent the latter's function as the waging of war against counter-revolutionaries according to Marxist principles, when in reality it was concerned with holding together the Bolshevist regime by the indiscriminate application of force whenever and wherever expedient. The further extension of the Cheka's activities after the end of the Civil War was accounted for by another fiction: the necessity for the Cheka to carry on its fight on a broader front against counter-revolutionaries who had only been forced underground, not annihilated, and had infiltrated and disguised their forces throughout the state apparatus. Latsis wrote in 1921: 'In all spheres of our life the counter-revolution has developed. It is therefore obvious that the work of VeCheKa must cover all spheres of Soviet life where counter-revolution has roots. And this means that there is no sphere of life not covered by the activity of VeCheKa. It must watch everything: military life, food, education, positively all economic organs, health, outbreaks of fire, communications, etc.'

But by the end of 1921, Lenin found it necessary to attempt a more ambitious deception concerning the police. He told the Ninth Congress of Soviets: 'Our failings are sometimes continuations of our virtues. This is the case with VeCheKa. It was virtuous when it defended the revolution against countless foreign enemies, when it was our striking weapon against countless plots. . . . But now, under present circumstances, it is imperative to restrict this institution to the purely political sphere. We say definitely that it is necessary to reform VeCheKa.' The Congress duly noted 'the heroic work of VeCheKa in the Civil War', and considered that the strengthening of Soviet authority, both internal and external, permitted the sphere of VeCheKa's activities to be narrowed down, and judicial organs to be made responsible for carrying out the fight against infractions of the law. In February 1922 the Cheka was replaced by the G.P.U. Events quickly demonstrated that nothing concerning the police except its name had been changed, but the myth of its constitutional respectability was now firmly emplanted in Soviet propaganda.

13 /

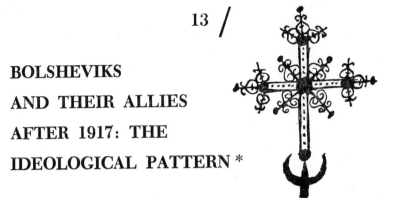

BOLSHEVIKS
AND THEIR ALLIES
AFTER 1917: THE
IDEOLOGICAL PATTERN *

In comparison with most new ruling groups that have appeared in history, the Bolsheviks made what seemed to be a remarkably thorough sweep of opposition and dissent in their first years of power in Russia, reaching the state of "monolithic unity," so often mentioned by party leaders, with extraordinary speed. But the thoroughness and the speed were only relative, as Dr. Utechin shows: although the revolutions of 1917 produced an abrupt and radical change in Russian historical development, they did not produce a fully developed ruling class in one, or even two, strokes. The creation of the much vaunted state of "monolithic unity" (characterized by the absence of opposition, dissent, and even debate) was an extended and complex process.

INTRODUCTION

THE PETROGRAD coup on 7 November 1917 and the series of more or less similar coups that followed throughout the country, brought to power in Russia the Bolshevik Party, 'a party of a new type', designed and trained by its creator and leader in such a way as to achieve as complete as possible a domination over the life of the country. Yet the victorious and now dominant party was by no means in all respects such as Lenin would have wished. One of the most important aspects in which the party differed from Lenin's idea was its lack of ideological unity. Far from being single-minded in matters of ideology, the party

* S. V. Utechin, "Bolsheviks and Their Allies after 1917: The Ideological Pattern," *Soviet Studies,* X (October, 1958), 113–35. Reprinted by permission of the author and the publisher.

The author is Senior Research Officer in Soviet Studies at the London School of Economics and Political Science. He is the author of *Everyman's Concise Encyclopedia of Russia* (1961).

members exhibited a remarkable variety of views; the differences ranged from those of emphasis to serious conflicts of outlook.

Moreover, the Bolshevik party was not running the country alone. In the civilian, military and economic administration, as well as in the field of propaganda, the Bolsheviks made use of persons and groups ideologically alien to themselves, but possessing the particular skills required for this or that function, who were for whatever reason prepared to collaborate with them. In those days recognition of the practical usefulness of such persons or groups was accompanied by a certain degree of toleration for their general views.

However, despite this toleration of heterodoxy within and without the party ranks, there was the ever-present tendency to impose the official ideology, and the obstacles in the path of those who might wish to give expression to a coherent system of unorthodox views were many and often insurmountable. It is therefore difficult to discover exactly what went on in the minds of those who made up what might be called the class of Lenin's collaborators, i.e. all those who had some position of power or influence in the apparatus of the Bolshevik dictatorship in its widest sense.

Nevertheless, certain trends and tendencies of thought are clearly distinguishable. They were mostly continuations of pre-1917 ideological traditions and their sub-divisions. There were the various branches of the Marxist tree: Leninism, Bogdanovism, Social-Democratism, and the singular offshoot of Makhayevism; there were Populism in its two main forms, radical and moderate (Neo-Populism), and Anarchism; there was the ideology of industrial managers and technicians—Technocratism; the etatist ideology in its new form of National Bolshevism; and finally the eccentric development of religious thought, Fyodorovism. In what follows we shall briefly consider in turn the roots, the main representatives and variations, the institutionalized forms (if any) and the fates of these ten trends of thought. No attempt is made to deal fully with Leninism, only such aspects of it being stressed as illuminate its distinction from the other Marxist trends.

LENINISM

The officially prevailing ideology was, of course, Leninism. In an article on the occasion of Lenin's fiftieth birthday in 1920, Stalin described Leninists as that group of Marxists which 'switches the centre of gravity of the problem from the outward recognition of Marxism to its implementation, its transmutation into life. Designing ways and means of realizing Marxism which correspond to circumstances, changing these ways and means when circumstances change—that is what this group principally pays attention to', he wrote. Accordingly, the complex of accepted ideas of this group contained a small number of basic propositions of Marxian social philosophy in a dogmatic and slogan-like form, and a large body of Lenin's ideas on organization and tactics for the conquest and maintenance of power by the party—an exposition of which falls outside the scope of this article. According to Stalin, many practitioners of Leninism did not particularly love theory; the practitioners (he said) tended to brush the theory aside.

When they did interest themselves in theory, it was Leninism rather than Marxism. The writings of Lenin himself, Stalin, Zinoviev and other Leninists were concentrated on current political problems which were analysed in terms of Lenin's organizational and tactical principles and of past experience in their application. When other subjects were treated, they were also related to the central subject of power—(the famous demand for 'partyness' in philosophy, literature, etc.). Virtuosity in political thinking and practice contrasts sharply with the crude and elementary ideas and forms in other fields. In education their attention was concentrated on liquidating illiteracy and on the superficial acquisition by broad masses of the people of the current Leninist slogans (Krupskaya was made the head of the 'Political Enlightenment' department of the Commissariat of Education); in the arts—such things as pulling down old monuments in the principal towns and replacing them by statues of revolutionaries quickly produced on government orders (known officially as 'monumental propaganda'!); in literature—the propagation of Demyan Bedny's utilitarian verses. Economic problems were treated, apart from the political, from a peculiar technological point of view—the technician and the bookkeeper personified for the Leninists economic wisdom. In accordance with the guiding principle of Leninist ethics—'morality is what serves the destruction of the old society of exploiters, and the uniting of all toilers around the proletariat which is creating the new society of communists'—practical morals were thought to be best based upon considerations of political expediency.

It was this system of ideas that largely dominated the Bolshevik party training and party propaganda in Lenin's lifetime, and still more so after his death. As Stalin consolidated his power, the ideological field was ever more exclusively occupied by the basic tenets of Leninism until, in the thirties, merged with National Bolshevism and hero worship, they produced Stalinism.

BOGDANOVISM

The second strongest ideology (in the degree to which it was able to express itself, in the influence it had upon official policy and in the organizational facilities at its disposal) among the former revolutionaries after 1917 was undoubtedly Bogdanovism in the broadest sense. This seems to be the most appropriate name for the trend of which A. A. Bogdanov (Malinovski) was the leading representative and which had originated in the realization, at the beginning of the century, by some of the leading young Marxists that the 'revisionists' both in Russia and abroad were right when they attacked orthodox Marxism for its philosophical insufficiency. This realization prompted Bogdanov and his friends to seek a better epistemological foundation for the Marxian system, and they believed they had found it in the teaching of Mach and Avenarius. This Russian brand of a blending of Marxism and Empiriocriticism found its first literary expression in a symposium 'Essays in Realistic Philosophy', published in 1904. Between 1904 and 1909 the adherents of this ideology vigorously pursued their theoretical investigations, finding more and more obsolete elements and gaps in the Marxian doctrine, and trying to replace them and fill the gaps by modern ideas or by products of their own thought. Thus, apart from several related epistemological systems (Bogdanov's Empiriomonism, P. S. Yushkevich's Empirio-symbolism), they developed a new logic instead of the obsolete Marxian dialectics (Ya. A. Berman), a new ontology (Bogdanov's Tectology, or 'universal organizational science' with extensive sociological content), ethics (S. Volski's 'Philosophy of Struggle'), and finally, a new religious teaching (A. V. Lunacharski and M. Gorki). The new trend was extended to literary criticism by V. M. Shulyatikov, Lunacharski and P. I. Lebedev-Polyanski, and to the study of history by M. N. Pokrovski. At the same time all these people considered themselves as Marxists and Social-Democrats, and most of them were among the leading members of the Bolshevik faction; so much that Plekhanov held Bogdanovism to be the official philosophy of Bolshevism, and accused Lenin of philosophical indifference and betrayal of Marxism. After 1909 Bogdanovism (in the broad sense in which we are here using this term) was the official ideology of the 'Vperyod' sub-faction, and after the latter's disintegration, of its Geneva group. After the break with the Leninists, the attention of Bogdanov, Lunacharski and their followers was concentrated on problems of creating, in conscious opposition to the existing bourgeois culture, a distinct 'proletarian culture'. Lunacharski and Lebedev-Polyanski nursed in the emigration a group of talented 'proletarian poets' from among genuine workers.

In 1917 most Bogdanovists (notable exceptions being Bogdanov himself and Gorki) again joined the Bolshevik party. Their leader in the party was Lunacharski, who entered the Bolshevik government as Commissar for Education. Lunacharski's popularity was such that he was apparently the only person—apart from Lenin and Trotski—whose appointment as People's Commissar was greeted with applause at the second congress of Soviets. The Commissariat of Education (or rather, 'Enlightenment'—*prosveshcheniye*) had to control and direct all the cultural activities in the state apart from those directly controlled by the party. Lunacharski summarized his views on the main problems confronting him in a pamphlet entitled 'Cultural Tasks of the Working Class', which was published by the VTsIK.

'The socialist culture of the future will be a culture of the whole of mankind', he wrote, 'not of a class, . . . harmonious, . . . of a classical type, where the content . . . developing itself in a healthy organic process receives a completely fitting form. The culture of the struggling proletariat is a sharply isolated class culture built on struggle . . . of a romantic type, where the content, being tensely determined, runs ahead of the form, because there is no time to care for a sufficiently . . . perfect form for this stormy and tragic content'. Common to both cultures was the struggle for the ideal, 'for the blossoming of collectivism of the mass life not on the principles of compulsion or of herdlikeness . . . but . . . on a completely new principle of an organic, or rather, super-organic, free and natural fusion of personalities in a super-personal unity'. The achievements of the proletarian culture so far were: first, the Marxian method; secondly, the gains in the political struggle; thirdly, the achievements in the economic struggle—trade unions and co-operatives; and the fourth form of proletarian culture was the struggle for enlightenment. For further successes the working class had to produce many specialists in intellectual and other cultural work, to create its own intelligentsia. But intellectuals of a non-proletarian background could also join in performing this noble task.

Four days after the seizure of power, on 29 October 1917, Lunacharski issued a declaration on the policy to be pursued by his Commissariat. The main reforms announced included the creation of a comprehensive school system in which schools of all levels, from primary to the university, would be integrated; all schools were to be taken over by local government bodies. In accordance with the original Bogdanovist impulse—to supplement Marxian thinking with modern ideas—the Commissariat of Education under Lunacharski and Pokrovski (who was appointed Deputy Commissar) embarked upon a policy of compulsory introduction into the cultural life of modernist principles: co-education, free education (Dalton Plan) and pupil's participation in the school administration, the labour principle, election of schoolmasters, etc. The department of Higher Education Establishments abolished all educational requirements for matriculation and opened universities and institutes to everybody of sixteen years or over, abolished all degrees, diplomas and state examinations, introduced the participation of students' representatives in all governing bodies, abolished the old faculties of law and replaced them by new faculties of social sciences, established Workers' Faculties, etc. The theatres were soon in the hands of the modernist producer V. Meyerhold in Moscow and Gorki's friend the actress M. F. Andreyeva in Petrograd. In poetry, the Futurists had the full backing of the authorities and were allowed to pose as a quasi-official trend.

When Stalinists finally prevailed in the party leadership, Lunacharski was dismissed from the post of Commissar for Education in 1929, but a radical change in educational policies came only in 1932 when Zhdanov was put in charge of cultural matters and began introducing that blend of Leninism and National Bolshevism which became typical of the cultural aspects of Stalinism. Pokrovski, who had dominated historical research and teaching (as the head of the historical section of the Communist Academy, of the Historical Institute of Red Professorship, the Central Administration of Archives, the Society of Marxist Historians, and finally, after the 'integration' of the Academy of Sciences in 1929, of its Institute of History) remained a deputy commissar for education until his death in 1932.

Apart from the Commissariat of Education, the main organizational centre of Bogdanovism was the so-called *Proletkult*, where the dominant influence was that of Bogdanov himself. Bogdanov's views on the proletarian culture differed from those of Lunacharski. Proletarian culture for him was identical with the culture of the future socialist society. The creation of a proletarian culture was a condition for a real proletarian revolution (in Lenin's view, on the contrary, it was much easier to bring about a 'cultural revolution' after a successful political one), or rather, the most important part of the revolution itself. In its content the proletarian culture must be creative rather than destructive. Cultural organizations of the proletariat must be independent of its political or economic organizations. 'Proletarian Cultural and Education Organizations' (*Proletkult*) were set up in 1917 before the Bolshevik coup. In his declaration on policy after the coup, Lunacharski said that 'the spontaneously created cultural and educational class institutions of workers, soldiers and peasants' were to enjoy full autonomy and be independent both of the central state authorities and the municipal authorities. At a conference convened by Lunacharski in 1918 a Central Committee of the *Proletkult* was elected with the Bogdanovist F. I. Kalinin as Chairman; after his death a few months later, Lebedev-Polyanski took over the office. The organization, which had several tens of thousands of members, managed to maintain its independence until 1919, when it was subordinated to the Commissariat of Education as one of its departments and had to co-ordinate its work with the department of extra-mural education headed by Krupskaya. The direction of the *Proletkult* was transferred to the Central Council of Trade Unions in 1925, and it was abolished altogether in 1932.

There were other forms of organized Bogdanovism. Influenced by Bogdanov's ideas on the organization of social experience, two leading members of the *Proletkult*—P. M. Kerzhentsev and A. K. Gastev—concentrated their energies from the early 1920s on the problems of scientific organization of productive work. Gastev, who had founded and was in charge of the Central Institute of Labour, thought that the first task was to educate in people the will to organizational work; this could be done by first concentrating on the study and organization of the simplest operations, such as blow and pressure. Thus the Institute would be able to train a generation of instructors who would act as 'older brothers' to the rest of the proletariat and help to bring elements of organization into its work. Kerzhentsev, on the other hand, insisted that the main problem was not the organization of the work of an individual but the organization of a whole enterprise, and, further, a planned shaping of the state's policy in its administrative and economic aspects. The concept of scientific organization of labour became identical for him with the concept of building up socialism. Socialism was for Kerzhentsev essentially the scientific organization of labour. In 1923 he and his followers founded the League of Scientific Organization of Labour to counterbalance Gastev's Institute, and after a few weeks it claimed several tens of thousands of members. Like the *Proletkult* itself, the Institute and the League were not abolished until the 1930s.

Another theory of a Bogdanovist kind (supplementing Marxian by modernist ideas) was the Winged Eros theory on the relations between the sexes in the new society put forward by another prominent member of the *Proletkult*, Alexandra Kollontay. She did not advocate, as is often supposed, promiscuity, but held that individuals should be able to associate with different people of the opposite sex for different purposes and according to the attraction of their different traits. Like all Bogdanovist tendencies, this one was gradually suppressed during the 1930s.

SOCIAL-DEMOCRATISM

In the election to the Constituent Assembly at the end of 1917 there were three main Social Democratic lists: those of Plekhanov's 'Unity' group, the official Menshevik party (consisting of former Internationalists and most of the 'revolutionary defencists') headed by Martov and F. Dan, and the group of Defencist Social-Democrats headed by A. N. Potresov. This division was symbolic; throughout the years of Lenin's rule there existed three main Social-Democratic trends among the former revolutionaries, reaching far beyond the limits of the three dwindling party groupings.

The first, Plekhanovist, trend was primarily concerned with the Marxian teaching. Its adherents were mainly engaged in collecting, editing, commenting on and popularizing the writings of Marx, Engels and Plekhanov, as well as in applying their theories to particular philosophical, sociological, literary and artistic problems. They wanted to preserve and propagate the ideas of their teachers in their entirety and purity, thus differing from both Leninists and Bogdanovists. The most prominent representatives of this trend were D. B. Ryazanov, L. I. Akselrod, A. M. Deborin and I. K. Luppol. Ryazanov joined the Bolshevik party, and most of their followers were also in the party. The main organizational centres of Plekhanovism were the Marx-Engels Institute, founded by Ryazanov in 1918, and the Philosophical section of the Socialist (later Communist) Academy established in 1919.

The second, Martovist, trend was not so much interested in Marxian theory itself as in its practical realization through a proletarian socialist revolution. Inasmuch as they thought that the social basis of Lenin's rule was the working class, and that the Leninists—though in a more or less wrong and often quite unpleasant way—were laying the foundations of a socialist order, they were prepared to co-operate with and to defend the Leninist revolution. In this sense, adherents of the Martovist Social-Democratic trend were not only the members of the official 'Centrist' Menshevik party (many of whom, perhaps the majority, joined the Bolsheviks in 1919–21), but also many Bolsheviks who had never had any connections with the official Menshevism. Those who took the Marxian teaching seriously, and wholly accepted it, believed in the historic mission of the proletariat and considered it their duty to make the proletariat fulfil its mission—all these should perhaps more properly be regarded as Martovists, even if they had always been in Lenin's party. They usually had little understanding of problems of power, and equally little interest in them. They were usually dissatisfied with Lenin's terroristic methods as applied to themselves, but justified them in relation to others. Those of them who were in the Menshevik party or who were in the more or less organized oppositions within the Bolshevik party (such as the Democratic Centralism Group or the Workers' Opposition) tried to impress upon the Leninists the necessity of concessions to themselves in order that they should be able to co-operate more effectively.

The third, Potresovist, trend began as a rejection on moral grounds of the principle, shared by Plekhanov and Lenin, of amoralism in politics and of Martov's accommodating attitude, for reasons of expediency, towards immoral practices of which he in principle disapproved. After the 1905 revolution it developed into a rejection of the official party view on the workers' legal organizations as merely a tool for furthering the party's ends. This was the starting point of the policy of 'liquidationism'. During the world war 'liquidationism' became 'defencism'. In 1917 and after the Bolshevik coup, quite logically, the problems of preserving and regaining democratic freedoms came to the forefront of Potresov's and his friends' political thinking. They had no illusions about the Leninist policy and sharply attacked the Martovists for having such illusions. They also recognized the reasons for the latter's illusions—the Martovists' clinging to the obsolete concepts of Marxist propaganda (Potresov's impression of the Menshevik conference in December 1917 was summarized in two words—'Dead souls!'). Reformist in their approach to practical problems before 1917, they were tempted to try the same approach under Lenin, particularly after the introduction of the NEP. They were mostly concentrated in co-operatives, then also in the trade unions and economic organs (V. G. Groman was one of the key figures in Gosplan). Even among the Bolsheviks there were people with almost Potresov's views, e.g., G. I. Myasnikov and his group. But not all Potresovists considered the reformist approach appropriate in conditions of Lenin's rule; many placed their hopes on a more or less distant new anti-Bolshevik revolution.

The fate of these three Social-Democratic trends was similar. Their respective leaders died (Plekhanov, 1918) or emigrated (Martov, 1920; Potresov, 1925) and the trends themselves were broken up in 1930, the former as a result of Stalin's intervention in the philosophical discussion of that year and the latter two in consequence of the Menshevik trial. Some adherents of these Social-Democratic trends were able to work in the Society of Old Bolsheviks or the Society of Former Political Hard Labour Prisoners and Exiles until these societies were dissolved in 1935.

MAKHAYEVISM

The flooding in 1917 and after of the ranks of the Bolshevik party with large numbers of unskilled workers, soldiers, agricultural labourers and urban *déclassés* greatly strengthened yet another ideology that had for long existed on the fringes of the party—Makhayevism. This ideology was given a systematic form by a former Polish Social-Democrat, Makhaiski (J. W. Machajski) while in banishment in Siberia in 1898–1900, though the anti-intellectual bias which was fundamental to it had been known in Russian Social-Democracy from its earliest beginnings. Another theorist of Makhayevism was E. Lozinski.

Makhayevist theory was an attempt, starting from the basic conceptions of orthodox Marxism, to find an answer to the question of the place occupied in the social organism by the intelligentsia. In Makhaiski's view, knowledge is a kind of means of production, and its possession by the intelligentsia means that the latter is a separate social class. In the process of production and distribution the intelligentsia appropriates a part of the surplus value; hence it is an exploiting class. This is the main thesis of Makhayevism. The interests of the intelligentsia are therefore opposed to the interests of the proletariat and the 'Socialist' phraseology of the intelligentsia is merely a device in the struggle for its own interests. It wants to use the proletariat for the socialization of the means of material production, which would then be managed by the intelligentsia without interference from the capitalists. But the intelligentsia does not want to 'socialize knowledge', the means of intellectual production; rather, they want to preserve it in their own monopolistic possession. Thus Socialism is the 'class ideal' of the intelligentsia, which wants to replace capitalists and to concentrate in its hands all means of domination over the proletariat. The proletariat, on the other hand, must strive to 'socialize knowledge' by removing the inequality of opportunity for acquiring it, and the practical way to this is the abolition of inheritance of any property. The proletariat must also make it impossible for the intelligentsia to appropriate surplus value—by a levelling of incomes. Everybody must receive the same remuneration for his work.

We do not need to go here into the Makhayevist views on the organization and tactics which the proletariat should adopt in order to achieve a Makhayevist revolution—they are basically syndicalist. But it is interesting to note that, until such a revolution, they expected the 'hungry masses' to be tempted to use every opportunity to destroy as much as possible of 'those cursed goods which they endlessly create and which are always taken away by the masters', and approved of such destruction. And the seizure of power by the proletariat would be used for seizing the property of the educated society, of the 'learned world'.

It is easy to see to what extent Makhayevist ideas influenced the thinking and behaviour of a large section of the Bolshevik party after 1917. They were the core of all the 'intellectual-baiting' tendencies. Moreover, they greatly influenced early Bolshevik legislation and party policy, whatever the explanations given at the time for various measures may have been. The first law on inheritance abolished inheritance altogether and merely provided (as a temporary measure until the full development of social security schemes) for a limited use of an estate for the maintenance of the unemployed relatives of the deceased. The attempts to introduce a maximum salary for party members not exceeding the earnings of a skilled worker were also, at least partly, due to the influence of Makhayevist ideas, as was the policy of the resettlement of workers into the houses and flats of the bourgeoisie and intellectuals, and vice versa. The Makhayevist cultural nihilism and vandalism were also characteristic of the outlook of many party members.

The Makhayevist trend was fashionable in the party, despite half-hearted reproofs from the party authorities, until 1936, when Stalin declared that the intellectual-baiting of the Makhayevists must no longer be applied to the new Soviet intelligentsia.

ANARCHISM

Anarchism was formally recognized by the Bolsheviks as an allied political trend during the 1917 revolution and the first period after the seizure of power. Anarchists, who in 1917 organized themselves in the Federation of Anarchist Groups, joined several Soviets and were influential in one of the most important of them—in Kronstadt, where they were as active as the Bolsheviks in undermining the authority of the Provisional Government. They took an active part in the latter's overthrow—there were four Anarchists in the Military Revolutionary Committee in Petrograd—and in the dispersal of the Constituent Assembly. The squad of sailors which dispersed the Assembly was commanded by an Anarchist, V. Zheleznyakov. Individual Anarchists went further and worked in the organs of the new regime (for example, A. Ge was a member of the VTsIK, later vice-chairman of the Cheka in Pyatigorsk). But the Anarchists' attitude towards the Bolsheviks was necessarily ambivalent, and already in 1918 some of them turned against the Bolshevik dictatorship while others continued to co-operate during at least a part of the Civil War (N. I. Makhno). Anarcho-Syndicalists (whose main theorist in Russia was D. I. Novomirski) in particular tried to co-operate with the Bolsheviks in what might be called the Martovite fashion, that is, co-operating in practice while offering ideological opposition. Until his death in 1921, Prince P. A. Kropotkin, the theorist of Anarcho-Communism, was one of the main living 'personifications of the Revolution', as it were, and as such he was useful to the Bolsheviks from the propaganda point of view. Anarchist organizations were finally suppressed in 1921, following the Kronstadt uprising, and only in the Society of Former Political Hard Labour Prisoners did a group of 'Communist-Anarchists' (led by A. A. Karelin) survive until 1929–30. Some theoretical and historical work was permitted to several leading Anarchist theorists (A. A. Borovoi, N. K. Lebedev) until the early 1930s. Indeed, as late as 1926, one Anarchist writer claimed that 'the October Revolution gave impetus to the Anarchist movement. A number of interesting trends and tendencies appeared in the stormy stream of Anarchist ideas under the impact of the colossal events'.

Anarcho-Syndicalist tendencies were, however, felt far outside Anarchist organizations, and many members of the Bolshevik party shared Syndicalist views. The Workers' Control in industry, as practised during the period of War Communism, was in fact unsuccessful workers' administration, and its enthusiasts were clearly Syndicalists. The Workers' Opposition, with its demand for a Congress of Producers which would administer the national economy, was rightly branded at the tenth party congress in 1921 as an Anarcho-Syndicalist deviation. But despite the tenth congress such views lingered throughout the 1920s.

RADICAL POPULISM

Radical Populism, like Anarchism, was at first a fully recognized political ideology. It was the official ideology of the party of Left Socialist Revolutionaries which had broken off from the Socialist Revolutionary party in the autumn of 1917 and allied itself with the Bolsheviks. The

Left SRs took an active part in the October coup (there were fourteen Left SRs among the sixty-six original members of the Military Revolutionary Committee in Petrograd, and P. I. Lazimir was its first chairman; Izmailov was chairman of the Committee of the Baltic Fleet), and a few days after the coup they entered into the coalition government with the Bolsheviks. This co-operation on the part of the Left SRs ensured to the Bolsheviks the support of a considerable part of the peasantry, whose most radical spokesmen they were. Their main concern was the partition of the landlords' estates; otherwise the policies they advocated were very similar to the Bolsheviks', especially the latter's Left wing.

The official coalition ended in 1918; the Left SRs were unable to swallow Lenin's opportunism over the Brest-Litovsk treaty, resigned from the government (though remaining in such state organs as the Cheka, where Aleksandrovich was Dzerzhinski's deputy) and organized a plot which was intended to renew the war with Germany through the assassination of the German ambassador. When this plot misfired, the party attempted to seize power in Moscow (in July), but failed and disintegrated. In 1920, however, they began once more to function openly, reviving the journal *Znamya* where they advocated 'dictatorship of the masses as against dictatorship of a party' and the formation of a trade union co-operative organization of the peasants. The movement was suppressed by 1922, but while it existed it was supported by some of the leading intellectuals—the famous poets Blok and Esenin, the literary critic and publicist Ivanov-Razumnik, etc.

In 1918 some Left SRs, led by N. Kovalskaya, A. Ustinov, A. Kolegayev and (prior to his death in Switzerland) the veteran Populist revolutionary M. A. Natanson, organized a 'Party of Revolutionary Communism' which accused the Bolsheviks of disregard for human personality, of 'being interested in the people's belly rather than in their spirit', and of Taylorism in industry; they were against the use of armed detachments for food procurement, and advocated the speedy formation of agrarian and factory communes. The party approved of the Bolshevik foreign policy, tried to co-operate with them as far as possible, and in 1920 joined the Bolshevik party. Another SR group which attempted direct co-operation with the Bolsheviks was the so-called Minority of the Party of Socialist Revolutionaries, who broke off from the main party in 1919, fearing—like the official Menshevik party—a victory of the Whites which would bring back the landlords. They published a journal *Narod* and the group was better known under this name. They tried at the same time to co-operate with the Bolsheviks and to compete with them ideologically—in this again resembling the official Menshevik party. The group disintegrated in 1922. Yet another group of Radical Populists— the Maximalists—, who had split off from the SR party in 1904, also co-operated with the Bolsheviks after October, and had representatives in the VTsIK. It disintegrated in 1920 and the majority joined the Bolshevik party.

After 1922 the former Left SRs (e.g., M. Spiridonova), the Maximalists and other former leading revolutionary Populists (e.g., N. A. Morozov), were merely permitted, so to speak, to 'personify the Revolution' in the Society of Former Political Hard Labour Prisoners and Exiles.

NEO-POPULISM

Neo-Populism was essentially a continuation of the Liberal Populism of the 1880s and 90s. The mass of statistical material collected by Zemstvo statisticians made possible a new approach to the problems of peasant life. Abstract ideological schemes as well as theories based on the study of entirely different societies (foreign or urban) waned in the face of the abundant factual information about the actual conditions of Russian peasants and the processes taking place in the peasant economy. A new complex of ideas gradually emerged, centred around the concept of the Peasant Labour Economy (*trudovoye krestyanskoye khozyaistvo*) worked out by A. N. Chelintsev, A. V. Chayanov and others.

The future of Russia, according to the Neo-Populists, lay in the future of her largest social class—the peasantry. The peasants were much more than just the object of care and help by the intelligentsia, as the Liberal Populists had tended to regard them. They were the subjects of continuous change in the internal organization and functioning of individual peasant economies, and this autonomous process was as much as anything else determining the social change in Russia. The Neo-Populists therefore saw their task as the continuous detailed analysis of the development of peasant economy, elucidation of its needs and assistance in their satisfaction. The intelligentsia's place was side by side with the peasantry, but if it wished to find this place it should free itself from all the usual ideological aberrations based on ignorance and prejudice.

The main strongholds of Neo-Populism were the agricultural co-operative organizations and the Central Statistical Administration which was in the hands of former Zemstvo statisticians until 1929. Its academic centre was the Agricultural Academy (near Moscow), where Professors Chayanov, N. D. Kondratyev and others organized in 1920 a Seminary for Agricultural Economics and Politics which was later (1927) transformed into a Research Institute and joined by Professors Chelintsev and Makarov who returned from the emigration. Frustrated during the period of War Communism, the Neo-Populists saw in the NEP the dawn of a new life. But the collectivization of agriculture put an end to the agricultural co-operatives and the academic work was stopped in 1930, when all leading Neo-Populists were arrested in connection with the so-called case of the Peasant Labour Party.

TECHNOCRATISM

Technocratic tendencies in Russia can be traced back to the last quarter of the 19th century. The swift progress of industrialization during the 1880s and 90s created a large category of industrial specialists—technical and commercial managers of big capitalist concerns. These soon acquired an influential position in the business world, and played an active, often leading, role in the organizations of various branches of industry (the mining industry of the South, oil and steel, etc.). Their main central organization was the Council of the Congresses of Industry and Commerce; another important form of organization of industrial specialists was the various voluntary societies for the promotion of industry and trade.

The most brilliant spokesman of the technical intelligentsia was the great scientist D. I. Mendeleyev. In the last years of his life he recorded in print his views on a wide range of subjects of philosophical and public interest, from epistemology to economic and educational policy, thus developing a complete ideology of what might be called Russian Technocratism. Mendeleyev was primarily interested in raising the wealth and well-being of Russia through the development of her industries. This could best be achieved through the application of scientific methods and a determined government policy of protection and encouragement. The form of government is relatively unimportant. Mendeleyev urged like-minded people—whom he calls realists (in contradistinction to both idealists and materialists) and gradualists—to abstain from 'politics mongering' (*politikanstvo*) and to concentrate on concrete practical work, making use of such opportunities as exist. The advance of science and technology, training scientifically-minded and patriotic public figures and organizing and expanding Russian industry, were for Mendeleyev the tasks worth undertaking.

The World War marked a new stage in the development of technocratic trends. As in the other belligerent countries, the government and the people of Russia realized in 1915 that the war they were fighting could not be conducted successfully unless measures were taken to adjust the country's economy to the abnormal conditions. The result was the creation in 1915–16 of special councils and committees for the state control of economic life, as well as of institutions of an unofficial character—the War Industries Committees. All these institutions employed in their headquarters, regional and local branches a great number of specialists of various kinds. Invested with wide powers (as were the officials of the Special Councils and their branches), or anticipating for themselves and for the social groups they represented a great increase in influence and social importance after the war (as did the personnel of the unofficial bodies), they engaged not only in the immediate work of mobilizing the war effort, but also in deliberation as to the ways the Russian economy should go in the years to come, and long-term economic planning: 'and it is here' wrote one of them, Professor Sirinov, 'that the whole might of the industrial public initiative has displayed itself, it is here that they have touched upon issues of enormous state importance.' Another active member of the Moscow War Industries Committee, Professor V. I. Grinevetski, wrote a book, *The Post-war Prospects of Russian Industry,* which in fact served as the basis for all subsequent economic planning.

The impact of the February revolution on both the official and the unofficial bodies was two-fold. On the one hand, wherever possible they were called upon to replace the old bureaucratic machinery which had been destroyed; on the other hand, all these institutions, as well as new combinations of them—the Economic Council and the Supreme Economic Committee in Petrograd, Supply Committees in the provinces and districts—were flooded by representatives of the so-called 'revolutionary democracy' whose interests were directed towards 'deepening Revolution' rather than towards the positive work of guiding the Russian economy. Any productive work was made all but impossible by this 'revolutionary democratic' majority. The democratic idea was never particularly attractive to the technical intelligentsia, and the failure of democracy in 1917 must have made even those who had tended towards it doubt the validity of the democratic premises, and strengthened the elite-ist tendencies in their thinking.

It was with such views that the majority of these 'bourgeois specialists' found themselves in the service of the Bolshevik state. With his usual acute sense of reality, Lenin advanced the theory that the capitalist economy, in its monopolistic stage, creates forms of economic management which precipitate socialist practice; it was therefore not necessary to destroy the apparatus of the economic management of the country, but simply to take it over. How this was done in practice is described in detail by L. N. Kritsman and G. V. Tsyperovich. Ministries, together with their experts, were subordinated to the *collegia* of the People's Commissariats. War-time institutions for the regulation of the national economy were transformed into Chief Administrations (*Glavniye upravleniya,* or for short, *Glavki*) of the respective branches. Some of the Chief Administrations were created out of former monopolistic associations of industrialists. In those branches where there had been no monopolistic development, or it was incomplete, it was made compulsory. Instead of the expected increased prestige and influence in public affairs, which would have corresponded to the importance of their function as managers of the national economy, the technical intelligentsia found that they were merely tolerated as a necessary evil under the new regime. Yet the very fact that their declared political enemies could not do without them must have further strengthened their belief in the social value of their class. Isolation from the political life of the country was another factor stimulating the development of their class consciousness. The official Leninist policy of suspicion, and the open hostility of the Makhayevist elements, made it extremely difficult for them to reconcile themselves to the Bolshevik regime. Hence their hopes that it might be succeeded by a system under which they would not have to fear interference with their work either from the party commissar or from the Works' Council, though they heeded Mendeleyev's reminder that in Russia it was often preferable not to be too outspoken, indeed not to talk about one's views at all unless there was a compelling reason to do so. The old technocratic ideas were thus strengthened by the conditions of life and work under Lenin.

The main organizational centres of technocratically-minded specialists were the State Planning Commission (*Gosplan*) and the Supreme Council of the National Economy, as well as the various societies of engineers and technicians; the main academic centres were the Moscow Technical High School (of which Grinevetski had been the director) and the Thermo-technical Institute set up in 1921. The most outstanding individual representatives of the group were specialists in fuel and power—P. I. Palchinski (who had been the virtual head of the Central War Industries Committee, and the Deputy Minister of Trade and Industry in Kerenski's government), L. K. Ramzin (who organized and headed the Thermo-technical Institute) and I. G. Aleksandrov (the future builder of the *Dneproges*). They took the leading part in working out the GOELRO plan of electrification and in the subsequent economic planning and management, developing further the ideas put forward by Mendeleyev and Grinevetski.

Organized technocratism was eliminated in 1928–30 in connection with the Shakhty and Industrial Party trials, when many leading people were shot or imprisoned and others reduced to purely technical functions.

FYODOROVISM

The teachings of the humble librarian of the Rumyantsev Museum in Moscow and universal erudite N. F. Fyodorov, who died in 1903, very strongly influenced the thinking and the activities of many of the intelligentsia, mostly from among 'bourgeois specialists', and it seems appropriate to name after him the trend of which he was the outstanding theorist.

The mainspring of Fyodorov's thinking, which permeated all his writings, was an irreconcilable attitude to death, and he developed a consistent all-round theory of the conquest of death, beginning with a liturgic theology, through a 'projectivist' system of philosophy, to practi-

cal suggestions for a course of action. Fyodorov held that the hostile
attitude of men and nations towards one another is a result of the pressure upon man of the menacing, death-bearing forces of nature; that
every man is chiefly concerned with his own preservation, and that owing to this men's energies are divided and therefore insufficient to solve
the great problem of ruling nature. The social order arising out of this
egoism is founded upon the separation of the conscious and directing
functions from the executive ones, and thus arise the distinctions of class
and social standing. For Fyodorov, the ideal social order should rest
upon a unity of consciousness and action; there should be no class distinctions, no coercion by military or police. In such an ideal regime every
man would do his duty fully aware of the tasks with which he is faced.

Fyodorov believed that the special task of scientific activity under
such a regime would be to study the deadly forces of nature with the
aim of turning them to the benefit of man. Once man has learned to
rule nature and so to do away with hunger and all other wants, the
causes of discord between men will automatically disappear. Mankind
could then concentrate all its forces upon the common task of regulating
the nature of the earth and even of the cosmos. Fyodorov believed that
in the ideal regime armies should still exist, but for the purpose of regulating the forces of nature rather than for the destruction of man by man.

This belief in the aims of science leads Fyodorov to what he considers to be mankind's supreme task—the resurrection of all ancestors.
He regarded as immoral the positivist theory of progress, which builds
the welfare of the future generations upon the sufferings of the past.
'One must live not for oneself (egoism) and not for others (altruism),
but with everyone and for everyone; this is the union of the living (sons)
for the resurrection of the dead (fathers)'. Fyodorov contended that
even the materialists cannot prove it is impossible to resurrect the dead,
and therefore they have no right to shirk the task. 'Put the engine together, and consciousness will return to it', he says. According to him,
the disintegration of the body and the dispersal of its particles are not
an obstacle to its reconstitution, since it is impossible for the particles
of the body to go beyond the limits of space.

Fyodorov's views appealed to the enthusiasts both of revolution and
of science. They were very widely shared, and even Marxists could accept many of Fyodorov's ideas as a logical development of some remarks in Marxist literature on the proper purpose of philosophy and on
life in a classless society. But the source of these ideas and the very
name of Fyodorov were usually unknown. It was suggested already in
the twenties that several of Fyodorov's plans were fulfilled in the Soviet Union, e.g. the bringing together of knowledge and action, or various technical plans. Fyodorov had spoken of regulating the weather and
thus ensuring good harvests; of utilization of solar energy and the electro-

magnetic energy of the earth; of interplanetary travel, etc.; and all these ideas were taken up and vigorously pursued in the early years of the Soviet power. There was even an attempt to create Labour Armies.

Even Fyodorov's central and most exalted idea, that of conquering death and resurrecting the dead, found followers. The most prominent of them was Krasin, who, at the funeral of Karpov publicly stated his belief that science would achieve the resurrection of the dead. It is worth noting that Krasin spoke of the resurrection not of all the dead but only of the most valuable ones—doubtless under the influence of the elite-ist thinking of both the Leninist and the technocratic trends. The great poet V. Mayakovski also believed in bodily resurrection, and his vision of it also bore elite-ist traits. M. Gorki was more cautious: 'I do not know whether death is really forever un-eliminable, I see no limits for the creative forces of reason and will . . . I have no reason to assume that man's perception and thinking apparatus will always remain as it is now . . . .' A concrete step towards realizing the task of resurrection was made by the famous scientist Academician Vernadski, who created the theory of the biosphere as a separate sphere in the structure of the earth. According to this theory, matter drawn by living organisms into the biosphere and assimilated is not lost after the disintegration of a particular organism, but retains certain peculiar characteristics and therefore remains in the biosphere (Fyodorov had only pointed out that it remained in space).

The main organizational centre of Fyodorovism was the Commission for the Study of the Natural Productive Forces of Russia. It was set up by the Academy of Sciences in 1915 as a part of the war effort, but it was intended that it should expand its work on a large scale in the postwar period. The initiative had come from Vernadski, who was appointed Chairman of the Commission and held this post in 1915–17 and 1926–30. The scope of the Commission's work was very broad and soon after the Bolsheviks came to power it began co-operating with the Bolshevik Government. Some of the enthusiasts of the Commission's work might even have expected their dreams to be more easily realizable under the new regime, which promised to give every encouragement to the most extravagant plans (the electrification plan, the prospecting for iron ore in the region of the famous Kursk Magnetic Anomaly, etc.). The Commission retained its semi-independent character until 1929, when it was, together with the rest of the Academy of Sciences, integrated into the Communist administrative system.

Another branch of organized Fyodorovism was the Local Studies movement. Fyodorov taught that in the future ideal society 'all social work will be accompanied by the study of the corresponding region of the world'. Extremely difficult material conditions in the large cities in the years of the Civil War forced many scientists to seek refuge in small towns or even in villages. Many of them soon found themselves heading groups and societies for local studies. The number of institutions for local studies rose from 160 in 1917 to 516 at the beginning of 1923, including 231 societies and circles and 285 museums. In 1921 the Commissariat of Education convened the first All-Russian conference of societies for local studies and in January 1922 a Central Bureau for Local Studies was set up by the Academy of Sciences. In 1923 the publication began of a special magazine *Krayevedeniye* (Local Studies). The local studies movement flourished throughout the 1920s until in 1931 it came under the direction of local Party and administrative organs; the organization was finally suppressed during the Great Purge.

Although organized Fyodorovism was thus eliminated by the early thirties, many Fyodorovist ideas on the control of nature were incorporated into the official Stalinist ideology.

NATIONAL BOLSHEVISM

The ideology of National Bolshevism first manifested itself in General Brusilov's appeal in October 1917 to the national-minded people to save the country from disintegration, to preserve its independence and territorial integrity, if necessary without and against the government. The government of the day was Kerenski's Provisional Government, but it was obviously irrelevant for Brusilov and like-minded people what government there was, and when the Soviet government proclaimed early in 1918 the slogan of the 'Socialist Fatherland in danger', even Purishkevich (who was in prison) expressed his willingness to serve the Bolsheviks in whatever capacity they would find suitable. Allied intervention in the Civil War enhanced these sentiments, and the majority of former officers who were commanding the Red Army (S. S. Kamenev, Brusilov, Admiral Altfater, etc.) adhered to the ideology of National Bolshevism. This ideology was given a systematic expression by two former prominent Constitutional Democrats—Professor N. A. Gredeskul in Russia and Professor N. V. Ustryalov in the emigration in Harbin—in 1920. Arguing against P. B. Struve, who was irreconcilably anti-Bolshevik, Ustryalov claimed that it was Struve himself who, in the famous symposium *Vekhi*, taught Ustryalov and his generation to disregard the various 'people-loving' ideologies of the intelligentsia and to hold the State in high esteem as a value in itself, irrespective of who was governing at the moment. In the emigration Ustryalov's followers started a *Smena vekh* (Change of Landmarks) movement of reconciliation with the Soviet Government. One of its most prominent adherents was the author Count Aleksei Tolstoi, who in 1922 published an open letter to the veteran Populist leader N. Chaikovski, in which he spoke of the Soviet power as of that 'real . . . power which alone is now defending Russian frontiers from violation by neighbours, maintaining the unity of the Russian state and, at the Geneva conference, alone defending Russia from possible enslavement and conquest by other countries'. Early in 1923 he returned to Russia.

With the beginning of the NEP period a new element entered the ideology of National Bolshevism—the idea that Russia was following the course of the French revolution and entering a period of 'normalization'. The economic policy of War Communism had always been considered by National Bolsheviks to be harmful, and now they rejoiced at the picture of Soviet Russia being 'like a radish—red outside and white inside'. Their hope was that Krasin and other business men would eventually replace the 'utopians' in the leadership of the party.

There was a concomitant to the Great Russian National Bolshevism in a number of similar movements among other nationalities. Local nationalisms were blended with the Bolshevik demagogy which offered 'self-determination' to all and sundry. Often these minority National Bolsheviks were given responsible positions in the Soviet administration in their respective territories. An interesting link between both varieties of National Bolshevism was provided by the well-known ethnographer, V. G. Bogoraz-Tan, who saw in the Bolshevik revolution the realization of his passion for free and full development of every nationality and ethnical group, however small in numbers. He was the moving spirit in the Committee for Assistance to the Peoples of the North (established 1924) and the Institute of the Peoples of the North, which both survived until the Great Purge.

In the 1920s and early 30s, the National Bolsheviks among the non-Russian nationalities were largely in control of the educational and cultural policies of their respective republics. But in turn most of them were accused of 'bourgeois nationalism' and by one means or another removed from positions of influence. Great Russian National Bolshevism was at first felt by the Communists to be much more alien, and was often branded as chauvinism, but in 1934 it was revived by Zhdanov, and in the following years become one of the main components of Stalinism.

CONCLUSION

The Great Purge of 1937–38 put an end to all remnants of organized heterodoxy, physically eliminated most heterodox thinkers, and silenced the rest. The revival of controversy in the 1940s was confined to artistic and scientific problems. Where practical activities (such as the study of natural resources or local studies) were carried on which in the past had been connected with the different trends, they were now cut off from their ideological origins. Only the thaw after Stalin's death produced a few tentative moves towards reviving some of the old trends, together, of course, with some attempts at fresh thinking.

DEVELOPMENT OF COLLECTIVIZATION IN A SOVIET VILLAGE *

Collectivization is one of the most dramatic episodes in the history of
the Soviet Union. Many of its aspects have been carefully studied, but
the full story of its development and operation has yet to be
assembled. The selection that follows presents a phase of the history
of a Ukrainian village and gives a valuable account of its
transformation as it was taken into the Soviet collectivization scheme.
In writing the book from which this selection is taken, Mr. Belov
relied on what he had learned as a youth in the village, on his
recollections, and on diaries that he had kept.

FROM PREREVOLUTIONARY DAYS
THROUGH THE CIVIL WAR

THE VILLAGE which is the site of the kolkhoz I want to describe
is situated in the western part of the Ukraine, in a small valley. In 1950
it numbered 772 households; their dwellings were spread out along the
banks of a stream for a distance of six kilometers (a little under four
miles).

Before the Revolution, part of the village lands belonged to the
landlord F. whose estate lay nearby; he owned 10,000 hectares (25,000
acres) of plowland and 2,000 hectares of forest in various parts of the

* Fedor Belov, *The History of a Soviet Collective Farm* (New York: Frederick A.
Praeger, 1955), pp. 1–26. Reprinted by permission of the copyright holder, the Committee for the Promotion of Advanced Slavic Cultural Studies.

The author was born in a Ukrainian village shortly after the Revolution of
1917, attended a local school, and worked on a collective farm in his youth. He later
went to Kiev for further education. During the war, he served in the Red army,
reaching the rank of captain. After the war, he returned to his village and worked
as chairman of a collective farm for three years. Then he returned to military duty
but soon decided to defect, escaping by way of Germany. He is now living in the
United States.

district. About 1,000 hectares of his property formed part of the lands of our village. On his estate he had 300 oxen, 200 horses and over 100 cows; he also owned a large brickyard, a lumber mill and several flour mills. His residence and farm buildings were located in the center of the village, dividing it into two parts which later became the sites of the two kolkhozes set up in the village. All of his farm and administrative buildings, such as dairies, granaries and workshops, were built of stone; other buildings on his estate were of brick, and some of these, among them the school, the hospital and several shops, are still standing. The bricks used in these buildings are marked A.F., the initials of F.'s wife—an unobtrusive reminder of the contrast between things past and things present, for almost all the newer structures of the village are built of clay.

The village was proud of its church, the largest and most beautiful one in the district. It had been built largely at the expense of the landlord. Religious festivals were important events in the life of the village, which in general was peaceful and predictable. The land was fertile, food was always plentiful and the peasants were able to supplement their income by selling the products of the home industries which they carried on during the winter.

The calm routine of village life was disrupted by the outbreak of war in 1914. The army took many of the men; some never returned, others came back crippled and embittered.

In the summer of 1917 the first deserters from the front appeared in the village. The soldiers brought back guns, Bolshevik leaflets and the seeds of disloyalty to the Tsar. One of them (who was subsequently shot by the Germans) secretly began to prepare an anti-government uprising in the village; the same sort of activity was going on in the surrounding villages, but before anything could be accomplished the ringleaders were arrested and sent to Siberia.

News of the revolutionary uprising of October 25, 1917, reached the village the following day and was greeted with enthusiasm; to the peasants it meant free land and an end to the war. On the very day the news arrived the landowner's manor house was looted, his stock farms were "requisitioned," and his vast orchard was cut down and sold to the peasants for wood; all his farm buildings were torn down and left in ruins while the land was distributed among the peasants who were prepared to live the new Soviet life.

But the triumphant and exciting days of the Revolution were quickly followed by evil days; the Germans came almost immediately, drove off most of the peasants' livestock and left the village devastated. Then came the Civil War, with robberies, murders and general economic ruin.

The political situation in the Ukraine at that time was so complex that the peasants, who were poorly educated and knew little of politics, were incapable of understanding it. No one knew whom to believe, whose leadership to follow. One government followed another, and the peasants hung on grimly and waited for the end of the confusion.

It was a long time before the peasants felt safe in relinquishing their guns, for it was not till 1923 that the village was free from the raids of armed bands, whether Communists, anti-Communists or ordinary brigands.

FROM THE END OF THE CIVIL WAR
TO COLLECTIVIZATION

Following the Civil War, with all its anxieties and confusion, the village gradually began to revive. After the famine of 1921 (I should mention that no one in the village died of hunger during this time), the village lands were repartitioned according to the new regulations. At that time the village numbered more than three thousand inhabitants, with total holdings of 4,380 hectares. This total included the homestead strips, or individual garden plots, which averaged six to seven hectares per household.

Our land produced good crops. On an average, the yields obtained per hectare were 30 to 40 centners of wheat, 25 to 30 centners of rye, 20 to 25 centners of barley, and 200 centners of beets. Every household had large surpluses of grain which it could dispose of as it saw fit; for the most part, the grain went to market for sale.

Since at that time the tax burden was light, the majority of the peasants were able to increase and improve their holdings. They built houses, barns and sheds, and bought agricultural implements. By 1926 the village had more than 500 cows, 300 horses, 600 swarms of bees, 2 watermills, 13 windmills, and 6 stores. More than 100 houses were fitted out with sheet-iron roofs, a sure sign of peasant prosperity. A villager who did not kill one or two pigs a year (for Christmas and Easter) was a rarity. As a rule, lard and eggs could be found in every home. These were the golden days of the NEP, which the peasants still look back upon with longing.

Church and national holidays were celebrated solemnly and joyously. During Christmas week nobody worked; everyone wore his best clothes; the best dishes were cooked for one's guests; and no one refused charity to the crippled beggars. Following the old tradition, the children went around singing carols in praise of Christ and collecting donations for the church. At Easter, the villagers greeted each other with the customary "Christ is risen!" instead of with "How do you do?" No one violated the traditions which had been established by the people and the church.

In the autumn, as a rule, two or three weddings took place in the village. They were celebrated in accordance with all the church canons

and national customs. A wedding lasted six or seven days, and while
it was being celebrated the relatives, friends and neighbors of the newly
married pair drank copious draughts of homemade liquor, consumed a
calf or a pig, and generally made merry.

A sugar refinery, which stood on the boundary between our lands
and those of the neighboring village, also contributed to the well-being
and prosperity of our village. Many of the households grew sugar beets
and sold them to the refinery, receiving in return a good cash income
as well as sugar, syrup and mash for the livestock. The refinery belonged to a man who had owned it since before the Revolution. In 1925
the refinery workers had a disagreement with him and "had a little fun
at his expense"; they forced him to carry them through the streets of
the neighboring village as if he were a horse, to the general amusement
the workers. Shortly after this incident the owner left, threatening that
"from now on you'll not have a refinery", and within a year the refinery
was closed. We were not told why, but everybody knew—the owner had
since begun to work in the main administration of the Ukrainian sugar
industry. All the advantages which the refinery had brought to the surrounding villages were gone. Its equipment was hauled away and the
buildings were gradually demolished. Only a few storage buildings and
the smokestack survived until the Second World War, when the Germans blew up the smokestack, a good orientation point for Soviet troops
or guerrillas.

In spite of the closing of the refinery, the life of the village went
on much as before. Almost the only change was that the peasants now
sowed more grain and oil-producing plants and less sugar beet. Each
peasant managed his farm in his own way, without any special directives, keeping to the tradition of his forefathers.

In the spring of 1928 the first wave of the "attack on the kulaks"
swept over our raion. As a rule, it was the Committees of the Poor and
the members of the Komsomol in the villages on whom the government
depended. In our village the Committee of the Poor was headed by one
of the poorest peasants, Kapan.

Kapan had appeared in our village after the Civil War; he had married a widow and squandered almost all her money on drink. He went
about dressed in a soldier's overcoat and a huge sheepskin cap, and
was always slightly tipsy. Somehow his appearance made one think
of a beast of prey about to pounce on its victim.

Eighteen of the poorest households joined the Committee of the
Poor. In many of these households the young people were members
of the Komsomol. Frequently, in the "attack on the kulaks," father and
son marched together. Though the Komsomol of the village had only
nine members, they were held in even greater awe by the villagers than
members of the Communist Party are today.

The "dekulakization" took place in the following manner: in the office of the village soviet, where the Committee of the Poor had its headquarters, a victim would be selected at a board meeting, and on the next day the entire group of active members would raid the victim's household. Such raids resembled those of the locusts which destroy everything in their path. The raiders made a clean sweep of everything—grain, agricultural implements, harness, livestock, furniture, and clothing. The entire company was armed with revolvers and long iron rods; with the latter they probed the walls, the floors, the stove, and so forth of the raided peasant's home, in search of "kulak property." The members of the kulak family would sometimes dress themselves in several layers of clothing hoping to save at least something, but the clothes would be taken off by force in spite of all pleas and tears. Articles taken from the kulak farms were sold at auction in the village club. Most of the peasants did not go to these sales, saying "one's happiness cannot be built on the tears of others." The stolen goods usually fell to the "active" peasants.

During this period twenty-one kulak households were "dekulakized" in the village. The members of nine households were sent to Siberia and Kazakhstan. (After the war some of them returned to the village.) The singing of the young girls was no longer heard in the evenings; at night the baying of the dogs on the ruined farms gave rise to a feeling of sadness and vague foreboding.

THE FIRST ATTEMPTS AT COLLECTIVIZATION

It was in the same year that the first attempts at collectivization began. A commune was set up, using two former kulak farms as a base. The commune consisted of thirteen families, with a total of seventy persons, the majority of whom were poor peasants, hired farmhands and orphans. The farm tools taken from the "dekulakized" farms were turned over to the commune, since its members had almost none of their own. The members ate in a communal dining hall, and income was divided in accordance with the principles of "cooperative communism." The entire proceeds of the members' labor, as well as all dwellings and facilities belonging to the commune, were shared by the commune members. The orphans and the homeless of the commune lived in a separate building called the "bachelor house." The same building was used for the club, from which propaganda was carried on among the peasants. At the head of the commune was a five-man council which managed the entire administrative and economic life of the commune and drew up ambitious plans for the future. But in spite of all propaganda, more peasants did not enter the commune. It was the same in other villages. The communal form of collective farming soon lost favor and Party efforts to promote it were gradually abandoned in the late twenties.

At about the same time the members of the Evangelist sect in the village set up another commune on a religious basis. This one included six families with a total of twenty-four persons. In order not to harm any peasants by taking their land, the commune asked the village soviet to give them the poorest lands. They built a community house, a store and dairy; they lived and worked as one family, in friendship and harmony. They taught their children at home, since disbelief in God and church were being taught at school. Many peasants who were not members of the sect attended their church and spoke well of them. They were against war and every kind of violence and falsehood.

Nevertheless the religious commune was broken up by an order from above; the authorities found in it the dangerous germ of "counterrevolution."

After the dissolution of the religious commune, a new form of collective farm, the TOZ, appeared in the village. TOZ's were created on a voluntary basis; usually they were joined by former commune members and poor peasants. In the spring of 1929, the TOZ in our village included thirty-four households which had pooled their lands and implements. In the distribution of the profits, not only the amount of labor performed by the members on the society's farm but also the means of production which they had contributed were taken into account. The income of each society member thus depended on the acreage he provided, on his livestock and implements, and on his labor contribution. Such distribution caused intense dissatisfaction in the households of the poor peasants who, because they did not have any livestock or implements, received very small incomes. These households fought for a distribution of profits according to the number of mouths and the amount of labor contributed; the other households, however, defended the existing system of distribution. In this way the TOZ soon split into two camps.

By the autumn of 1929 the TOZ numbered fifty-seven households and received a charter from the government. Notwithstanding special advantages such as reduced taxes, however, the TOZ gained no new members after that time; by the end of 1929 eleven households had withdrawn, six of them leaving the village entirely to seek their fortunes in the Soviet Far East. Soon other households followed the example of the first group, and the TOZ was in danger of collapse.

The experience in our village with these early types of collective farms was typical of what was taking place in many other Soviet villages at this time.

The Party and the government, finding that collective farms could not be created on a voluntary basis, and realizing that the continued existence of individual farms alongside the collective farms would have an adverse psychological effect on the members of the collective farms, inaugurated a policy of general collectivization in the spring of 1930. In that year many middle-peasant households which refused to enter a collective were reclassified as kulaks. The second wave of the "attack on the kulak" began; in our village over forty households were destroyed, and the "dangerous elements" (that is, the most independent members) were sent into exile. By fanning class enmity, the government succeeded in promoting bitter civil war in the village. Incidentally this policy produced a fertile soil for crime—before long our village had experienced several robberies, eight cases of arson and fourteen murders.

In the winter of 1930, the TOZ was reorganized as an artel, the form of collective farm which the government decided should be generally adopted and which evolved into the present-day kolkhoz.

General collectivization in our village was brought about in the following manner: Two representatives of the Party arrived in the village. All the inhabitants were summoned by the ringing of the church bell to a meeting at which the policy of general collectivization was announced. At the meeting, however, someone distributed leaflets entitled "This Is How It Will Be on a Collective Farm." The leaflet showed a picture of a mother and child, the mother bent under the burden of overwork. The upshot was that although the meeting lasted two days, from the viewpoint of the Party representatives nothing was accomplished.

After this setback the Party representatives divided the village into two sections and worked each one separately. Two more officials were sent to reinforce the first two. A meeting of our section of the village was held in a stable which had previously belonged to a kulak. The meeting dragged on until dark. Suddenly someone threw a brick at the lamp, and in the dark the peasants began to beat the Party representatives who jumped out the window and escaped from the village barely alive. The following day seven people were arrested. The militia was called in and stayed in the village until the peasants, realizing their helplessness, calmed down.

It was difficult, however, for the Party and government to break down the old principles and traditions. The peasants stubbornly clung to their possessions. But "there are no fortresses which Bolsheviks cannot storm." Heavy taxes and fear of the future drove even the middle-peasant households into the collective farm. Those households which refused to join were loaded with burdensome taxes and allotted the poorest lands. The independent peasants feared particularly "the household plan," a special tax regulation under which monetary payments in kind were required to be made on twenty-four hours' notice; after the expiration of the time limit, the delinquent farm was subject to a raid by the Committee of the Poor and the Komsomol members.

THE FIRST KOLKHOZES AND
THE FAMINE OF 1932–1933

By the end of 1930 there were two kolkhozes in our village. Though at first these collectives embraced at most only 70 per cent of the peasant households, in the months that followed they gradually absorbed more and more of them.

In these kolkhozes the great bulk of the land was held and worked communally, but each peasant household owned a house of some sort, a small plot of ground and perhaps some livestock. All the members of the kolkhoz were required to work on the kolkhoz a certain number of days each month; the rest of the time they were allowed to work on their own holdings. They derived their income partly from what they grew on their garden strips and partly from their work in the kolkhoz.

When the harvest was over, and after the farm had met its obligations to the state and to various special funds (for insurance, seed, forage, etc.) and had sold on the market whatever undesignated produce was left, the remaining produce and the farm's monetary income were divided among the kolkhoz members according to the number of "labor days" each one had contributed to the farm's work. One day's actual work might be worth anywhere from one half to two or more labor days, depending on the difficulty of the task involved and the degree of skill required.

Our kolkhoz was built on the site of the former commune, the acreage of which had been increased at the expense of households which had been evicted to other parts of the village. The farm and administrative buildings of the collective were constructed from sheds which had formerly belonged to kulaks, the farm buildings of collectivized peasants, and other miscellaneous sources. Tombstones and stone crosses from the cemetery were used for the foundations of the buildings; for the roofs, the sheet-iron was ripped off the former kulak dwelling on the kolkhoz land. Willow and linden wood, of which the village had an ample supply, was also used in the farm's construction. By the summer of 1931, the kolkhoz had its own stud farm with space for 120 horses, a large barn for grain and a steam-operated flour mill. It included in its membership 85 per cent of all the peasant households of our section of the village, and had 90 horses, 24 oxen, 80 sheep, 160 swarms of bees, and several cows and pigs.

It was in 1930 that the kolkhoz members first received their portions out of the "communal kettle." After they had received their earnings, at the rate of 1 kilogram of grain and 55 kopecks per labor day, one of them remarked, "You will live, but you will be very, very thin."

In the spring of 1931 a tractor worked the fields of the kolkhoz for the first time. The tractor was "capable of plowing every kind of hard soil and virgin sod," as Party representatives told us at the meeting in celebration of its arrival. The peasants did not then know that these "steel horses" would carry away a good part of the harvest in return for their work and would devalue still further the "collective yardstick," the labor day.

By late 1932 more than 80 per cent of the peasant households in the raion had been collectivized. In the twenty-four villages of the raion there were fifty-two kolkhozes and three state farms (sovkhozes). That year the peasants harvested a good crop and had hopes that the calculations would work out to their advantage and would help strengthen them economically. These hopes were in vain. The kolkhoz workers received only 200 grams of flour per labor day for the first half of the year; the remaining grain, including the seed fund, was taken by the government. The peasants were told that industrialization of the country, then in full swing, demanded grain and sacrifices from them.

That autumn the "red broom" passed over the kolkhozes and the individual plots, sweeping the "surplus" for the state out of the barns and corn-cribs. In the search for "surpluses," everything was collected. The farms were cleaned out even more thoroughly than the kulaks had been. As a result, famine, which was to become intense by the spring of 1933, already began to be felt in the fall of 1932.

The famine of 1932–1933 was the most terrible and destructive that the Ukrainian people have ever experienced. The peasants ate dogs, horses, rotten potatoes, the bark of trees, grass—anything they could find. Incidents of cannibalism were not uncommon. The people were like wild beasts, ready to devour one another. And no matter what they did, they went on dying, dying, dying.

They died singly and in families. They died everywhere—in the yards, on streetcars, and on trains. There was no one to bury these victims of the Stalinist famine. People traveled for thousands of kilometers in search of food—to Siberia, and Caucasus. Many perished by the wayside or fell into the hands of the militia. To protect what little grain they had from the raids of the militia, the peasants often banded together in groups of thirty or forty persons and defended their gleanings with sticks and knives.

I was thirteen years old then, and I shall never forget what I saw. One memory especially stands out: a baby lying at his mother's breast, trying to wake her.

A man is capable of forgetting a great deal, but these terrible scenes of starvation will be forgotten by no one who saw them. The worst time came during May and June 1933. In the fields of the kolkhoz a bumper crop was ripening, but the peasants were too weak to live until the new grain was ripe. Many went out to the waving fields of wheat and rye, tore off the half-ripened ears and ate them. But they were so weak that the indigestible grain was fatal and they would drop dead on the spot. In our village alone the famine claimed 479 lives.

There was no one to gather the bumper crop of 1933, since the people who remained alive were too weak and exhausted. More than a hundred persons—office and factory workers from Leningrad—were sent to assist on the kolkhoz; two representatives of the Party arrived to help organize the harvesting. Out of the first threshing, the kolkhoz members were given 500 grams of flour per labor day for the first six months of the year; food was also prepared for them daily at their place of work.

During this period the peasants had to bear another burden: the forced loans to the government. Although the loans were relatively small that year, they were particularly burdensome, coming as they did on top of the famine and general impoverishment.

That summer (1933) the entire administration of the kolkhoz—the bookkeeper, the warehouseman, the manager of the flour mill, and even the chairman himself—were put on trial on charges of plundering the kolkhoz property and produce. All the accused were sentenced to terms of seven to ten years, and a new administration was elected.

In the autumn, after all the farm work had been completed, a "harvest day" was held. Cash prizes amounting in all to 5,000 rubles were distributed among the kolkhoz workers. Several pigs and sheep were also given out as prizes. or especially good work in the organization of the harvesting, the two Party representatives each received from the kolkhoz 15 kilograms of honey and 200 kilograms of grain and 1 ruble, 5 kopecks in cash for each labor day they had contributed. Thus ended that sorrowful year in the history of the kolkhoz.

LIFE ON THE KOLKHOZ BEFORE THE WAR

After 1934 a gradual improvement began in the economic life of the kolkhoz and its members. The economic conditions of a kolkhoz depend to a large degree on its acreage distribution, that is, on the amount of land which can be sown to the most profitable crops, and on the character of its organization and management. The peasants naturally took a great interest in the election of the chairman and the board of managers of the kolkhoz.

Of the forty-six kolkhozes in the raion, in only seven did the chairmen manage their farms for a period of four or more years. The others were all replaced during their first or second year of work. The principal reason for this fact was that many of the chairmen enriched themselves at the expense of the collectives. They drank heavily and bribed the raion officials with kolkhoz property. The new chairman of our kolkhoz, Dmitri A., differed from his predecessors. He was a simple man, strict and strong willed; no one could reproach him for illegal or unjust actions. He never drank, and he disliked drinking in his subordinates; he never tried to bribe the raion authorities. Since his kolkhoz was among the leading ones of the raion, the authorities had to reckon with him. He loved order and accuracy, and woe to anyone who ignored his directives. He would throw his cap down at the feet of a culprit for emphasis, but never used abusive or profane language. His conduct won the love and respect of all the members of the collective farm, and he managed our kolkhoz continuously for seven years, 1934–1941.

During the first two years of his management, a cattle farm, a pig farm and a sheep farm were added to the kolkhoz. A twelve hectare pond in which fish were bred was constructed, and an orchard and vegetable garden covering forty hectares were planted. In subsequent years the sale of fish alone provided the kolkhoz with an annual income of as much as 90,000 rubles. Thanks to the creation of a sound economic base, the kolkhoz earned an annual income of 600,000 to 700,000 rubles until the war.

The principal cash income was derived from technical crops such as sugar beets and vegetables, and from dairy products and fish. Vegetables, honey, vegetable oil, and fruit were shipped to Leningrad, Minsk and Kiev. To obtain space on railroad cars for the transportation of the produce to districts where the selling price was high was almost impossible by ordinary means and required considerable ingenuity—a knowledge of what strings to pull and whose palm to grease—on the part of the kolkhoz chairman. "If you don't grease, you don't travel," says a Soviet proverb; and indeed it was constantly necessary to "grease." Two or three literate kolkhoz members and a member of the inspection committee always accompanied the produce to market. The proceeds of the sale, along with an account signed by everyone concerned, were kept in the kolkhoz safe. Since it had a good cash income, the kolkhoz improved and expanded its holdings. The flour mill was modernized, reaching a capacity of forty tons of grist every twenty-four hours. A creamery, sawmill, workshops, and other buildings were put up. The kolkhoz members received 3 to 6 rubles in cash per labor day.

The kolkhoz enjoyed its greatest prosperity during the years 1936–1938. In these years it had a five-field system of crop rotation and planted an area of 72 hectares in sugar beets. The total vegetable plantings ran as high as 200 hectares.

Since it had excellent draft power—160 horses and 80 oxen—the kolkhoz tried to cultivate its land with its own motive power and thus avoid the large payments in kind for the use of the tractors provided by the Machine-Tractor Stations (MTS). Since the tractor station was not large—one tractor brigade (four tractors) serviced two or three kolkhozes —the collective performed about 55 per cent of its cultivation with its own power. The total payments in kind for the work of the tractors amounted to no more than 1,200 to 1,300 centners of grain annually. It should be mentioned, too, that because of its fine stock of draft animals the kolkhoz had thousands of tons of manure for its fields, which contributed to its success.

Having a surplus of grain, the kolkhoz members decided at the general meeting to sell it to the state each year and with the credit thus obtained to buy machinery and necessary implements. The kolkhoz had such surpluses up until 1939, when a new system of deliveries of agricultural products was initiated. Thereafter the amount of obligatory deliveries of individual products was based not, as before, on the area of land sown to each crop, but on the total area of arable land. Moreover, differences in the fertility and composition of the land on different farms were ignored in computing the amount of the deliveries under the new regulations. Under this system only those kolkhozes with fertile land could operate profitably; the others were doomed to poverty. For example, although the value of the labor day on our kolkhoz was usually about three to six kilograms of grain and 3 to 5 rubles in cash, there were other collectives in our raion in which the labor day was equal to only one to two kilograms of grain and 70 to 90 kopecks in cash.

During the years 1935–1939 shock brigades, Stakhanovites and the so-called Five Hundreds were created. Five Hundreds were squads that undertook to raise 500 centners of sugar beets or more from one hectare; the administration of the kolkhoz was obliged to render them assistance. For instance, in 1936 a woman squad-leader on our farm undertook to raise 1,000 centners of sugar beets from one hectare. A particularly good piece of land was allotted to her squad, special fertilizers were provided, three manurings were made, and so on. Not only the kolkhoz but the entire raion watched over this squad; the agronomists never left the area where it worked, and during the dry days the area was artificially watered.

The achievement of a record harvest of beets could not be managed, however, without considerable connivance. Since it soon became evident that 1,000 centners of beets would not be obtained from the single hectare, the board of managers of the kolkhoz, on orders from the raion, made up the missing centners from the communal area. As a result, the squad "grew" 1,017 centners of beets from one hectare. After such a "victory" the squad-leader was rewarded. She became a deputy of the oblast executive committee, and her name was constantly brought up in speeches at conferences where she was elected to the presidium. At one of these conferences, she undertook a new responsibility—the raising of 1,200 centners from a single hectare. She brought her speech to a close with the words "I have bestowed and will bestow." Of course, this did not get by without laughter, but the laughter was hastily stifled by applause. The next year, however, did not bring her further fame, because certain of the kolkhoz workers blocked the making up of the additional centners necessary to "achieve" her target.

The raion press made much of such people, and they were widely praised and advertised as the vanguard of socialism. When collective farmers read in the papers about new "records," they only smile; they know how these records and these Stakhanovites are created.

Each kolkhoz bears a name, either of an individual or of some place or event connected with Soviet history. Our kolkhoz, unfortunately, had chosen the name of a Party leader who subsequently fell into disgrace; in 1937, therefore, the kolkhoz was forced to choose a new name. Wishing to avoid a repetition of the incident, the management this time chose the name of a hero of the Civil War, safely dead and thus less likely to suffer Party disgrace. Another kolkhoz with which I was acquainted had to change its name three times before it hit finally on an acceptable one —that of the Ukrainian poet Shevchenko.

A campaign to increase the number of cows had been started in 1936 among the collectives of the raion. Heifers were distributed to the kolkhoz members on a three-year deferred payment plan, but some peasants refused to take them because of lack of space and feed. Nonetheless, as a result of this campaign more than 80 per cent of the collective farmers had their own cows and heifers.

In general, from the mid-1930's until 1941, the majority of kolkhoz members in the Ukraine lived relatively well. They were never in need of bread and other foodstuffs. If the market provided insufficient clothes and shoes, the shortage was made good by items made locally. In 1939 and 1940, however, the state demanded more grain from the kolkhozes than they had contributed before. The alliance with Germany, to which the grain was sent, stirred up dissatisfaction and disapproval among the peasants. The sharp changes in the amount delivered to the state and the fluctuating remuneration for the labor day constantly aroused a fear of tomorrow's fate among the kolkhoz members and drove them to steal grain and conceal it.

On the eve of war, our kolkhoz presented the following picture: its collective livestock consisted of 180 horses, 44 cows, 90 oxen, about 300 calves, more than 400 pigs, about 100 sheep, and more than 60 chickens. It had three automobiles, a flour mill, a sawmill, a creamery, machine and wood-working shops and other buildings. It was considered a "leading" kolkhoz in the raion and had participated in the all-Union agricultural exhibitions from 1935 to 1939; its chairman had attended several republic and oblast conferences of agricultural leaders.

THE DESTRUCTION OF THE KOLKHOZ AND
THE OCCUPATION OF THE VILLAGE BY THE GERMANS

At the beginning of the war most of our collective livestock was driven to the east and turned over to other kolkhozes. (Not one head of livestock was returned at the end of the war.) Most of the remaining animals were slaughtered and the meat was distributed among the kolkhoz members. Before the arrival of the Germans in the village, the kolkhoz was dismantled; all the farm buildings were torn down and the building materials were carried away by the peasants. The implements, agricultural machinery and harness, and even the tractors, were also divided among the kolkhoz members. The allotment of the collective property was carried out under the supervision of Fyodor B., a former deacon of the church, who created a special commission for this work. The allotment of the lands to the peasants was supervised by a temporary committee elected by a special assembly of the village. This committee, which was composed of two schoolteachers, the former secretary of the village soviet and several peasants, managed the village until the Germans came.

In 1941 each peasant harvested the crop from his own strip of land. Some former kulaks moved back into their homes without disturbances; they did not demand their former lands and submitted to the generally established rules. In the same year more than forty deserters from the front appeared in the village, hoping to settle down to a new life as free peasants. When the German troops came, the village greeted them "with bread and salt" and hailed them as liberators.

At first the Germans were friendly; they accepted the food they were offered, clicked their cameras and roared, "Stalin kaput." But the "liberation" did not last long. In the winter of 1942 the Germans ordered the restoration of the kolkhozes. They commanded the peasants to surrender the implements and machinery previously distributed and threatened to execute those who evaded the order. Regulations in the two restored kolkhozes in our villages, under the management of a certain Hungarian whom the people nicknamed "Fritz," became stricter than ever. Five o'clock in the morning was the time set for going out to the fields, and nine at night for returning; for lateness, the culprit was given three or four lashes. Subsequently the Germans took away all the cows, chickens, pigs, and beehives from the individual peasant households and put them back in the kolkhoz.

As a result of such actions, the peasants' attitude toward the Germans changed to one of hostility; there was much stealing from the kolkhozes; the local population worked together in this and protected one another from German retribution. There were exceptions when the lure of reward in the form of money or land would induce a man to denounce his neighbor, but they were few. Many peasants joined the partisans, while others awaited with impatience the return of the Russians. Following the liberation of our village by Soviet troops, the active collaborators with the Germans were tried and banished to Siberia; the "emigrants" from the front were shot.

All told, the village suffered the following losses from the war: forty-four homes were burned, two bridges and two club buildings were destroyed and over three hundred male inhabitants were killed. The Germans did not bring the peasants the expected land and freedom. They brought only suffering to the peasant masses.

THE RESTORATION OF THE KOLKHOZ

In the first days after the liberation from the Germans in 1944, the kolkhoz presented the following picture: Out of the five livestock barns, only one horse-stable was still intact. All the agricultural implements had been plundered. The farm had no sheep, poultry, or bees, and only 16 horses, 13 oxen, and 23 pigs. The families of the former kulaks who had settled in their old homes were forcibly evicted. The other kolkhoz in the village was in similar straits.

Promptly after the departure of the Germans, the kolkhoz was again set up. This was not, however, simply the re-establishment of the prewar kolkhoz; it was the creation of a new organization, since the entire process had to be started over from the beginning, just as in 1930.

In theory, the formation of a new kolkhoz begins with the creation of a group of founders. The organizers of this initial group may be the Party and soviet workers who are carrying out educational work, or they may be the peasants themselves. The minimum number of founders has varied at different periods. Before 1930, the number of founders could not be less then five; after 1930, however, the minimum number was increased to fifteen. The founders of a kolkhoz are supposed to work out its regulations in accordance with a model statute. The peasants are "urged" to become members and, voluntarily or not, most of them join. After the regulations have been discussed and approved in the presence of at least two-thirds of the total membership, the approved regulations are signed by the chairman and the board of managers or by the founders themselves. This procedure for organizing a kolkhoz was not followed in reality, however.

The role of founders of the kolkhoz after the liberation of the village was played by the old prewar board of managers, who were later elected anew by the general meeting of the collective. All the peasants of the village were told to write to the founders and declare their desire to enter a kolkhoz. Everyone who had reached the age of sixteen wrote such a declaration. Each "new" member was accepted and approved by a general meeting and required to pay an entrance fee of 30 rubles. Discussion and approval of the regulations, however, did not take place until 1948, at which time they were recorded in the raion "register of kolkhoz regulations." Since everybody was already working and following the dictates of the board of managers, the entire procedure as carried out was a mere formality.

A chairman, Vasili B., was appointed by the raion Party committee as soon as the kolkhoz was re-established in 1944, and afterwards he was approved by the general meeting. He was forty-five years of age, fat, uncouth, and illiterate. His swearing, which was incessant, he called "mathematics." He was proud of the fact that the kolkhoz members were afraid of his "mathematics" and that it served him as a useful weapon. The peasants wondered why this man remained on special orders in the rear and was not sent to the front; such people, it seems, were valued by the raion Party committee as obedient and devoted tools.

Much had to be done to get things back into working order. Before the Germans withdrew, they had distributed among the peasants all grain they could not take with them, together with whatever animals and implements remained. Even before the kolkhoz was re-established, the government organized the collection of the grain donations for the army. A good deal of grain was collected in this way, partly because everybody had plenty at that time and partly because they felt patriotic.

The major problems were to obtain adequate building materials to restore the farms and to restock the kolkhoz herds. A commission was organized by the board of managers to take the individual farmer's agricultural implements and all their building materials, most of which had been kolkhoz property in the first place anyway. But this was not nearly enough, and the kolkhoz had no money to buy more. It obtained a government credit of 800,000 rubles for three years, however, and permission to purchase 110 cubic meters of lumber from a nearby forest. The lumber proved to be a great disappointment, because it was hornbeam—unsuitable for building purposes since it rots completely within four or five years. As a result almost all building at that time was done with *saman*, a brick made from a mixture of clay, straw and horsehair or some other fibrous material.

Not all the cattle were taken back into the kolkhoz; the peasants were allowed to keep some. Every peasant who had a cow was assigned some of the useless hornbeam to use in constructing his cowshed. The peasants also had to agree to sell all the offspring of their animals to the kolkhoz, and were prohibited from slaughtering them or selling them on the market. This was one way in which the collective built up its herds; another was by illegal purchases on the market, and a third was by sending representatives to the newly-acquired areas in the western Ukraine, which had formerly been part of Poland or Czechoslovakia. There were as yet no kolkhozes in these areas, and the peasants were quite willing to sell their cattle, since the representatives from the kolkhozes further east told them that if they didn't sell they would have to give them up for nothing when kolkhozes were formed in their areas. The purchases of cattle were conducted legally: from the raion executive committee and from their own farms the kolkhoz representatives received special documents, which they then presented to the local authorities in the new regions. Because of the activities of the Banderists, however, things did not always go smoothly. During the period 1944–1947 the Banderists robbed or killed so many kolkhoz representatives that many farms were afraid to send their people to the newly occupied areas.

The Banderist movement was most active in the early post-war years, spreading over almost the entire western region of the Ukraine. It was partly an anti-Soviet political movement, but many Banderists were nothing but bandits. In our village eight people perished at their hands. They plundered kolkhozes and killed officials and soldiers. The Party worker sent into areas where they were strong rarely survived. They pulled some extraordinary feats: at the time of the elections for the Supreme Soviet in 1946, in spite of the guards at the voting places, they raided our village and carried off the ballot boxes, while on another occasion they robbed the State Bank in Stalino in broad daylight and got away with three million rubles in government money. In 1947 the regular army rid the principal raions of the Banderists but they still continued to stage periodic robberies.

Another of the postwar difficulties of the kolkhoz was the replacement of equipment. In many cases implements had to be manufactured at home on a makeshift basis. Harrow teeth were made from railroad spikes; sometimes the kolkhoz bought these illegally from the railroad gangs but more often they were stolen. Steel for sickles and scythes was taken from wrecked tanks.

Knowing the great need of the kolkhozes for all sorts of materials, hundreds of speculators made the rounds of the farms, offering glass, iron, boards, harness, machines, and even tractors. Since none of these things was provided by the government, they had to be bought from the speculators at exorbitant prices.

The kolkhoz was forced to engage in a variety of illegal activities in order to exist and fulfill its obligations. The drought of 1946 further increased its troubles; the state grain deliveries took so much that the peasants received only 300 grams of grain and 60 kopecks in cash per labor day; the seed and forage funds, moreover, were cleaned out. The farm was told to look for seed locally, despite the fact that neighboring farms were in the same plight and were doing the same thing.

Because the peasants received so little food and money, they became almost entirely dependent for their livelihood on their homestead plots. Labor discipline went to pieces, and the peasants refused to work on the collective land. The chairman found that not even his best "mathematics" was effective in this situation, and he had to threaten the peasants with trial and expulsion from the collective. This was sometimes effective, because although many people wanted to leave the kolkhoz they did not want to be expelled, for in such a case they were given no official documents, without which it was impossible to move about the country.

When I came back to the village in January 1947 in the company of two other army officers, we were struck by the contrast between living conditions then and before the war. The whole village was seething with discontent, which was particularly directed against the administration, both of the two farms and of the village. It was a measure of the strength of this discontent that the peasants managed to force the local Party leadership to let them elect new people to the posts of chairman of the village soviet and chairmen of the two kolkhozes in the village.

Thus all the top posts in the village passed into the hands of former front-line officers, who strove to improve the economic position of the collective farmers. Bohdan K., a young, energetic and intelligent officer who immediately won the respect of the peasants was elected chairman of the village soviet. Volodymyr T., a retired colonel, became chairman of one of the kolkhozes; the other chairmanship fell to me.

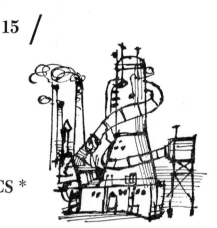

15 /

INTERPRETING
SOVIET STATISTICS *

Economic development has received such high priority in the Soviet
Union that its study must be given high priority elsewhere. The
questions involved in such a study are many and complex, the answers
to most of which require at least some study of Soviet statistics—and
therein lies the difficulty. Even before World War II, Colin Clark and
other economists questioned the reliability and validity of some Soviet
statistics; and since that war, even more work has been done on them.
Dr. Jasny has had much experience in interpreting the troublesome
features and in devising reliable means of handling them.

I HAVE BEEN asked how a reasonably correct picture of the Soviet
economy can be obtained in spite of the inadequacy—to use a neutral
word—of the relevant statistical material.

The answer is: why, it is simple. You examine carefully the statistics
that are released, correct those false and inaccurate statistics that it is
possible to correct, discard those which are beyond repair, putting in
their place and in the gaps which have been deliberately left, your own
estimates—made with the help of correct and corrected official statistics
and other suitable evidence—and you then get a set of statistics permitting more or less definite conclusions.

It takes time, certainly. This is better counted in years rather than
weeks or months. The present writer has been at it for more than 15
years and cannot yet see the end.

* Naum Jasny, "Interpreting Soviet Statistics," *Soviet Survey* (October–December,
1958), pp. 9–14. Reprinted by permission of the author and the publisher.
    The author is a noted analyst of the Soviet economy. Among his many works
on the subject are *The Socialized Agriculture of the U.S.S.R.* (1949), *The Soviet
Economy during the Plan Era* (1951), and *The 1956 Soviet Statistical Handbook
—A Commentary* (1957).

One quality that the analyst needs, sometimes referred to as 'the feel for figures,' is a constructive mind which, coupled with a sense of reality, can, by a process that is both conscious and intuitive, fit together the single bricks to make a more or less comprehensive structure.

It is essential to approach this work with a reasonable lack of bias and a readiness to go your own way, whatever the demands from the outside. Those with a bloodless indifference to both sides in the present titanic conflict will most likely lack other indispensable qualifications for the task. They may well be opportunists, responding to public pressures. Only that analyst will be successful who is able not merely to reject demands from the outside, but also to conquer his own inclination to see black or pink, as the case may be.

Errors, and indeed relatively great errors, are inevitable in an analysis in which one is compelled to use such a crooked item as Soviet statistics. It is best to acknowledge such errors frankly, to get them entirely out of one's system, so that they cannot affect—and distort—further work.

These tiresome preliminaries settled, it is possible to get a fairly correct idea of what is going on. But there is a vast difference between the knowledge of the analyst and the knowledge which has become common property. Soviet problems are usually presented in a context of heated controversy; it is at times extremely difficult to get correct findings accepted, and in this way their usefulness is diminished.

In spite of the immense amount of research into the Soviet economy being done in the United States, the sputniks came as a complete surprise except to a very few. The explanation lies largely in the bias both of those who are unwilling to give the Soviet régime due credit for its achievements, and those whose sympathies tend in the opposite direction. In either case the prevalence of wishful thinking, and the readiness of the opportunist to fall in with it, can clearly have deplorable results.

During many years of Stalin's reign and for some time thereafter almost no statistics were released in the USSR. This policy was changed in 1956, and since then a great volume of statistics has been published. They are markedly selective; for example estimates of the population, both total and sub-divided into rural and urban, were published in 1956, but the age and sex composition was withheld. Among the items not covered at all or only inadequately covered by Soviet statistics are such important items as nominal wages and indices of farm production, not to speak of practically everything connected with the armed forces. A reasonably correct official price index exists only for the retail prices of consumer goods in 1947–57, with 1940 as the base year; lack of information about prices will, it is expected—and with justification—prevent even a superficial analysis of the most important economic items, such as the budget.

The nature of Soviet statistics is in itself controversial. One extreme, and perhaps the less dangerous one, is represented by those who believe that *all* Soviet statistics are falsified. The other camp insists that Soviet statistics are not false, but that their acknowledged defects arise from methodological deficiencies. In fact, Soviet statistics cover the full range from correct to falsified, with every kind of intermediate grade in between. Concealment of the methods of calculating the data, and of all the details of the calculations (for national income, for example, only one figure is announced for each year), frequent unannounced changes in concepts and coverage, and last but not least, the marked element of distortion introduced by the language used in commenting on the statistics, immensely enhance the difficulties.

The degree of distortion in Soviet statistics depends in the first place on the importance that an item has in Soviet propaganda and on the extent to which reality departs from the Soviet rulers' wishes or from what they want the reality to be believed to be. Other differences in reliability are related to the time factor. Correct statistics have a much greater propaganda value than false statistics; hence the release of false statistics declines in periods favourable for the régime, and soars in unfavourable periods.

The idea that all Soviet statistics are a falsification is obviously absurd. It is held mainly by strangers in the field of statistics, or by those with an anti-Soviet attitude who give free rein to their fantasy in describing what is going on (or not going on) in the USSR. This is of course much easier than making the sustained effort needed to separate the wheat from the chaff in Soviet data.

The idea that Soviet statistics do not contain falsifications—the other extreme—could have grown up only at a time when the study of the Soviet economy in the West was in its early stages. It is for reasons unconnected with research that the idea has survived until today. If this attitude towards Soviet statistics has not made the analytical work of its adherents entirely valueless, this is because they have largely disregarded the distorted official data—sometimes to an even greater extent than the present writer does.

The bulk of Soviet statistics, so far as they are released at all, are correct. Their shortcomings, if any, consist in unexpected and unannounced changes in concepts. Transport statistics, for example, seem to be entirely correct. Statistics of industrial production *in physical terms* are almost completely correct as well. Soviet statistics of acreages under cultivation and livestock herds have never been seriously doubted (possibly only because of the inability to provide proof of their unreliability).

On the other hand, most of the statistics relating to aggregate quantities, such as the indices for national income and industrial production, are incorrect. Although such data may not cover a large number of categories, they are precisely the figures to which a statesman, scholar, or journalist would in the first place turn.

Falsification reaches astronomical dimensions in statistics of real wages and real incomes. The great achievements of the USSR in industrialisation were obtained by imposing immense sacrifices on the population. Even Khrushchev admitted as much in his speech on the expansion of output of textiles and shoes in May 1958 (*Pravda*, 10 May 1958). Nevertheless, Soviet statistics are made to demonstrate immense increases in real wages and real incomes of the peasants. For example, the fantastic claim was officially made that in one year only (1948) real wages more than doubled, although such an increase is physically impossible; the actual growth is unlikely to have exceeded 15 per cent. In 1939 it was announced that real wages had more than doubled during the second five year plan; a rise of 25 per cent would have been more in line with facts. To reinforce this claim the turnover in State and co-operative trade in 1928–40 (which did not increase at constant prices by much more than 50 per cent) was advertised as having grown 4.6-fold.

Falsifications and exaggerations are, in fact, strewn over the whole economy. An astonishing case was a table in an official statistical handbook, *Socialist Agriculture*, (Moscow, 1939) reproduced in 1948 by M. M. Lifits, Minister of Trade, in his pamphlet *Soviet Trade*. It showed a rapid rise in per capita sales of the most important consumers' goods by the peasants in 1933–38. The table left no doubt that physical quantities were involved. Only after several years of work did the present writer realise that the quantities sold were measured in rubles of rapidly declining purchasing power.

The Soviet economy has shown great rates of growth since 1946. In the decade before the war only the years 1934–36 were of similar nature. The period of the great purges, 1936–40, were years of near stagnation, while the period of full-scale collectivisation connected with the drive to industrialise (the years 1930–32), was characterised by rapidly declining rates of growth. As might be expected, statistics covering the good periods showed in general only relatively moderate exaggerations and occasionally there were no exaggerations at all. On the other hand, the indices for the unfavourable periods are as a rule exaggerated immensely. Long-range indices for the most important items, such as national income, industrial output and investment, embody all—even the most stupendous—exaggerations of the unfavourable periods and consequently they too are greatly exaggerated.

Unexpected and usually unannounced changes in concepts are most frequent in regard to farm products. For about 20 years, until 1954, the Soviets operated with the so-called 'biological' or 'factual' yield of grain (for a somewhat shorter period for other crops); this departed from reality by quite substantial but never announced percentages. Recently some non-meat food was included in the estimates of meat production to make them more presentable. The milk covered by statistics was also recently expanded, without any explanation or announcement.

The idea that the errors in Soviet statistics are not deliberate implies that the Moscow central statistical office is staffed by infants. The people working there are better statisticians than most of those analysing Soviet statistics in the West. They know better than most Western analysts the weak spots in their statistics, the great extent of falsifications, the immense contradictions between them. Most Soviet statisticians would be only too happy to release honest statistics, but they operate on orders and have no choice. They may and no doubt do congratulate themselves on the great effectiveness of Soviet propaganda. The Soviet 1956 statistical handbook was published in many hundreds of thousands of copies in many languages—three editions in English alone. (Both I and my publisher would be satisfied if a few thousand copies of my *Commentary* on this handbook were to be sold.) The immensely distorted indices for the aggregates mentioned above are also repeated in virtually every speech and article, certainly in every book.

The methods used in the tiresome and frustrating work of checking Soviet data vary. Here only the most important will be discussed.

The Soviet economy, as that of any other country, represents a body with an endless web of inter-connected links. Many farm products serve as the raw materials of the food industries. The output of these reaches the consumer via the retail trade. In between these two series of linked stages is the operation of the transport system. In short, there is a chain in which each stage is tied in with the preceding and the succeeding link. Other examples of such important chains of inter-connected links are: iron ore and coking coal—pig iron—steel—machinery—investment in equipment, or building materials—construction as part of investment.

In dealing with the economy of a country with good statistics, an analyst will devote attention to such chains and inter-connections only in specific cases, for example, when he is interested in the proportions of total farm output reaching the market. In general the existence of proper tie-ins is taken for granted. In work on the Soviet economy, examination of the tie-ins (most frequently the ascertainment of their insufficiency) is a major, if not the major, tool.

The degree of inexactness varies in each chain from link to link, from zero in some cases to immense proportions in others. Proper tie-ins between the individual links may consequently be absent, sometimes glaringly absent. The table on p. 34 of *Economy of the USSR in 1956*, the official statistical handbook (this is the basic table of the handbook), gives the Major Indicators of Development of the National Economy of the USSR in 1913–56. Some of the indicators for 1956 (1913 and 1928 = 100) in the table are as follows:

	1913–56	1928–56
Numbers of wage and salary earners	443	446
Fixed investment of the State	....	3527
Basic funds	1480	1089
National income	1922	1615
Gross industrial production	3021	2288
Freight transports (5 carriers)	1136	1092

Of the six series, two, those of wage and salary earners and freight transports, are reasonably correct. The other four indices are extremely high relative to those for wage and salary earners and freight transports. The contradiction in regard to the number of wage and salary earners cannot be cleared up by general considerations. It is obvious, on the other hand, that gross industrial production could not have increased in 1928–56 more than twice as much as freight transports. The transport system is engaged primarily in transporting industrial goods and the raw materials required for them. Moreover, the five carriers for which the index is calculated do not include transport by horse, which declined greatly over the period. Similarly, home industry, which is as a rule conducted without or with relatively little use of transport by the five registered carriers, was still quite important in 1928, but has been greatly reduced since. Transports by the five carriers must consequently have grown substantially more than industrial production.

The official indices for gross industrial production and freight transports by the five carriers imply that raw materials and finished industrial goods were making their own way from the farm to the factory, from factory to factory, and from factory to retail stores. This does not occur even in a socialist state, and since the index for freight transports is accepted as correct, the index showing a roughly 8-fold increase in industrial production in 1928–56, calculated by D. Shimkin *et al* of the U.S. Bureau of Census as well as by this writer, appears to accord well with the roughly 11-fold increase in freight transports by the five carriers.

The official claim of a 16-fold growth in national income in 1928–56, makes even less sense relatively to the 11-fold increase in freight transports by the five carriers, than does the 23-fold increase in industrial output. Again it may be said that, all things considered, the 4.5-fold increase in national income calculated by this writer, and the even smaller percentage rises calculated by other analysts, seem to tie in well with the officially calculated 11-fold increase in freight transports by the five carriers.

Most of the marked discrepancies between individual links in the chains and conditions point to distortions. Few of them yield reasonably exact data, as for example, determination of the grain harvest from the utilisation end. Usually only a broad idea is obtained, indicating the direction in which research must be conducted.

Statistics of the national economy are normally prepared by statistical organisations. Since research on the Soviet economy in the West is mostly conducted by individuals or at best by small groups, the handling of even the available material causes great difficulties which are aggravated by the Soviet habit of concealment (wise from the Soviet point of view). A really thorough covering of the whole economy is impossible in these conditions. The choice for the Western analyst is usually between having relatively more thorough results, at prohibitive costs and with a long delay, and the use of short-cut methods (basing indices on small samples, employing semi-detective methods such as pinning down the implications, not intended for disclosure, in statements, etc.). Judiciously handled, short-cut methods yield satisfactory results, but very few analysts are able to make use of them, especially in the field of Soviet economics, and the results obtained by those who are qualified for such tasks are looked upon with more or less distrust. If this were not so, a discussion would not have been conducted in 1957–58 in the pages of *The Times* on the reliability of the funny Soviet index of industrial production (torn to shreds by Colin Clark as far back as 1939, as well as by his numerous successors thereafter).

Whatever findings on the Soviet economy are available are at best incomplete, and the disagreements between Western students in some cases substantial. The growth of national income in the five years 1951–55, for example, is estimated by this writer at 9 per cent per year (the official figure is 11.5 per cent). Probably not many of his colleagues would agree with this estimate. The estimate of 6–7 per cent per year is generally accepted in the United States.

One of the easiest tasks is a rough calculation of real paid-out wages. Nominal wages, even when they were concealed, could have been roughly estimated from one or another tied-in item, such as retail trade. Most prices of consumer goods and services can be found, too, although a great deal more time is needed for this task than most analysts are prepared to devote. A usable index for Soviet real wages was not calculated before 1951. Calculation of peasants' incomes meets with the difficulty, which cannot be entirely surmounted, of estimating the output from their private plots and livestock; there has been a complete black-out on this since 1940. With the prices used for the index of real wages, an index of retail prices can be constructed (by changing weights), but only one attempt has been made so far, and even this needs revision.

Official estimates of the real grain crops have not been disclosed even now. The present writer's estimate for the years before World War II turned out to be accurate, while those for the post-war years were too high. Still, it was useful to have the estimate of the 1950 grain crop of 92 million tons, in face of the official estimate of 124.5 million tons, although the crop later turned out to have been equal only to about 80 million tons (implied in official data), or 85 million tons (this writer's latest estimate). Calculation of the grain crops does not actually meet with serious difficulties for one who is familiar with the utilisation of grain; there are only six items (food, feed, seed, technical uses, foreign trade, and waste) to consider. With the relatively small number of important farm products, and with the data on acreages and livestock herds usually available, even estimating the index for farm production available for sale and for consumption in the farm home is really not a very big task.

The calculation most frequently attempted has been that of industrial production. It has been undertaken for both gross and net output, and both by more thorough and by short-cut methods. A full coverage is impossible because of the absence of data on the output of armaments and of the great variety of machines produced and the frequent changes in models. Impressively, the results reached by most analysts for the period 1928–50 are fairly close to each other. A successful appraisal of the growth in industrial output in 1928–37 was even reached by something resembling a trick (evaluating a contradiction between two widely-diverging estimates of the share of Soviet industrial production in total world production in the same year in two different editions of the same official statistical handbook).

There are numerous factors causing considerable difficulties in estimating construction and investment. But too great errors can be avoided, because changes in investment more or less parallel changes in construction, and for construction a good check is available in the output of building materials. The main difficulties are encountered in estimating the shift of investment from 1928, when the private sector accounted for a large part of total investment, and, say, 1932, by which time this share had dwindled greatly. There are also great distortions in the official data pertaining to changes in investment during the purges (1936–40) and the subsequent years until 1946, distortions which it is not easy to eliminate completely.

All estimates of Soviet national income thus far made in the West have been produced by crude methods. The results differ greatly, depending on the selection of weights. Still, with due allowance made for this fact, the estimates do give a fair order of magnitude, while the official index for, say, 1928–55, is exaggerated more than two-fold.

In conclusion, it seems to me that I may have taken too lightly those questions on which my own mind has been made up, and that therefore the task will look too easy. I really do not see how an outsider can find his way among the various estimates, official and unofficial. Machinery output represents almost 40 per cent of total Soviet industrial production. According to official calculations, the production of machinery (including other metal-processing) grew from 1950 to 1955, a period of considerably improved Soviet statistics, by as much as 120 per cent. One organisation devoted to research into the Soviet economy has given, for the output of machinery (excluding armaments) an increase of 14 per cent (1928 weights) or 23 per cent (1955 weights) in those years. Statisticians in the U.S. Bureau of Census calculated for the output of machinery, including armaments, an increase of 72 per cent for the same period. (Let it be added that the output of armaments is unlikely to have grown during the period in question much more than the average for all machinery.) There you are: 120, 72, 14 or 23. Take your choice.

16

THE NEW SOVIET INTELLIGENTSIA: ORIGINS AND RECRUITMENT *

Just as it is inappropriate to apply certain Western European terms to Russia, so it is inappropriate to apply some Russian prerevolutionary terms to contemporary Russia; yet that is often done. The term "intelligentsia," for example, is used officially, but as the Soviet government employs it, the term has a meaning different from the one it had before 1917: it now designates both the white-collar and the professional groups. More important than the semantic problem involved in the use of the term "Soviet intelligentsia" is another: the potential social and political importance of the new intelligentsia as a class. In Soviet theory, there are and can be no classes in the Soviet Union. Nonetheless, it is evident that the Soviet intelligentsia may evolve into a class, as "class" is understood in Western social science, for apparently its members now have a favored material position which they are seeking to preserve and enhance. Whether or not they can make the next step—win political power—remains to be seen.

WHEN ENGELS was describing the origins of socialism in the nineteenth century (in that part of *Anti-Duehring* which was later published separately as *From Utopian to scientific socialism*) he put his finger on one particularly relevant spot: the disillusionment with the results of the French revolution among the Western intelligentsia. What

* Leopold Labedz, "The New Soviet Intelligentsia," *Soviet Survey* (July–September, 1959), pp. 103–11, abridged. Reprinted by permission of the author and the publisher.

The author is Associate Editor of *Survey* (formerly *Soviet Survey*). He was born in Russia and received his education in Poland, France, Italy, and England. In addition to performing his editorial duties, he is now doing research on Soviet society at the London School of Economics and Political Science.

they expected, he said, was the rule of *liberté, egalité, fraternité,* the king-dom of reason, and what they got was a bourgeois-dominated society. To the disenchantment with the old slogans they reacted by producing the new ideological blueprints of utopian socialism. But these were useless. Only by transforming socialist theory by putting it on a 'scientific' basis, could socialist society be created.

How far the theory of 'scientific socialism,' constructed in the nine-teenth century from the materials of German classical philosophy, English political economy, and the French revolutionary tradition, re-sulted in a jump from the realm of necessity into the realm of freedom can be seen now, when Khrushchev is proclaming that the stage of transi-tion to full communism has been reached. This, on any possible interpre-tation of the canonical texts (including the official interpretation), must be accompanied by the disappearance of the distinction between mental and manual work. In other words, it logically implies the disappearance of the 'new Soviet intelligentsia' as a separate social category.

Apart from being the officially proclaimed 'guide to action,' the original Marxist doctrine is also a constant source of embarrassment, as it invites comparison between the doctrinal indications about the classless society (scanty as they are in Marx) and actual Soviet social develop-ments. The new social structure, gradually emerging, offers few indica-tions that it is approaching the prescribed target. Social planning is even more difficult than economic planning, and the social consequences of revolutionary upheavals rarely correspond to the hopes of the revolu-tionaries (or, for that matter, to the expectations of the counter-revolu-tionaries).

At first, doctrinally at least, the situation was not too complex. True, the revolution had occurred in a country where the production forces required to construct a socialist society still had to be built. The destruc-tion of the old order was accompanied by the annihilation of landowners and capitalists, and the Decree of 10 November 1919 proclaimed that 'all classes and class divisions of citizens, all class privileges and disabili-ties, as well as all civil ranks, are abolished. . . .' After the introduction of NEP Lenin decribed the new Soviet social order as consisting of work-ers, peasants, and the 'new bourgeoisie'. This new bourgeoisie, *kulaks* in the country and *nepmen* in the town, was eliminated with the end of NEP and the collectivisation of the countryside.

There was, however, another problem in the twenties, that of the 'bourgeois *spets*,' i.e., of all those highly qualified specialists who were needed to run society, the economy, and the state. Trotsky's use of Tsarist officers in the Red Army was, of course, the first instance of the dilemma. The old specialists were regarded as being essentially hostile; but their services were needed for the time being, although they were to be dis-pensed with as soon as the new technical cadres were educated. The old specialists, according to the Leninist analysis, belonged to the bourgeois intelligentsia, a category eventually as much condemned to extinction as the bourgeoisie itself.

The pre-revolutionary intelligentsia in Russia was the nursery of revolutionary ideas, but its character and composition had been changing. Before the revolution its features already differed from those when the *raznochintsy* largely determined its dominant traits. With the progress of industrialisation it was becoming less *freischwebende*, and professional people were becoming more numerous. However, it was still the vehicle of the Russian revolutionary tradition.

Engels' remark that the working class, by taking power, abolishes itself as a class, is more appropriate to the revolutionary intelligentsia. The Bolshevik revolution signified its end, as it did the end of the entire pre-revolutionary intelligentsia. Pasternak's *Doctor Zhivago* is a poignant illustration of this process.

According to the *Political Dictionary* (Moscow, 1958, p. 211) 'The intelligentsia is a social stratum consisting of people who are professionally occupied with mental labour. . . . It is not a separate class as it does not occupy an independent position in the system of social production. . . . Under capitalism the majority of the intelligentsia serves the possessing classes; bourgeois scientists and teachers elaborate and spread the ruling capitalist ideology, infuse bourgeois morality into the consciousness of the masses, and attempt to justify the rule of the bourgeoisie. . . . After the October revolution the communist party successfully solved the task of re-educating part of the old intelligentsia in a socialist spirit and created the new Soviet intelligentsia.'

In the early thirties, after the beginning of the Plan era, policy towards the intelligentsia seemed to have changed in many respects. *Uravnilovka* became a petty bourgeois sin, discrimination on the basis of social origin was somewhat attenuated, Stalin decided that *kadry reshayut vse*. In 1934 he announced the arrival of socialism, the first stage on the road to classless society. As a corollary to this (after some vacillations) the Stalinist theory of Soviet society was made part of the official orthodoxy. Soviet society was now said to consist of two friendly classes, workers and peasants, and of a stratum, 'the new Soviet intelligentsia.' Long-term orthodoxy remained unchanged. *The Big Soviet Encyclopedia* (Vol. 27, 1937, p. 608) declared: 'When full Communism is achieved . . . there will be no intelligentsia as a separate social stratum.'

The *Yezhovshchina* hit the intelligentsia harder than any other category, particularly the remaining members of the pre-revolutionary intelligentsia. But the 'new Soviet intelligentsia' continued to increase numerically with the progress of industrialization. The orthodox class analysis could not easily account for this. According to its criteria, a class was determined by its relation to the means of production. But this criterion could not account for the existence and expansion of a separate social category whose relation to the means of production was exactly the same as that of the workers, while its social characteristics were basically different. Its inclusion in the Stalinist theory of the Soviet social structure acknowledged the reality, but it resulted in an internally inconsistent and embarrassing definition. The more the Soviet economy progressed along the road of industrialisation, the more difficult did it become to square the facts of (social) life with the requirements of orthodoxy. A modification of the original articles of faith was called for. The new edition of the *Encyclopedia* (Vol. 18, 1953, p. 270) registered the supplementary qualification with an adjective: 'The work of I. V. Stalin, *The Economic Problems of Socialism* . . . has shown the way to liquidate the essential (*sushchestvennoe*) difference between mental and manual labour in Soviet Society.'

Da liegt der Hund begraben. The adjective 'essential' opens a way out for the utopian element in the doctrine. No wonder that it has been incorporated in the official orthodox formulas and has remained there ever since.

The Khrushchev era has not yet provided many instances of the 'creative development of Marxism,' the official euphemism for the modification of orthodox tenets which can no longer be held against the intractable reality. The original formula about the disappearance of the difference between intellectual and physical labour has been maintained, now qualified by 'essential,' but the announcement that the second, full stage of communism is approaching, makes it necessary for the formula to be related more specifically to the impending realisation of the prophecy.

The Soviet ideological functionaries are therefore trying hard to find a satisfactory way of handling this delicate problem. The current treatment is reflected in two authoritative pronouncements made at the special session of the department of social sciences of the Academy of Sciences, by Ostrovitianov and Fedoseev. Ostrovitianov said:

In order to build communism it is necessary to overcome the essential difference between mental and physical work, to raise the cultural-technical level of all toilers to the level of engineer-technicians and agronomists. As is known, the social and class content of the opposition between mental and physical work has already been eliminated in our country. However, there remain fairly substantial differences in the character of the work of the two major groups of the population: one which is predominantly occupied with mental labour, and the other predominantly occupied with physical labour.

Fedoseev repeated the perennial thesis that 'in the socialist society intellectual and manual workers are drawing together at an accelerated pace.' This is due to 'the reduction in the number of unskilled workers.

With the development of mechanisation and automation, physical labour becomes lighter and, with socialist relations of production, its character draws closer to that of engineer-technical labour. On the other hand, the preparation of highly qualified specialists must proceed on the basis of a harmonious conjunction of mental and physical labour.' Polytechnisation and Khrushchev's educational reform are said to be accomplishing this process of social symbiosis among the more intellectual occupations. The distinction between the two kinds of labour is neatly defined in another recent Soviet book devoted to the subject: M. Danielyan, *On the opposition between mental and physical labour* (Erevan, 1957). According to this work, physical labour consists of work 'expended on the direct production of material goods,' while intellectual labour is 'expended on organisation, leadership, supervision, performance of various social and state functions on a social scale as well as on the level of a single enterprise' (p. 6).

How all this can be logically sorted out is, of course, a mystery. When physical labour is mechanised under capitalism, the worker becomes an automaton, a man-machine, exclaims *Voprosy Filosofii* (1958, 4, p. 150). But under communism it leads to the disappearance of the difference between mental and physical labour. Obviously conveyer belts have vastly more enlightening possibilities in the land of socialism.

As to intellectual labour which, according to the above definition, is concerned with 'organisation, leadership and supervision,' it is difficult to see how it can merge with work concerned with 'the direct production of material goods' without abandoning these three functions, on which productivity in modern industry rests.

So, however grim the prospects of the Soviet intelligentsia may be according to the theory, which logically demands its disappearance, in practice, of course, there is no question of the theory being implemented, for this would involve the dismantling of the state organisation, Party leadership, and supervision of the economy.

The doctrinal blueprint is obviously an ideological myth, and one which is becoming less and less consistent. What are the hard facts which can be discerned behind it? What are the characteristic features of the 'new Soviet intelligentsia' in terms of its origins and recruitment, income and status differentiation, its group consciousness and homogeneity? Or is it merely a blanket term to designate various social categories having little in common? If there are common characteristics, what relevance have they to the distribution of power in the Soviet system? What light can the answers to such questions shed on the prospects of further social change in the Soviet Union? Or is 'intelligentsia' an ideological term legitimised because of its historical connotations, but really helping to camouflage and confuse the real lines of social divisions?

It is enough to put these questions to see that even though the evidence is thin and inconclusive, it is better to ask them than to use the term 'intelligensia' as a ragbag concept, much as the word 'bureaucracy' was used by the revolutionary romantics.

There is little point in starting with a definition. Most analysts of the phenomenon of the 'old' intelligentsia agree that it was not to be defined as a class or an estate, that it had a certain level of education and an 'active' attitude towards general ideas, that it was socially heterogeneous and relatively unattached. But whether one takes as a starting point Lenin or Miliukov, Mannheim or Alfred Weber, Arnost Blaha or Chalasinski, all of whom devoted special studies to the problem, it is clear that their definitions do not fit the new intelligentsia, that this is a genuinely different phenomenon, and that its analysis can only result in confusion if it leans too heavily on semantics and the assumption of continuity. The question to be asked now is not only how much continuity can be discerned between the old and the new intelligentsia, but also which sub-groups of the new intelligentsia display the traditional characteristics of the old intelligentsia and which reveal their discontinuity.

The eschatological opposition between 'capitalism' and 'socialism' tends to obscure the fact that although industrialisation has occurred in a variety of social contexts and has been promoted by widely different methods, it possesses certain common functional imperatives which set limits upon the variability of social organisation. These include recruitment and motivation of the managerial and technical cadres, who not only have to be educated but given incentives to perform their roles and authority to do so effectively. The Party found in practice that it had to develop an appropriate system of economic incentives (*printsip lichnoi materyalnoi zainteresovannosti*), and a parade of prestige and deference to maintain authority in the hierarchical system. It could easily dispense with independently minded intellectuals, but it needed the technical specialists. It found, however, that 'of the highly qualified technological and scientific intelligentsia, the writers and artists, it was only individual members who immediately and unconditionally came over to the side of the Soviet Government. . . . A considerable part of the old intelligentsia adopted a hostile, or at best a waiting attitude.' Thus the Party embarked upon an operation designed 'to bring about a radical change in the class composition of the student body.' Early in 1919 the first 'workers faculty' (*Rabfak*) was created. In 1920 *Rabfaks* were attached to all universities (VUZY) in the RSFSR, and those who passed through them were given priority right in entering the VUZY. It is claimed that in the academic year 1924/25 they constituted 43.3% of all the entrants to the higher educational establishments, a proportion which increased to 49.3% by 1928.

The policy of 'proletarianisation' of professional personnel had as its background the fact that of 15,500 university trained engineers working in Soviet industry in that year, only 138 were Party members. However, the social composition of VUZY students changed less than one might suspect from these figures. In 1928 workers or their descendants constituted 25.4%, peasants and their descendants 23.9%, and the descendants of the intelligentsia and others 50.7% of the newly enrolled students. A decade later, in 1938, the respective figures were 33.9%, 21.6%, and 44.5%. Of the 100,600 specialists engaged in industry in 1928, 13,700 had higher education and 10,500 had a secondary specialised education.

During the first Five Year Plan the educational target for engineers was 176,000 (there were only 24,000 in 1930). It was claimed that 170,000 specialists with higher qualifications were in fact trained, of whom 65.2% were of worker and peasant origin in 1932 (twice as many as in 1929 but including 'specialists with secondary qualifications'). However, the policy of forcible proletarianisation had by that time to be relaxed; here too the social composition of the professional personnel shows a distinct divergence from what might be expected. In 1940 50.4% were descendants of the old intelligentsia and other heterogeneous elements, while the rest were of proletarian and peasant origin. That in fact the percentage of the children of the old intelligentsia in the ranks of the new intelligentsia was even greater than is suggested by these figures can be inferred from other factors. Discriminatory practices in education created an additional incentive to surmount all obstacles and get into the university, and work hard when they got there. It was the one avenue of social mobility open to them, and their inclinations were reinforced by the high value traditionally placed on education among the old intelligentsia. They had to fight hard to overcome the handicap of their social origin and in order to succeed they had to have some additional drive. They had to work harder and, of course, be even more zealous politically than other students to acquire a protective colouring. The mechanism of the process had obvious similarities to that of social mobility through education in systems where the 'built-in' bias is against the lower classes. Only in this case it worked in the obverse sense, with different categories, and the Soviet 'lucky Jims' were handicapped by having political as well as social skeletons in the family cupboard.

This mechanism of compensation was obvious enough in the case of members of the old intelligentsia who jumped on the bandwagon. For their descendants the need to stress political loyalty in order to have a career or at least the possibility of a career was socially no less paramount. The Party card was therefore a more desirable object for the members of the intelligentsia than for workers or peasants (and also more difficult to obtain), as it gave an outward guarantee of political respectability. The influx into the Party of the new intelligentsia was as much due to this as to the deliberate effort of its leadership to effect a managerial-political personal union in order to solve the problem of political reliability and control. It was a paradoxical analogue of Michels' analysis of the German social-democratic party as an avenue of social mobility for workers deprived of the chance to rise through higher education. It is understandable that where conditions were reversed, and political criteria came to play a paramount role, it was the intelligentsia who often tried to use the 'workers party' as a vehicle for its own social mobility. The number of Party members among specialists with higher or secondary education rose steadily both in absolute terms and as a percentage of the total. They constituted 10.4% in 1929, 25.1% in 1932, and 33.0% in 1956. They also constituted a growing percentage of the Party cadres. In 1956 there were already 1,878,000 of them in the Party, and by 1959—2,300,000 (of the total claimed for the whole country of 7.5 millions). Of 224,000 scientific workers in 1955, 97,000 (or 43%) were members of the Party, against 54,000 (or 37%) in 1947. The trend is even more striking among those with the highest qualifications: in 1947 members of the Party constituted 31% of all the doctors, 36% of all the *dotsents*, and 32% of all the professors. In 1956 the respective figures were 55%, 60% and 59%.

The first five-year plan concentrated on the engineering-technical cadres, the second showed some shift towards the training of medical and pedagogical staffs. 'By the end of the second five-year plan the old specialists had finally melted into the enormous army of the Soviet intelligentsia.' The *Rabfaks*, which by 1934 had trained almost a quarter of a million, entered the last period of their existence. Their number and their output diminished, and in 1940 they ceased to be. The last year for which figures on the social origin of students in higher educational establishments were published was 1937/38. Since then no official data have been available. In 1958 Khrushchev, in his memorandum on the educational reform, mentioned that in some universities the percentage of students whose parents are non-manual workers (i.e., belong to the 'new Soviet intelligentsia') reaches sixty to seventy.

The modification of the policy of enforced occupational mobility reflects the requirements of Soviet industrial development. But the new educational reform is presented as a step which will rectify 'the serious shortcomings which have appeared in the selection of pupils for the higher educational establishments,' and thus presumably deprive the children of the intelligentsia of their illegitimate advantages. This remains to be seen. The experience of the last forty years, when the obstacles put in their way were even higher, and did not produce an intelligentsia consisting exclusively of the children of peasants and workers conforming to the propaganda stereotype, is enough to justify scepticism. Among the new Soviet intelligentsia, *vydvizhentsy* are as likely to try to pass on their status to their children as the descendants of the old intelligentsia. They may have approved the principle of selection by social origin when they were its beneficiaries, but not necessarily when it may put *their* children at a disadvantage.

With the relaxation of terror the intelligentsia acquires greater security of tenure. Technological progress necessitates continued emphasis on the production of highly skilled specialists, and these are more likely to come from intellectually more sophisticated homes. Thus although the middle and lower grades of specialists have lost their scarcity value, this does not necessarily mean that as a result of Khrushchev's educational reform the children of the intelligentsia will display a downward mobility trend. They may even be relatively more successful in by-passing obstacles on the road to higher education than were the children of the old intelligentsia. Unlike the latter, they cannot be described as 'counter-revolutionary' on account of their social origin. Even without nepotism they have a distinct advantage over their predecessors.

The upper layer of the Soviet intelligentsia is thus horizontally divided, according to educational criteria, into highly skilled specialists and those with secondary specialized education. More recently a new term has come into use (both in the Soviet Union and in the People's Democracies) which divides them vertically; the two categories are the technical intelligentsia and the creative intelligentsia. The former obviously describes technical occupations, the latter refers to 'humanistic' occupations, writers, artists, historians, journalists, philosophers, lecturers in Marxism-Leninism, etc. It is in this group that the element of continuity with the old intelligentsia is to be sought, as, in conditions of modern specialisation, they are the most likely to display interest in general, social, and political ideas. In the Soviet system they may be regarded as the nearest substitute for intellectuals, although they are not often free to apply an individual critical judgment to general ideas and are thus more passive and less creative—reproductive rather than productive.

But apart from the specialists with higher education and those with secondary specialised education, i.e., of the professional personnel which is now listed as 7.5 million strong, what other categories are included in the new Soviet intelligentsia?

Konstantinov, discussing Khrushchev's theses at the 21st Congress, stated that 'at present the Soviet intelligentsia counts in its ranks more than 15 million people.' Who are the remaining 7.5 million?

In a paper presented to the Third World Congress of Sociology ('Changes in the Class Structure of the Population of the Soviet Union'), Academician V. S. Nemchinov reported that in 1955 the intelligentsia (families included) amounted to 14.1% of the population. He also disclosed that the working class (including farm workers) accounted for 44.2% of the population. This is a rather revealing breakdown, because the percentage of workers and employees given in the Soviet Statistical

Yearbook for 1955 is 58.3% of the total population (p. 19), which is, of course, the sum of the percentages given by Nemchinov. In other words, it seems that, at least for statistical purposes, the concept of the new Soviet intelligentsia is identical with the concept of 'employees' in Soviet usage. As all the workers in the Soviet Union are employed by the state and all the employees are working for the state, it is clear that some other criterion than 'work' and 'employment' must be used to differentiate between them for the purposes of a statistical breakdown. My own efforts in a conversation with Nemchinov to find out the criteria for the inclusion or exclusion of occupational categories used for his figures were not successful. It is clear that 'workers' are those doing manual work, and 'employees' are engaged in mental labour, in other words, all these co-terminal concepts are 'in the final analysis' reduced to the simple Marxian dichotomy. This makes it difficult to analyse the actual social situation in realistic terms. The remaining 7.5 million members of the 'new Soviet intelligentsia' undoubtedly consist of various kinds of clerks, the counter-parts of the Western 'white-collar' or 'blackcoated' workers. As in the West, their social aspirations and their actual status do not coincide. In the West, as one observer put it:

There are many indications that the division between manual and non-manual work is still a factor of enduring significance in the determination of class consciousness, despite changes in the relative economic position of the two groups. The differences between office and factory work are not merely technical but social. . . . Along the division between manual and non-manual work there has been no lack of competition for status.

In the Soviet Union the situation of 'status ambiguity' is even more pronounced. Official ideology sticks to the fiction of the workers' state; at the same time there has been a steady rise in the numbers of the intelligentsia, and the traditional status values have persisted. This derives, as Mr. Lockwood points out (in reference to Britain) from the social relations of modern industry, and more specifically from the structure of industrial organisation, especially from the relations of authority within the enterprise. Like his counterpart in the West, the Soviet clerk falls upon the distinction between manual and non-manual labour and exploits it symbolically in order to maintain his status. And this applies not only to such occupations as *zamglavbukha* (assistant to the chief accountant) or *zammag* (deputy storekeeper), which exist in the West, but also to a host of other occupations, basically clerical, but which are peculiarly Soviet and do not exist in the West, such as *normirovshchik* (norm-controller) or *planovik* (low-grade superviser of plan fulfilment at the grass-roots level).

Nemchinov divided the intelligentsia into three groups, and gave the following table:

	1929	1940	1955
1. Technicians, agronomists and animal husbandry	13%	17%	19%
2. Educationalists, medical and cultural workers	48%	59%	69%
3. Administrative workers in state, co-operative, and public organisations	39%	24%	12%
TOTAL:	100	100	100

It is difficult to square these figures with other known data. They imply that the plan era showed a marked decrease in the relative number of various bureaucracies, which is contrary to every known indication. After NEP the state extended its scope. The Party has grown enormously, and so must its apparatus have done. The budgetary allocations on administration were growing until recently, when they became stationary. And, finally, Konstantinov's division of the Soviet intelligentsia into two halves, each of 7.5 million, contradicts this table. The categories in the first and second groups must all have higher or secondary specialised education, and so have some in the third; together they accounted for more than 88% of the total intelligentsia in 1955. How is it then that in 1959 they account for only 50%? Has there been an enormous increase in the non-specialised intelligentsia since 1955? All Soviet assertions suggest the contrary, and even if one is sceptical about the accuracy of official claims, there can be little doubt about the fact itself of increased specialisation.

The reason for these semantic and statistical casuistries is obviously the embarrassing necessity to square doctrinal dicta with actual developments. Most embarrassing from this point of view (but from no other) is the fact that on the official reckoning the numbers of the intelligentsia are now about equal to those of the industrial workers, and are growing faster. Somehow this has to be adjusted to the pronouncements about the impending classless society.

Lenin wrote that in the transition to a classless society the social group of specialists will remain until the highest stage of communism has been reached. The higher (second) stage of full communism is, according to Khrushchev, not a distant but a close prospect, and Soviet society has already entered it. But the 'social group of specialists' (together with the state and other categories condemned to wither away) show no signs of being put into 'the museum of antiquities.' It is perhaps the central contradiction in Marx that the society he visualized was to be based on a high degree of productivity, requiring modern division of labour and progressive specialisation, and was at the same time to solve the problem of 'alienation,' partly due to the division of labour into mental and physical, by a harmonious combination of various activities by individuals. This is not a realistic prospect in Soviet (or any other) society. A different degree of intellectual and physical effort is, of course, always present in human labour, mechanisation may replace some forms of manual labour but it does not do away with skill-differentiation and specialisation which, if anything, accentuates the division between those occupations with a high intellectual, and those with a low intellectual component. 'Alienation', in the sense used by Marx and attributed by him solely to the iniquities of capitalism, continues with progressive specialisation, independently of the change in property relations. The Soviet navvies do not seem to be much nearer to the Nesmeyanovs and Kurchatovs. It is not surprising that a more outspoken Soviet author wrote recently: 'Forecasting the disappearance of the division of labour, V. I. Lenin clearly saw that communism will come to it "only in many years". And in fact many years have gone by since 1920 and the division of labour is still obvious in our society.'

17

LEGAL STATUS OF
THE CHURCH IN
SOVIET RUSSIA *

Soviet policy on organized religion has attracted much attention, and
rightly so, for one of the principal aims of that policy is to end
religious belief and to train Russian youth in the spirit of atheism. The
regime has sought, on the one hand, to monopolize and use all means
of directing the minds of the young and, on the other hand, to
eliminate wherever possible the influence of the church. The legal
status of the church has not changed substantially since 1939, the year
in which the following article was written, but the spirit in which the
law is applied has become somewhat more lenient. The Russian
Orthodox church has been permitted to reopen some theological
schools, monasteries, and churches; but its legal rights have not
changed, nor has the basic policy of the government with
respect to religion.

I THE THEORETICAL BACKGROUND OF THE SOVIET
LEGISLATION AFFECTING RELIGION

THE ADOPTION of a new constitution of the Soviet Union, in
December 1936, was understood by many foreign observers as a turning
point in the treatment of the Church and religion by the soviet government. As a matter of fact, however, the main provisions of the new soviet
federal constitution dealing with religion were not an innovation but were

* Vladimir Gsovski, "Legal Status of the Church in Soviet Russia," *Fordham Law
Review*, VIII, No. 1 (January, 1939), 1–28. Reprinted by permission of the publisher.

    The author (1891–1961) made Russian and East European law his lifelong
concern. He studied law in his native Russia and served as specialist in Russian
and East European law in the Library of Congress during the last thirty years of his

taken word for word from the constitutions of the principal constituent republics of the Soviet Union. Prior to 1936 the soviet federal constitution did not deal with religion. The new constitution restated the rather uniform provisions of the constitutions of the individual republics. It did not promise any change in soviet legislation concerning religion but merely sanctioned the *status quo* of the Church in Russia.

This status is by no means simple. The soviet laws directly dealing with religion and the Church are not the only factor determining the status. The theoretic evaluation of religion in the communist philosophy of the soviet rulers has contributed largely to the manner in which the laws were interpreted and applied. Finally, general laws and practices justifying the interference of the soviet authorities with the life of the soviet citizen set up important restrictions to the exercise of worship. A true picture of the status of the Church in Soviet Russia cannot be presented unless all these factors are taken into consideration.

In studying the situation a non-soviet scholar must bear in mind that the soviets have used common political and legal terms to designate concepts which are at variance with the traditional meaning we have for these terms. This is especially true of the so-called "separation of Church and State" declared in the soviet law.

The idea of the separation of the Church from the State in America emerged from the struggle for religious freedom and tolerance. This principle does not imply suppression of worship but is designed to safeguard liberty in the exercise of faith. The State is presumed not to be hostile or beneficent to any specific Church but equally benevolent to every Church. Interference of the authorities is supposed to be restricted to the protection of public order and peace among the adherents of various denominations.

Yet the soviet legislators were inspired by quite different ideas. They postulated that religious belief and worship run counter to the main objectives of the soviet government: against the planned socialist reconstruction of society, and against the prospective philosophy of the citizens of the soviet land. For the soviet leaders, "any religion is a kind of bourgeois ideology inimical in its very substance to the proletarian concept of life . . . to the socialist reconstruction of society . . . a remnant of capitalism in the mind of men that sanctifies in the name of a non-existing God all the other remnants thereof."

According to Lenin:

The saying of Marx: "Religion is the opium for the people," is the cornerstone of the Marxist point of view on the matter of religion. All contemporary reli-

---

life. At the time of his death, he was Chief of the European Law Division in the Law Library of the Library of Congress. Perhaps the most noteworthy of his many publications is the massive two-volume work *Soviet Civil Law* (1948–1949).

gion and churches, all and every kind of religious organization Marxism has always viewed as organs of bourgeois reaction, serving as a defence of exploitation and the drugging of the working class.

The difference between so called purified religion and crude religion is the same as between a blue devil and a violet one, no more.

Religion "forbids knowledge"; it "imposes upon the toilers a false concept of the world . . . distorting and perverting their concept of the world, the laws of nature and the development of human society."

Consequently the communists presume that "religion and communism are two hostile forces facing each other, two worlds engaged in an irreconcilable fight, two enemies whereof communism shall never extend its hand to religion." They think that "where religion is victorious communism is weak. The communist regime will only come into being in a society freed from religion."

All religions are equally condemned by the communists but Christianity is especially disapproved. Thus the program of atheistic work, adopted by the convention of the Union of the Militant Atheists in 1926 called for

exposing religious morals, as a morality imposed in a special manner upon the toilers by the ruling class. Contemporary Christianity for example, as a system of morals, represents by itself nothing but such concept of duty as is in the interest of the ruling exploiters. The morals proposed to the toilers by Christianity, are bourgeois—exploiter morals, training the exploited classes for all those qualities which, from the point of view of the exploiter, his victim should have: silence, passiveness, meekness, patience. It is necessary to condemn categorically, as the worst type of popery, every effort of approachment of Christianity to communism. Religion must be rejected for good, without reservation or camouflage.

Again, the Marxian philosophy purported to see in religion as in many other manifestations of spiritual life a result of material conditions of life, or to be more precise, economic conditions destined to disappear with the achievement of socialism. This is the simplified explanation offered by Engels and Lenin to the paramount human demand for God.

According to Engels:

Now all religion is nothing else than the fantastic reflection, in the minds of men, of those external forces which dominate their everyday existence, a reflection in which the earthly forces assume the form of supernatural forces.

Lenin went on to develop this idea:

God (as He appeared in history and life) is before all a complex of ideas produced by the stupefying oppression of man both by the outer nature and class exploitations,—a complex of ideas which pacifies the class struggle.

Economic slavery is the true source of the religious humbugging of man

. . . the oppression of religion over humanity is but the product and reflex of economic oppression within society. . . .

Taking religion and ethics for mere "reflexes" of social conditions the communists, and especially Lenin, evaluated religion as well as ethics primarily by the significance for the "class struggle," as they called the political struggle for socialism-communism.

Again Lenin argues:

Our ethics is completely subordinate to the interests of the class struggle of the proletariat. Our ethics is deduced from the interests of the class struggle. . . . Ethics is something that serves for the destruction of the old exploiting society and unites all the toilers around the proletariat which creates a new communist society.

Elsewhere Lenin pointed out the relation between religion and social oppression of the working classes.

Consequently the communist rulers called occasionally for moderation in the direct anti-religious activities and for centering the attention upon the socialist reconstruction of the society. Yet these relaxations had a short life. The sweeping change in the economic condition did not work according to the Marxian scheme. Thus, the presumed factor of religious belief (capitalism) is supposed to have been done away with at the present stage of the soviet regime, according to Stalin. However, the religious belief is still in evidence in Soviet Russia and is shared by the working people. As late as May, 1937, *Pravda,* the official organ of the communist party, denounced as "rotten" the theory "that religion at the present time has ceased to play any part in the Soviet Union, that workers and peasants, members of the collective farms, have grown up in a cultural way and therefore have no need of anti-religious propaganda."

Yaroslavsky, the official leader of the anti-religious activities in the Soviet Union, stated about the same time no less definitely, that according to the data of the Union of Godless "in the towns more than half of the workers, about two thirds of the adult population above sixteen class themselves with atheists. *In the villages,* on the other hand, probably *more than half,* about two thirds believe in God, and that means not only old men and women, as some think, but among the young in the villages the percentage is very high." According to the same writer "another mischievous theory is that only old men and women are believers. This is not true." So Yaroslavsky called for vigilance and for making the anti-religious work more active and effective.

In brief, "the soviet power is against all religion" as stated by "The Godless," the organ of the Soviet Union of Militant Atheists. Consequently, it is an unvarying proposition for the soviet rulers to combat the religious concept of life as an error and the Church as an inimical force. Atheism and materialism are integral parts of the communist teaching and are its prospective standards for the popular mentality. The stress is laid at one time upon propaganda and at another time upon direct persecution and suppression. To deprive the churches of any possibility of exercising an influence upon the people even outside of politics is the real tenor of all the acts of the soviet government. To create conditions for replacement of religion by atheism is its real aim.

In the writings of Lenin there are passages which on the surface may lead one to believe that he supported religious tolerance. However, such a conclusion is not true. These writings antedated by a decade or so, the establishment of the communist rule in Russia. At that time, Lenin's party was carrying its struggle against a non-communist state and against a bourgeois government. He proposed then (1905 to 1909) to abstain from incorporating atheism in the final program of his party. He insisted instead that such a bourgeois government should recognize religion as [the] "private affair" of a citizen. However, he made it clear that this is "a socialist-proletariat's demand upon the contemporaneous state and the contemporary church." He especially emphasized, in putting this demand forward, that the struggle of his party against religion is not a private affair. In other words, he sought in the separation of the Church from the State a measure which, if adopted by the capitalist state, would give a better chance for his party to fight religion. But religious approach to the problems of life or religion as a concept of the world, must be fought, according to Lenin, without compromise. He did not expect from a "proletarian state" any neutrality toward religion. He vehemently condemned the attempts made by some of the Russian Marxists in 1908–1909 to create a link between socialism and religion.

For Lenin a good church was worse than a corrupted one. It is religion itself and not the occasional abuses by the members of churches that is attacked by Lenin. He says:

Any religious idea, any idea of a "good God," any coquetry even with a "good God" is an abominably nasty thing which is met especially tolerantly (often benevolently) by the "democratic bourgeoisie" and is just for that reason the most dangerous abomination, most odious infection.

The foregoing maxims by the soviet leaders explain why, on the one hand, the first soviet decrees affecting religion were couched in a language resembling religious tolerance but, on the other hand, sought to undermine the very existence of the Church in Russia. Thus, beginning with the first decree, "On separation of the Church from the State and the school from the Church," issued January 23, 1918 (in the third month of the soviet regime), such a separation did not seek virtually to establish a religious freedom. It is true that the declaratory statements made in this decree as well as in the Soviet Constitution adopted in July, 1918, if taken by themselves, would not mean a menace to religious freedom. However, the other provisions of the same decree, and especially of the instructions accompanying its enactment and developing the details, filled these statements with a different meaning. The practice and the subsequent legislation which developed these provisions into a coherent system of regulations purported to deprive churches in Russia of the fundamental background of the normal life of an ecclesiastic community. In 1929 the constitutions of the major soviet republics were amended to make clear the prohibition of religious propaganda. The original text of the R.S.F.S.R. Constitution was as follows:

To insure for the toilers religious freedom, the Church is separated from the State and the school from the Church, *while freedom of religious and anti-religious propaganda is secured to all the citizens.*

In 1929 "freedom of religious propaganda" was omitted from the text and the italicized part became modified to *"while freedom of religious persuasion and of anti-religious propaganda is secured to all the citizens."* It was officially announced that from now on religious propaganda is that which "exceeds the limits of religious freedom recognized by law." The new federal constitution of 1936 contains provisions which are very close to the modified text.

Moreover, the isolated regulations restricting the religious activities were codified in a single law of April 8, 1929, "On Religious Associations." It created a regime of separation of Church and State which resembles outlawry of the Church rather than religious freedom. It sought to submit the Church to the scrupulous control of the atheistically minded governmental agencies and to beset the life of religious communities with difficulties both actual and legal. The comparatively liberal decree of January 23, 1918, still remains on the statute books, but the more recent legislation made its liberal portions ineffective. Again, the outlawry of the Church was never stated in any official act of the soviet government, but it presents itself as the sum total of the individual provisions of the soviet laws, as well as the practices of the soviet authorities and of the semi-official Union of the Militant Atheists.

Let us examine these provisions by topics and follow within each topic the development of the soviet legislation beginning with the first decree on the separation of Church and State down to the present time.

II PROVISIONS OF THE SOVIET LAWS AFFECTING RELIGION

The conditions set forth by soviet law for an open existence of ecclesiastical communities may be summarized as follows:

1. Dismemberment of the Church

In the first place, the soviet statutes do not recognize the Church as an organized aggregation of parishes of a given denomination. On the contrary, the aim to break up the churches into purely local, isolated units is very much in evidence. In so far as soviet citizens are permitted to unite for religious purposes, or to form ecclesiastical bodies, the units must be strictly local in character. The religious activities of a "religious association," as soviet law calls a religious community, and of its minister, are limited by a narrow territory. It knows only parishes and not churches. The soviet statute provides: "A citizen may be a member of one religious association only [society or group]" and persons who are members of several religious associations may be prosecuted under Section 187 of the Penal Code. Only those members of the congregation who reside in the same city and vicinity or in the same village, or in several villages of the same township (*raion*), can form a religious association. A religious association can use only one church building (or other premises for prayers).

Performance of religious ceremonies by an association outside of its residence or outside of the church building requires special permission from the authorities.

It is true that the statutory law states that "religious associations may organize local, All-Russian or All-Union conventions and conferences," but it is only allowed "by special permission issued for each case separately" by the soviet authorities. Again, such conventions and the executive bodies elected by them have fewer rights than the local religious associations whose limitations are dealt with *infra*. They may not organize any collection even of voluntary donations from believers, or, have, by rent or otherwise, any religious property, whether churches, temples, synagogues, or mosques. Even vestments and other articles of worship are forbidden to them. It is especially emphasized that their decisions and decrees cannot be enforced and are subject to the good will of the members of the congregation. Ecclesiastic authorities have in the eyes of soviet law no jurisdiction over the parishes with regard to religious properties and no legal status whatsoever if they are not corporations, and can not own in their names any property or association. In any event no such convention took place during the last ten years. Thus whenever the soviet law uses the term "religious association" only the isolated parishes are meant. Only a separate parish has some kind of status in Soviet Russia. But as will be evident from the following analysis, even the legal capacity of a local parish appears to be extremely limited and beset with impediments that make the normal parochial life difficult and the proper exercise of faith questionable, to say the least. In the first place the parishes are deprived of any material basis for their existence.

2. Deprivation of Church of Any Property

Beginning with the first soviet decree on separation of Church and State of January 23, 1918, the churches in Russia were deprived not only of all their properties but also of the capacity to own anything in the future, including church buildings, utensils, vestments, and other objects destined for purely liturgical or other ceremonial use.

"Religious associations do not enjoy the right of a juridical person," states the soviet statute. By this is meant that religious associations are not corporations, and can not own in their names any property or enter into contracts. All properties owned or possessed by the churches in Russia prior to the seizure of power by the bolsheviks in November, 1917, were "nationalized"—that is, declared forfeited to the government without compensation. For the future a distinction was drawn between properties which although owned by the Church are devoid of immediate religious significance, *i.e.*, not directly used for ceremonial purposes, and those properties termed by the soviet law as "necessary for the performance of the cult." To the first class belong properties which constitute the material basis of existence of the churches as organizations, and furnish subsistence for the clergy, such as cash, bank accounts, land, buildings other than churches, printing offices, candle factories, etc. The churches are not only denied ownership of such objects, but they cannot hold under any title whatsoever. For example, renting a house or printing office is forbidden. In brief, the Church in Russia can not use any income-bearing property or property of material value.

To the other group of properties—those "necessary for the performance of the cult"—belong church buildings, chalices, vestments, and similar objects of liturgical or other ceremonial significance. These properties are also nationalized, but the soviet law leaves to the free discretion of local governmental agencies the decision to permit the use of such objects by members of a given denomination, or to take these objects away from them. If such objects have, in the opinion of the soviet agencies, an historical or artistic value, they are taken away as a rule and placed in a museum, where they are exposed to what is nothing less than desecration and sacrilege in the eyes of the faithful. For example, the relic of a saint was exposed side by side with a mummified animal. If such objects have a material value they have to be turned over to the government treasury.

Governmental ownership of any object "necessary for the cult" applies not only to such objects possessed by the Church prior to the revolution, but also to any object given to or acquired for the Church under the soviet regime. A donation of a religious object to a church in Soviet Russia makes that gift automatically the property of the soviet state, subject to disposal by the soviet government authorities.

Consequently the only way for soviet citizens to possess a place of worship is to get it from the local soviet under a contract. If premises for this purpose are hired from private persons the contract requires also the approval of the local soviet. The soviet statutes state that the use of church buildings is granted "free of charge." However, this refers to the building itself, while in the cities a rental must be paid for the land occupied by the building, and everywhere the churches are subject to the local tax of one-half per cent of the value of the building annually as well as other taxes. The heavy burden of financial liability arising from these taxes, from obligatory insurance, and other fees and dues is imposed directly upon the individual members of a religious association who signed the contract for the use of the church building. Since a religious association is not a corporation or juridical entity, the church buildings and liturgical objects are not given to the association itself but to its members, at least twenty of whom must be the signers of the contract and assume all responsibility arising therefrom. Again, the members of the executive body of a religious association are personally responsible for the upkeep of the building and other expenses connected with the activities of their religious community and especially for the church building and other "properties necessary for the cult" which are entrusted to them as governmental property. They are held responsible for loss which may occur in such properties, even though without any culpability on their part. The soviet practices occasionally went so far as to make the executives responsible for larceny committed in the church building by non-members unless it was proved that the larceny could not have been prevented due to "elemental forces" (the soviet term for "Act of God").

Failure to meet promptly one of the terms of the contract may result in the withdrawal of the church from use by members of the religious association. Moreover, a church once given to the religious association may be withdrawn practically at the volition of the soviet authorities. For a time it was an established rule that the church could be withdrawn in case of arrest of a single member of the executive body of the association, regardless of the grounds of arrest.

The only transactions permitted to be made in the interest of a religious association are as follows:

Transactions for the management and use of religious property such as hiring of watchmen, buying of fuel, repair of the building and objects destined for the rite, purchase of products or property necessary for a religious rite or ceremony. . . . No contract embodying such arrangements may contain in its text any reference to commercial or industrial transactions, even if these are of a kind directly connected with the affairs of the cult, such as the renting of a candle factory or of a printing works for the purpose of printing religious books, etc.

To summarize: Any parish or religious community in Soviet Russia must exist on current, irregular donations alone, with no lawful possibility of accumulation and savings and no other way of possessing

premises for prayer than by holding them on contract. Again, collection
of money for religious purposes is beset with special difficulties:

> Members of a group of believers or of a religious association may pool
> money together and collect *voluntary donations* in the building of the church
> or outside of it, but *only among the members* of their religious association and
> only for the purposes connected with the upkeep of the church building and
> property incidental to the cult, and with hiring of the clergy and maintenance
> of the executive board.

Establishment of regular membership fees is termed under soviet law
"compulsory collection of money" and as such is forbidden under a
penalty.

It is to be noted that although soviet law denies to churches the right
to become juridical persons it does not confine itself to the mere declaration that legal transactions made in their name are null and void, but
imposes a penalty for the violation of this rule.

From the above it is evident that the name "religious association"
used by the soviet law does not imply a real status of an association in
our sense of the word. Denial of rights of a juridical person or of legal
entity to a duly registered parish places it in a position beset with un-
solvable contradictions. Let us discuss just one point. Members of a
congregation are permitted to pool money by voluntary donation to
cover the expenses of the upkeep of a church which they received by
contract. In the normal course of business the receipt of donations
does not coincide in time with the payment of these expenses. Consequently the executives of a religious association have some cash on hand.
Now, who is the owner of this money? It is not the parish because it
has no right of juridical person and cannot therefore own any property.
Nor does such money belong to the donors, collectors, or the executives
of the association. It is evident that no satisfactory answer to the question can be given. In one case the Commissariat of Justice decided that
money collected for a synagogue can be deposited with a bank "in the
name of individual citizens."

The general conclusion would be that the soviet law is designed to
establish a complete control of the soviet government over any property
needed for the church including the most indispensable objects of ceremonial significance. Any parish can possess only such objects as the
soviet government deems it necessary to permit.

The available information justifies the conclusion, that a very insignif-
icant portion of the ecclesiastic properties is left to the faithful. As
far as the non-religious properties are concerned the largest church in
Russia (the Russian Eastern Orthodox Church) which enjoyed a privileged position under Imperial regimes possessed as a matter of fact a
very small part of the national wealth. For example, less than one

per cent (.68%) of crop area and pastures belonged to the Church and other public bodies in the forty-nine most important agricultural provinces of European Russia, according to a soviet writer. The artistic splendor of the churches and monasteries which for centuries were the depositories of the Russian religious art—the only Russian art prior to the Eighteenth Century—made the Russian Church appear more wealthy than it actually was. Such churches have been largely withdrawn from religious use and many have been destroyed, *e.g.*, the Cathedral of Our Lord the Saviour and many other churches in Moscow. Valuable articles and artistic paintings were for the most part removed in 1922–1923. An extensive campaign for the closing of churches was carried out, especially in 1929–1930. From the scattered reports to be found in the soviet press the following very incomplete figures are deduced which nevertheless give an idea of how far the campaign went: Prior to 1921 about six hundred and seventy-three monasteries and churches were closed in the R.S.F.S.R. alone; in 1927 one hundred thirty-four; in 1928 some six hundred; but, in 1929 one thousand four hundred and forty. Some newly created big industrial centers have no churches at all, *e.g.*, Magnitogorsk, two hundred thousand inhabitants; Karaganda, one hundred twenty thousand; Stalinsk, two hundred thousand. The destruction of religious paintings was also conducted on a rather large scale. In 1930 the soviet press continually reported the burning of icons and religious books in small villages in such quantities as twelve carloads, eight carloads, two thousand icons and one thousand religious books, four thousand icons.

3. Governmental Control over the Religious Organizations

Along with the nationalization of church buildings and other articles intended for worship, the decree on separation of Church and State of January 23, 1918, contained a clause which permitted the administration to place these religious properties at the service of the believers by a contract. However, neither the decree nor the instruction accompanying it outlined how the believers must be organized to take advantage of this provision. There seems to be a reason for this omission. The bulk of the population of Russia belonged to the Russian Orthodox Church, which is a ritual version of Christianity. For them exercise of worship was closely connected with a definite ecclesiastic rite which can be performed properly only in premises especially decorated and equipped. Consecrated articles, religious images and symbols were indispensable for the service. The compilers of the decree by establishing the governmental control over all the religious properties sought to interrupt the continuity of the parochial life. If the instructions of the soviet government were virtually followed, the churches and other religious properties had to be first taken by the soviet authorities and then perhaps turned over to a rather indefinite group of citizens designated in the soviet decrees as "believers" or "group of believers."

As was a matter of fact, however, it depended largely upon the pleasure of the local authorities whether an existing parish was actually dispossessed of such properties (and these were occasionally mutilated) or merely whether an inventory of such properties was required and the parish continued to use its properties and its activities.

The organization of the "believers" was not regulated by a definite law. Nor was the status of the ecclesiastic authorities and the parishes settled. The decree of January 23, 1918, merely stated that "all the religious and ecclesiastic societies are subject to the general conditions governing private societies and associations" except for the right of a juridical person of which the religious associations were deprived. Such general conditions were set up first in 1923 but the religious associations were placed under special rules different from those established for other private associations.

According to these rules a religious community could have been recognized either if it had received as a "group of believers" a church under previous regulations or if it had formed under the new law a religious association and presented for registration its constitution drawn according to a pattern established by the soviet authorities. Religious communities which failed to do so within three months were considered dissolved.

Finally when the law of April 8, 1929 was introduced the "group of believers" and the "religious associations" were brought under uniform rules and a new "registration" was required of them. All religious communities which did not obtain the registration under the new law prior to May 1, 1930 were considered dissolved. According to this law, religious associations may begin their activities "only after the registration."

Consequently a parish in Soviet Russia has to pass from two to three registrations to survive. These registrations were not a matter of mere making record of their existence but at each of them the administration was at liberty to deny to a parish its further existence. The conditions of the last registration were especially burdensome. The law of 1929 codified all the scattered rulings hitherto issued for the bringing of the parochial life under the control of administration and setting narrow limits for the activities of religious organizations.

For registration in the first place a list of all members of the association with their signed consent thereto was required. Mere listing of the parishioners is not sufficient; from each of them his consent must be obtained. Some local regulations, for example in Armenia, Azarbaydjan and Turkmenistan, require as was the rule before the R.S.F. S.R., indication of the social and material standing from 1914 of each founder of the association and the class of people to which he belonged before the revolution. Then the narrow territorial limits for the activities of the association must be indicated. Complete information concerning the occupation of each executive since 1914 (*i.e.,* for sixteen years) must be supplied with indication whether he or she was subject to punishment. A more detailed separate questionnaire has to be filed for the priest who can begin to officiate only after this has been done. Furthermore, "the registering body may exclude any individual executive of a religious association." In other words only those persons can manage the affairs of a religious community who are approved by the atheistically minded soviet authorities.

Any change in membership, executives or clergy of the association must be reported to the authorities within seven days and besides a general report must be presented annually. Again, no more than three executives are allowed for each association. The local administration has the right to make an examination of the activities, records, bookkeeping, etc., of a religious association at any time. The executives are elected by the general assembly of the religious associations by open ballot. For each such general assembly a permission by local authorities must be obtained in advance and the subject matters of the discussion must be indicated. The authorities can send to this assembly their representative who has broad power to close the assembly.

The jurisdiction of the executives is strictly defined by the law. They are elected "for the performance of functions connected with the management and usage of the properties necessary for the exercise of the cult and for outside representation." The right of representation, however, must be taken in a very limited sense because the churches cannot be officially represented at any convention, committee or other public body in Soviet Russia.

To conclude the matter of registration the fulfillment of all the conditions required by law for registration does not make recognition obligatory for the administration; the "registration" still can be denied. The law does not even require the indication of a reason for such denial. The only duty imposed upon the registering body is to serve its decision on the applicants within a month. Thus "registration" is in effect a license. The existence of a religious community is entirely in the hands of administration. It may deny the registration as well as close a duly registered association if it deems that "it deviates from the rules established for such associations."

In brief the activities of a religious community are under a permanent surveillance of the soviet administrative authorities, and its existence is left to the free discretion of such authorities.

4. Limitations Set Up for Activities of Religious Organizations

The most salient point of the law is the narrow field left to the activities of a religious association. They are confined to what soviet law terms "performance of the cult" and that which appears in the eyes of soviet writers and in practice bare performance of religious ceremonies, God's service or common prayer.

The Church must keep away from any charity, brotherly intercourse of fellow members, self-education and teaching of religious doctrine even to its own members and their children. The religious associations may not organize poor houses, alumni, or mutual funds to cover funeral expenses.

The editor of a semi-official commentary on the law says:

The activities of all the religious associations are reduced to the performance of the cult (prayer and performance of ceremonies and similar things). Activities exceeding the limits of satisfaction of these needs are not permitted.

Similar comments were made after the adoption of the new 1936 Soviet Constitution.

Again some limitation is set up for the performance of religious ceremonies or display of religious symbols and holy images. They are not permitted "in any governmental, public, cooperative or *private* institutions or enterprises." Exception is made only for the extreme unction of persons "dangerously ill or dying" in hospitals and prisons and for display of images in the museums. At the time when some private commercial and industrial enterprises were permitted in Soviet Russia, no crucifixes or any other holy image (icon) could be placed in their premises, a well established custom in the pre-bolshevist days. Even in a kitchen jointly used by several families, which is very common in present Russia because of the prevailing housing conditions, no such image can be put. A prayer can not be pronounced in commonly used premises of an apartment without the agreement of all those who occupy the place. Performance of religious rites or installation of religious pictures in a governmental institution entails penalty under Section 126 of the Penal Code. It must be noted that at the present time all commercial and industrial enterprises in Russia are governmental. Moreover, tolling of the bells is prohibited in the majority of large cities by city ordinance.

A special permit of authorities is required for God's service in any other premises than a church as well as for "religious processions" or "performance of religious ceremonies or rites in the open air," both of which were very customary forms of worship in the pre-revolutionary villages. Permission must be asked for two weeks in advance. Exception is made for funerals and "for religious processions which are an inevitable part of the church service and are made only around the church . . . provided they do not disturb normal street traffic." The last clause gives again a chance for the interference of the authorities. A permit of the authorities is also required for services outside the residence of the religious association. Finally an important actual obstacle to the observance of church ceremonies, especially to the attendance of Sunday service is the result of the so-called five-day or six-day working week in the majority of soviet enterprises and institutions. Under this labor regime the rest days do not as a rule coincide with Sundays but with various weekdays according to a complicated schedule. In enterprises working under the regime of a normal seven-day week the rest days might not coincide with Sundays. Neither Christmas nor Easter are holydays in Soviet Russia, to say nothing about other festivals. According to the Soviet Labor Code failure to appear for a single working day is a legitimate reason for dismissal. Consequently celebration of a religious festival may result in loss of employment.

5. Prohibition of Teaching of Religion

Among the activities prohibited to the Church, the teaching of religion is undoubtedly a substantial part of the exercise of faith and one of the foremost purposes of an ecclesiastic body. If the Church or its ministers cannot teach religion who else could do it? But this was the exact aim of the soviet rulers—to cut the younger generation off from religion. The following program indicates that it is not religious tolerance but atheism and materialism that form the official aim of soviet education. An editorial of the official organ of the Commissariat of Education stated recently:

It is not the non-religious but an atheistic education of children that is wanted. It is recommended . . . in general to permeate the entire instruction with the spirit of militant atheism.

Yaroslavsky stated the same objective in a more radical way:

Therefore we cultivate in the children a hatred for those ties which religion imposes. . . . We demand of the child to be a fighter against religion anywhere, at the school and in the family.

In accordance with the communist aims the soviet statutes prohibit "the teaching of any form of religious belief in governmental, public and private teaching and educational establishments" and prohibit also in general "teaching of religious doctrine to persons under eighteen years of age."

The decree on separation of Church and State on January 23, 1918 which is still on the statute books stated that "citizens may give and receive religious instructions privately." This provision, however, soon became void because of other subsequent regulations. Thus any private instruction of children in groups comprising over three children was forbidden in 1923. Until 1929 teaching of religion privately in groups of not over three children was not directly prohibited insofar as it did not have a character of organized group instruction. However, the law of April 8, 1929 put an end to this. Only teaching of religion by parents to their own children is not expressly prohibited now. Any other teaching is a crime.

It is stated in the law that "religious instruction is permitted exclusively in special theological courses" which can be opened by a special permit of the high soviet authorities. However, such special theological courses do not answer the need for religious instruction of the population. Besides, the available information shows that only a score of such courses were opened, with a very small number of students, because of the prevailing general conditions in Soviet Russia.

The soviet regulations are not confined to the negative combat of religion, to the prohibition of religious instruction. A positive task of an atheistic education is clearly set forth in the program for the soviet schools. The following is the program on this point for the so-called Pedagogical *Technikums,* that is, training schools for the soviet teachers as outlined by regulation of the Commissariat for the Education of March 28, 1929:

> The whole scholastic system, the whole system of professional and technical education, including also pedagogical *technikums,* must be placed on the forefront of anti-religious activity. . . . The militant attack on religion must have a systematic character . . . to create in students a definite materialistic mentality. The contents of all scientific disciplines studied at the Pedagogical *Technikums* must—without a single exception—strengthen this mentality. The program of every branch of science must be established in agreement with this principle.

Consequently a religious man is barred from teaching activities in Soviet Russia. The recent reports by the soviet press show that there was no change in this respect after the adoption of the new constitution.

Soviet teachers were summoned recently to intensify anti-religious work among children by the authoritative organ of the Commissariat of Education. The aim of the soviet education was outlined there as follows:

Teaching must be so conducted that by the end of his schooling the pupil has a clear understanding that, though religions differ in form, they all in essence lead to the same end; all are ideologies of slavery, all implacably contradict science and all are directed against the interests of toilers.

Thus the soviet legislation is designed not only to bar the church from religious instruction but to put an end to the teaching of religious doctrine in general. Atheistic education and atheistic propaganda are the objectives of the official program of the communist party and are carried on not only "through the machinery of the soviet state", according to the soviet writers, but also through the trade unions and a special "Union of Militant Atheists" sponsored by the government.

III PERSECUTION OF THE CLERGY

In addition to the restrictions set up by the soviet legislation to the activities of religious communities a number of direct limitations and special heavy financial burdens were imposed upon the clergy of all denominations and the monks, up to the time of the 1936 constitution. It is true the decree of separation of Church and State of January 23, 1918, announced: "All restrictions connected with religious persuasion or absence of religious persuasion are abolished." However, this was superfluous in the first place, and, besides, was not carried out. It was superfluous because by the decree of the Provisional Government of Russia of March 20, 1917, all the discriminations against the citizen because of religion or race existing under Imperial regime were already abolished. The announcement was not fulfilled because beginning with the first soviet constitution of July, 1918, and up to the 1936 constitution the soviet laws deprived of franchise "present and former clergymen of all denominations (ministers, deacons, rabbis, etc.), monks and nuns." In 1929, 248,000 persons were disfranchised on this ground, and 161,000 in 1931, the decrease being officially explained "in the national decrease of the number of ministers."

The disfranchise did not affect merely the right of vote. The disfranchised persons (*lishentsy*) constituted a special class of the soviet citizens, a kind of outcast, whose right to work, earn, and even to get food was considerably restricted. Thus they could not be members of the trade unions and could not therefore be lawfully employed, especially in the governmental enterprises. Special regulations prohibited the clergy from holding any position in the institutions under the control of the Commissariats of Justice, Education, Agriculture, Food and the Interior. They had to pay in increased rent for their apartments —from five to ten times higher than the "toilers." They could not rent rooms or apartments in municipalized or nationalized buildings, that is, in the prevailing number of buildings in the cities. Persons living in such buildings could not accept ministers of religion as lodgers. When for quite a long time food and other commodities were distributed by rations on cards, the disfranchised persons were deprived of such cards. The right to work and employment affected not only the disfranchised persons but also the members of their families. Their children were practically barred from education, especially in the higher institutions. Finally, the disfranchised persons paid a special, high income tax and an agricultural tax; and those 21 to 40 years old were forced to pay a military tax in peacetime and to enroll in the labor militia in war time.

The new 1936 constitution no longer contains a clause disfranchising the clergy. Still statements were made in the soviet press to the effect that clergymen must not be considered "toilers," that is, treated equally with others, and the fact remains that for twenty years the restrictions followed every minister of religion and member of his family.

Again these well defined limitations are not the only hardships which a religious man faces no less than a priest in Soviet Russia. The soviet State is "theoclastic" in its very nature, in its ideology: it is neither tolerant nor indifferent towards religion but aims to fight actively the belief in God.

The soviet legislation as expounded in the previous chapter leaves a too narrow margin for worship, if any. In any event it runs counter to the traditional exercise of faith and made almost any attempt to continue religious activities along the customary path appear a transgression of the rules established by the government. Such an attempt was in the eyes of the soviet atheistic authorities a manifestation of an anti-soviet frame of mind. If the State inscribes atheism on its banners, any religious activity, although non-political in itself, arouses the suspicion of the government. A religious procession on the day of a patron saint of the local church, ecclesiastic celebrations of a marriage, baptism, etc., are looked upon by the soviets with such suspicion. Likewise in many cases obedience to the government means for a religious man the abandonment of traditional mode of worship: the teaching of religious doctrine to children, for example, or work on Easter or Christmas, or the acceptance of desecration such as the removal of consecrated objects from the Church by non-qualified persons, or the opening of coffins containing the relics of a saint. Observance of the ecclesiastic tradition runs counter to the loyalty to the government which aims to eradicate religion. Therefore, a religious man is suspected in soviet Russia of being inimical to the government and any accusation of the violation of the "separation of State and Church" almost automatically involves accusation of counter-revolution.

The soviet penal system offers rather wide possibilities for prosecution of "counter-revolutionary" crimes. First, the notion of such crimes is much broader than that of a political crime in many other countries. The indicia of individual crimes are couched in very general terms and in addition to the definitions of particular crimes there is a general "species" definition of a counter-revolutionary crime. It embraces among other things "any act directed . . . to weaken" the authority of the soviet government or "the basic economic, political, and national conquests of the proletarian revolution." According to the official annotators of the Code, the indirect intention suffices; that is, it suffices if the perpetrator knew that his act may have endangered these conquests. There is besides another even broader group definition of "crimes against the administration." Moreover, the soviet court has the power to sentence for an act not expressly dealt with in the Penal Code if it merely resembles a crime mentioned in the Code. Finally, "propaganda or agitation containing an appeal to overthrow, undermine, or weaken the soviet authority or to commit individual counter-revolutionary crimes, or the dissemination, preparation, or possession of literature containing such matter . . . if done . . . by utilizing religious or racial prejudices" entails the death penalty. Incitement of "religious enmity or discord" or possession of literature of that nature entails either imprisonment or under extenuating circumstances, the death penalty. These sections were often used wherever the violation of separation of Church and State was involved. Secondly, side by side with the courts, a special government department functions in Soviet Russia which has a broad power to inflict heavy penalties without any judicial procedure—without a trial—and this department is not bound by any substantive or adjective law. Its name is varied: *Cheka* from 1917 to 1921, *G.P.U.* from 1921 to 1923, *O.G.P.U.* from 1923 to 1934, when it became Federal Commissariat of the Interior—*Narkomvnudel* or N.K.V.D. This institution had for several years first the actual power and later the right to put to death after a secret procedure, or sentence to penal servitude (labor camps) or exile. At the present time *Narkomvnudel* has the authority of confining in a "labor camp" equal to penal servitude for a period up to five years with an unlimited facility of renewal or prolongation of the term of exile, or, to a definite locality without confinement and prohibiting residence in certain places for the same period. The statute is silent on the death penalty. The *Narkomvnudel* can undertake an investigation and arrest on a charge of any crime. After the investigation is completed it can either dispose of the case by inflicting one of the above-mentioned penalties or transfer the case for trial to the court. This is a matter of unrestricted volition of the *Narkomvnudel*. There are no rules of substantive or adjective law for such procedure. The cases involving "substantive activities" must, however, be tried not by the regular court but by a court-martial. For some special crimes there are also special courts assigned.

The *Narkomvnudel* is also in charge of all penal institutions (labor camps as well as prisons, reformatories, etc., where the sentences of the regular courts are served), of the entire police, of the offices registering births and deaths, celebrating marriages and granting divorces, of the grant of the right of residence in large cities (passport system), and of special troops. Consequently the soviet citizen does not have to be guilty of a particular crime to be deprived of liberty and serve long term penal servitude if the *Narkomvnudel* considers him dangerous to the soviet regime. Both the courts armed with the elastic instrument of the soviet penal law and the *Narkomvnudel* with its broad power are watching with suspicion the activities of the religious men in Russia. Both are set in motion whenever the soviet government thinks that religion gains in the mind of the people.

That a high number of prelates of churches, priests, monks and active parishioners were sentenced by the soviet courts for various penalties is beyond dispute. What the voluminous anti-religious and clergy-wrestling soviet literature tries to prove is that the reason for their prosecution was anti-soviet activities. It is true that indictments and sentences pronounced them guilty of counter-revolution, or of direct treason, as it was in numerous cases in 1937 under the new constitution. However, the entire set-up of the soviet penal system does not offer any convincing evidence that these accusations are justified.

To conclude: Separation of State and Church declared in the soviet decrees means actually the suppression of the Church by an atheistic state. The soviet legislation on religion is a legislation of militant atheism which sought to eradicate religion from the human mind. It beset the existence of ecclesiastic organizations with unsurmountable obstacles. If, nevertheless, religious belief has survived in Russia, the soviet rulers have no more credit for it than the pagan Emperors of Rome for the survival of Christendom.

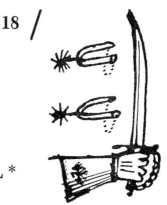

18 /

THE HISTORICAL
BACKGROUND
OF SOVIET
THOUGHT CONTROL *

Historians habitually stress the possibility of finding the roots of the
present in the past, while some sociologists and political scientists
believe it possible to study the present without any reference to the
past. In the following selection, Professor Karpovich seems to step
out of the conventional role of historian by questioning the belief that
Soviet totalitarianism is the product of Russia's past; however, he is
still working in the historian's manner, looking for both continuities
and discontinuities. Even if the beginnings of Soviet totalitarianism
should be satisfactorily traced in Russian history, there would remain
yet other questions; for example, is the source to be found in
Muscovite absolutism or in what Professor Toynbee has called
"Byzantine totalitarianism"?

I

EVERY PHASE of historical investigation seems to have its own
peculiar danger to be avoided. In the case of attempts at establishing
historical continuity, such a danger is that of over-simplification. Far too
often, a pattern of historical continuity is being based on superficial
similarities between a past and a present phenomenon each taken out
of its historical context. What is easily forgotten is that change no less
than continuity is of the very essence of history, and that any study of
the historical background should involve significant differences as well as
similarities.

Indeed, there are cases with reference to which differences can be

* Michael Karpovich, "The Historical Background of Soviet Thought Control," *The
Soviet Union: Background, Ideology, Reality,* edited by Waldemar Gurian (Notre
Dame: University of Notre Dame Press, 1951), pp. 16–30. Reprinted by permission
of the publisher.
For biographical note on the author, see pp. 91–92.

of greater importance than similarities. "Plus ça change, plus c'est la même chose" is by no means a generally applicable historical law. And perhaps its applicability is particularly doubtful in the case of the Soviet regime.

Not only was the Revolution that brought it into being one of the most radical of all revolutions in human history, but it also had some historically novel features. In none of the earlier revolutions do we see such a consciousness of design and such a degree of organization as in the Bolshevik coup d'état in Russia, and likewise none of the earlier revolutionary regimes once established had at its disposal means of propaganda and suppression even remotely similar to those which the development of modern technology placed in the hands of the Soviet government.

In a sense, the Soviet regime is unprecedented, and this alone should put us on guard against all attempts to link it with the historical past in too simple a fashion. I have in mind such current assertions as that the Communist dictatorship is a legitimate successor to tsarist autocracy, the collective farm a modernized version of the traditional Russian village commune, and the present-day Soviet expansion a mere continuation of the old Russian imperialism. Tempting as these analogies are, they are historically incorrect—and I would add, politically misleading.

It might be equally tempting to interpret the Soviet system of ideological and cultural control in terms of traditional Russian institutions and habits of thought. In fact, such attempts have been made on more than one occasion.

Thus, in a book on the history of Russian literature recently published in this country, I read the following:

Whoever attempts to understand the intricate conditions of literary life in the Soviet Union should not overlook the particular auspices under which modern Russian literature with its traditions began in the eighteenth century.*

What the author has in mind is the educational function of the eighteenth-century Russian monarchy. The fact itself can not be denied. Beginning with Peter the Great and through the reign of Catherine II, the imperial government was the leading agency in the process of Russia's westernization. It established schools, theaters, museums, libraries, academies and learned societies; it ordered translations of foreign books and started periodical publications; it exercised a general patronage over arts and letters. And yet, an attempt to establish historical continuity between this imperial patronage of the eighteenth-century Russia and the Soviet system of thought control is bound to fail.

To begin with, this imperial patronage was not a uniquely Russian phenomenon. There was no substantial difference between what the

---

* Marc Slonim, *The Epic of Russian Literature*, p. 46.

Russian sovereigns of the period were trying to do and the cultural policy of Louis XIV or that of the West European enlightened despots. If governmental activity in cultural matters loomed larger in Russia than in the West, and at times assumed a more drastic character, it was because in Russia more had to be achieved, and in a shorter period of time.

In the second place, as time went on, the importance of governmental tutelage in Russian cultural life was decreasing rather than increasing. One of its results was to call into being public activity which, while following the governmental lead, still tried to preserve a certain degree of independence. Modern historical research has shown that already in Peter's days there was more of such public activity than has generally been assumed, and by Catherine's time, this activity became a factor of no small importance.

It was then that the cultural elite of Russia first came into an open conflict with the government—not so much on political as on cultural grounds. Modern Russian civilization was coming of age, and its standard-bearers were no longer prepared to remain under the governmental tutelage. Thus, in the historical perspective, the latter appears as a passing phase only, and therefore it can not be invoked as a "national Russian tradition" to explain the present-day cultural policy of the Soviet regime.

In the early nineteenth century, the civilizing mission of the Russian monarchy largely came to an end. From that time on, except for the promotion of education on various levels, its intervention in the cultural life of the country took the form of a more or less repressive censorship. On occasions, but on occasions only, it still tried to issue positive ideological directives, but one should not be misled into attaching too much importance to these sporadic and largely inefficient efforts. Neither the obscurantist bigotry of Alexander I's later years (for which one can find parallels both in Restoration France and in the Germany of the Metternichian period) nor Nicholas I's "Autocracy, Orthodoxy and Nationality" was a potent factor in shaping Russia's cultural development in the mid-nineteenth century. Even in schools, which were all government-supported and government-controlled, one hardly can find evidence of sustained and successful indoctrination.

With regard to literature, the oldtime Russian censorship was negative, and not positive. Its purpose was to prevent the writers from expressing certain ideas or from discussing certain problems, but, apart from its own paid literary agents (a phenomenon not limited to Russia of Nicholas I's time), the government did not attempt to tell the writers what to say and how to say it. One can find a few exceptions, but they rather prove the rule. I shall cite but one. In 1826 Pushkin submitted to Nicholas I, who had offered to be his own censor, the manuscript of his historical tragedy "Boris Godunov." In returning the manuscript to Push-

kin, Count Benckendorf, the actual head of the political police, communicated to the poet the following imperial resolution: "I believe that
Pushkin would have achieved his aim had he rewritten his comedy
(*sic*) as an historical novel in the manner of Walter Scott." To this
Pushkin sent a courteous reply in which he expressed his agreement with
the Emperor's criticism, but then he added: "I regret that I am not
able to rewrite anything once written." One must remember that Pushkin
had returned from exile only a year before that, that he had been
suspected of being in sympathy with the Decembrist uprising, and that
he still was under police surveillance. Under these conditions, his letter
was a rather daring act. And yet nothing happened either to Pushkin or
to "Boris Godunov." Pushkin simply put the manuscript aside, and a few
years later it was published, with some minor changes imposed by the
censor, but essentially in the form in which Pushkin had written it—
as a tragedy, not as an historical novel "in the manner of Walter Scott."

It does not require much imagination to picture to oneself the
fate of a Soviet writer who, under any circumstances, would have dared
to disregard a piece of literary advice coming from Stalin through the
intermediacy of Beria.

The reign of Nicholas I has been called the "apogee of autocracy"
in Russia. It certainly was that period in modern Russian history when
governmental repression and censorship were at their highest. And yet,
as one studies the intellectual history of the time, one is surprised at
the large margin of liberty that could be preserved. Annoying and even
harmful as the censorship was, it still was neither all-embracing nor all-
penetrating. It did not succeed in stifling independent creative activity or
in preventing the growth of the critical spirit. And it failed in its efforts to
erect a "Chinese wall" (the mid-nineteenth century version of the "iron
curtain") between the educated Russian society and the West. On this
last point, the evidence is decisive. It shows that the Russian cultural
elite of the time kept abreast of all the literary and political developments in Europe. Annenkov, an outstanding intellectual of the period, tells
in his memoirs how surprised he was to find out upon his return to
Russia from Western Europe that his Russian friends were well read in
the latest French Socialist literature. Annenkov was not the only one to
have benefited from a direct contact with Western life and thought.
Herzen, Ogarev, Bakunin, Stankevich, Granovsky, Turgenev, among
many others, were permitted to go abroad—in some cases in spite of the
fact that previously they had been either accused or suspected of subversive political activity.

Personal contact abroad was not the only way of acquiring information about Western developments and trends of thought. Importation
of West European books and periodicals was constant and substantial.
They came to Russia both in a legal and illegal way. Thus, from the diary

of young Chernyshevsky we learn that in 1848–49, when governmental reaction was in full swing, he could follow the revolutionary events in France by reading current French periodicals in a St. Petersburg cafe. About the same time, one of the highest secret agents of the Russian political police reported to the government that he discovered a large-scale traffic in forbidden foreign books.

Apparently, one has to revise the traditional idea about the omnipotence of Nicholas I's political police. In the light of our recent historical experience, its activities begin to look like a decidedly amateurish performance. This circumstance helps to explain the fundamental paradox of Nicholas' reign. A time of strongest political reaction, it simultaneously was the most fruitful—or in some respects the most seminal—period in modern Russia's cultural and intellectual history. Herzen has called it "an amazing period of outward slavery and inner emancipation." Had he said "political slavery" and "intellectual emancipation," his formula would have gained in precision. The emancipation process was not limited to the realm of individual thought and sentiment. It found its tangible expression in the great achievements of Russian scholarship, literature and art, and, more surprisingly, in the formation of some basic trends of political thought. It also gave birth to that not easily definable social phenomenon which subsequently became known as the Russian intelligentsia. Whatever it was, it prided itself in particular on its nonconformism and independence.

All this happened under the stern rule of Nicholas I. That the boundaries of freedom in Russia were expanding steadily in the course of the decades that followed—is a familiar story which does not need to be retold.

II

What it all amounts to is that the old Russian monarchy, even at its worst, was not a totalitarian state. Nor was it an "ideocracy" dedicated to the realization, either at home or abroad, of a definite "philosophy." Time and again reference has been made to the supposedly "theocratic" character of Russian autocracy. It is significant, however, that in support of this assertion one usually has been forced to go back to the sixteenth century and to quote from Ivan the Terrible. The generalization remains debatable even with reference to Muscovite Russia, and it certainly is not applicable to the modern period of Russian history. There was no counterpart to Marxism-Leninism-Stalinism in pre-revolutionary Russian governmental policies.

Of equal importance is the fact that at no time in its existence was Russian autocracy in a position to develop the technique of totalitarianism. Even had it wished to establish an all-embracing system of thought control, it could not do so simply because it lacked the appropriate means. Thus, in this field the Bolsheviks could learn but little from their historical predecessors.

For the origins of the Soviet system of thought control one must look somewhere else. Here, as in the case of other basic features of the Soviet regime, a study of the more immediate background promises to be more rewarding. Generally speaking, one should concentrate more on the history of the Communist Party—of its origin, growth and rise to power—rather than go back to the Byzantine and Mongol legacy in Russian history, to Ivan the Terrible or the supposed mysteries of the Russian soul.

Paradoxical as it might sound, the present-day system of ideological control in the Soviet Union can be understood much better in the light of the history of the Russian revolutionary underground than if one tries to link it with tsarist censorship. This is not the place to discuss at length the nature of this underground—a subject on which there is a rather abundant literature. For my present purpose it is sufficient to remind the reader that, in the course of its existence which lasted from the 1860's to the first decade of the twentieth century, this underground succeeded in shaping the peculiar psychology and mentality of several generations of Russian revolutionaries. Among the outstanding traits which the underground was breeding, were maximalism, ideological fanaticism and, in some cases, authoritarianism. By maximalism I mean an impatient desire to strive for the immediate realization of the ideal in its entirety, a contempt for gradualism, for the intermediate stages of progress and partial achievements. Coupled with this was a tendency to attach a tremendous importance to the revolutionary theory which assumed the character of a quasi-religious philosophy demanding from its adherents an unreserved allegiance and excluding the possibility of ideological compromises. And finally, in some of its aspects, the revolutionary struggle of the time tended to produce a conspiratorial variety of authoritarianism, reflected both in the concept of the party's organization and in the belief in force as an instrument to be used for the creation of a new world.

Lenin inherited all these features from the pre-Marxian Russian revolutionary underground. The peculiarity of the place he occupies in the history of Russian revolutionary socialism consists precisely in that he has produced an amalgam of certain features of Marxism with certain features of the native revolutionary tradition.

From the latter, Lenin took its maximalism and its ideological fanaticism while rejecting the ethical motivation that had been so important in the Populism (*Narodnichestvo*) of the 1870's. He also chose revolutionary authoritarianism in preference to the libertarian and democratic tendencies of the movement. All Lenin's pronouncements in favor of "democracy" to the contrary, one cannot help feeling that from the outset there was in him an unusually strong authoritarian and dictatorial strain. Except for a few individuals like Tkachev and Nechaev, both repudiated by the majority of their fellow-revolutionaries, Lenin's "will to power" was a novel phenomenon in Russian revolutionary history.

From Marxism, Lenin chose dogmatic materialism, relativist class ethics and elements of revolutionary authoritarianism (the "dictatorship of the proletariat") while virtually neglecting its evolutionary as well as its democratic features. In the compound which resulted, seeds of totalitarianism could be found in abundance.

Their presence is equally obvious in the methods that subsequently were used by Lenin in his attempt to build a revolutionary party designed as an instrument for the conquest of power. From this point of view, the factional disputes and squabbles of the period, at that time of interest only to those directly concerned, have acquired a considerable historical importance. In shaping his party, Lenin to a large extent was predetermining the main features of the revolutionary regime to come.

Of particular significance to the discussion of the present problem, is Lenin's constant concern for the preservation of theoretical conformity within the party. Not only the political and social demands of the party program, but their "philosophical" premises as well had to be rigidly adhered to by all the members in the spirit of a monolithic solidarity. When some of the Bolshevik intellectuals attempted to combine Marxism with certain trends in modern philosophy, Lenin came forward with a vitriolic attack on this dangerous heresy and an ardent defense of the old-fashioned materialism as the only possible base for revolutionary action. One must read his *Materialism and Empirio-Criticism* (1909) to appreciate the importance which revolutionary theory had in his eyes as well as the degree of his intellectual intolerance. And this was not the only case when Lenin was prepared to read out of the party those who disagreed with him not on political, but on philosophical and other intellectual issues.

What happened after 1917 was the inevitable extension of this intra-party totalitarianism into the national life of the country. It was but natural for the party which now became the actual ruling body of Russia to impart its own spirit and technique to the various phases of national policy, including that in the cultural field. Moreover, such a development was implied in the very design of the revolution as it had been conceived by Lenin and accepted by his followers. This revolution was not to limit itself to a thoroughgoing political, social and economic change. It also aimed at a re-education of the people, the creation of a new type of man. Here as in other cases, the Bolsheviks with their "voluntaristic" tendency, were not prepared to wait till, in accordance with the orthodox Marxian doctrine, the new economic "base" would produce a corresponding cultural "superstructure." The process had to be assisted and speeded up by an immediate and powerful state intervention. Hence the paramount importance ascribed to the "educational" function of the Communist Party.

We know now that an all-embracing system of thought control is inherent in the very nature of a totalitarian state. It cannot recognize the autonomy of culture, neither can it acknowledge the existence of politically neutral spheres of human activity: everything must be subordinated to the political aims of the regime. What still is not realized by many is the historical fact that Lenin was the virtual creator of the totalitarian state and the Soviet regime, its *first* example. No doubt, the full implications both of the theory and practice of totalitarianism did not become clear in Soviet Russia until their flowering during the period of Stalin's supremacy. But not only the seeds, but also some fruits of the doctrine can be found already in the earlier stages of the regime. If at that time the new government could not apply itself to the task of "re-educating" the people with the same vigor as later, this was due primarily to two circumstances. In the first place, an apparatus of control had to be established, and, in view of the magnitude of the task, this required a considerable amount of time. Secondly, both during the civil war and the ensuing period of economic recuperation, the regime had too many pressing immediate problems to face, and as yet was not sufficiently strong, to be able to devote enough energy and attention to matters of cultural control. It should not be forgotten, however, that some of the most valuable fields of intellectual activity—vulnerable from the point of view of the official ideology—were submitted to strict regulation from the outset. In the universities, chairs of philosophy were abolished and subsequently replaced by those of "dialectical materialism," while no other teaching or writing than that based on Marxism (in its officially approved version) was permitted in the field of social sciences.

Human memory is short, and by now the early purges of Soviet historians, for instance, have been forgotten. Had it been otherwise the outside world would have been less shocked by the recent purge in Soviet genetics. It should have been viewed as a logical working out of the same fundamental premises which underlay the earlier Soviet attempts at thought control. Equally logical is Stalin's last intervention in the intellectual field—a ruling as to how Soviet philologists should approach the study of language. Neither should one be surprised by the fact that from the determination of the ideological "general line" the Central Committee of the Communist Party has passed to prescribing artistic styles in literature, painting, music and architecture. Absurd as these phenomena might seem if taken out of their context, they all fall within the same general pattern of a totalitarian political system. They all can be traced back to the same "original sin"—the utopian ideal of a human society in which the totality of cultural endeavors is being planned, regulated and shaped by an omnipotent and omniscient ruling elite.

III

Besides those elements of the Russian revolutionary tradition which have contributed to the make-up of Bolshevism, one can establish still another link between the Soviet system of thought control and certain features of pre-revolutionary Russia. In this case, the connection can be found in the field of Russian intellectual history.

I have in mind the temporary prevalence among the Russian intellectuals, particularly those of the radical brand, of a strongly utilitarian and politically colored approach to cultural values. The official Soviet spokesmen themselves repeatedly have acknowledged their indebtedness to that trend of thought in nineteenth-century Russia. As one of the more recent examples, one can cite Zhdanov's speech at the All-Union Congress of Soviet Writers held in August, 1946. There, buttressing his argument with references to both Lenin and Stalin, Zhdanov spoke of "the tremendous significance of the great Russian revolutionary-democratic writers and critics" who "had repudiated so-called 'pure art' and 'art for art's sake.'" Among others, he cited the names of Belinsky, Chernyshevsky and Dobroliubov. As far as Belinsky is concerned, only the last phase of his literary activity gives him a right to be included in the list, and even then, he did not go to the extremes that were reached by his successors. For the full blooming of the "civic art" theory, one has to turn to the radical intellectuals of the 1860's, the time of the famous battle between "fathers and sons," the heyday of "Nihilism." It was then that the issue was joined between the "idealists" of the older generation and the "critical realists" of the younger, and significantly the central problem of the debate was that of the relation between art and society.

In the heat of polemics, both sides exaggerated their mutual differences and defined their respective positions in a needlessly sharp fashion. In particular, the attack of the "sons" on the "art for art's sake" theory was hitting off the mark as it would be difficult to find a representative of pure aestheticism among the Russian intellectuals of the first half of the nineteenth century. For obvious historical reasons, there was no place for an ivory tower in the Russian intellectual landscape of the time. Pushkin who was disparaged by some of the younger critics as "pure artist" had compared the poet to an echo, and in his poetical testament ("The Monument") he had pointed out his defense of liberty and his advocacy of "mercy to the fallen" as his claim to national recognition. Gogol wanted to make his art an instrument of Russia's moral and religious regeneration. To the Russian romanticists, art was a way to penetrate the mysteries of the universe as well as to bring harmony into the discordant human life.

The real issue, obscured by the polemics, was that of the *autonomy of culture*. If properly understood, the position of the greatest Russian writers from Pushkin to Turgenev was precisely the defense of this autonomy. None of them wanted to separate himself from national life or to deny the writer's social obligations. But they all felt that the writer (or the artist) could discharge his duty toward his own society and humanity in general only under conditions of complete artistic freedom —only if he was permitted to perform his function of his own free will and not under the pressure of a political or social command.

They all had a keen appreciation of the fact that art, while not separated from human life and society, still had a peculiar sphere of its own, that the artistic activity was an activity *sui generis*, subject to the laws of its internal development and having its own ways of expression. And finally, they realized that human life was not limited to politics, and that therefore a strictly utilitarian and predominantly "civic" approach to art was an illegitimate narrowing of its scope and a despoilment of cultural riches. They were prepared to defend the "eternal values" as against an exclusive preoccupation with the evil of the day.

It was along these lines that the "revolutionary democrats" differed from their opponents. They believed that society had a right to dictate to the writer not only *what* he should write about, but also *how* he should write. The subject-matter must lie within the field of pressing social and political problems, and the form must be that of realistic art as the only one corresponding with the spirit of the "scientific age" and satisfying the needs of the mass reader. They ruled out as useless or even harmful such branches of literature as "pure" lyric poetry, and such intellectual pursuits as metaphysical or religious speculation. They displayed an inability to appreciate the peculiar nature of art as a specific form of man's creative activity, and, by virtually rejecting aesthetic criteria, they reduced literary criticism to a discussion of the social value of a given work of art, praising it for its "progressive" tendency or rejecting it because of its "reactionary" character. In short, they stood for a complete subordination of culture to politics.

One can understand how such a frame of mind arose among the radical Russian intellectuals of the period, dedicated as they were to the task of combating the established political and social order and yet deprived of a possibility to express and propagate their views in a more direct and open fashion. For them, this attitude served both as a mechanism of self-defense and a weapon of attack. Just the same, the harm done by it to Russian intellectual and cultural life is an indisputable historical fact. Apart from its immediate detrimental effects, it paved the way for the Soviet system of thought control—to the extent to which it survived among certain limited circles of Russian intellectuals, to the time of the Revolution.

The affinity between the Soviet attitude toward cultural values and that of the "revolutionary democrats" of the 1860's is quite obvious. In both cases, we meet with the same denial of the autonomy of culture, the same politically colored utilitarian approach to art and literature, the same dogmatic exclusion of wide fields of intellectual interests, and the same belief in the efficacy of "social command." But while recognizing this historical connection, one should be on guard against jumping to the conclusion that it makes the Soviet system of thought control a natural result and final consummation of a Russian "national tradition."

To begin with, even at the time when the influence of this exclusive, civic-mindedness was at its highest, it by no means was shared by all the important representatives of Russian culture. On the contrary, one might say that while it was widespread among the rank and file of the intelligentsia, it was conspicuously absent at the heights of Russian cultural life. It was not shared by such great novelists as Turgenev, Tolstoy and Dostoevsky or, with the single possible exception of Nekrasov, by any outstanding poet of the period.

In the second place, and this has a more direct bearing on the problem of historical continuity, the hegemony of civic-mindedness proved to be a passing phase in Russian intellectual history, tending to fade away as the specific conditions which had called it into being began to undergo a significant transformation. At the turn of the century, a radical change took place in the Russian intellectual climate with the advent of new philosophical, literary and artistic trends which are usually grouped together under the name of Symbolism of Neo-Romanticism.

The movement was far from being homogeneous, but in all its different aspects alike it represented the abandonment of the exclusive civic-mindedness of the preceding decades, a revolt against the tyranny of politics and radical conformism, and an affirmation of the autonomy of culture. It has been interpreted by Soviet literary historians (and not only by them) as a spiritual reaction, a betrayal of their progressive mission by the intellectuals, an escape from reality, and a symbol of decadence.

As I see it, it was a sign of intellectual progress and growing intellectual maturity. It brought about a renaissance of Russian arts and letters, it widened the horizons of the country's intellectual elite while by no means making it divorced from reality, and it contributed to that variety and richness of cultural life which could be found in Russia in the early twentieth century. That very diversity of intellectual pursuits, and in particular, the differentiation between culture and politics, which to some critics is the ground for condemnation, should be viewed as the natural and welcome result of the country's historical evolution toward a healthier social and political order.

Be that as it may, the fact remains that on the eve of the Revolution the political utilitarianism of the "revolutionary democrats" of the 1860's ceased to be a living tradition and did not play any longer an important part in national culture. If it still lingered in the restricted circles of some old-fashioned radicals, this was a typical example of an intellectual lag and a glaring anachronism.

That this outworn ideology could be revived and made official and obligatory by those who came into power in November, 1917, in no sense can be ascribed to its intrinsic vitality and superiority. It did not win in a free competition of ideas. It simply was imposed on the nation by a governmental fiat and by means of a forcible elimination of all the competing trends of thought. The fruits of this "restoration" are there for all to see. A deadly unformity of ideas and expression has taken the place of the former variety and richness. From this point of view, the cultural policy of the Soviet regime appears as a profound intellectual reaction.

SOVIET NATIONALITY POLICY: THE CASE HISTORY OF BELORUSSIA *

Among the most important aspects of Soviet policy is that involving the treatment of the nationality problem. The Tsarist regime made a failure of its efforts to cope with the problem, a failure that was inevitable since its program of Russification of minorities engendered so much hatred that it actually provoked rather than retarded the growth of nationalism among the non-Russians. The Bolsheviks made the solution of the nationality problem one of their planks, holding out the promise of "liberation from Tsarist and Great Russian oppression." One of the first acts of the new Soviet regime was to issue a "Decree of the Rights of the People of Russia," signed on November 15, 1917, by Lenin and Stalin, affirming the right of national minorities to develop their own cultures and to decide their own fate —even to the point of forming independent states. Since then the Soviet government has implemented a comprehensive nationality program, in the course of which it has apparently tried to encourage national cultural development while stifling any tendency to question the dictates of Moscow. The consequences of such a course are shown by Professor Vakar.

BELORUSSIANS, or White Russians, are a subdivision of the East Slavic stock to which the Ukrainians (or Little Russians) and the Russians (Great Russians) also belong. As the smallest member of that family,

* Nicholas Vakar, "Soviet Nationality Policy: The Case History of Belorussia," *Problems of Communism*, III, No. 5 (September, 1954), 25–33. Reprinted by permission of the author and the publisher.
The author is Professor of Russian Civilization and Literature at Wheaton Col-

they inhabit a territory of 207,600 sq. km. (79,846 sq. miles) surrounded by Poland in the west, Lithuania and Latvia in the north, Russia in the east, and the Ukraine in the south. . . . No one knows exactly how many Belorussians there are. The last general censuses recorded only 989,900 Belorussians in Poland (1931), and 5,267,400 in the U.S.S.R. (1939), although the total was revised by the Soviets up to approximately 8,500,000 as of June 1, 1941. No data have been published since, but circumspect judgment based on indirect evidence would suggest that the total number of Bellorussian-speaking people in the U.S.S.R. does not exceed 6 millions today (a ratio of approximately 1:20 between Belorussians and Great Russians).

Facts of geography and demography, however, have little power against the Belorussian nationalists' views of their family and legitimate home. They are convinced that:

1. Belorussians are an ethnic group of pure Balto-Slavic descent, thus having an inalienable right to both the Baltic and the Slavic heritage.

2. The name Belorussia is inadequate and either ought to be replaced by Kryvia or—as a lesser evil—ought to be translated White Ruthenia, not White Russia.

3. Ancient Belorussia was an early home of "democratic ideas" and "social equality" unknown to other Slavic tribes; the Belorussian (Kryvian) people were already politically independent in the ninth century; from the thirteenth century on, they dominated the Grand Duchy of Lithuania which, in fact, was a Belorussian Lithuanian state; in the fifteenth and sixteenth centuries Belorussian writings "overshadowed all Slavic literatures."

4. The aggressive policies of Warsaw on the one hand, and Moscow on the other, were responsible for the decline of the Old Belorussian culture; today, "bitter memories of the past make the Belorussian turn from Poland and Russia with equal disgust."

5. The Allied Powers at the Versailles Peace Conference were mistaken in rejecting the Belorussian claim for independence; a Belorussian state would have been a "stabilizing factor" in Eastern Europe, indeed "might have prevented or circumscribed World War II . . ."

The student of history may not agree. His view will only inflame the ardors of believers in the national myth. Belorussian nationalism has become a latent force which can neither be negated nor dismissed. If nobody else, the Soviet leaders themselves have acknowledged its existence. The viability of Belorussian nationalism is demonstrated by the Kremlin's efforts to bring it under control, neutralize it, and finally liquidate it with all the means at their disposal.

---

lege. He was born in Russia and received his higher education in that country and in the United States. His interests include both linguistics and history. He has made a special study of White Russia (Belorussia), out of which came his historical work *Belorussia* (1956) and *A Bibliographical Guide to Belorussia* (1956).

FIRST ATTEMPTS AT INDEPENDENCE

It is significant that none of the nationalist claims enumerated above had been made before the Russian Revolution.

National self-determination among the peoples of the Tsarist empire was, for many reasons, a slow and belated process. By no means were the Belorussians in the front row of the movement which swept Europe in the nineteenth century. Their intellectual elite had been either polonized or russianized, while the common people farmed as of old, undisturbed in their customs and beliefs, and faithful to the native idiom. Since the Belorussian area was almost totally agrarian, there was no middle class. The standards of living and of literacy were among the lowest in the empire. The people did not remember their "glorious past" and were not even sure of their own identity. When asked who they were, they simply described themselves as "local residents" (*tutashni, tuteishi*). The administration treated people of the Greek Orthodox faith as Russians, and those of the Roman Catholic faith as Polish.

Not until the middle of the nineteenth century did Polish and Russian scholarship discover that the inhabitants of the region were neither Poles nor Russians. Used hitherto in a geographical sense, "Belorussian" became an ethnographical term around which, by the end of the century, a movement of national self-determination began to crystallize.

The movement followed a natural course from ethnic to literary, and from cultural to political nationalism. It had not reached a very advanced stage when World War I, the Russian Revolution, and the institution of the democratic Provisional Government in Petrograd drastically changed the situation. Young Belorussian leadership split over socio-economic issues. The nationalist faction's claims did not go beyond "cultural autonomy" or "a territorial status" within the political boundaries of Russia. But even these optimum claims proved incompatible with the popular mood. In the free elections held throughout Russia in the spring of 1917, not a single seat was won in the municipal and rural councils (*zemstvos*) by the nationalists. A few months later, in the general elections to the Constituent Assembly, their ticket collected barely 29,000 votes in all Belorussia. To be sure, there already were Belorussian clubs, schools, newspapers, and writers of national fame. But the idea of nationality was bound up with the mother tongue—that is, with cultural and literary rather than political unity—and at that was hindered by the absence of a literary standard, even of a grammar for the schools. In many quarters, the Belorussian idiom was still regarded as a lower form of Russian and not as an independent language.

The Bolshevik *coup d'état* in November, 1917 gave Belorussian nationalism the momentum it needed in two opposite, though equally effective, ways. The Bolsheviks were seeking to enroll the dynamic forces of both socialism and nationalism for world revolution. They urged "the oppressed nations" to fight "for the freedom of self-determination, *i.e.*, the freedom of secession," and to break up empires. To them, "the nationality question was a subordinate one" and the Belorussians, like the other peoples of Russia, were offered immediate statehood provided they adopt a Soviet system of government. At the time it was not too clear what the Soviet system of government might be; in any event, this was a minor consideration from the nationalists' point of view. Tongue in cheek, a group of the nationalist leaders gladly joined hands with the Soviet Commissariat of Nationalities (at that time headed by Stalin) in preparing the administration of the forthcoming Belorussian republic, a Soviet and socialist state but a sovereign one—so the Bolshevik promise went.

For anti-Soviet leaders, on the other hand, the quick establishment of a sovereign Belorussian state was now the only way to save the country from communism. They turned to the Central Powers which occupied the land (in accordance with the treaty of Brest-Litovsk of February, 1918). The Austro-German military command obliged and a Belorussian National Republic (BNR) was proclaimed in Minsk on March 25, 1918. All ties with Russia were severed, and claims were laid upon all territories where Belorussian was spoken. A national flag was adopted. The state seal bore the symbol (*pahonia*) of the ancient Lithuanian Russian state, and postage stamps of three denominations were printed. Sovereign power having thus been consummated, the self-imposed government sat down to do business as best it could. The occupation authorities had given it considerable leeway in domestic affairs and even in foreign relations. A number of reforms had to be hastily enacted to promote Belorussian culture and to awaken the national consciousness of the people: decrees were issued, making Belorussian the state language, granting equality rights to the minority groups, reforming the educational system, paving the ground for elections to a state legislature, abolishing private land-ownership, nationalizing forests, lakes, and natural resources, establishing an eight-hour work-day, *etc.*

These reforms took place during the summer and fall of 1918, up to the time the Germans were defeated in the West. In December, however, the German occupation troops were withdrawn, spelling doom for the Belorussian National Republic.

The communists moved in quickly. A Belorussian Workers' and Peasants' Government had been formed in Moscow by the Belorussian Department of the Commissariat for the Nationalities, consisting chiefly of former members of the Belorussian National Committee in Minsk. On January 1, 1919 it outlawed the BNR, proclaimed a Belorussian Soviet Socialist Republic, and called an All-Belorussian Congress of Workers, Peasants and Soldiers, to confirm the "will of the people." However, the delegates of Smolensk, Mogilev and Vitebsk provinces rejected the idea of an independent statehood and the territory of the Republic shrank to six counties of Minsk province alone. Only three months later the Red Army was routed, and Belorussia conquered by the Poles.

Although independent statehood had been unsolicited and short-lived, it had stirred the pride and imagination of the people. Political independence seemed no longer something to attain, but something to regain. A myth rapidly grew around the BNR and the B.S.S.R.: the 25th of March for the anti-Soviet population, and the 1st of January for the Soviet side, became Independence Days to be celebrated for years to come.

THE RISE AND DECLINE OF BELORUSSIAN NATIONALISM

The treaty of Riga (March 18, 1921) cut Belorussia in halves, one Polish, another Soviet. Sad as was this circumstance for the people, the Belorussian national movement gained rather than lost from the partition of the national territory.

The Poles had no clear idea as to how they should treat the Belorussian minority. They were not prepared to grant it territorial status within the Polish state, but they believed that they might use Belorussianism for two purposes: first, counteracting the Russian influence in the eastern provinces, and secondly, attracting the Soviet Belorussians to the Polish side. Consequently, Belorussian leaders were given financial and other support to proceed with the belorussification of the borderland (kresy) under the supervision of the Polish authority.

Meanwhile, beyond the border the B.S.S.R. was restored as a sovereign state and at first enjoyed equal status with Russia itself. The national administration was given full freedom in belorussifying the country, even in treating the Russians as a second-place minority. Presently, everything reminiscent of "old Russia" was destroyed, remodeled, or re-formed. The Russian language was banned from schools, courts, and offices, even from homes. The people were ordered to bring their dialects into line with the national standard, still in the making itself. People who spoke a mixed idiom were criticized as "Muscovites" and deprived of rights. Moscow remained undisturbed; in fact, it was pleased. Twice it even increased the territory of Soviet Belorussia, raising its land area to 125,703 sq. km. (48,347 sq. miles) and its population to 5,439,400 by 1926.

The nationalists, it seemed, could not have made a better bargain. The price they were paying the Kremlin—enforcement of the communist program—meant little to them: there were few Belorussians among the "capitalists" who perished in the "class struggle." On the other hand, there was much to be gained through lip service to "Marxism-Leninism." The leaders of the former BNR gave up their hopes for a "democratic Belorussia," and returned from exile (1925). Given at once responsible positions in the Soviet administration, they enthusiastically joined hands with local communists in building "the Belorussian home."

The Poles obviously were not able to outbid the Soviets, and the Belorussian movement in Poland got out of hand. In 1928 the Polish government, fearing open revolt, cracked down on the 100,000-member Belorussian Workers' and Peasants' Society (*Hramada*) which worked closely with the communist underground. As soon as the leaders were jailed the Kremlin offered to exchange them for Poles arrested in the U.S.S.R. Shipped out to Minsk by the Poles, leaders of the *Hramada* were received as national martyrs and heroes.

In time virtually the whole nationalist leadership—the elite of Young Belorussia—was gathered in Minsk under the protection of the Communist International. They felt that their strategy had been vindicated and that their investment in "world revolution" had paid off. Hadn't they succeeded in *nationalizing* communism? Their national home, though Soviet in structure, was even more Belorussian than they had hoped.

In the meantime, the Kremlin had been losing faith in the imminence of world-wide revolution, and the safety of the Soviet Union became the prime concern of the party. Belorussian nationalism as an instrument for fomenting unrest in neighboring Poland was no longer of use to the regime. Nationalism among the minorities became, in fact, a target of increasing attack since it constituted an obstacle to the newly emerging doctrine of "Soviet patriotism." The problem was solved in the manner that has since become only too familiar to observers of the Soviet system. By the fall of 1929, the whole Belorussian leadership—including the most glorified leaders of the *Hramada*—found itself behind prison walls. No legal procedure was observed. Thousands of scholars, writers, teachers, even students were arrested and deported, or liquidated in jail. Indeed, it seemed as though the Kremlin had deliberately gathered the entire Belorussian elite in Minsk to liquidate it all at once.

The nationalist movement was beheaded by the very power which, only a decade before, had given it a new lease on life. Persecution of the survivors continued through the 1930's, and even the Communist Party of Belorussia was scratched to the bone. The Party First Secretary Sharangovich was shot. The Chairman of the Council of People's Commissars Haladzed was murdered in jail. Zhylunovich, president of the B.S.S.R. and one of the founders of the Communist Party of Belorussia, was imprisoned and died "awaiting trial." The actual founder of the B.S.S.R., Charviakov, shot himself to avoid torture and shameful "confession." Scores of prominent communists followed them to the grave or to Siberian labor camps. All had been accused of bourgeois nationalism, espionage, and sabotage, and disappeared in the wake of those whom they themselves had liquidated only a few years before.

Of the intellectual elite, with the exception of a dozen writers and scholars who "repented" and whose talents communism still could use, not a single man who had labored under the Soviets for the establishment of the "Belorussian national home" was free and alive. Their offices were handed over to the younger generation, ideologically conditioned to un-questioning obedience to Moscow. Literature, theatre, radio, the fine arts, and the press were brought under central control in "unions" of writers, artists, composers, architects, and others, each under the iron thumb of a party delegate. Belorussian institutions were preserved in outward form, indeed grew in number, but were filled with a new sub-stance. The history of Belorussia was ordered rewritten in line with the history of the U.S.S.R. National culture was tolerated, even encouraged, on condition that it be, in Stalin's words, "nationalist in form and socialist in content."

Belorussian nationalism seemed sufficiently "socialized" when, in 1939, World War II broke out, and the Soviet armies marched into pros-trate Poland to "liberate" their oppressed brethren, the Ukrainians and the Belorussians. After Poland's defeat, the Soviet Union, according to its treaty with Nazi Germany, incorporated West Belorussia. The incor-poration of these territories raised new political and cultural problems for the Soviet masters.

WORLD WAR II: UNIFICATION AND DISPERSION

It has been observed that certain symbols are used not because cer-tain things are believed to exist, but rather certain things are believed to exist because certain symbols are used. The maxim, it would seem, was not unknown to Poland and the Kremlin, but they interpreted it in op-posite ways.

The Poles believed that by removing the symbols of Belorussian in-dependence they might open people's eyes to the fact that such a thing as a Belorussian nation never was nor could be. On the other hand, the Soviets cultivated the symbols of Belorussianism in the firm conviction that they would induce the people to believe in a nation which had, in fact, ceased to exist. In accordance with their respective theories, the Poles destroyed the shell but did not touch the animal, while the Soviets removed the animal and kept the shell. The Polish policy left the Belo-russians without legitimate outlets for any but Polish activities. The Soviets let Belorussian institutions survive, but filled them with a dummy per-sonnel. As a result, Belorussian nationalism became in Poland an uneasy spirit in search of a body, while in the Soviet Union, the body was pre-served intact, but the spirit crushed. However tamed Soviet Belorussia may have appeared, her meeting with the hard-tempered spirit of West Belorussia represented a menacing problem to the Kremlin.

For obvious reasons, the Kremlin wanted the union of West Belorussia with the U.S.S.R. to appear voluntary. The occupation authorities announced that the people would be entirely free to decide their political future. The West Belorussian nationalists, even those with a long anti-Soviet record, were neither harried nor incommoded. On the contrary, they were invited to take part in the election campaign for a National Assembly which in turn was to decide the "question" of incorporation. Some pro-nationalists who knew better had fled to Germany or to Lithuania, but others were only too glad to contribute to the historical "reunion" of their people. No communication with the B.S.S.R. was permitted, but the symbols of Belorussian national sovereignty were displayed all over the occupied territory. There was little knowledge of communism, and little fear of it among the people embittered against the Poles. Belorussian patriotism was skillfully played upon by swarms of propagandists sent over from the U.S.S.R.

On election day, October 22, a tremendous effort was made to drive the entire West Belorussian electorate to the ballot boxes. Where persuasion and allurement failed, coercion was used. According to the official data, 2,672,280 persons, or 96,7% of the electorate went to the polls: 2,409,522 voted for the "national ticket," favoring incorporation, and 247,-245 against it, while 14,932 ballots were disallowed for "technical errors." In all, 927 representatives to the National Assembly were elected, 804 men and 123 women, one delegate for every 5,000 inhabitants of West Belorussia. It is noteworthy that although the Polish population was estimated at 40 percent, only 110 Poles were included among the candidates, that is, 11.9 percent of the total number of nominees. On October 28, the National Assembly convened in Bialystok, and "decided" unanimously to demand the incorporation of West Belorussia into the U.S.S.R.

At about this time, the news was released that the U.S.S.R. had handed over to Lithuania the city of Vilna and adjacent lands—2,850 sq. miles with a population of 457,500. The Act, alienating a territory which the West Belorussians considered their own, had been signed on October 10th, but its publication was withheld until after the elections. It was too late for the National Assembly to protest, had it chosen to do so.

Meantime, representatives had been dispatched to Moscow, where all was in readiness for a formal incorporation ceremony. On November 2 "the Extraordinary Fifth Session of the U.S.S.R. Supreme Soviet acceded to the request of the masses of the people of West Belorussia and accepted them into the Union of Soviet Socialist Republics."

The fate of the country was sealed, but in the first months the Kremlin did not press its program of sovietization too vigorously. The economy was nationalized, but small trade was left free and collectivization of farming delayed. As the winter progressed, however, the process of sovietization was accelerated. The last vestiges of Polish administration were removed. The Polish colonists (*osadnicy*) were treated as "enemies of the people" and liquidated, even the many who had thoroughly as-similated into Belorussian life, whose children no longer could speak Polish. One eye-witness reports:

In the severe winter, we saw Polish women, locked in freight cars, without heat or food, throw the frozen bodies of their children through the windows at the feet of the Soviet guards.

Jewish cultural and economic clubs were either disbanded or their activi-ties restricted; of four Yiddish newspapers published in 1935, only one was left in Minsk. The more prominent West Belorussian leaders were invited to Minsk and quietly disappeared. In April, the "invitation" was extended to writers and artists; those who unwarily showed dissatisfaction with the "Stalinized" forms of national culture were deported and others given a period of grace to mold themselves into the Soviet pattern.

Polish money was outlawed; virtually the entire savings of the people were expropriated. Everybody was thus forced to look for work and to accept such conditions and wages as were offered by the only employer— the state. "An immediate and universal proletarianization of the city re-sulted, and wages became the only source of income," according to the same witness quoted above. Another writes:

In February the business section of the city [Pinsk] resembled a cemetery; stores closed, street lights unlit, people afraid to walk at night. At the public market (bazar) one could sell and buy old watches, dresses, decks of cards, frying pans, pillows, all kinds of junk which had suddenly assumed a new value . . . Bread lines appeared . . . The arrests continued. No one was sure of what might happen to him . . . In March, two thousand people were de-ported, all relatives of the previously arrested.

With the incorporation of Lithuania into the Soviet Union on August 3, 1940, the last nationalist stronghold in Vilna was liquidated. The purges then spread from city to village; the community leaders, the rural in-telligentsia, and practically everyone who had been politically active in the past were removed.

Farmers owning more than one horse and more than one cow were classified as kulaks and deported to eastern regions of the U.S.S.R. Others left the village rather than be enrolled in the collective farms, and went to work in the city. According to available evidence, less than half of the population in many localities were left to work in the fields. The individual owner-manager and the unskilled laborer were liquidated, and only a quaking fringe of handicraft-workers was left outside the planned mass-production of goods and services.

The Communist Party was expanded and the more trustworthy recruits, in the eyes of Moscow, appointed to national offices. Literature, the fine arts, the press, indeed all cultural activities fell under party con-trol, and the "national ideology" under its direction. Libraries were purged, schools supplied with new textbooks, and the literary standard was unified. Growing popular unrest was quelled by mass deportations, arrests, and executions. Communications with the original B.S.S.R. remained restrictive. Economically, the country was worse off than it had ever been under the Poles, and the general atmosphere was one of despondency, hatred, and fear. Politically, however, the situation seemed well in hand.

The Soviet press boasted of the new successes and achievements, filling its pages with acknowledgments of the "eternal debt of the Belorussian people to the Communist Party and to Stalin" for the "complete fulfillment of the national dream."

OCCUPATION AND "LIBERATION"

The Germans attacked the U.S.S.R. on June 22, 1941, and in about three weeks the whole territory of Belorussia was overrun.

There is little quarrel among historians that the Belorussian population offered no resistance, indeed welcomed the invader and hastened to cooperate with him. The Soviet civil authorities had fled, leaving the people to their own devices, but the German armies had no difficulty in maintaining order in the rear. A kind of self-government sprang up in the urban and rural communities, left free by the military command to look after their own affairs. The economic situation deteriorated, especially in the cities, but people obviously enjoyed "a breath of freedom" not known before, and the feeling grew that there might be better opportunities for self-development after the war. "Unfortunately," as one witness put it, "the favorable attitude toward the Germans continued only as long as there was military government; the so-called *Reichskommissarn* quickly destroyed the good will of the people." The incompetent and inhuman Nazi civil administration caused a complete reversal of the popular attitude within less than a year. Treated as a sub-human race, persecuted and abused, often reduced to caveman existence in the woods and swamps, the Belorussian people had no recourse but to join hands with the Soviets in a guerrilla warfare for survival.

From the abundant evidence gathered on this period the following observations can be made:

1. With liberation from communism, the country's whole economic and social structure collapsed. There were no individual and no public bodies ready to represent the nation or to take over the responsibilities of administration on more than a community level. Reared in the habit of obedience, the human mass patiently waited for orders from whatever new authority might be imposed on them.

2. Without waiting for orders, however, and much against the German will, collective farming was spontaneously discontinued all over the territory of Belorussia. In the areas where no occupation authority appeared,

there was a return to the pre-revolutionary pattern of government, the *mir*, as if the years of Soviet power had brought no change in the people's minds and habits.

3. Although brought up in one totalitarian system and dominated by another, the people, to the extent that they were left free to manage their own affairs, set out quietly to build a democratic order, however rudimentary in form and limited in purpose it may have been.

4. Belorussian nationalism made a poor showing, though slightly better in the western than in the eastern part of the country. A score of die-hard nationalists did return from exile—some of them well-known—but they were not able to stir the hopes and imagination of the people. Perhaps in the popular mind symbols of Belorussianism had been too long associated, indeed too often confused, with communism. Moreover, the former exiles, perfectly vocal in their denunciations of the Soviet system, were surprisingly tongue-tied in acknowledging German wrongs. To the common man, their position suggested that they were either powerless or cowardly and treacherous. In any event, despite some loud claims to the contrary, there is no documentary evidence of the guerrilla leaders ever formulating a nationalist program, whether they fought the Soviets or the Germans. In fact, instances have been recorded of Belorussian bands fighting both communism and "Belorussianism" at the same time.

It was not that the Belorussian had lost pride in himself and his way of life. More than ever, his patriotism had ethnic and cultural overtones. But the old political symbols had worn out, and between the Germans and the Soviets the country had no choice. When in June 1944 an All-Belorussian Convention was convened in Minsk to confirm the Act of Independence of March 25, 1918, and to form a Belorussian government, there was little reaction among the people. A few days later the Germans withdrew and the country became Soviet again.

THE SOVIETS AGAIN

By this time the communists had learned a lesson. They realized that active subversive nationalism and latent nationalism require different modes of suppression. Subversive groups in the country were liquidated more or less effectively, although they kept the MGB and NKVD busy for several years. On the other hand, attempts were made to neutralize refugee opinion and action abroad by raising the symbols of Belorussian independence to a new height: Soviet Belorussia was given a new national flag and, along with one other Soviet republic (the Ukraine), made a member of the United Nations on an ostensibly equal footing with the U.S.S.R. itself.

The B.S.S.R. government and party Central Committee have been reshuffled several times, and most of the responsible positions have been filled by persons of non-Belorussian origin. Government decrees which by law should be published in both the Belorussian and Russian languages, are often in Russian alone. The army, institutions of higher learning, and most official correspondence also use only Russian. The new Belorussian dictionary (1953) is mostly a transliteration of Russian words. There are reports that people avoid speaking Belorussian in the streets lest they be suspected of "bourgeois nationalism." The history of Belorussia is once again being rewritten, to emphasize even more strongly the historical "debt" of the country to Russia. Belorussian scholarship is instructed to stress the indebtedness of modern Belorussian literature to Belinsky, Turgenev, Nekrasov, Leo Tolstoy, Maxim Gorky, and other Russian classics." Writings of the prerevolutionary period are condemned as "petty-bourgeois," and un-Belorussian. Belorussian patriotism is consistently divorced from its historical past, and the national heroes of Russia glorified. Cultural institutions have undergone transformation. As a neutral observer remarked, "The bottle displays Belorussian labels, but the beverage is from a Russian mixer."

This course may stamp out latent nationalism among the educated. For the peasantry, a policy of mass migration has been adopted. Whole communities in East Prussia (Kaliningrad province) have been resettled with Belorussian farmers. Thousands more of the peasants have been transferred to new settlements in West Siberia and Central Asia. This year a drive is being sponsored for the "voluntary migration" of new thousands of Belorussian lumberjacks with their families to the Karelo-Finnish S.S.R. and the northern provinces of the R.S.F.S.R. In their stead, immigrants from other Soviet republics have been moved in to take over Belorussian industries and farming. The apparent theory is that nationalism latent among the minorities will be less harmful when dispersed. Statistical data are not available, but enough information has leaked out to show that the demographic picture of Belorussia has changed significantly since World War II.

The history of Belorussian nationalism raises a number of interesting questions, none of them easily answered: How intense are the national sentiments of Belorussians? What is their nature? Are they purely cultural—that is, do they represent a striving for cultural autonomy? Or are they also political—that is, anti-Soviet and anti-Russian? Has Soviet communism succeeded in strengthening or in destroying Belorussian nationalism?

Whatever the final answer to these questions, there is no doubt that the Kremlin is not willing to wait and see—that it is bent on eradicating any manifestation of national consciousness which threatens its power or could do so in the future. It is ironical, perhaps, that while the German Nazis found Belorussian nationalism virtually non-existent, their oppressive policies, as well as the policies of the Soviet regime, were instrumental in arousing national feeling among the Belorussian people. Of course this sentiment cannot express itself in sharply-defined political goals. There is no way of telling whether persistent national feeling and yearnings for cultural self-expression also reflect a desire for political autonomy in the hearts of the people. At the present time, there is little or no evidence of such strivings among the Kremlin's Belorussian subjects. The Belorussian intelligentsia—the principal source of national consciousness —has been decimated by the Soviet regime. All channels for the expression of Belorussian cultural values have been destroyed. Real or potential, the spectre of Belorussianism—as well as any other nationalism that threatens to disrupt the monolithic structure of the U.S.S.R.—continues to haunt the leaders of the "freest country in the world."

20 /

THE SOVIET UNION
AND THE WAR
IN THE WEST *

Soviet military and political operations during World War II
were cloaked in unmatched secrecy, and the Soviet government has
done little in the years since the war to lift the veil. It has recently
begun to release certain diplomatic correspondence of the period
and to publish a serious history of the Soviet war effort. Yet, for a
broad interpretation, one must still rely on the work of competent
non-Soviet analysts like Dr. Matloff.

As TENSIONS mount in the atomic age and shadows lengthen
over Europe and Asia, the problem of coexistence with the Soviet Union
in a shrinking world has emerged as the most pressing issue of the day.
After two world wars, the widening rift between the Soviet Union and
the West since 1945 has caused a wave of disillusionment and frustration.
A growing chorus of opinion on both sides of the Atlantic has charged
that the peace was lost as a result of political and strategic mistakes of
World War II. It becomes all the more important, therefore, at this stage
of the cold war to take stock of the wartime association of the Soviet
Union with the West—its origins, development, and break-down.

THE THREE PARTNERS

The story of Allied collaboration in the war against Germany is,
simply put, the search for a common denominator among three sovereign partners faced with a common enemy. It is important to remember

* Maurice Matloff, "The Soviet Union and the War in the West," *U.S. Naval Insti-*
tute Proceedings, LXXXII (March, 1956), 261–71. Copyright © 1956 by U.S.
Naval Institute. Reprinted by permission of the author and the publisher.
    The author is Senior Historical Advisor, Post-World War II Branch, Office
of Military History, United States Department of the Army. He is co-author, with

that the Grand Alliance was forged in war and essentially for war purposes. It was, therefore, a war marriage, a "marriage of expediency." A common bond of danger drew the three countries together in 1941. But each member of the Grand Alliance, as a result of differing traditions, policies, interests, geography, and resources, looked at the European war through different spectacles.

Great Britain, the island empire, dependent upon the sea lanes for its very existence and situated precariously on the edge of Hitler's *Festung Europe*, was the first to enter the war against Germany. For centuries it had put its faith in the balance of power. It could be expected to seek to revive and rally the smaller nations and to continue to put its weight against any strong power that threatened to upset the balance on the continent. It had special political and economic interests in the Mediterranean and the Middle East through which ran its lifeline to the Empire in the East. Its economy, while highly industrialized, was, in comparison with that of the United States, small-scale. In any global war Great Britain's resources would be stretched thin. Keenly conscious of its heavy manpower losses in the ground battles of World War I, Great Britain was anxious to avoid a repetition of these. By necessity and choice, its leaders put their faith in the Navy, the Air Force, and the mechanized and armored forces, rather than a large ground army. Experienced in war, diplomacy, and empire, Great Britain had a long history of alliances with European powers. Its military were accustomed to work closely with the political leadership, and its policy in war could be expected to give political matters a primary place. Even though thrown on the military defensive and with its back to the wall when the United States entered the war, British military and political strategy were operating together wherever possible. Reduced to their fundamentals, British political aims toward occupied Europe were twofold and, as it turned out, somewhat contradictory. For the short run the British sought to encourage resistance and rebellion; but, in the long run, they hoped, once the cancer of Hitlerism had been excised from the European body politic, for a general return, with appropriate reforms, to the *status quo ante bellum*.

Across the Atlantic lay the other Western power in the alliance, the *United States*—young, impatient, rich in resources, highly industrialized, the country with the technical "know-how." It was now to undergo a major experience in coalition warfare. This was the country whose whole tradition in war had been first to declare, then to prepare. Traditionally opposed to becoming involved in European quarrels, it nevertheless had strong bonds of culture, language, and tradition with Western Europe—especially England. Based on its experience in World War I, the American

Edwin M. Snell, of *Strategic Planning for Coalition Warfare, 1941–42* (1953) and author of *Strategic Planning for Coalition Warfare 1943–44* (1959). Both volumes are in the series entitled *United States Army in World War II*.

approach to European war seemed to be to hold off as long as possible, enter it only long enough to give the bully or bullies who started it a sound thrashing, get the boys home, and then try to remain as uninvolved as before. To most Americans, therefore, war was an aberration—an un-welcome disturber of normalcy. In the pre-World War II period, the national policy was deeply influenced by popular beliefs that the United States should neither enter into military alliances nor maintain forces capable of offensive action. But, even in this atmosphere of disillusion-ment, that legalistic-moral strain which has so influenced the American approach to foreign affairs, to which George Kennan has pointed, re-mained strong. If only the nations of the world would subscribe to princi-ples and declarations of justice and morality, agree to disarm and to out-law war, all would be well with the world. This idealistic strain reflected in Wilsonian policies toward Europe during and after World War I was imbedded in the pragmatism of President Roosevelt and was to find its echo in his foreign policies in World War II. Two other factors distin-guished American policy from the beginning of the conflict. The loose relationship between the President and the military—in accord with what might be termed the American doctrine of the separation of military and political powers—offered a sharp contrast with the closely knit politico-military systems of Great Britain and of the U.S.S.R. And sec-ondly, the President and his military staff could never forget the war against Japan, which, to most Americans, appeared to be a more natural enemy than Germany. This compulsion was to play an important part in the relations among the Big Three and in the development of war strategy. Given the considerations of domestic politics and the added pressure of the Japanese war, the United States simply could not fight a long war in Europe.

And then there was the *Soviet Union,* essentially a land power with completely internal lines of communications. It represented an enigmatic, restless, and dynamic force, devoted to a political and economic ideology different from that of the Western partners. Possessing an enormous pop-ulation and great resources, its industrial program, however, was still incomplete. Lacking air and naval traditions, it put its faith in geography, the endurance of its people, and its army in the desperate battle for survival. Born in revolution and come to power in a civil and foreign war, the Soviet Union had developed into a baffling hybrid in Western eyes —a combination of "Russian national socialism," Marxist concepts, and policies and practices lingering from Czarist days. Dedicated to the propo-sition that war was inevitable in capitalist society until the world revolu-tion ushered in a new millennial order, Bolshevism lived in an undeclared state of war with the capitalist world. In fact, it is a popular misconcep-tion to regard the "cold war" and "iron curtain" as purely postwar phe-nomena. In a very real sense they go back to November, 1917. As we get more perspective on the Russian role in World War II, it becomes evident that the period of its defensive struggle against Germany was merely a pause, an interlude, in its twin drives for security and expansion. These drives appear to have been at work in its war with Finland and even in the uneasy period of its pact with Hitler. One of the main reasons for the break with the Fuehrer was the aggressive action of the Soviet Union in pushing farther west in Europe—in asserting its claims to Poland and the Balkans—moves which Hitler, confronted with a stubborn Britain on the west, considered too dangerous to be permitted to continue. Until attacked by Germany, the Soviet war effort can be characterized therefore as warfare in pursuit of aggrandizement. The Nazi invasion only reinforced the Soviet desire to strengthen its position in Eastern Europe —an objective whose roots lay deep in Russian history and was never lost sight of in World War II. But for almost two years after the German attack the Soviet Union was engaged in a desperate fight for its very existence, and while political and territorial ambitions were by no means absent, military considerations were more immediately paramount. Still fearful of capitalist encirclement, suspicious of friend and foe alike, its position in what Major General J. R. Deane so fittingly called "The Strange Alliance" would be uneasy.

1941–1942: ROOTS AND ORIGINS

Of the three main phases in the story of the partnership, 1941–42 is the fascinating period of roots and origins. This period witnessed the formation of the Grand Alliance and saw the beginnings of the pattern of collaboration between the Soviet Union and the West—a pattern which in large measure was to obtain for the remainder of the war. For the Allies this was a period of defensive strategy—a strategy of scarcity. The basic fear was the fear of defeat; the great concern, the survival of the Soviet Union.

From the beginning, the inner web of the Grand Alliance was the close relationship between the United States and Great Britain. The Russians remained outside of the Combined Chiefs system—developed for the day-to-day coordination of the Western effort in the global war. Above that system were the Prime Minister and the President, whose association became as close and warm as their relationship with the enigmatic Stalin remained formal and distant. Unlike the Western partners, the Soviet Union would be at war on only one front. With their forces far apart, the West and East were operating at long range. From the start, the troubled relations of the past, the lack of free intercourse, the legacy of suspicion made genuine understanding difficult. A curious "arms-length" war partnership came into being.

The divergent approaches toward the European war were most clearly reflected in the emergence of the peripheral theory, espoused by Churchill and the British staff, and the theory of mass and concentration advocated by Marshall and his staff. For each the geography and manpower of the Soviet Union early became the key to victory, and both justified their theories and plans in terms of relieving the pressure upon the Russians most expediently. But neither side could readily win the other to its concept of strategy, and the long debate which ensued led to a delicate relationship and a bone of contention with the Soviet Union. From the beginning the Russians, locked in a death struggle on the Eastern front, had no doubts about the proper Western strategy. They wanted a second front; they wanted it soon; and they wanted it in the West. Each Anglo-American postponement of this second front added fuel to the fire.

In the first round of debate in 1942, the British notion of an invasion of North Africa won out over the American notion of a cross-Channel attack. When TORCH won out, Churchill felt the full weight of Stalin's disapproval in a stormy interview in Moscow.

Irritations also developed over lend-lease. The Western Allies offered their assistance generously and without question when the Russians were fighting with their backs to the wall, and, in return, the Soviets gave little, if any, information. In addition, the Russians never showed much sympathy with, or understanding of, the pressing problems and competing demands on the Western partners for shipping, aircraft, and materiel in their global war. When, therefore, deliveries fell behind schedule in 1942, Soviet suspicions mounted even as Western sensitivity increased. In spite of these annoyances, however, lend-lease did form a narrow bridge of cooperation between the partners throughout the war.

By the close of 1942, certain characteristics of the war relations had become apparent. Though Western Allied plans were tied to the outcome of the struggle on the Eastern front, the West had still not agreed on strategy, and its plans had not been coordinated with those of the Soviets. The Russians, on the other hand, even in the darkest days of 1942, had turned down the offer of Roosevelt and Churchill to send an Anglo-American air force to support the Soviet forces in the Caucasus. Soviet representatives made it quite plain that Western military forces were not wanted in Soviet territory to fight alongside Soviet soldiers. It became clear that the political aspect of the project—the "comradeship in arms" in a strategically important area—which made it desirable from the viewpoint of the Prime Minister, made it undesirable from the Soviet point of view. To the West the Soviet Union looked not for closer military cooperation and fraternization but for more lend-lease and a Second Front. Its expectations for both had not been met.

On the part of the West a guilt complex was rising—resulting from the failure to fulfill Soviet hopes and from the burden of sacrifice borne by the Soviets in the fighting. The two Western approaches to war had had their first conflict, and British opportunism or peripheral strategy had scored the first victory. But this was only the first round, and the issue was not yet squarely joined. That British notions of strategy had tended to prevail was not surprising. Its forces had been earlier mobilized and were in the theaters in far greater numbers than the American. The Americans were still mobilizing their manpower and resources. The better part of a year after Pearl Harbor passed before their forces gained any appreciable weight or effect in the theaters. In the absence of a common agreed strategic plan, the only links with the Soviet Union were supplies, common subscription to general principles and declarations, such as those of the Atlantic Charter and Declaration of the United Nations, and, above all, the common enemy.

The TORCH decision, which disappointed American military hopes, also complicated relations with the Soviet Union. Sensitive as they were to Soviet reactions, the West was relieved to learn that Stalin did not protest their dealing with Darlan. On the contrary, Stalin went so far as to pass on to Churchill the illuminating observation that in war it was justifiable not only to use Darlan but, to quote an old Russian proverb, "Even the Devil himself and his grandma." The fact that the West had tried to compensate for the immediate effects of TORCH on aid to the Soviet Union through such friendly gestures as offering direct military assistance in the Caucasus, developing the Persian Gulf route, and building up the Alaska-Siberia air ferry route meant little. The Western Allies were beginning to learn that there was no banking good will with the Soviet Union. They could expect no real improvement in military relations with the U.S.S.R. except where such collaboration would clearly contribute to the one common interest—the early defeat of Germany. In other words, what the Russians wanted, above all else, was the Second Front. That question remained critical.

THE SOVIET UNION AND
THE MID-WAR DEBATE: 1943–1944

In 1943 the debate over European strategy and the collaboration of the Allies entered a new phase. If the strategic ideas of each partner remained basically the same, the circumstances of their application changed. This mid-war period—roughly down to the landing in Normandy—was the period of relative plenty. The power to call the turn and choose the time and place to do battle passed from the Axis powers to the Allied coalition.

The great debate on European strategy between the Americans and the British—opened by the decision for TORCH—endured clear down to the summer of 1944. Soviet behavior and tactics during this mid-war debate were for the West as puzzling as they were disturbing. Its curious position as half-ally—in the alliance but outside the regular Anglo-

American CCS-conference network—meant that the Soviet Union did not directly participate in most of the debates. But it appears clear that, interested as it was in the outcome, it resorted to a variety of tactics and pressures *vis-à-vis* the Western partners to influence the result. At the end of each of their conferences the Western partners would announce to the Soviet Union the general decisions reached and their expectations for the Second Front. For a while Soviet hopes would rise, but cycles of irritation followed those of good feeling as the promises and prospects of the Second Front gradually receded from 1943 to 1944. A chain reaction of displeasure would be generated throughout the whole mass of Soviet officialdom which came into contact with the West and would color dealings on all levels and problems—even those remotely associated with the issue at hand. There is fleeting evidence—difficult to weigh—suggesting that at least at one point the Soviet Union may even have seriously considered a separate peace with Germany and entered into tentative negotiations. The Soviet press kept up its campaign of registering displeasure at the delay of the Second Front, at times even going so far as to question the good faith of the Allies, especially of the British. Shortly after the Washington (TRIDENT) Conference in May, the Soviet Government tried a diplomatic gambit, going so far as to recall its ambassadors both from London and Washington. But perhaps the most puzzling move of all was its tactic at the Moscow Conference in October, 1943. Here the foreign ministers of the three partners came together to lay the groundwork for the later meeting of the Big Three at Teheran. To the great surprise of the Americans, the Soviet representatives hinted that they might be willing to accept increased pressure in the Mediterranean, even at the expense of a delay in OVERLORD, and accept aggressive action in Italy as a Second Front. In the weeks that followed, as the Allies prepared for the showdown on issues in European strategy, General Deane, Chief of the American Military Mission in Moscow, reported to Washington further hints along the same line. Certainly, on the eve of Teheran, the Americans, concerned over what seemed to them to be signs of British lukewarmness to OVERLORD, were disturbed by the threat of a reversal in the Soviet position—a turnabout that, if true, would strengthen the British strategic case. But the negotiations at Teheran were soon to suggest that this latest move was only a maneuver, perhaps designed to throw the Western partners off balance and stiffen the American stand for the long-promised but often-delayed Second Front. Aware of Anglo-American differences in European strategy, the Soviets were apparently not averse to sending up a trial balloon—especially one that might in the process of playing off one Western partner against the other enable it to win through to its own ends.

Teheran was *the* decisive conference in European strategy. There for the first time in the war, the President, the Prime Minister, and their staffs met with Marshal Stalin and his staff. The Prime Minister made eloquent appeals for operations in Italy, the Aegean, and the eastern Mediterranean, even at the expense of a delay in OVERLORD. But the U.S.S.R., for reasons of its own, unequivocally put its weight behind the American concept of strategy. Confident of its capabilities, it asserted its full power as an equal number of the coalition. Stalin came out strongly in favor of OVERLORD and limiting further operations in the Mediterranean solely to the one directly assisting OVERLORD, namely, an invasion of southern France. In turn, the Russians promised to launch an all-out offensive on the East front to go with them. Stalin's stand put the capstone on Anglo-American strategy. In a sense, therefore, he fixed Western strategy. The final blueprint for Allied victory in Europe had taken shape. Germany was to be crushed by a great pincers—the Anglo-American drive on the west and a Soviet drive from the east. Stalin's blunt query put to the Western leaders about the name of the commander also speeded Roosevelt's decision. General Eisenhower was named the commander for OVERLORD and preparations for the big blow began.

The resolution of the mid-war debate on European strategy broadened the range of opportunities for military cooperation—hitherto limited almost exclusively to the field of lend-lease. But the end of the debate did not, *ipso facto,* lead to closer collaboration with the Soviet Union. Despite the military agreement reached at the highest levels at Teheran, it proved difficult in practice to extend the coordination very far. General Deane has recorded in detail the exasperating slowness, the delays, suspicions, and obstacles encountered by the U.S. Military Mission in trying to bring the partners closer together on a military level as the western and eastern drives began to take shape. In each case it was the Western partners who took the initiative, and in practically every case results were obtained only as a result of heavy Western pressure and protracted negotiation. One fascinating example, unique in the annals of coalition warfare, concerned the initiation of the shuttle-bombing project. Suspicious as ever of foreigners and foreign aircraft on Soviet soil, the Russians insisted on setting up a complicated procedure of group visas for the American airmen who entered the Soviet Union—a system which broke down in practice. With all its bureaucratic red tape—Soviet style—this project was, however, one of the rare cases during World War II when military cooperation between the Russians and the Anglo-Americans was attempted on an operational level.

If by the summer of 1944 Stalin could rejoice in the direction Allied strategy and operations had taken, he could also take satisfaction that his own share in them had not been made at the expense of any commitment on post-war policy. During the crucial mid-war debate, territorial and political questions concerning central and eastern Europe had simply been left open. Though Stalin showed no disposition to abandon his ambitions, he did not press them at either the Moscow or Teheran Conferences. He continued to subscribe to Western declarations—Declaration of Iran, the "Four Power" Declaration, and the like. Whatever doubts he may have entertained about the practicability of the unconditional surrender formula, announced unexpectedly by the President in January, 1943, he subscribed to that too.

Behind the Anglo-American debate of mid-war, significant changes had taken place in the balance of military power within the coalition— a phenomenon which had as important implications for the determination of war strategy as for the future relations among the partners in the wartime coalition. At the close of 1943, the Americans, with their mighty industrial and military machine now in high gear, had, with Soviet help, made the British yield to their notions of continental strategy. The growing flow of American military strength and supplies to the European theater assured the triumph of the American staff concept of a concentrated, decisive military war—an objective reinforced by the addition, from Casablanca onward, of the unconditional surrender concept. Despite the impressive flow of lend-lease to the Soviet Union in mid-war, the long delay in opening the Second Front, added to the heavy Soviet losses, had continued to keep the West on the defensive in its dealings with the Soviet Union. Capitalizing on lend-lease, its production behind the Urals, the sacrifice of its armies and people, and the effects of a war of attrition on the German invaders, the Soviet Union had shown unexpected strength and recuperative powers. Steadily gathering strength and confidence after Stalingrad, the Soviet bear had been able to make its weight felt in the strategic scales at a critical point in Allied councils. At the end of the period massive Russian armies were driving West. The Soviet Union was coming into its own. Britain had practically completed its mobilization at the end of 1943, and strains and stresses had begun to show up in its economy. The Americans in mid-war drew up to and threatened to pass the British in deployed strength in the European theater. Britain's military power, along with her notions of fighting the war, was being outstripped. Via the military doctrine of concentration, the strategists of the Kremlin and of the Pentagon had found common ground. Teheran, which fixed the final European strategy, marked the beginning of a wartime realignment in the European power balance. The foundations of the Alliance were changing.

1944–1945: THE MILITARY PAY-OFF

This brings us to the third phase of Allied relations in the war in the West, the last nine months of the conflict—the period of the military pay-off. This is the period when the problems of winning the war began to come up against the problems of winning the peace. In this phase, the course of the war started to shape the conditions of the peace. The main outline of events is familiar—how, after the successful landing in Normandy on June 6, 1944, the Western Allied forces broke out of their beachheads and knifed across the Continent, while the Russians picked up capital after capital in east and central Europe, beating the advancing Americans to Berlin, Vienna, and Prague, and flowed into the Balkans to fill the vacuum left by the retreating Germans. The direction of their movement suggested that the flow of their power against key political and strategic positions was more than merely coincidental. The curtain began to lift on the divergent national objectives and war aims of the Allies—objectives hitherto obscured by the common military danger, the military strategy hammered out on "the anvil of necessity," and the political declarations to which they had subscribed.

The full impact of American concepts was to be felt even more strongly from the summer of 1944 to the surrender of Germany in May, 1945. Once the Allied forces had become firmly ensconced on the European continent, the war became, for General Marshall and his staff, essentially a matter of logistics and tactics, with the Supreme Allied Commander to take over and make his decisions as military exigencies in the field dictated. But to Churchill, warily watching the swift Soviet advance into Poland and the Balkans, the war had become more than ever a contest for great political stakes, and he wished Western Allied strength diverted to forestall the Russian surge. As the strategy unrolled in the field, the two approaches to the war boiled down therefore to a question of military tactics versus political maneuvers.

Had the President joined with the Prime Minister, as he often had in the past, the American military staff's concentration on bringing the war against Germany to a swift military conclusion might still have been tempered and the war steered into more direct political channels. But the President would not, and the Prime Minister by himself could not. There are many reasons which may account for the President's position —reasons of health, desire to get on with the Japanese conflict, desire to get on with the tasks of peace, etc. But of none of these can we yet be certain. In any case, let me suggest this: By 1944–45 the Commander in Chief was caught on the horns of a political dilemma confronting any American President involved in an extended coalition war abroad. There is reason to believe that he was not unconcerned about the unilateral efforts of the Soviet Union to put its impress on the shape of post-war Europe—as witness his stand on the reconstruction of the Polish Government. But from the viewpoint of domestic political considerations he had to fight a quick and decisive war—one that would justify American entry and the dispatch of American troops abroad. Once the bullies were beaten, it was doubtful whether the American people would countenance any prolonged occupation in Europe, or a more active role in southeastern Europe as the Prime Minister desired. Besides the President's policy for peace seemed to lie in the same direction as Wilson's—national self-determination and an international organization to maintain the peace—not in reliance on the balance of power. To achieve this aim he had to take the calculated risk of being able to handle Stalin and winning and maintaining the friendship of the U.S.S.R. While the Prime Minister appeared willing to go a long way in the same direction, he also seemed to hedge more in the traditional balance of power theory. Whatever the explanation may be, the fact remains that American national policy in the final year placed no obstacle in the way of a decisive ending of the European conflict.

The inability of the Prime Minister in the last year of the war to reverse the trend bore eloquent testimony to the changed relationships between American and British military weight and to the shifting bases of the Grand Alliance. If the military power which the American staff had managed to conserve for the big blow on the Continent gave the United States a powerful weapon, it did not choose to use it for political purpose; the Prime Minister had the purpose but not the power. After the middle of 1944, the British production became increasingly unbalanced, and the British fought the remainder of the war with a contracting economy. Clearly the last year of the war saw the foundations of the coalition in further transition, British influence on the wane, and the United States and the Soviet Union emerging as the two strongest military powers in Europe.

In the absence of political instructions to the contrary, the American military staff fell back upon the task of applying the given resources and manpower to getting the disagreeable business over with as quickly as possible. Thus the war against Germany was to be concluded—on the Western side—as the American military chiefs had wished to wage it from the beginning—a conventional war of concentration, a technical soldier's game. On the Eastern side, the war was also to be concluded as it had been fought from the beginning—a combination of political and military strategy, and the Soviets began to gather in the fruits of victory.

In the closing months of the war, there were signs that the West was beginning to re-analyze its approach toward the Soviet Union. Day-to-day coordination as the troops drew closer became more feasible but remained difficult. From a variety of sources came appeals for a greater firmness in American policy toward the Soviet Union, and a firmer note began to creep into its dealings. What negotiations with the Soviets on bomblines in southern Europe could not produce, General Eaker's strong arbitrary action established. From Moscow, General Deane, frustrated as ever in trying to establish closer coordination with the Russians, strongly urged a reversal of policy on lend-lease, a *quid pro quo*. To General Eisenhower, in January, 1945, General Marshall recommended forgetting diplomatic niceties in future dealings with the Russians and urged on him a direct approach "in simple Main Street Abilene style." It is one of the ironies of historical fate that President Roosevelt, pragmatist that he was and flexible on most issues, should go down in history as almost inflexible on the Russian issue. But his last message to Churchill, written an hour before his death, with the Polish crisis evidently very much on his mind, while expressing the optimistic hope that this problem like others with the Soviet Union would also pass and that the course toward the Russians had so far been correct, at the same time urged firmness. Taken in the context of their wartime correspondence, some of Roosevelt's last exchanges with Stalin were most sharp.

But these were only straws in the wind and symptomatic of the fact that the three powers approached the end of the war quite far apart on European issues. American policy remained opposed—in principle—to recognizing territorial settlements before the peace conference and the firm establishment of the new international organization. The United States, as Roosevelt categorically announced at Yalta and Truman's approach confirmed at Potsdam, was determined to withdraw its troops from Europe soon—within two years after the end of the fighting. The British were more amenable to recognizing at least the moderate Soviet demands. They were even willing to enter into temporary expedients with the Soviet Union, like dividing up the control of the Balkan states on a percentage basis—a curious, but short-lived wartime application of the sphere of influence principle. The Soviets began to show their political hand more openly and strongly. What they could not get by negotiation, they sought by direct and unilateral action. Their policies in 1945 were tuned to capitalize on the weakness of Europe and the dichotomy in Western thinking. Part of their success was inevitable with the shift of the power balance, and part helped along by the failure of the West to agree. From this point of view, the much publicized and debated conferences of Yalta and Potsdam—about which so much controversy revolves—must be regarded not as the causes but the symptoms of Western weakness and growing Soviet strength and influence.

THE BALANCE SHEET

What, then, are some of the conclusions to be drawn from the study thus far of the experience of the Western Allies with the Soviet Union in the past European war? In treating the wartime relations of the Soviet Union, the Western scholar is dealing with a phenomenon where only that part of the iceberg that appears above the water is clearly visible. Many questions are still unanswered. The experience of World War II sheds light but provides no clear-cut answer on the problem of motivation —which has so preoccupied Western students of the Soviet Union. Has the prime motivating force been national security, Russian imperialism,

Soviet power politics, or Communist world revolution? Certainly whatever the ultimate or theoretical goal—necessarily held in abeyance during the wartime period of crisis—the initial objective was to secure a firm hold on Eastern Europe—the borderlands. The territorial aims it had sought from Hitler it sought from the Grand Alliance. Success whetted its appetite and emboldened it. Before the war was over it was striving for a firm hold on Central Europe—Germany as well as Poland. It appeared ominously to be reaching out not only to close the historic exits to the Soviet Union but also to open a gateway to the West—perhaps the first steps—now that it had achieved the inner concentric belt—in what may be a program for control of all Eurasia. At Potsdam it even put in a bid for Italian colonies in the Mediterranean. Certainly where Soviet security stopped and expansion began was not clear in Western, perhaps not even in Soviet, eyes. In the light of World War II experience it is probably safest to assume that Soviet foreign policy is multi-motivated.

If Soviet objectives were consistent, its tactics were varied. The same power could flit first from an effort to cooperate with Western powers against Hitler, after Munich, to a non-aggression pact with Germany, and after June, 1941, to a wartime partnership of sorts with the West. But it is also clear that it had one foot in the alliance and the other out. What it could not obtain by negotiation with the partners, it sought by unilateral action. Within its own theory of dynamics, it found the capability of surviving on the defensive and of asserting itself in the offensive. Throughout it showed a determination to fight the war its own way. In fact, it may well be argued that the European war was really composed of two wars—the one fought by the West and the other by the Soviet Union; that there never really was an Allied strategy in World War II; that Soviet strategy remained tangential to that of the West and just happened on a military basis to be compatible with it. The same power that on V-E day could acknowledge the great achievement of the West and toast Allied unity and its leaders could, within two years after the end of the conflict, cancel V-E day as a national celebration, subject Roosevelt as well as Churchill, popular wartime figures, to violent attack, claim that the West had launched OVERLORD to forestall the Soviet advance on Berlin, and again reassert the need of the Soviet state to remain prepared for attack from a hostile world. It may prove correct in the history of the Soviet foreign relations to view its wartime relationships as a phase of the cold war—a war that began as far back as November, 1917—and Soviet participation in the Grand Alliance as a temporary cycle of attraction with part of the West under the compulsion of necessity. In any event, World War II which gave the Soviet Union its greatest test also gave it its greatest opportunity for extending its sphere of control—an opportunity its leaders did not hesitate to grasp.

On the part of the West in its relationships with the Soviet Union, it would appear to be true, in retrospect, that mistakes were made. Certainly Soviet strength and capabilities were miscalculated, its political ambitions underestimated. More flexibility in objectives, plans, and methods would appear to have been desirable. Certain concepts and policies with which the West began the war or introduced in its earlier phases were probably held too long and rigidly—notably the generous lend-lease policy and the unconditional surrender concept. But even here, simple pat judgments in postwar writing must be carefully reassessed. Much has been made, for example, in postwar writing of the external effects of unconditional surrender as a war aim—in prolonging the war and adding to its costs. But there is another aspect which must also be weighed in the scales of historical judgment. Leaving aside its external consequences, this formula was to have important effects within the Allied coalition. It served to conceal further the divergent postwar national objectives back of the common goal—the defeat of Germany. Its limitations as a political formula began to show up in the last year of the war when the time had come—perhaps was long overdue—to replace a common war aim with a common peace aim. But it is, of course, still a moot point whether anything more or less than the single-track idea of unconditional surrender would have succeeded in this "strange alliance." The question of the Balkans versus the cross-Channel invasion about which so much controversy has raged in the postwar period is also a complex and highly debatable issue and must be carefully re-examined in the light of the known evidence. Suffice it to say here, this is purely a postwar debate—the Balkan question was never argued out in frank military or political terms by the Western Allies during World War II. But all these so-called mistakes must, of course, be taken in the context of their times. And far more important than the alleged mistakes reflected in the "hard-pressed" strategic and political decisions of the war in and out of conferences was the inability of a wartime relationship to bridge the gap between West and East—the legacy of suspicion, of divergent conceptions of international morality, power, war, and peace, and the failure of an Allied military victory to prevent the further weakening of the West—a weakening begun in World War I. It should be noted that the weakening of Great Britain and its close dependence on the United States were well underway before the close of 1943—when peripheral strategy, to which the Prime Minister was so devoted, was still in its heyday. It should also be noted that proponents of the strategy of the "indirect approach" have uniformly oversimplified the American strategic case, glossing over its compulsions and strong points, even as they have closed one eye to World War II experience with Mediterranean operations—which gave a striking demonstration of how great the costs of a war of attrition can be. It also seems clear that, with all the advantages of hindsight and all the persuasive and eloquent arguments that have been marshalled against the alleged American political and strategic naïveté in World War II, there is no certainty that the war could have been programmed to produce a faster or cheaper victory over Germany and at the same time have put the West in a fundamentally more secure position in postwar Europe *vis-à-vis* the Soviet Union. In a sense the cards were stacked against the West from the beginning, and the emergence of the Soviet Union as the strongest continental power was an almost inevitable product of the shift in the power balance, a shift which had its roots in World War I. World War II, which marked the defeat of Germany and the further decline of the Western European states, only reinforced the shift begun with the weakening of the Western states in World War I and the decline in the European political system in the years between the two world wars.

The war ended with the United States and the United Kingdom—close partners that they were—almost as far apart on European problems as the West was from the East. The war ended with the United States giving up two bargaining weapons—*vis-à-vis* the Soviet Union—represented in lend-lease and the United States troops abroad—one the path of appeasement, the other of force. Puzzling as its behavior had been earlier in the war, in success the Soviet Union was a bigger question mark than ever. Henceforth Europe would look to the two powers—the one from the new world, the other from the old—that had emerged out of the war to positions of world leadership—the one as reluctant to grasp the nettle as the other was eager.

The events of 1945 demonstrated the capacity of allies with divergent aims to wage a war that was completely successful on a military plane. Their military strategy, as we have seen, was a hybrid product—a composite of American directness, British caution, and Soviet bluntness. It had found its common denominator in the defeat of Germany—by a giant nutcracker squeeze on the Continent. But as the forces of the coalition partners came closer and the defeat of Germany more certain, their political differences became more apparent, and the cement which held them together—the "common bond of danger"—began to crumble. What the West and East had set out to do in common was to defeat Germany, and this they had successfully accomplished. By May 8, 1945, Germany surrendered. But Poland and eastern Europe were already in the grip of another dictator, and Germany, which had brought the East and West together, was already a bone of contention between them. The shooting war was over, but, in the eyes of the West, Europe had been liberated only to the Elbe. Out of the strange comradeship-in-arms was to come a new rivalry for power. A firm peace was still to be won.

21 /

PEACE-MAKING, 1946 *

The Soviet government is as secretive about its diplomacy as it is
about its military operations. Just as one must turn to the accounts of
those who dealt with the U.S.S.R. in the military sphere for a glimpse
of Soviet military operations and planning, so must one turn to the
accounts of those who dealt with Soviet diplomats for a glimpse of
Soviet diplomacy at work. Such a glimpse is here provided by
Professor Mosely. What he has to say is relevant not only to the study
of Soviet diplomacy but also to a study of the beginnings of
the cold war.

THE FIRST DAYS of December, 1946, saw the completion of the
first round of the peace treaties. Except for the verification of the texts
and the final arrangements for signature, the treaties with Italy, Rumania,
Bulgaria, Hungary and Finland were now ready, after fifteen months
of back-breaking and often heart-breaking effort. The initial installment
of peace-making had, in fact, taken more than fifteen months, for several
of the thorniest questions—notably, the disposition of the Italian colonies,
freedom of commercial navigation on the Danube, and Italian reparation
—had received their preliminary going-over at Potsdam. And at least
one question—the disposition of the Italian colonies—had been postponed for later settlement.

The period of negotiation saw four lengthy sessions of the Council of

* Philip E. Mosely, "Peace-Making, 1946," *International Organization*, I (February,
1947), 22–32. Reprinted by permission of the author and the publisher. This article
is also included in Philip E. Mosely's *The Kremlin and World Politics: Studies in
Soviet Policy and Action* (New York: Vintage Russian Library, 1960).
The author has successfully combined several careers—teaching, scholarship,
public service, and administration—all of them having Russia, past and present, as
their center of interest. He is now Director of Studies for the Council on Foreign
Relations and Adjunct Professor of International Relations at the Russian Institute

Foreign Ministers, at London in September–October, 1945, at Paris in April–May and June–July, 1946, and at New York in November–December, 1946. The procedure of peace-making was also one of the principal topics at the Conference of the three Foreign Ministers at Moscow, in December, 1945. In addition, the Deputies of the Foreign Ministers had been at work almost continuously since mid-January, 1946, and numerous committees of the Council had held hundreds of meetings on special aspects of the treaties. Finally, a conference of 21 Allied states, meeting in Paris from July 29 to October 15, had reviewed the draft treaties and presented its recommendations in great detail.

At the end of this wearisome process relief at the thought that the first round of peace-making had actually been completed prevailed over disappointment at the amount of time it had consumed and the tensions it had brought to light. But there was no room for complacency when it was realized that the settlements with Germany and Japan and the establishment of Austrian and Korean independence were still to be worked out.

The comparisons which have usually been drawn between the present process of treaty-making and that of 1919 have not been to the advantage of the statesmen of the present. It is easy to point out that the Treaty of Versailles was drafted and imposed upon Germany in a matter of some five months. It is usually forgotten that an Allied decision on German reparations was reached only in 1921 and that a temporarily workable arrangement was negotiated in 1924. Similarly, the settlement with Turkey which became a reality in 1923 was very different from the terms which had originally been laid down in Paris. Of course, any such comparisons have meaning only if they take into consideration the contribution made by the peace-making process to a lasting peace between victors and defeated and among the victors.

The Paris Conference of 1919, which began as a conference of all the victor states, conducted its real work in private meetings of the Big Five, later the Big Four, and for a time the Big Three, for the great powers had to make peace with each other before they could impose it on the defeated countries. Unlike the general conference of 1919, which had mainly a ceremonial role, the Paris Conference of 1946 worked for long hours and with grim seriousness.

In the peace-making of 1945–46 it was recognized from the outset that in the absence of prior agreements among the principal victors it was necessary for them first to harmonize their views on the main lines of the settlements. The Potsdam arrangements provided for the drafting of the treaties by a Council of Foreign Ministers of the five principal victors.

---

of Columbia University. During and immediately following World War II he was an official in the Department of State, taking part as advisor in many of the wartime and postwar Allied meetings. His interest in diplomatic history is illustrated by his *Russian Diplomacy and the Opening of the Eastern Question in 1838 and 1839* (1934).

The expectation was that the Ministers, at a first meeting, would block in the broad outlines of the settlements, leaving it to their Deputies and staffs to fill in the detailed provisions of the treaties. At a second meeting the Ministers would review the work of the Deputies and decide any outstanding questions. The draft treaties would then be examined in a general conference of the Allied states, and the recommendations of the conference would be studied by the Council in preparing the final drafts.

The treaty-making arrangements contained one further provision of great importance. It was agreed at Potsdam that in the drafting of the five treaties decisions would be taken by the powers which had been signatory to the surrender terms, except that for the drafting of the Italian treaty France would be considered a signatory to the armistice. This meant that within the Council of Five four governments would be responsible for drafting the treaty with Italy, three for the treaties with Rumania, Bulgaria and Hungary, and two for the treaty with Finland. This flexible and apparently expeditious program, to which France and China gave their concurrence, soon ran into unforeseen difficulties.

At the opening meeting of its first session in London, on September 11, 1945, the Council agreed unanimously that all five Ministers would be present at, and participate in, the discussions of all the treaties, while decisions would be adopted on the basis of the "four-three-two" formula. After nine days of discussion, during which the outlines of the Italian and Rumanian settlements were reviewed inconclusively and a beginning was made on a review of those with Hungary and Bulgaria, Mr. Molotov suddenly demanded that the Council reverse its previous decision on procedure. He now insisted that the Council's decision of September 11 had been "illegal" and that it was "a violation of the Potsdam decisions" for the French and Chinese representatives to attend discussions of treaties on which they did not have deciding votes. From then on, for nearly two weeks, the Soviet delegation pressed, with all five Ministers present, for the complete exclusion of the Chinese and the partial exclusion of the French Foreign Minister. It must be said in passing that there had been nothing in the conduct of the two Ministers to justify this abrupt change in the Soviet attitude. The Chinese had been largely silent although they had submitted written drafts of treaties, and the French had played a similarly cooperative role.

During the remaining days of the London session little headway was made on questions of substance. The Council meetings were largely devoted, on Soviet insistence, to discussions of procedure, in which vehement and endlessly reiterated accusations of "destroying Allied unity" took the place of any reasoned consideration of the question on its merits. The search for a reasonable compromise was pressed by the other Ministers, especially by Mr. Byrnes, but no suggestions found favor with Mr. Molotov. It can be assumed, however, that, if far-reaching concessions of

substance had been made at once to the various Soviet demands, the procedural roadblock would have been removed just as suddenly as it had
appeared.

After several days of discussion and of searching for a compromise
which would have met the Soviet demand at least half-way without com-
pounding the indignity inflicted on the representatives of France and
China, Mr. Byrnes and Mr. Bevin agreed, with obvious reluctance and
solely in order to get on with the work at hand, to accept Mr. Molotov's
demand, subject to one condition, and they secured the consent of the
French and Chinese representatives to this unwelcome change. The only
condition which Mr. Byrnes advanced was that, in order to avoid a repetition of this "misunderstanding" at a later stage, the council should agree
on a somewhat fuller statement of the arrangements for the future peace
conference at the same time that it accepted the new Soviet interpretation
of the Potsdam formula.

Having come so close to winning its contention, the Soviet delegation
now presented an even more extreme demand. Mr. Molotov now insisted
that the record of the Council's decision of September 11 must be revised
by deleting the decision of that date on the procedure of the Council and
substituting it for the new Soviet text, which would then appear in the
final record of the session as having been accepted on the date of September 11! All entries in the agreed records subsequent to that date were also
to be revised to eliminate all references to the "illegal" participation of
the French and Chinese Ministers in the work of the Council and to make
it appear that the new Soviet version of the "four-three-two" formula had
been applied from the first meeting of the Council. It is hardly necessary
to recall that the Council had issued numerous communiqués which had
reported the French and Chinese Ministers present and in the chair, and
that both of them continued to be present and to occupy the chair by
rotation throughout the debates over the Soviet proposal for their exclusion! This most unusual proposal was rejected, as the Soviet representative no doubt intended it to be, and the Council adjourned its London
session *sine die* and without approving a final record of its decisions or
issuing a communiqué.

In retrospect, as at the time, it can only be assumed that Mr. Molotov
was so dissatisfied with the course of the first days' discussions, particularly with the poor welcome received by his proposals to transfer Trieste
outright to Yugoslavia, to establish a Soviet trusteeship over Tripolitania,
and, in effect, to repeal the Yalta Declaration insofar as it made provision
for the establishment of representative regimes in Rumania and Bulgaria,
that he made up his mind to suspend the Potsdam agreement to expedite
the five treaties and embarked on a campaign to test the nerves and the
degree of determination of the other four governments. It is interesting
to note, however, that although the London session failed to agree on a

final protocol, the substantive decisions of that session, few though they were, actually formed the basis of the work of the Deputies when they finally began their labors in January, 1946.

During the discussions of the Soviet re-interpretation of the "four-three-two" formula Secretary Byrnes had urged the Council also to clarify the arrangements for the peace conference, but the Soviet Foreign Minister refused even to discuss this question until the Council adopted without condition his own proposals on procedure. Three months later this intransigence was somewhat relaxed. In December, 1945, at Moscow the compromise proposal which Mr. Byrnes had advanced at London was adopted with minor modifications, thus enabling the Council to resume its work. The role of the peace conference was further clarified in January, 1946, through an exchange of letters between M. Bidault and Mr. Byrnes, the latter acting for the three Ministers who had participated in the Moscow Conference. With this clarification, which emphasized the right of the future peace conference to examine all aspects of the draft treaties, the French government accepted the Moscow formula. The Chinese government also gave its concurrence, while reserving its rights with respect to the settlements with Germany and Japan.

The Moscow Protocol contained one provision which was dubious in language and in law. It stated that "the peace treaties will come into force immediately after they have been ratified by the Allied states signatory to the respective armistices . . ." This unfortunate departure from customary international practice would have allowed any Allied state except the Big Four to claim the benefits of the Italian treaty without accepting any obligations on its own part. The lapsus was pointed out at the Paris Conference, which, by a simple majority, recommended adoption of a new article which provided that "the provisions of the present treaty shall not confer any rights or benefits on any State named in the Preamble . . . unless such State becomes a party to the treaty by deposit of its instrument of ratification." This necessary correction of the Moscow Protocol was inserted into the Italian draft treaty by the Council of Ministers in December, 1946. Without this safeguarding clause the Yugoslav government, which had withdrawn in protest from the final plenary session of the Paris Conference and had announced that it would not sign the treaty with Italy unless it conformed more closely to Yugoslav demands, would have received the territorial and other benefits of the treaty without undertaking any obligations on its part toward Italy or the Free Territory of Trieste.

The Moscow re-interpretation of the "four-three-two" formula was applied in the work of the Council of Deputies, which began its work in London in mid-January, 1946. The French Deputy took part only in drafting the Italian treaty, while the Finnish treaty was considered only by the Soviet and British Deputies. Since one of the delegations was not empowered to change by one iota the positions previously adopted by its Minister, the Deputies' range of effective negotiation was narrowly circumscribed. However, their intensive study of the treaty problems resulted in the first detailed examination of the numerous treaty proposals, in clarifying a large number of technical and legal points, and in clearing the ground for the major decisions, which, in the circumstances, could only be taken by the Foreign Ministers in person.

When the Ministers resumed their meetings at Paris in late April, it was uncertain whether the Soviet delegation would again insist on the strict application of the "four-three-two" formula. At the first meeting, however, Mr. Molotov brushed aside this question, over which he had broken off the London session, by moving that all four Ministers participate in all meetings of the Council. M. Bidault was, of course, in the chair at the first meeting; the Paris press had shown some sensitiveness on this question; a constitutional referendum and an election were approaching. In practice the French representative took almost no part in the discussion of the treaties with the four satellites, while the American delegation, which continued to abstain from discussion of the Finnish treaty, was subsequently free to offer from the floor of the conference certain recommendations on that treaty.

In the work of the Council of Foreign Ministers the governments of the smaller Allies had no direct part, while on the other hand Italy received a much fairer hearing than Germany had been granted in 1919. At its London session the Council had invited the various Allied governments to submit their suggestions and recommendations in writing. Most of the governments presented memoranda, usually dealing with their direct claims and interests. In addition, Australia, New Zealand and the Union of South Africa had requested, and received at that session, an opportunity to present their views orally to the Council on the Yugoslav-Italian boundary. On this occasion Mr. Evatt of Australia advanced the claim of the smaller Allied states to participate fully in the deliberations of the Council. His proposal, if adopted, would have meant entrusting the drafting of the treaties to a general conference, as in 1919. It is doubtful whether such a procedure would have had much effect on the actual process of treaty-drafting, or whether most of the Allied states would have relished this enlargement of their political role. When they were eventually confronted at Paris with the full range of problems over which the Big Four had tussled for nearly a year, many of the Allied delegations were none too happy over their added responsibilities.

On a few matters, mainly territorial in character, the Council heard, at a formative stage, the views of an ex-enemy state, long since accepted, it is true, as a co-belligerent on the Allied side. On the future boundary between Yugoslavia and Italy the views of the two governments were heard four times in the Council. On the Italo-Austrian boundary both governments presented detailed memoranda and were heard both by the Deputies and by the Conference. The Italian government also presented its views in detail on the Franco-Italian boundary, on reparations and war damages, and on many other problems. In addition, special commissions of the Council carried out on-the-spot investigations of the Yugoslav-Italian and Franco-Italian boundary questions. Proposals for similar consultations with representatives of the four eastern satellites were turned aside by the Soviet delegation. Finally, each of the five governments presented its case at length in full sessions of the conference and, by invitation, before various of its commissions. At Paris their delegations had full freedom of personal access to the various Allied delegations, unlike the situation of the German delegation in 1919. Full hearings naturally did not lighten the burdens imposed on them by many of the provisions of the treaties, and several of the ex-enemy delegations showed great diffidence in pressing their views, presumably because of the limited degree of independence exercised by their governments within their countries. Only Bulgaria proved able and willing to present far-reaching claims of its own.

As the Council of Ministers progressed haltingly through its agenda at the two Paris sessions, between April and July, the question of the future peace conference came to occupy an important place in its discussions. For a long time the Soviet representative maintained that the date for the conference could be set only when the draft treaties had been agreed down to the last detail. Since several score of major and minor matters were still in dispute, it sometimes seemed as if the conference could never be called. Secretary Byrnes maintained that the Potsdam and Moscow agreements merely called for the great powers doing all they could to advance the drafting of the treaties, and that these agreements had been intended to facilitate the calling of the conference, not to prevent the other Allies from having their say on the treaties.

Meanwhile, the Council had agreed to postpone the disposition of the Italian colonies for consideration during the year following the coming into force of the treaty with Italy, and had accepted the international status for Trieste as a way out of another dead-lock. In early July two decisions were taken in a single meeting of the Council, which prepared the way for the calling of the conference. An agreement was reached on Italy's reparation deliveries to the Soviet Union only a few hours after it had been agreed to set the opening of the conference for July 29, without waiting for a complete agreement to be reached on all provisions of the treaties.

This decision automatically gave a far wider range of effective deliberation to the conference than could have been foreseen at Potsdam almost one year before. The conference, as it turned out, had before it two main groups of issues, some on which the Council had reached agreement and others on which separate and unagreed drafts were submitted. In addition, the conference was able to assert its right to present recommendations of its own on subjects which had not been covered in the drafts submitted to it.

The decision to call the conference, itself the result of long negotiation, was only a prelude to further disputes. After the decision had been taken the actual despatch of invitations was held up for several days, during which the Soviet delegation fought hard to secure the adoption by the Council of its proposed draft rules of procedure to govern the work of the conference. In the arguments which followed the Soviet delegation implied more than once that the acceptance of these rules should be regarded as a condition for the issuance of the invitations and for the admission of the Allied governments to the conference. Mr. Byrnes defended the traditional right of a conference to determine its own rules of procedure, but he was willing to meet Mr. Molotov more than half-way by agreeing on draft rules which would then be circulated to the participating governments as a suggestion, and by promising to vote for the adoption of the agreed draft in the conference.

Concurrently, a further controversy developed over the organization of the conference. The Soviet draft rules provided, in effect, for the plenary conference to assemble only in the opening and closing sessions, and for the real work of the conference to be carried on in five commissions, one for each treaty, each commission to be composed of those states which were recognized by the Council as having "actively waged war" against the respective ex-enemy state. This arrangement, if adopted, would have had some curious consequences. Byelorussia and Ukraine, for instance, would have had full memberships on each of the five commissions, while France would have been a member only of the Italian commission, and Norway of none. It was pointed out repeatedly that these narrow limitations on the organization of the conference were not in harmony with the provisions of the Moscow Protocol of December, 1945, or of the Byrnes-Bidault exchange of letters of January, 1946.

It was finally agreed to abandon the idea of having a separate commission for each treaty and to adopt a somewhat more functional arrangement. The Council agreed to recommend the establishment of five Political Commissions, one for each treaty, two Economic Commissions, one each for the Italian treaty and for the Balkan and Finnish treaties, a Military Commission, and a Legal and Drafting Commission. In the upshot France was represented on all the commissions, while a Norwegian delegate served on the Legal and Drafting Commission. There were also discussions as to whether recommendations could be voted only by the commissions with, in the case of the two Balkan commissions, their more limited membership, or also by the plenary conference. In the end it was agreed that both the commissions and the conference would be able to vote on recommendations.

As soon as the conference had met and had passed to the working stage, the Soviet delegation again pressed for the adoption of the more restrictive rules which it had advocated and then abandoned in the Council of Ministers. Many days were consumed in controversy, and at times it seemed as if the conference would not be able to complete its organization, much less proceed to the work at hand. The Soviet representatives again accused the other members of the Council of having violated agreements, despite the clear record of the Council's decisions. After the smoke and fury had cleared away, the rules adopted were substantially those which had been proposed by the Council in July. In the course of the debates over procedure Mr. Byrnes had gone beyond the other Big Four delegations in asserting his desire to strengthen the role of the conference; he stated that, in the later deliberations of the Ministers, he would support recommendations made by a two-thirds majority of the conference even if they ran counter to the vote of the American delegation in the conference.

The conference served the purpose for which it had been planned. It gave recognition to the views of the Allies upon the making of the treaties. Its role was, of course, limited from the outset by the fact that the Big Four entered it pledged to vote for the decisions which they had already arrived at. Such questions as Italy's boundaries with Yugoslavia, Austria and France, the surrender of the Italian colonies, and the reparation deliveries to the Soviet Union by Italy, Hungary, Rumania and Finland, could not have been effectively modified by the conference. On the other hand, the conference made important recommendations on Italian reparation deliveries to other Allied countries, on compensation for Allied properties in ex-enemy countries, on freedom of commercial navigation on the Danube, on the cession to Czechoslovakia of the bridgehead opposite Bratislava, on the Trieste statute, and on numerous economic and legal provisions. During the conference the Italian and Austrian governments also arrived at an agreement on the status of the German-speaking population of the South Tyrol, or Upper Adige, which the Council of Ministers, in December, agreed to mention in the Italian treaty.

The obligation of the Big Four to "support" the Council's decisions in the discussions of the conference was interpreted by the Soviet delegation to mean that the other three delegations were under obligation to exert all their influence to win the votes of other delegations for the support of agreed decisions. The Soviet-led "Slav bloc," which emerged as a striking feature of the conference, showed good teamwork and careful timing. Other great-power delegations interpreted the pledge of "support" to mean that they would cast their votes for the agreed decisions but that they were under no obligation to "strong-arm" other Allied delegations into voting in the same way. Many of the Allied delegations, in fact, cast their votes in a manner intended to demonstrate their independence from domination by any great power. This circumstance did not prevent the Soviet delegation and press from asserting that other members of the Big Four were exerting all kinds of improper pressure on other delegations and were using other delegates as "stooges" to raise obstacles to the acceptance by the conference of the agreed decisions of the Council. In this respect Soviet resentment appears to have been directed particularly against Mr. Evatt, who, taking the Council's invitation literally, had presented a large number of draft amendments to the treaties.

At its close the conference referred back to the Foreign Ministers a long series of recommendations, some supported by a two-thirds vote, others by a simple majority. Many of the recommendations represented real improvements of substance or language over the previous work of the Council, in which there had developed a reluctance to bring up suggestions for technical or textual improvements in view of the slight chance of their being considered by all four delegations on their merits.

For a time it was hoped that during the latter part of the conference its recommendations could be considered at once by the Council of Ministers, which could then incorporate those which it adopted into the final texts of the treaties, the latter then to be signed before the conference disbanded. For political and technical reasons this schedule proved to be impossible to follow, and instead it was agreed to hold a further meeting of the Council on November 4, in New York. When the Foreign Ministers resumed their labors they were again confronted by most of the same questions which had been before them so often before. It was anyone's guess whether the Council could complete the drafts of the treaties at that session or at any later one. After three weeks of zestless leafing through of old controversies it at last became evident that the Soviet delegation was now prepared to make certain concessions in order to conclude the treaties. It is a fair comment to say that if the same compromises could have been reached during the first three or six months after Potsdam a great contribution would have been made to inter-Allied unity and to the feeling of confidence throughout the United Nations. As it was, the completion of the treaties was received, if not with indifference, at least without any noticeable upsurge of enthusiasm.

Could the procedural difficulties which were so conspicuous in the treaty-making process have been foreseen and avoided? It seems fair to conclude that if the original arrangements had been interpreted in a reasonable and conciliatory spirit they would have been adequate to the purpose. Likewise, once the initial obstacles raised by Molotov at London had been by-passed at Moscow, much more progress could have been made if the Soviet delegation to the meetings of the Deputies had been empowered to advance, or even to consider, possible adjustments and compromises. Unfortunately, in a negotiation of this kind, the most reluctant government determines the maximum rate of progress. In the work of the Council of Foreign Ministers the search for a basis of settlement could begin only after the Soviet delegation had become convinced that further delay was no longer working to the advantage of Soviet interests.

Since the Soviet method of negotiation, illustrated in the history of Council of Ministers, is based on an assumption that relations between states are regulated by the rivalry of competing systems, their negotiators tend to turn every decision, whether vital or trifling, into a test of endurance and will-power. One by-product of this approach is ordinarily to confine negotiation to formal across-the-table debate and to rule out the less formal methods which might assist in reaching an understanding.

At the end of the first fifteen months of treaty-making the advantages to the Soviet Union of further delays tended to be out-weighed by growing disadvantages. In the intervening period the balance of political forces in Western Europe and Italy had been tested in free elections, while Soviet predominance in the countries of Eastern Europe had been heavily reinforced by many forms of political and economic action. The peace treaties contained no provisions which would admit of a challenge to the predominant control of the Soviet Union over the affairs of the four eastern satellites, but the Italian treaty had not added greatly to the pressures which the Soviet Union could bring to bear on Italy. In many respects the treaties simply registered the consequences of a new division of power which had come into being in Europe during the final stages of the war. The implications of this new division of power were of a nature to discourage those who feel that exclusive spheres of power, whether they be regarded as offensive or defensive in the motivations alleged to justify them, must be held to a minimum through cooperative action of the great powers if the general structure of international cooperation and security is to function effectively in the post-war world.

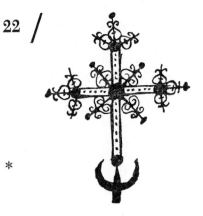

PERMANENT FEATURES OF SOVIET FOREIGN POLICY *

The study of the history of Soviet foreign policy may, like any other study, be undertaken as an end in itself, or it may be motivated by the desire to find materials for an explanation of the present policy of the Soviet Union in relation to the past and to predict its future course with some accuracy. The search is a difficult but not a hopeless one, as is proved in Professor Gurian's perceptive analysis of the constants in Soviet foreign policy.

In FEBRUARY, 1914, P. N. Durnovo, the former Russian Minister of the Interior and elder statesman, addressed to Tsar Nicholas II a memorandum in which he argued that not Germany, but Britain was Russia's enemy, and, therefore, that a German-Russian war ought to be avoided. Great Britain, he elaborated, was the supporter of revolutionary forces and a war with Germany would only promote revolution. 'Strange as it may seem, Britain, monarchical and conservative to the marrow at home, has in her foreign relations always acted as the protector of the most demagogic tendencies, invariably encouraging all popular movements that aim at the weakening of the monarchical principle.' Durnovo believed that Russia was in no way prepared for a world war, and emphasized: 'It is our firm conviction . . . that there must inevitably break out in the defeated country a social revolution which, by the very

* Waldemar Gurian, "Permanent Features of Soviet Foreign Policy," *Yearbook of World Affairs*, I (1947), 1–36, abridged. Reprinted by permission of the publisher and Mrs. Waldemar Gurian.

The author (1902–1954) was born in Russia, but lived in Germany from the age of nine until Hitler's ascent to power. Then, after a stay in Switzerland, he came to the United States, where he served as Professor of Politics at the University of Notre Dame and as editor of the *Review of Politics*. A man of many interests and much energy, he was a journalist, teacher, and scholarly writer. Much of his life was given to the study of nazism and communism. He was the editor of *The Soviet Union* (1951) and *Soviet Imperialism* (1953), and the author of *Bolshevism* (1952) and many other works in English and German.

nature of things, will spread to the country of the victor . . . An especially favourable soil for social upheavals is found in Russia where the masses undoubtedly profess, unconsciously, the principles of Socialism . . . A political revolution [he meant a change to a parliamentary-democratic regime] is not possible in Russia, and any revolutionary movement must inevitably degenerate into a Socialist movement. . . . The Russian masses, whether workmen or peasants, are not looking for political rights which they neither want nor comprehend.'

This memorandum has been regarded as a remarkable prophecy, but it shows that Durnovo anticipated correctly the general trend of Russian internal developments and, at the same time, misjudged the future relations of Russia, Great Britain and the world. The war against Germany brought about the collapse of the Tsarist regime in March, 1917. After a few months the democratic liberal Provisional Government gave place to Lenin's Soviet regime, which, although it destroyed all political liberties, promised to fulfil the elementary social aspirations of the masses. But this revolution did not succeed in spreading among the victors— neither Germany, victorious over Russia, nor Great Britain nor the other Western victors over Germany became Communist. Great Britain did not support Russian world-revolutionary propaganda, but, on the contrary, opposed it most energetically, in contrast to her nineteenth-century attitude of favouring liberal and democratic movements on the Continent, the attitude which Durnovo had in mind. What Durnovo feared and Lenin hoped for did not materialise—no world revolution ended World War I.

In 1946 the situation was radically changed. The Soviet Union succeeded where Nicholas II failed—Germany has been defeated. Does this mean that the Soviets can now accomplish what was beyond their power after World War I? Will social and pro-Communist revolutions sweep the world? Will the revolutionary potential of the period after World War I become a revolutionary reality after World War II? Will the foreign policy of Lenin, who emphasized from the beginning of his rule that world revolution could not be expected at once, and that it was necessary to manœuvre patiently for it, win after almost three decades? Or will this foreign policy obtain a victory which Lenin did not expect? Will it only succeed in building up a gigantic empire which, though with a peculiar tradition and self-interpretation, is an empire among other empires?

These questions determine the approach of the present article to the fundamental problems of Soviet foreign policy. Who is right among the students of Soviet affairs—those who with Timasheff believe that Russian nationalism has won and that, in spite of temporary comebacks, Communism with its international and world revolutionary hopes is on the retreat, or those who with Dallin assume that Stalinism is only a new method of realising the old programme? According to Dallin, conquest and power politics have replaced the old belief in proletarian solidarity and the efficiency of the propaganda and of the organisational work of the Third International with its sections, the various Communist parties.

. . . . .

During World War I, Lenin maintained an uncompromising opposition to all the policies of the Tsarist regime. He was a defeatist, believing that all Powers were imperialist Powers, and that, therefore, humanity would not be interested in the victory of any side. He even used nationalist arguments to justify his defeatism. In the Autumn of 1914 he wrote in an article, which has escaped general notice, that the Great Russians should be proud to liberate themselves from the yoke of the Tsars and to realise democracy and Socialism. Such a successful revolution would be the basis of true Russian patriotism. After the Bolsheviks came to power in October, 1917, Lenin abandoned his defeatism; he stated that he had become a defender of Russia (an *oboronetz*); for now Russia, under the Soviet Government, had become the basis for the progress of humanity towards Socialism. Lenin also realised that the October victory of the forces fighting for Socialism in Russia did not mean that this victory would be assured in all other countries, or even in Russia herself. He was very proud when he was able to announce that the Soviet regime had outlasted the days of the Parisian commune. And he emphasised that it would be wrong to sacrifice the 'healthy born baby'—the regime of the October revolution—to the hopes of international revolution. The opportunity of developing his views on foreign policy was given to him by the debate on the separate peace with Imperial Germany. From the beginning, Lenin opposed all those who believed that a peace with an imperialist power, a peace that would obviously favour the imperialists and sacrifice the revolutionary forces inside Germany as well as in the German-occupied eastern territories of Poland, the Baltic States and the Ukraine, must be rejected. He took the attitude that the Soviets had no reason to expect an immediate world revolution. He emphasised that it was necessary to take power relations into consideration—the Russian peasants and workers had no army and were too tired to oppose the advancing German forces—and he claimed that to ignore realities would result only in worse peace conditions and, perhaps, even in the total destruction of the Soviet regime.

The Brest-Litovsk crisis is the key to the understanding of Soviet foreign policy. Lenin did not give up his world-revolutionary aim. The very belief in the world-revolutionary utopia, in the ultimately inevitable victory of Communism, justified careful adaptation to existing realities, that is to say, power politics. The foundations of Soviet patriotism are laid. Russia becomes the fatherland of Communists, because she is controlled by a Communist government. As the history of the Third International will show, this first proletarian government demands that its foreign policy be regarded as the policy of the international proletariat by all Communists in all other countries. The Soviet regime is at the same time the Government of Russia, and the power which works for the future world order of justice. Soviet nationalism is the complement of Communist internationalism.

During the crisis of Brest-Litovsk, Lenin realised what his opponents, the Left-Communists under Bukharin, had overlooked. He understood that the world revolution would not come at once, simply by means of appeals and propaganda. Later on, he recognised as a mistake his belief of 1918 that a world revolution would develop in a few months as a result of the World War. In 1919 he founded the general staff of the world revolution, the Third International. After the end of the civil war in Russia (1921), he postponed his revolutionary aims again and inaugurated the N.E.P. (New Economic Policy); for he realised that Russia needed a breathing spell, and that she had to learn from the capitalist countries which she hoped to overcome. To this end, Lenin even accepted a policy of granting business enterprises as concessions to foreign capitalists.

The crisis of Brest-Litovsk reveals the two-fold aspect of the foreign policy of the Soviet doctrinaire—utopianism and cynical realism. The doctrinaire and utopian aspect consists in the acceptance of the Marxian-Leninist analysis of capitalism and of imperialism as the highest stage of capitalism in which it begins to disintegrate. This analysis may be supplemented by some actual experiences. Lenin died before the emergence of Fascism, but the fundamental terminology and doctrine remain unchanged. The Communist party is the vanguard of the proletariat. The proletariat will found the new society in which the realisation of the interests of humanity will supplant domination by a few capitalists. There are distinctions between capitalist, semi-capitalist and feudal countries. There is the possibility of an uneven development which would permit the acceleration of evolution, the skipping over of social stages, and telescoping into one period the destruction of the feudal order and the overcoming of a bourgeois democracy (as in Russia).

This doctrine gives wonderful opportunities for changes and reversals. It can be claimed that periods were wrongly interpreted—e.g., what was in reality a feudal period had been regarded as a half-democratic one. The advances made by a democratic order were overlooked by left-wing radicals, who in an infantile way were over-enthusiastic and became drunk with their own oratory. The Communist dialectic also made it possible to say that there were betrayers who prevented the right development, who were not bold enough, and who had become enslaved by their comfortable life. Lenin himself had pointed out that the imperialists win over the leaders of Socialist parties and of the working class by corrupting them, and creating for them better conditions of life. This explanation by way of betrayal is then used against everybody who is accused of preventing the expected Communist success or who opposes the policies of the dominant Communist group, from Ruth Fischer and Brandler to Trotsky and Bukharin-Rykov. This doctrinaire terminology has done much harm to the policies of Russia. It can be quoted against the Soviet leaders. Dallin does not have to forge statements of Stalin in favour of world revolution and of the victory of Communism throughout the world. This terminology has impressed and sometimes misled the leaders of the Soviet Union themselves. Stalin obviously believed that the Russo-Finnish war would not last long, because he overestimated Communist revolutionary influences among the Finnish masses. Apparently the Soviet leaders miscalculated Communist influences in Nazi Germany. Only during World War II did they advance the theory of people's imperialism. This people's imperialism poisoned the working class of a nation and made it responsible for the exploitation of other nations.

The indestructible character of utopian beliefs is based upon the assumption that such beliefs offer keys to the necessary development of history which will end in a moral way—realising what is most useful and at the same time just. This attitude permits the development of a cynical realism. There is certainty that the opponents will disappear. But the time and means of destruction are not known. It is therefore possible to co-operate with the opponent as long as he is strong enough and the Communist army has not yet gained enough strength and experience. But it is also perfectly right to annihilate him as soon as the opportunity to do so arises. Lenin used the sealed car given him by the German General Staff in 1917 in order to come to Russia for the overthrow of the Provisional Government, in whose disappearance he as well as Ludendorff —for rather different reasons—was interested. He did not thereby become an eternal ally of Ludendorff. Co-operation with Churchill during World War II provided no obstacle in restoring him to the position of World Enemy No. 1 after the war. The Soviet historian Tarle praised Churchill in 1944 as the founder of Anglo-Russian co-operation and attacked him bitterly in 1946 as the most dangerous exponent of British imperialism. Soviet propaganda justifies the most devious shifts and the most spectacular changes of views by reference to the eternal principles of social and historic development. This cynical realism makes the understanding of Soviet policy somewhat difficult for those who do not share its peculiar utopian and doctrinaire basis, a basis that makes it ruthless and intensifies its amoralism. For everything may be justified by the utopian aim, and the most brutal actions and unexpected changes may be attributed to considerations of humanity and justified by an analysis of the existing conditions.

Has the character of the cynical realism of Soviet policies changed since Lenin? I think that no change in fundamentals can be observed. But a change in the emphasis of propaganda appeals can be discovered.

The gulf between utopia and the present order is perceived with greater clarity. Lenin himself passed from a belief that the world revolution would come in a few months to the conviction of the necessity of the NEP. Bolshevik education in the realities of the world has continued. Stalin and Vyshinsky emphasise that the proletarian State will continue to live in a non-proletarian and capitalist world which will try to destroy it, and which will even exercise a corrupting influence inside its frontiers. Thus, the State and its power must be emphasised, and the withering away of the State becomes an even more distant goal. The institutions and policies of the destructive revolutionary period during which the young power of the Bolsheviks felt compelled to differentiate itself most emphatically from the hated Tsarist regime had to be abandoned. Typical of this development is the recent assumption by Stalin and his associates of the titles of Prime Minister and Minister, titles which Lenin regarded as particularly hateful and gladly abandoned. The earlier utopian experiments have been dropped for the time being and are replaced by policies that will enhance the State's material power. The present cannot be sacrificed to the future. The healthy child of Lenin, the Soviet regime, has meanwhile become quite a strong young man, and Stalin acts in Lenin's spirit when he refuses to sacrifice him to hopes and promises which may not be fulfilled.

The determining influence in the various tendencies of Soviet foreign policy is the fact that the Soviet regime remains the proletarian-Socialist regime in capitalist surroundings. An attempt will be made in this article to analyse the various trends in Soviet foreign policy by enumerating and interpreting the most important events in the relations of the Soviets with other Powers. There is no pretence of completeness in this analysis and no discussion of details, some of which may be found in such works as those of Fischer, Milyukov, Taracouzio, Dallin and Yakhontoff.

. . . . .

Are there permanent features and trends in Soviet politics? The abstract ideological justification always remains the same, as we have seen. The Soviet regime is always for world peace, but this world peace can be established only by a universal victory of the proletariat under the leadership of the Communist vanguard; for the imperialistic Powers are always inclined to pursue policies leading to conflicts and wars. These Powers are conspiring to encircle the Soviet regime, for it threatens their social order by the very existence of a more progressive one which, despite all backwardness in detail, represents the Socialist society of the future. Therefore, they are anxious to nip it in the bud, particularly after it has become stronger and started to win influence among all nations.

Of course, this fundamental scheme can be manipulated for the justification of the most varied policies. It can be used for justifying an isolationist Soviet policy—for the U.S.S.R. must keep aloof from capitalist intrigues and manœuvres in which she is not interested. The Soviet regime has to watch its own interests. Its very survival and gain of time for further development represent a victory of world revolution. The same fundamental scheme can be also used to justify co-operation with those among the Powers which are least dangerous for the Soviet regime. After Hitler's rise to power, the Soviet leaders discovered that according to Lenin, formal bourgeois democracy is better than the complete absence of freedom of speech and association. The League of Nations, democratic parties, even the hated and despised Social Fascists, as the Social Democrats were formerly called, were then regarded as allies against a greater danger—the danger of Nazi Germany. Before 1933, the same fundamental attitude was used to justify participation in the anti-Versailles front: England and France, at that time, were regarded as the most dangerous planners of interventions and intrigues.

The Soviet conception of history and social development permits extraordinary flexibility. But one attribute remains unchanged: the Soviet Union is always regarded as a regime *sui generis* with a particular mission that sets it apart from all other regimes. Between them and the Soviet Union there is always mistrust and suspicion. Belief in its universal mission and its peculiarity has been a permanent feature of Soviet policy. Mistrust and suspicion are not a psychological feature of some Soviet leaders of special or limited world experience, they are the consequence of the foundations of the regime. The regime has as its basis a unique character and a missionary claim which cannot be shared and accepted by other Powers. The Marxian theorists believe that even when capitalist States are not in an open state of war against the Soviet Union, such a state of peace merely disguises a form of war between the capitalist Powers and the Soviet Union. These periods of 'peace' are sometimes marked by disagreements among the 'enemy' States, and divisions in the ranks of the 'enemy' may be exploited to gain a breathing spell for the Soviets by means of temporary alliances. Temporary compromises can be made, as, for instance, during the first years of the Soviet regime when a common front against Great Britain bound Turkey and the Soviets together, or during World War II when it was necessary to defeat Hitler, a common enemy of Russia and the West. But such compromises do not mean lasting understanding and co-operation; for, in this case, the Soviet Union would lose the basis of its existence. Lenin always opposed those leftist infants who refused to participate in representative bodies and elections, because those bodies and elections were instruments of capitalism. But, at the same time, he emphasised that the Bolsheviks entered representative bodies and participated in elections not in order to co-operate but to exploit the possibilities of propaganda, to develop their own organisation and to prepare for the seizure of power. Co-operation on the part of the Soviets has a provisional character, and this provisional character and dependence upon circumstances has been developed into a conscious method by the doctrinaire basis of Soviet policies. Changes and manœuvres are also practised by other regimes, but in the Soviet Union they are elevated to the rank of an ethical principle. The belief in their own mission makes the Soviets inclined to misinterpret the behaviour of others; even when foreign nations have no aggressive designs, they are looked upon as devils and planners of evil. Or their passivity is interpreted as proof of the fact that the capitalists are decadent, no longer able to act in unison, and that the world has entered the period of decadent imperialism.

This distrust was originally caused by the distinction between the Socialists and proletarian world to which the future belongs, and the capitalist and bourgeois world which has become an evil force. With its continued existence, Soviet hostility to the bourgeois regimes assumes a more concrete character. The world proletariat is identified with the Soviet regime and the ruling party of the regime. No possibility is recognised of making a distinction between the world revolution and the Russian regime. The Soviet regime needs the world revolution and at the same time it is the most important instrument of the world revolution. The difference between the interests of the world revolution and the interests of the regime disappear. Many ex-Communists have in bitter disappointment complained that the Third International became an instrument of the Russian Communist Party, and it was in vain that the Trotskyites appealed to the Comintern against the leadership of the Russian Communist Party. The use of propaganda and military methods by the Soviet regime was determined by considerations of power. In 1919 the Red armies were not strong enough to reconquer permanently the Baltic States, whereas today they are strong enough to control Eastern Central Europe. But, from the start, these military operations were accompanied by propaganda waves. The power elements of Soviet policies which emphasise the State and its instruments, increased due to the fact that the world revolution did not come, whereas the regime in Russia lasted; but the multi-national character of the Soviet Union was stressed in order to keep the various peoples of the Union together and to contrast the Union with Tsarism as well as with imperialism. Accusations of Great Russian nationalism on the one side and tendencies toward separatism and hate against Great Russians on the other side were used according to the necessities of the struggle inside the Communist party. During World War II the party was intentionally kept somewhat in the background. But even before the war, Stalin had used the slogan of the Bolshevik outside the party in order to maintain the influence of the regime over the masses and persons outside the party. After the war, the fear has arisen that too much emphasis on patriotism can become a threat to the regime, and therefore the emphasis is now again more upon the party doctrine, schooling in Marxism, Leninism and Stalinism. The inter-relationship between Soviet nationalism and Soviet belief in Marxian-Leninist views on world development is another permanent feature of the regime.

This interrelation is often overlooked, because the reasons for the changed attitude of the Soviets toward the past are not correctly estimated. Originally, the Soviet regime was weak and had to emphasise its differ-ences from the unforgotten and recent Tsarist regime. For example, to have resumed the Tsarist policy of conquering the Dardanelles in 1918–19 would simply have been impossible. There was not enough power in the hands of the Soviets. The lack of military power had to be replaced by propaganda, for instance, by promises to grant to the oppressed non-Russian nationalities of the Empire an absolute right of secession.

But with the strengthening and stabilisation of the regime, the policy of unifying all peoples of the former Russian Empire and also of expand-ing, where possible, beyond its boundaries reappeared. That is no trans-formation of the world revolutionary belief into a nationalist one. Practical limitations change the emphasis upon world revolution to an emphasis on the defence of the Soviet Union and the strengthening of its power and influence. This is done not only by the domestic Five-Year plans, but also by expansion in various forms, the erection of new Soviet repub-lics, and the creation of zones of influence of different types.

Only if the fundamental attitude of the Soviet Union is understood, can the significance of the tactical changes in its foreign policy be grasped. After World War II, the wishful belief of living in a world-revolutionary situation has again increased. This revolutionary situation requires re-newed emphasis on the unique character of the Soviet Union. Changes in leadership and tactics of the Communist parties show that a more aggressive policy is being conducted. Browder, the dismissed leader of the American Communists, was charged with opportunism and with neg-lecting to carry on class warfare against the capitalist regime. But this aggressive policy is at the same time a policy destined to aid the expan-sion and the international influence of the Soviet Union. The Union needs security, it must appear as equal to all the Great Powers in all parts of the world. Therefore, it pursues the policy of creating and maintaining 'a *cordon sanitaire* in reverse' by establishing pro-Soviet governments on her Western frontiers and by concluding trade agreements which give a monopolist position to the Soviet Union. Thus, the Soviet Union is eager to appear in the Security Council of UNO as the Power which does not fear being isolated in the midst of Powers who are either un-willing to face the continuing Fascist danger or who perhaps contemplate aggressive action against the U.S.S.R. These tactics, which emphasise the unique character of the Soviet regime, explain the eagerness of Vyshinsky, during the London meeting of the Security Council in 1946, to raise issues on which Russia was bound to be defeated.

It is a paradoxical fact that this aggressive revolutionary attitude makes old problems of Russian expansionist policy reappear. In 1917 Stalin and Lenin signed an appeal to the Mohammedans that stressed the fact that Constantinople ought to remain a Moslem city, and thereby emphasised the distinction between the new regime and oppressive Tsarism. Milyukov was attacked by the Bolshevik party for his demand that the Dardanelles be put under Russian control, and was nicknamed Dardanelski. That has been radically changed. The strong Soviet Union of today is seeking to reach the Mediterranean, to control the Dardanelles, to win concessions and at least a sphere of influence in Iran. But these changes appear as the consequence of the successful Bolshevik regime in Russia. Russia must obtain security, equal rights and equal influence in a world of capitalist Powers. This fight for security and influence requires methods which the newly-born and weak regime rejected; secrecy of negotiations and exclusion from international conferences of smaller Powers, which would only support the opponents of Russia, are demanded by the U.S.S.R.; for she has now become one of the Big Three. These policies can be accepted by those who emphasise the unique Socialist character of the Soviet Union as well as by those who are interested in Russia's power and strength, who are nationalist, and therefore proud of the achievements of the Red armies, not because they are Red, but the armies of the successor of the Russian Empire. A similar co-operation based on completely different fundamental attitudes existed before; in 1920, the Nationalist General Brussilov favoured helping the Soviet regime after it had become involved in war with Poland. Brussilov certainly did not share the world revolutionary hopes of Lenin.

Oscillation between more aggressive and more restrained foreign policies permits the adoption of the most flexible methods, and the use of several lines at the same time. Lenin had always recommended such tactics. He had opposed those who, during the period of the Bolshevik fight for power, recommended either exclusively legal or exclusively illegal methods. He had also emphasised the combination of both methods in the fight of the Third International for world revolution. The legal aspect of Communism stresses democracy, uses the existing rights to organise groups, to participate in elections and electoral campaigns, to publish newspapers, etc. The Communist party appears as a party fighting for social reforms, opposing exploitation, supporting peace movements, opposing imperialist expansion, and revealing, if it is exposed by police measures, the limitations of capitalist democracy. But, at the same time, illegal organisations and groups are built up in order to be ready for the eventuality of suppression of Communist and pro-Communist groups, and also for revolutionary situations in which power can be taken over.

What influence does this combination of methods have on Soviet foreign policy? On the one hand, its policy involves formal observance of international law and treaty obligations. This legal propriety is publicly emphasised. A democratic terminology is used. Official Russian policy denied any responsibility for the policy of the Third International. Activities of the Comintern and statements on party congresses, for example, the fact that the Soviet Ambassador in Paris, Rakovsky, signed the world revolutionary programme of the opposition directed against Stalin (1927), have caused much trouble for the Commissariat of Foreign Affairs, for this Commissariat has been anxious to appear as a strict adherent to legal methods and traditional diplomatic forms. On the other hand, it is obvious that the machinery of the Comintern, the various Communist parties, formed a most important, though not officially and publicly admitted, instrument in the hands of the leaders of Russian foreign policy. Of course, they were repudiated as long as they were not successful—the Communist parties in the Baltic States were not favoured, at least, in the market place, when in 1939 the Soviet Union took over only military and naval bases and disclaimed plans of incorporation and Sovietisation. But when there was a possibility of taking over, the situation soon changed. Communist parties or pro-Soviet groups became the masters, openly supported by the Soviet Government. The armies advancing in Poland during the war of 1920 were accompanied by a committee, prepared to assume the role of the Polish Government, among whom the Polish aristocrat, Dzhershinsky, the chief of the Tcheka, played a decisive role. A similar committee was recognised as the Finnish Government, after, in 1939, the Finnish cabinet had rejected Russian demands for military bases and frontier adjustments.

The fact that the tactics have changed from the old practice of using partisan elements to the current endeavour to form democratic coalition governments does not alter the fundamental policy. In these governments the moderate groups are dominated by the strictly disciplined Communist nucleus. Sometimes, the Communists try to use non-Communist parties, for example, in Iran or Bulgaria. Sometimes, as in the Germany of 1946, an appeal to the whole working population, backed by the army of occupation, is believed to be useful in accomplishing a Communist merger with the Social Democrats. But the basic method has remained the same from the beginning of the Soviet regime. Movements outside the boundaries of the Soviet Union are used for Russian foreign policy. This manipulation is of course covered up by the formula that there is a natural harmony between democratic social aspirations and Soviet policies. Soviet foreign policy is simply regarded as the policy of the world proletariat, for the defence against Fascism, for peace and democracy. Moreover, at the very beginning of the regime, as in Poland in 1920 (without success), or in Georgia in 1921 (with success), the Red armies brought with them the pro-Communist, pro-Soviet committees and governing bodies that were to be established in countries dominated by anti-Soviet Governments. What has changed is the power of the Red Army. Obviously the Red Army of 1945–46 cannot be compared with the Red Army of 1919–20 which was easily driven from the Baltic States, and defeated in Poland after spectacular initial successes.

This co-existence of several political lines and agents intended to carry them out makes changes in Soviet foreign policy very easy. If the revolutionary hopes are not realised—after, for instance, the German Republican Government had overcome the critical situation of 1928—then the legal public line is emphasised, and even a great moderation in the pursuit of this line is adopted. The leaders of the Union then argued that, in such circumstances, the peoples of the Soviet Union were exhausted, and that much had to be done before the Union could catch up with the technically more advanced capitalist Powers. A new breathing spell was therefore necessary. The governments of the Baltic States were recognised after 1920. Or, if there is fear of immediate intervention, attempts are made, as after Hitler's rise to power, to secure the help of one capitalist group, of the Western Powers, against Germany. The co-existence of several policies which can be exchanged, if one of them has failed or new situations have arisen, gives to Soviet policy the aspect of being unpredictable. But this unpredictable character is only the consequence of the Soviet endeavour to exploit all situations by calculating them in advance. If the interpretation that a revolutionary situation has arisen proves to be wrong, then the policy required by the 'relative stabilisation of capitalism' or by the unshaken power of non-proletarian middle class and peasant groups, can be introduced. The newly formed governments sponsored by the Soviet vanish as suddenly as they have been formed. The classic example is the disappearance of the pro-Communist Finnish Government of Kuusinen in 1940 after it had failed to establish itself in spite of Soviet recognition.

Such changes in the long run may rouse the suspicion of the non-Soviet world, but they do not matter inside Russian. For any direct influence of public discussion and public opinion has been eliminated in the Soviet Union. This tendency to manufacture public opinion existed from the beginning. At first, Lenin and his party had to appear as acting in response to the Soviet majority. Within limits, they had to tolerate other Socialist parties. Even inside the Communist party it was not easy to enforce public unanimity by strict party discipline. But this situation has changed. All other parties have been eliminated. Due to his unquestioned authority, Lenin was able to tolerate some discussion inside the party, but that was impossible for Stalin, who had to impose his authority on elements who were inclined to regard him only as one of the many lieutenants of the great Lenin. There are, of course, disagreements and discussions inside the party which also reflect the moods of the population and its different groups. But they no longer come out into the open. Disagreements aired publicly, as in 1939 by Zhdanov, a member of the Politbureau, who expressed doubts concerning the negotiations with Great

Britain and France, are prearranged in order to influence the attitude of other Powers, and to create currents in international public opinion. The public unanimity makes sudden changes and shifts possible; for no one can publicly raise the question of consistency, or of the responsibility for the failure of previous policies.

The permanent features of Soviet foreign policy which derive from this fundamental structure of the Soviet regime show that the interplay of utopianism and cynical realism determines its development and changes. The utopian element has played a decisive role in strengthening the regime and in building the totalitarian and one-party State. The claims of the one-party and the ruthless energy necessary for their realisation were produced by the belief in the world historic mission of the Communists, the vanguard and brain of the proletariat, the class destined to bring about the just and classless society. The fact that this Utopia cannot be accomplished at once, but can result only from long development and from a protracted period of struggles with class enemies, makes the rise of a cynical adaptation to, and exploitation of, existing power relations possible. Therefore, the emphasis upon the Soviet Union and its power is only apparently a shift away from the utopian world revolution— it is seen by the Soviet leaders only as a tactical manœuvre, a 'breathing spell'. But this self-interpretation of the trends of Soviet policies, and particularly of Soviet foreign policy, should not be accepted by the other Powers. Co-operation with the Soviet Union can be based upon the view that the tactical adaptation will more and more postpone, and finally overcome the fight for world revolution.

True, the difficulty remains: what about the power politics of the Soviet Union, even if they are not seen in the light of the Marxist perspective of the future? In its first years, the Soviet regime was glad to survive, after the dissipation of the early dreams of the imperialist World War being transformed into a class war, with Lenin at the helm of the Universal Soviet Republic. The Soviet Union emphasised internal politics despite all efforts of the Comintern. Parts of the old Russian Empire were abandoned. In the peace treaty of Riga with Poland, territories which were regarded as Russian were given up. The Baltic States were recognised; no real efforts were made to regain Bessarabia from Roumania. Friendship with Turkey was maintained, even at the cost of territorial concessions (Kars; Ardahan). Then the period of fear of Nazi intervention followed. Opposition to the treaty of Versailles and the League of Nations was dropped. After Munich, this policy was replaced by a policy of neutrality, of reaching an understanding with Germany in order to avoid participation in war, and thus to achieve the position of arbiter in the coming world conflict. This period was also the period of a territorial expansion, tolerated by Germany. From 1941–45 the Soviet Union was involved in war against the Hitler Reich, and there followed co-operation

with Great Britain and with the U.S.A. The period of the war, its conclusion and early aftermath reveal that Russia has resumed her expansion.
She has imposed her domination and control over Eastern and Central
Europe. How far will this domination reach? This domination is accompanied by claims in the Far and Near East, particularly in the Mediterranean and Iran. Has the Soviet Union become an aggressive imperialist
Power in the belief that it can expand further, in its dissatisfaction with
its present limits?

The answer to this question depends not upon the Soviet Union alone.
The history of its foreign policy has shown that, in spite of errors in detail
and hesitations due to revolutionary utopianism, it has always taken into
account existing power conditions. These involve not only the resistance
of other Powers against its policies, but also their inability or ability to
maintain internal stability, to solve social problems and to organise collaboration with each other. The existence of the German-Anglo-American
antagonism made possible the expansionist policy of Russia after 1939. It
is clear that Soviet foreign policy is today again based on the calculation
that the other Powers will not remain united. The Soviets also hope that
the fluid conditions of the post-war period will operate in their favour.
They can manœuvre and exploit uncertainties and the general exhaustion.
The absence of a counter-balance against them on the European Continent is to their advantage. Moreover, they can raise the accusation that
blocks and alliance systems are built up in order to prepare an anti-
Soviet policy. But if the aggressive policy fails or becomes impracticable,
as it meets with too much resistance, then a withdrawal can take place.
Emphasis can be laid on internal reconstruction—on new attempts to
catch up with the production of the U.S.A.—an aim the realisation of
which still lies in the distant future, as the figures in Stalin's production
programme speech of 1946 show. The U.S.S.R. can be satisfied with having changed the *cordon sanitaire* and replaced it by a system under its
own influence. It can be satisfied with the defeat of Germany, and can
consider the future of Germany an open question. Russia can work for
a united Germany under Communist control or for a weakened Germany
on which she will still retain a strong Communist influence to meet the
claims of France. She can replace aggressive isolationism, to which she
tended after the war, by a more co-operative attitude, giving up her
most radical demands and therefore accepting compromises, which will
at least maintain her position in the Far East and Middle East. She can
become more co-operative in UNO and claim that she is anxious to preserve peace and international goodwill. She can adopt this attitude, and
postpone the fulfilment of her aims to a future which, as her leaders believe, will necessarily come. She can rely upon the ally which has so far
helped her to overcome all crises and to utilise all breathing spells—time.

What caused the adoption of the current aggressive foreign policy,

which has antagonised public opinion outside her frontiers and has endangered the goodwill created by the heroic fight of Russia's armies and
peoples, particularly in England and the U.S.A.? That is the great mystery
of the Kremlin, for time seems to work for the Soviet Union, as the calculation of future population figures shows. The intransigent policies of
1945–46 can only be explained by overestimation of revolutionary possibilities in the post-war world, and by the internal situation. External
tension permits the maintenance of the balance between the various
tendencies inside the party, as well as between the party on the one side
and the army command and the technical bureaucracy on the other; the
claim that capitalist Powers continue to threaten the security of the
Soviet Union gives excuses for the continuance of sacrifices and of the low
standard of living which cannot be greatly raised, even after the victory.
But it is impossible to discuss the conflicts inside the leading groups. We
are too little informed about what is going on behind the iron curtain
which hides all debates among the members of the ruling élite and its
various groups in the U.S.S.R. Nobody, apart from those directly concerned, knows the real meaning of certain changes in the leading personnel
(the removal of Beria, the rise of Bulganin, the apparent eclipse of
Zhdanov). Until now, the Soviet leaders have succeeded in combining
the world revolutionary line with a realisation of traditional Russian demands in Europe and Asia. 'Breathing spells', warnings against 'dizziness
by success', can be applied if the power constellation in the world shows
that Russia will meet an energetic resistance, which her leaders would
regard as endangering the Soviet regime.

CORRELATION TABLES

CORRELATION OF *READINGS IN RUSSIAN HISTORY*, VOLS. I AND II, WITH REPRESENTATIVE TEXTS

Clarkson, Jesse D., *A History of Russia*, Random House, 1961

Chapter Nos.	Related selections in READINGS IN RUSSIAN HISTORY	Chapter Nos.	Related selections in READINGS IN RUSSIAN HISTORY
1	I: 1–6	19	II: 1–5
2	I: 2, 7–11	20	II: 5, 6, 8, 9
3	I: 9–11	21	II: 1
4	I: 2, 11	22	II: 9
5	I: 11, 12	23	II: 10
6	I: 13, 14, 17	24	II: 11
7	I: 15, 17	25	II: 11, 13
8	I: 16, 17	26	II: 12, 13
9 } 10	I: 6, 16–18	27	II: 12, 13, 17, 18
		28	II: 13, 22
11 } 12	I: 5, 19	29	II: 14, 18, 19, 22
		30	II: 12, 14–18, 22
13	I: 20–22	31	II: 14–16, 18
14	I: 21–24	32	I: 2; II: 18, 19
15	I: 25–28	33	II: 22
16	I: 17; II: 2	34	I: 2, 5; II: 17, 19, 20, 22
17	I: 17; II: 1	35	II: 17, 21, 22
18	II: 3, 4, 6, 7, 9	36	II: 15–18

Florinsky, Michael T., *Russia: A History and an Interpretation*, 2 vols., Macmillan, 1953

Chapter Nos.	Related selections in READINGS IN RUSSIAN HISTORY	Chapter Nos.	Related selections in READINGS IN RUSSIAN HISTORY
Intro.	I: 1, 3–6	8	I: 13, 15, 16
1	I: 2, 7–11	9 } 10	I: 16, 17
2	I: 2, 11		
3	I: 11, 12	11	I: 17, 18
4 } 5	I: 14	12 } 13 14 15	I: 5, 6, 19
6	I: 7, 8		
7	I: 14, 17		

329

Florinsky, *Russia: A History and an Interpretation* (cont.)

Chapter Nos.	Related selections in READINGS IN RUSSIAN HISTORY	Chapter Nos.	Related selections in READINGS IN RUSSIAN HISTORY
16	I: 20	31	I: 6, 26
17		32	I: 27
18		33	II: 1
19		34	II: 1, 2
20	I: 21–23	35	I: 4, 5
21		36	II: 3
22		37	
23		38	II: 4, 5
24		39	II: 4–7
25	I: 24	40	II: 7
26		41	II: 1, 9
27	II: 2	42	
28	I: 25, 28	43	II: 8, 10, 11
29		44	
30	II: 2	45	

Harcave, Sidney, *Russia: A History*, 4th ed., Lippincott, 1959

Chapter Nos.	Related selections in READINGS IN RUSSIAN HISTORY	Chapter Nos.	Related selections in READINGS IN RUSSIAN HISTORY
1	I: 1, 3–6, 9	16	II: 3, 4
2	I: 2, 7–12	17	II: 1, 2, 5
3	I: 4, 5, 13–18	18	II: 3, 8
4	I: 7, 8, 12, 18	19	II: 1, 6, 7
5	I: 5, 19	20	II: 6, 7
6	I: 20, 21	21	II: 9, 10
7	I: 21	22	II: 10
8	I: 23	23	II: 11
9	I: 21, 22	24	II: 11–13, 18, 19, 22
10	I: 24	25	II: 12, 13
11	I: 28	26	II: 12, 14, 17, 19, 22
12	I: 25, 27, 28; II: 2	27	II: 14, 15, 17
13	I: 6, 26	28	II: 14–18
14	I: 5	29	I: 5; II: 20
15	II: 1–3	30	II: 15, 16, 21, 22

Pares, Bernard, *A History of Russia*, definitive ed., Knopf, 1953

Chapter Nos.	Related selections in READINGS IN RUSSIAN HISTORY	Chapter Nos.	Related selections in READINGS IN RUSSIAN HISTORY
1	I: 1, 3–6, 9	3	I: 11
2	I: 2, 7–11	4	

Pares, A *History of Russia* (cont.)

Chapter Nos.	Related selections in READINGS IN RUSSIAN HISTORY	Chapter Nos.	Related selections in READINGS IN RUSSIAN HISTORY
5	I: 12–14	17	I: 24
6	I: 15	18	I: 6, 25–28; II: 2
7	I: 16, 17	19	II: 1, 2
8	I: 2, 16	20	II: 1, 3
9	I: 17, 18	21	II: 1, 2, 4–7
10	I: 2, 16	22	II: 8
11 } 12	I: 19	23	II: 1, 9
		24	II: 10, 11
13	I: 20	25	II: 12–14, 17, 18, 22
14	I: 21, 22	26	II: 14–19, 22
15 } 16	I: 23	27	II: 20, 22
		Epilogue	II: 21

Treadgold, Donald W., *Twentieth Century Russia*, Rand McNally, 1959

Chapter Nos.	Related selections in READINGS IN RUSSIAN HISTORY	Chapter Nos.	Related selections in READINGS IN RUSSIAN HISTORY
Intro.	I: 1–8	13 } 14	II: 12–14
1	I: 1–8; II: 1, 2		
2	II: 3–7	15	II: 22
3	II: 6	16	II: 17
4	II: 6, 7	17	II: 14, 15
5	II: 8	18	II: 14–16
6	II: 9	19	II: 19
7	II: 1, 2, 5	20 } 21	II: 22
8	II: 10		
9	II: 11	22	II: 17
10 } 11 } 12	II: 12	23	II: 20
		24	II: 20–22
		25	II: 21, 22

Vernadsky, George, *A History of Russia*, 4th ed., Yale University Press, 1954

Chapter Nos.	Related selections in READINGS IN RUSSIAN HISTORY	Chapter Nos.	Related selections in READINGS IN RUSSIAN HISTORY
Intro.	I: 1, 3–6	6	I: 5, 19, 20, 23
1	I: 2, 9–11	7	I: 21, 22
2	I: 7–11	8	I: 22, 26
3	I: 11, 12	9	I: 24–28
4	I: 13–17	10	II: 3, 8
5	I: 5, 16–18	11	II: 1, 2, 4–7, 9

Vernadsky, *A History of Russia* (cont.)

Chapter Nos.	Related selections in READINGS IN RUSSIAN HISTORY	Chapter Nos.	Related selections in READINGS IN RUSSIAN HISTORY
12	II: 9	15	II: 14, 15, 18
13	II: 10, 11	16	II: 17, 18
14	II: 12–16, 19	17	II: 20–22

Walsh, Warren B., *Russia and the Soviet Union*, University of Michigan Press, 1958

Chapter Nos.	Related selections in READINGS IN RUSSIAN HISTORY	Chapter Nos.	Related selections in READINGS IN RUSSIAN HISTORY
1	I: 1, 3–6, 11	15	I: 5; II: 3
2	I: 2, 9–11	16	II: 1, 4–7
3	I: 7, 8, 11	17	II: 5, 8
4	I: 12–14, 17	18	II: 1, 9
5	I: 4, 5, 15	19	II: 10
6	I: 16–18	20	II: 11
7	I: 19	21	II: 12, 18, 19
8	I: 20–22	22	II: 12–14, 17, 18
9	I: 21–23	23	II: 13
10	I: 24	24	II: 14–16
11	I: 6, 25, 26, 28; II: 1	25	II: 22
12	I: 27	26	I: 5; II: 20, 22
13	I: 26; II: 1	27	II: 15, 19
14	II: 1	28	II: 21, 22

Wren, Melvin C., *The Course of Russian History*, Macmillan, 1958

Chapter Nos.	Related selections in READINGS IN RUSSIAN HISTORY	Chapter Nos.	Related selections in READINGS IN RUSSIAN HISTORY
1	I: 1, 4–6	17	I: 24
2	I: 2, 6	18	I: 28
3	I: 3, 6, 9	19 } 20	I: 25–28
4 } 5 6 7	I: 2, 7–11	21	I: 17; II: 1, 2
		22	I: 4; II: 3
		23	II: 2–7
8	I: 12, 13, 17	24	II: 4, 5, 7
9	I: 12–14, 17	25	II: 6–9
10	I: 15, 17	26	II: 9, 10
11	I: 16, 17	27	II: 11, 13
12	I: 16–18	28	II: 12, 13, 16–19
13	I: 5, 19	29	II: 14, 15
14	I: 20, 21	30	II: 16, 17, 19
15 } 16	I: 21–23	31	I: 5; II: 22
		32	II: 20, 21